Warlords

Warlords

AN EXTRAORDINARY RE-CREATION OF WORLD WAR II
THROUGH THE EYES AND MINDS OF
HITLER, CHURCHILL, ROOSEVELT, AND STALIN

Simon Berthon and Joanna Potts

DA CAPO PRESS
A Member of the Perseus Books Group

Cataloging-in-Publication data for this book is available from the Library of Congress.

First Da Capo Press paperback edition 2007
First published in the United Kingdom by Methuen Publishing Limited
ISBN-13: 978-0-306-81538-6
ISBN-10: 0-306-81538-9

Published by Da Capo Press
A Member of the Perseus Books Group
http://www.dacapopress.com

Da Capo Press books are available at special discounts for bulk purchases in the U.S.
by corporations, institutions, and other organizations. For more information, please
contact the Special Markets Department at the Perseus Books Group, 11 Cambridge
Center, Cambridge, MA 02142, or call (800) 255-1514 or (617) 252-5298, or e-mail
special.markets@perseusbooks.com.

10 9 8 7 6 5 4 3 2 1

CONTENTS

FOREWORD

Today's politicians often complain that reporting of their trade is too "personalized." Analysis of "issues," they say, is sacrificed to the promotion of beauty contests between leaders and impertinent gossip about their relationships. In these early years of the 21st century, it is a curious axe to grind. The seminal decision of the contemporary trans-atlantic alliance, to go to war in Iraq, was a very personal one by an American president, who had inherited unfinished business from his father, and a British prime minister, who, as the emerging record makes ever clearer, flew solo in taking his country into battle. Above all, Tony Blair was influenced by the call of a "special relationship" with George W. Bush. Their conjunction of minds led to Britons and Americans fighting, and dying, side by side in Iraq.

This book unashamedly takes the view that, in the war of 1939–45, the personal decisions of the four titans at its heart also dictated its outbreak, its course and its consequences. Hitler alone decided to invade Poland; in the summer of 1940 his mental processes alone led to the turn against the Soviet Union. Stalin—no one else—made a pact with Hitler; it was his psychological and strategic vision which concluded that Hitler would not invade the Soviet Union in 1941 and left his country defenseless. In the summer of 1940 there would probably have been a different outcome if Halifax, not Churchill, had become prime minister on that fateful day of 10 May. And however much Roosevelt trimmed and tacked before he was finally hurled into war, it was he who decided that Nazi Germany, not Japan, was enemy number one; and he who took the personal gamble that unlimited generosity was the way to win Stalin's collaboration in creating a new post-imperial world of peace and free nations.

These four men stood at the head of the 20th century's dominant ideologies as they collided in the Second World War: totalitarianism of right and left, liberal democracy, social democracy, European colonialism and economic imperialism. In the war between these ideologies tens of millions of people fought and died. This book is about the heart of that conflict: the ever-changing relationships of the four warlords and their war of the mind.

In trying to understand these men, I have accumulated debts. Professor John Lukacs's brilliant book, *The Duel: Hitler vs Churchill*, of which he kindly allowed me to make a film some years ago, made the subject an addiction. While that was about the mind games of enemies, the parallel duels of allies seemed equally beguiling and, in a succeeding project, *Allies at War*, on the tempestuous relationship between the French leader, Charles de Gaulle, and Churchill and Roosevelt, I owed an enormous amount to the unrivaled knowledge and wisdom of Professor Warren Kimball who introduced me in particular to the complexities of the two great democrats. For *Warlords* I am immensely grateful to a third historian, Professor Geoffrey Roberts, who has offered consistently shrewd advice in interpreting Stalin which I should sometimes have followed more closely.

Many people have helped in facilitating access to primary sources and contributing to original research: Professor Alexander Chubarian; Andrew Riley and the staff of the Churchill Archives Centre at Churchill College, Cambridge; the staff of the Borthwick Institute at the University of York; the staff of the Manuscripts Division at the Library of Congress; Professor Georgy Kumanev; Dr Mikhail Myagkov; the staff of the National Archives, Kew; the staff of the National Archives, Washington, D.C.; Christine Penney and the staff of the Special Collections Department at the University of Birmingham; Wilderstein Preservation; the staff of the Franklin D. Roosevelt Library; Professor Oleg Rzheshevsky; Cordula Schacht; the Countess of Avon; Lady Soames; and the family of Edward Wood, the first Earl of Halifax.

Janice Hadlow and Tim Gardam provided illuminating insights and vital early support; Hamish Mykura and Ralph Lee have brought their great intelligence to bear in the friendliest of ways. The team at 3BM Television has been as wonderful as always and special thanks are due to Simon Battersby, Frances Craig, Denysse Edwardes, Dan Korn, Oystein Lagerstrom, Glynis Robertson and Julia Yershova.

Above all I would like to thank my collaborator from the beginning of this project and co-author, Joanna Potts, without whose research, drafts and determination this book would not have been written. We would both like to thank Emma Musgrave at Politico's, our proofreader, Jonathan Wadman, and our agent, Andrew Lownie, who have shown that they really care.

And finally my thanks and love to Penelope, Helena and Olivia and my gratitude for their forbearance with an obsession that will now be parked firmly out of sight, if not entirely out of mind.

Simon Berthon
May 2005

PROLOGUE

May 10, 1940

Just after midnight, Friday, May 10, 1940. Two imposing steam engines at the head of ten luxuriously appointed coaches in bottle-green livery slid towards a junction 140 miles west of Berlin. The train had been traveling north from Hanover towards Hamburg, but now a set of points switched it to the west. It smoothly and slowly changed direction. On board this special train, code-named *Amerika*, was Adolf Hitler. The Führer was on a one-way ticket to Armageddon.

With Hitler was his personal secretary, Christa Schroeder, a breezy and attractive young woman of 32 who was full of admiration for the charm and vitality of the "boss." She wrote an excited letter to a friend describing her great adventure. The day before, the "inner" circle in Hitler's office in the *Reich* Chancellery, of which she was thrilled to be part, had only been told that they were going "on a trip." Its destination and length were a secret. Once the train had left Berlin, they asked the "boss" if they were going to Norway, the main theater of battle on that day between Germany and Great Britain. Teasingly Hitler appeared to confirm their guess: "If you behave you will be allowed to take a seal hide home with you."[1]

At dawn the train arrived at a station whose name plates had been removed. It turned out to be Euskirchen, 30 miles from the German frontier. Hitler and his party transferred to cars which took them through villages whose names were also missing and replaced by military signs. Finally they headed up a dirt track overshadowed by birches towards a small, flat clearing high in the forest spotted with concrete bunkers and posts. They had reached their destination: Felsennest, Hitler's new headquarters.

In the background the rumble of artillery started up. Hitler pointed a uniformed arm westwards and announced: "Gentlemen, the offensive against the western powers has begun."[2] The governments of Belgium, Holland and France were about to wake up to 136 highly trained and well-equipped German divisions storming across their frontiers. The "phoney war" was over; the *Blitzkrieg* had begun. Hitler's unique mind had plunged the world for the next five years into the deadliest war ever.

As the Luftwaffe's squadrons blackened the sky over Felsennest and the forces of the Wehrmacht poured down roads and tracks towards the west, a young man was taking an early morning ride among the deer of Richmond Park on the southwest fringes of London. He was John Colville, aged 25, and like Christa Schroeder he was a private secretary; in his case to another European boss, the British Prime Minister Neville Chamberlain. But, Colville knew, not for long. As he dismounted, his groom told him that Holland and Belgium had been invaded by the Nazis. Colville felt the heat of the political turmoil surging through Westminster and, as he noted in his diary, one thing was becoming depressingly obvious: "If the PM does go, I am afraid that it must be Winston."[3]

Winston Churchill, who had returned to the British Cabinet as First Lord of the Admiralty on the outbreak of war on September 3, 1939, was considered reckless, untrustworthy and insufferable by much of the political establishment. But Churchill woke up on this fateful day, knowing that by its end and barring accidents he would achieve his life's ambition of becoming British prime minister.

Churchill's opportunity had arisen only from a fiasco for which he bore the heaviest responsibility: the campaign in Norway, in which the British navy had been outwitted by German paratroopers. Its aim was to cut Germany's link to supplies of steel and iron ore from Sweden. But while British warships lumbered up the Norwegian coast and deposited their ill-supported land forces, Hitler struck from the air, forcing his opponents into a humiliating retreat. The Norwegian failure hardened political opinion in London that Chamberlain was not a man for battle; whatever Churchill's disadvantages, nobody could mistake that he was the type of leader the nation needed—a warlord who had long understood that the enemy was Hitler.

The day before, as Hitler's inner circle took the train out of Berlin, Churchill had his decisive encounter at 10 Downing Street with Chamberlain and the Foreign Secretary, Lord Halifax. Chamberlain, faced by a political rebellion in the House of Commons and unable to command the support of the Labour opposition for a national government, knew that his goose was cooked and he must resign. Halifax, the wily aristocratic diplomat, was the man the British establishment wanted to succeed him; but he realized that he was unsuited to be a war leader and let go his chance.

As the *Blitzkrieg* erupted on May 10, Chamberlain tried to renege at the last minute, arguing that crisis required continuity. But the Labour and Liberal opposition would have none of it and even his own ministers had lost confidence in him. At 6 p.m. Churchill's ministerial car took him from the Admiralty to Buckingham Palace. The journey was less than a mile but the most significant of his life; for him, like Hitler, there was no return. "I suppose you don't know why I have sent for you?" the king asked. "Sir," Churchill replied, a playful sparkle in his eye, "I can't imagine why." King George VI laughed. "I want to ask you to form a government."[4]

The billboards of the evening papers proclaimed the shocking news that Nazi forces were smashing into France, Holland and Belgium. "I hope that it is not too late," Churchill told his detective, W. H. Thompson, with a tear in his eye, as they returned to the Admiralty. "I am very much afraid that it is."[5]

Churchill was British prime minister, and in the drawing rooms of London and the world beyond, a rainbow of reactions arced over the political world. "Churchill appears to be a godsend," wrote Ivan Maisky, the Soviet ambassador in London, "but later on he could become a great obstacle if and when they desire to conclude peace."[6] John Colville was immediately invited by Churchill to stay on at 10 Downing Street, but the young man was full of trepidation, consoled only by the thought that Chamberlain and Halifax were staying on under the new upstart regime. "There will at least be some restraint on our new War Lord," he noted in his diary that evening; "he may, of course, be the man of drive and energy the country believes him to be ... but it is a terrible risk."[7] In Berlin Hitler's propaganda chief, Joseph Goebbels, who also kept a daily diary, concluded, "Churchill really has been made Prime Minister. The position is clear! That's what we like."[8] There is no record of Hitler's immediate reaction, but he had already formed his view of Churchill: he was an antique imperialist, a blusterer and, as Norway showed, a loser.

Three thousand miles across the Atlantic in Washington the new prime minister was regarded as a suspect character. President Franklin Roosevelt called an emergency meeting of his Cabinet in response to the shattering double strike of Hitler's *Blitzkrieg* and Churchill's succession. The interior secretary, Harold Ickes, recorded Roosevelt's verdict: "I suppose he is the best man England has even if he is drunk half of his time."[9] Ickes mordantly added that Churchill was "apparently very unreliable when under the influence of drink."[10]

Whether or not Churchill was an unreliable alcoholic, Roosevelt knew that he was now the front line against Hitler. Yet, as well as suspecting him of being a drunk, he harbored a dislike for him that stretched back more than 20 years. Its roots lay in Roosevelt's memory of his one and only face-to-face meeting with Churchill when in 1918, as American under-secretary for the navy and before he was disabled, he had visited France and Britain. In London he gave a speech at a dinner at Gray's Inn, bastion of the British legal establishment. Churchill, then a far more famous public figure, was in the audience. Roosevelt later remarked that he behaved like a "stinker … lording it all over us."[11]

The two men had not seen each other since and in the 1930s appeared to be polar opposites. Roosevelt was the charismatic president, Churchill the has-been stuck in the political wilderness; Roosevelt the scourge of European colonialism, Churchill the die-hard defender of the British Empire. But one thing united them. They had both understood from early on that Hitler presented a new and terrible force with which peaceful co-existence would be impossible.

There had been a coincidence in Roosevelt's and Hitler's rises to power. On March 4, 1933, Roosevelt was inaugurated as president for the first time. The next day Hitler tightened his grip on the German nation after a slim but sufficient win at the polls. But it was not until three years later, when German troops marched into the Rhineland on March 7, 1936, that Roosevelt's anxieties crystallized. The United States was a neutral country;

its people wanted no entanglements in Europe's squabbles. Roosevelt could only express his fears in private. One important confidante was his distant cousin and close companion, Daisy Suckley. He wrote to her: "The news from Germany is bad and though my official people all tell me there is no danger of actual war I always remember their saying all the same things in July 1914."[12]

The president could only watch as Hitler's onward march trampled through the enfeebled leaders of Britain and France. In March 1938 he told a colleague: "As someone remarked to me—'If a Chief of Police makes a deal with the leading gangsters and the deal results in no more hold-ups, that Chief of Police will be called a great man—but if the gangsters do not live up to their word the Chief of Police will go to jail.' Some people are, I think, taking very long chances."[13] After a speech by Hitler at the height of the Munich crisis in September Roosevelt conveyed to Suckley his visceral contempt for the Nazi leaders: "Did you hear Hitler today, his shrieks, his histrionics, and the effect on the huge audience? They did not applaud—they made noises like animals."[14]

When Churchill returned to the British Cabinet as First Lord of the Admiralty on the outbreak of war, Roosevelt immediately understood that he would become an important protagonist in resisting the Nazis and started a transatlantic cable correspondence with him. In his first message he wrote: "My dear Churchill, it is because you and I occupied similar positions in the World War that I want you to know how glad I am that you are back again in the Admiralty."[15] Privately Roosevelt told the American ambassador to Britain, Joseph Kennedy: "I have always disliked him since the time I went to England in 1918. ... I'm giving him attention now because there is a strong possibility that he will become Prime Minister and I want to get my hand in now."[16] On May 10, 1940, Roosevelt's forecast was vindicated.

On the other side of the globe, the world's fourth great leader was also taking stock of the cataclysm of May 10. In Moscow Hitler's collaborator, Joseph Stalin, dutifully dispatched his deputy, Vyacheslav Molotov, to the German embassy with a personal message for the Führer. "He realised that Germany must protect herself against British-French attack," the ambassador, Count von der Schulenburg, reported back to Hitler, "he had no doubt of our success."[17] These honeyed words of congratulation from one ally to another were a front; obligatory praise that masked a deep anxiety. The truth was that Stalin and Hitler, though neither of them yet fully realized it, were nine months into a psychological duel that would have devastating consequences for themselves, their nations and the world.

It had been instigated the previous summer by Hitler. During July 1939 the world's most celebrated Wagner fan attended no fewer than seven performances of his favorite composer and then retreated to spend the balmy days of high summer at his mountain retreat, the Berghof in Obersalzberg. Encamped in one of the world's loveliest places, Hitler planned the brutal invasion of Poland, his "little war" as he called it and one that he was determined to have. The urge for war had been building ever since the Munich agreement the year before, when, rather than being pleased by British and French appeasement over Czechoslovakia, Hitler had felt deprived of the chance to flex his military muscles.

No one was going to restrain him over Poland and his generals had told him he must attack before the autumn rains came. Only one thing stood in his way: Britain and France had said they would go to war for Poland, raising the specter that the Soviet Union might also turn against him and propel him into a war on two fronts. This was the very thing imprinted in Hitler's mind as having helped to lose Germany the First World War 20 years before.

Now in the pure air of the mountains, Hitler began to think the unthinkable—a pact with his greatest ideological enemy. In August 1939 he put out feelers to Moscow.

Not surprisingly Stalin was deeply suspicious of Hitler's approach. He kept him waiting, spending hours reading *Mein Kampf*, Hitler's autobiography and manifesto written fifteen years before, underlining key passages; among them Hitler's views of the early Bolshevik leaders, men like Stalin himself: "Never forget that the rulers of present-day Russia are common blood-stained criminals, that they are the scum of humanity."[18]

But Stalin could see that Hitler was now desperate for a deal and offering to send his foreign minister, Joachim von Ribbentrop, to Moscow. The British and French, by contrast, who were also courting him, had only managed to send a delegation of generals and admirals to Moscow. Stalin decided that Hitler's offer was too enticing to resist and invited Ribbentrop to Russia. Goebbels, aware of the fearful prospect of a two-front war, noted in his diary: "Non-aggression pact with Moscow perfect. Ribbentrop in Moscow on Wednesday. That is something! We're on top again. Now we can sleep more easily."[19]

On 23 August Ribbentrop landed in Moscow. Shortly after midnight on the morning of the 24th the Nazi–Soviet pact was signed and with it a secret protocol under which Germany and Russia would carve Poland into two. Hitler phoned Ribbentrop: "This will hit like a bombshell."[20] But as Goebbels noted, it was not strength but fear of Stalin knifing him in the back that had forced Hitler into history's biggest U-turn: "The Führer believes he's in the position of scrounging for favours and beggars can't be choosers. In times of famine the devil feeds on flies."[21]

In the Kremlin, Stalin proposed a cynical toast to Ribbentrop and the pact with the Nazis: "I know how much the German nation loves its Führer; I should therefore like to drink his health."[22] But like Hitler, Stalin was also acting from fear, in his case that Hitler would attack him. That evening he told his inner circle: "Of course it's all a game to see who can fool whom. He thinks he's outsmarted me but actually it's I who've tricked him."[23] There was a curious postscript to the celebrations. Hitler had sent his personal photographer, Heinrich Hoffman, to film Stalin's earlobes to see whether they were "ingrown and Jewish, or separate and Aryan." They were separate; Stalin passed Hitler's test.[24]

Stalin had found a bedfellow for whose cunning he had held a long and sneaking admiration. Back in 1934, he had observed Hitler eliminate his rivals within the Nazi party in the so-called night of the long knives and remarked: "Did you hear what happened in Germany? Some fellow that Hitler! Splendid! That's a deed of some skill!"[25] Hitler had felt no such mutual admiration. In his early years in power he was set on the dreams of *Mein Kampf*: an alliance with Britain's sea empire while he expanded to the east and built his German land empire on the continent. Only when that plan had clearly failed did Hitler begin to see in Stalin someone with whom he might one day do business.

Stalin was the first of the two to be a mass murderer. In May 1937 as his terror began to move into top gear, he compared his victims with the *boyar* landowners massacred by Ivan the Terrible 400 years before: "Who's going to remember all this riff-raff in ten or 20 years time? No one. Who remembers the names now of the *boyars* Ivan the Terrible got rid of? No one."[26] A week before he invaded Poland, during a conference with his generals Hitler made an eerily similar remark: "Genghis Khan had millions of men and women killed by his own will and with a gay heart. History sees him only as a great state-builder. ... And who, after all, speaks today of the annihilation of the Armenians?"[27]

For both men, mass murder was just another weapon in the ideological struggle. The state, whether Communist or Nazi, was supreme; individuals were its disposable tools. They even extended this idea to their domestic lives. Hitler had secret mistresses, most notably Eva Braun, but in public no woman was allowed to come between him and his nation. One of his secretaries recalled that he used to emphasize again and again: "My lover is Germany."[28] Stalin married twice and had children, but the suicide of his second wife, Nadya, in 1932 further brutalized him. Echoing Hitler, he once remarked: "A true Bolshevik shouldn't and couldn't have a family because he should give himself wholly to the party." Stalin told his son, Vasily: "I'm not Stalin ... Stalin is Soviet power."[29]

The Nazi–Soviet pact inextricably linked these two extreme proponents of totalitarian violence. Eight days after its signing Hitler invaded Poland and Stalin publicly supported his Nazi collaborator, announcing to the world in the Communist Party newspaper *Pravda*: "It is not Germany who has attacked England and France, but England and France who have attacked Germany." The enslavement of Poland united them in blood. SS units killed 60,000 Jews and members of the Polish ruling class. It was Hitler's first experience of mass murder and profoundly influenced him, showing him his followers would actually do it. Stalin's secret police, the NKVD, long versed in mass killing, would carry out similar massacres in the east of Poland. Among their victims were more than 20,000 Polish officers and political prisoners whose bodies would be discovered three years later.

Stalin had entered his pact with Hitler with open eyes and never doubted he was supping with the devil. However, he believed the pact offered the

Soviet Union both protection and opportunity, telling his inner circle just a week after the Nazis invaded Poland: "A war is on between two groups of capitalist countries. ... Hitler, without understanding it or desiring it, is shaking and undermining the capitalist system. ... We can manoeuvre, pit one side against the other to set them fighting with each other as fiercely as possible." He was also eyeing up a further desirable outcome, the chance to expand his communist empire: "What would be the harm if, as a result of the rout of Poland, we were to extend the socialist system onto new territories and populations?"[30]

For Hitler the pact also opened the door to conquest. Having cleared the potential threat to his rear, he could now turn all his energy and attention to planning the invasion of France. On October 1, 1939, Goebbels noted that he was even starting to hint at a desire for long-term collaboration with Stalin: "Conference with the Führer in private. He is convinced of Russia's loyalty. After all Stalin is set to pocket a huge profit."[31] However, Stalin saw no such potential loyalty in Hitler. *Mein Kampf* was still etched in his mind, above all Hitler's youthful ambitions to conquer Russian territory for the new German *Reich*: "If we speak of territory in Europe today, we can primarily have in mind only Russia and her vassal border states."[32]

Because he calculated that Hitler might still one day turn on him, Stalin set out to build a line of buffer zones to protect himself against possible Nazi attack. He forced the Baltic states, Lithuania, Estonia and Latvia, to accept Russian garrisons and on October 3, 1939, told a Latvian delegation: "There has been an unexpected turn, but one cannot rely upon it. We must be prepared in time. Others, who were not prepared, paid for it. The Germans might attack."[33]

Stalin also tried to bully Finland into giving him a swath of territory to provide a salient around Leningrad as a further buffer. When the Finns refused, Stalin sent in the Red Army. It was a disaster. Within days thousands of frozen Russian corpses littered the snow and, although the Finns were finally beaten by sheer weight of numbers and machinery, they managed to kill 125,000 Russian soldiers in the bloody "winter war."

Stalin's reaction was to order his political commissars to the front to shoot the Soviet commanders, but the real fault was his own as his terror had eliminated the Red Army's best officers. For Hitler, the Soviet army's incompetence offered yet more comfort, Goebbels noting on March 15, 1940: "The Russians can never become dangerous for us. If Stalin shoots his own generals, we won't need to do it. So far we've had nothing but advantages from our alliance with Russia."[34]

Now on May 10, 1940, Hitler had struck. The fierce and mutually destructive war of the capitalist and fascist states over which Stalin had drooled eight months before was under way. As always the meticulous creature of habit, he stayed up through the small hours, keeping his *apparatchiks* away from the comforts of bed and sleep. As the sun set on May 10, 1940, he could only wait, watch and hope that Germany on one side and Britain and France on the other would spend years tearing each other apart.

For Hitler May 10 exceeded even his most optimistic dreams. He had been especially nervous about the prospects of the assault against the Belgian block fortifications at Eben-Emael. Preparations for this operation had been so meticulous that a scale model had been built of the area.[35] The atmosphere in Führer headquarters was electric. Had they managed to take the enemy by surprise? By midday reports were streaming in of conquest and success. "The tension is released," wrote Goebbels, "this struggle decides 1000 years of German history."[36] Hitler could believe that providence was guiding him towards his destiny. In London Churchill felt the same. He worked late into the night piecing together his new administration and would later recall that he felt a "profound sense of relief" that he was now the British nation's supreme leader and warlord.[37]

Within 24 hours the entire character of the war had been transformed. A prime minister had fallen and Hitler's war machine was sweeping victoriously towards the Channel. The world seemed to hang in the balance between the two overlords of Europe, Winston Churchill and Adolf Hitler. Yet, though no one understood it, they were the last hurrah of one great period of history, the age of European empires. It was the two warlords of the future watching from the wings, Roosevelt and Stalin, who in the coming five years would emerge the ultimate victors and usher in a new age of two ideologically opposed superpowers.

CHAPTER ONE

May 13–July 31, 1940

Monday, May 13, 1940. Hitler's *Panzer* divisions burst from the forests of the Ardennes, the wooded barrier which the French high command had considered impenetrable. They crushed the skimpy defenses and began their lightning wheel towards the Channel. At midday Hitler gathered with his generals in the briefing room at Felsennest. For once he listened carefully as General Alfred Jodl informed him that German troops had successfully crossed the river Meuse.

The Führer erupted into elation and began barking orders to his exhausted commanders. They were allowed no pause as he set about formulating Directive II, the instructions for the second phase of the campaign. The Wehrmacht was to "thrust in all possible strength north."[1] The "sickle cut" strategy of slicing British and French forces in two was beginning to work. "There—at Felsennest," Hitler later declared, "I knew what I was doing."[2]

That afternoon Winston Churchill stood up to give his first speech to Parliament as prime minister. "There was usually something of an actor in his make-up," noted Ivan Maisky, who was present in the viewing gallery, "but on this occasion he was really and sincerely agitated. His voice even broke from time to time."[3] "I have nothing to offer but blood, toil, tears and sweat," Churchill declared in words that became immortal.[4] But at the time the reaction in the chamber was muted. The Tory establishment still saw Churchill as a renegade and adventurer and his oratory was not to everyone's taste; some in Westminster would have happily agreed with the Nazi propagandists' description of him as a "puffed-up pig," an animal which, as it happened, Churchill greatly admired.[5]

On returning to the Admiralty—he was yet to move into Downing Street—Churchill noticed that a small crowd had gathered. "Good luck, Winnie. God bless you!" they cried as he walked past. Churchill dissolved into tears. "Poor people," he said quietly to his Chief of Staff General Ismay, "they trust me, and I can give them nothing but disaster for quite a long time."[6] As the War Cabinet met late in the evening the news pouring in from the continent was unimaginably grim. Yet, anxious as he was, Churchill was clear about his war aims. He had one objective, behind which everything would fall: the destruction of Adolf Hitler.

"Of course," noted John Colville, the man who three days before had been reluctant to accept the position of private secretary to the new prime minister, "it must be admitted that Winston's administration, with all its faults, has drive."[7] Great Britain was now being led by a man whose commitment to ultimate victory was absolute; the question was how to achieve it as the French army and its famed Maginot line collapsed to the fury of the *Blitzkrieg*.

Churchill had only one answer. One morning in that month of May his son Randolph called on him at breakfast time and found him upstairs "shaving with his old fashioned Valet razor. He had a tough beard and as usual was hacking away." Father told son to sit down and read the papers while he finished shaving. After further minutes of hacking away Churchill turned to Randolph and said: "I think I see my way through." Astounded, Randolph asked his father whether he meant that defeat could be avoided, which seemed possible, or victory won, which seemed incredible. Churchill flung the razor into the basin and said: "Of course, I mean we can beat them." Randolph replied that he was all for it but did not see how it could be done. With great intensity Churchill turned around and said: "I shall drag the United States in."[8]

Just a few days into his premiership Churchill had decided that he must invest his hopes in one man, Franklin Roosevelt. Over the next year and a half, while the two great proponents of 20th-century totalitarianism, Hitler and Stalin, engaged in their psychological duel which would reach its climax with the Nazi invasion of Russia, the two great leaders of twentieth-century democracy waged a parallel psychological duel as Churchill tried to lure Roosevelt into war. This private mental war embracing all four warlords would become the decisive factor in determining the outcome of the world's greatest conflict.

On May 15, 1940, Churchill made his first plea to Roosevelt. He had been awoken at 7 a.m. by a frantic telephone call from France. "The road to Paris is open," Paul Reynaud, the French prime minister, told him, unable to contain his panic, "the battle is lost."[9] With the appalling realization that just five days after Hitler had struck, France was skidding to defeat, Churchill tried to shock Roosevelt into coming immediately to the rescue: "If necessary, we shall continue the war alone, and we are not afraid of that. But I trust you realise," he warned, "that the voice and force of the United States may count for nothing if they are withheld too long." He concluded with a vast shopping list of weapons and supplies. By far the most important request was for the loan of some 40 or 50 American destroyers which had been mothballed since the First World War.[10] The destroyer loan would become the first big test of the prime minister's relationship with the president.

At Cabinet that day Churchill steered his colleagues towards a secondary and more surprising ambition. He said that preparations should be made immediately to forge working relations with Joseph Stalin. While his entreaties to America were to be expected, the Soviet Union seemed a less orthodox target, especially for Churchill, who in 1919 had been instrumental in sending British troops to Russia to help the opponents of Bolshevism in their bloody civil war. But in the 1930s Churchill had come to believe that the Nazis presented a far more menacing threat to British interests, and the world beyond, than the Bolsheviks. While out of office he had made it his business to cultivate the Soviet ambassador to Britain, Ivan Maisky, and pleaded with Chamberlain's government to make a pact with Stalin against Hitler. In the fight against Hitler, any ally was welcome.

While Churchill single-mindedly prepared to fight the Nazis, Hitler was ambiguous towards the British; in the coming days and weeks this would prove a fatal flaw. On May 17, 1940, as his armies continued to sweep all before them, he visited the forward headquarters of army group A at Bastogne. General Gunther Blumentritt witnessed an extraordinary talk by the Führer. "Hitler was in a very good humour," Blumentritt later recalled, "and gave us the opinion that the war would be finished in six weeks." All of this was as expected, but the assembled officers were shocked as Hitler continued: "After that I wish to conclude a reasonable peace with France and then the way will be free for an agreement with Britain." Surprised glances were exchanged as Hitler began to talk of his admiration for the British Empire. "All I want from Great Britain," he announced, "is that she should acknowledge Germany's position on the continent."[11] "If he wants nothing else," General von Rundstedt commented with a sigh of relief after Hitler had departed, "then we shall have peace at last."[12]

But, though he failed to realize it, Hitler was asking for something to which Churchill could never agree. Back in 1935, before the Nazis had even embarked on territorial expansion, he had told a friend: "If Hitler means that we should come to an understanding with Germany to dominate Europe, I think this would be contrary to the whole of our history."[13] Now Hitler was trying to impose that understanding by what he envisaged as a short, brutal war. At this point everything was going well, almost too well. By 9:30 p.m. Hitler was back at Felsennest, holding his final military conference of the day. The army chief of staff, General Franz Halder, noted in his diary: "frightened by his own success, he is afraid to take any chance and so would rather pull the reins on us."[14] Hitler was beginning to hesitate.

In London Churchill was a whirl of action. That morning he had returned from a fleeting visit to Paris where he had been confronted by the defeatism of France's generals. Government offices were burning official papers, a sure sign that moves were afoot to leave the capital. For Churchill, a Francophile who had held such strong faith in the French army and its wall of defense, the blow was shattering.

While he informed the War Cabinet of the smell of defeat in Paris, news came in that German troops had marched into the Belgian capital, Brussels. Then came another devastating disappointment: Joseph Kennedy, the American ambassador in London, arrived with a telegram from Washington. "With regard to the possible loan of 40 or 50 of our older destroyers," Roosevelt wrote in response to Churchill's plea, "a step of that kind could not be taken."[15] The president's refusal was understandable. America was still a land of peace, bound by neutrality laws passed in the 1930s by the United States Congress. Roosevelt had worked a way around those laws to enable America to sell weapons to Britain and France, but the loan of destroyers was too great a political risk. That year, 1940, was a presidential election year and Roosevelt had more or less made up his mind to stand again for an unprecedented third term. He was treading warily.

At 11:30 a.m. on May 18 the War Cabinet met at 10 Downing Street. Churchill's confidence in the face of mounting adversity was beginning at least to reassure those close to him. "Winston is full of fight and thrives on crisis," noted John Colville, who had undergone a total change of heart in just a few days.[16] The prime minister's only problem seemed that he wanted to do everything himself. "Winston would be a better PM," judged the Secretary of State for War, Anthony Eden, "if he did not try to argue the details of war himself. His courage is proud and his spirit too."[17]

Churchill told his Cabinet colleagues that he had chosen a new emissary to Moscow to restore the diplomatic relations which had been disrupted by Russia's war with Finland. The envoy was to be Sir Stafford Cripps, an austere, public school–educated socialist, who had become a leading figure in the Labour Party. Churchill hoped that Stalin would favor Cripps as someone who inhabited the same political universe. It was a bad choice. Cripps could hardly have been further removed from the murderous, hard-drinking coterie with which the Soviet leader surrounded himself. But whether Britain's emissary was a vodka-swilling chorus girl or political fellow traveller was not the point. The question was whether Churchill had anything concrete to offer and, for the moment, his cupboard was bare. On the other hand the pact with Hitler had allowed Stalin to march his troops into half of Poland. While Churchill's key investment was in Roosevelt, Stalin's remained in Hitler.

The Nazi tide rolled on. On May 20 the German army reached the Channel coast. The British Expeditionary Force, along with tens of thousands of French soldiers in northern France, was now cut off, its backs to the sea. The next day Hitler was asked by Grand Admiral Erich Raeder, Commander-in-Chief of the German navy, whether he was seriously contemplating a seaborne invasion of England across the Channel. Hitler gave no sign of even entertaining such an idea. He expected the British, and Churchill, to accept the fact that he had beaten them and to start negotiating a peace deal.

On May 21 General Halder recorded a similar message from the Führer: "Enemy No. 1 for us is France. We are seeking to arrive at an understanding with Britain on the basis of a division of the world."[18] Britain could have its sea empire; Hitler would have Europe. That day at Felsennest he radiated happiness: "What glorious countryside this is! This morning for the first time in 20 years I heard again the trill of nightingales."[19] In London John Colville noted: "At Admiralty House there was chaos ... I have not seen Winston so depressed ... he said: 'In all the history of war I have never seen such mismanagement.'"[20]

The surrounded British Expeditionary Force was now retreating towards the French ports of Boulogne, Calais and Dunkirk. On the morning of May 24 Boulogne fell. The Permanent Under-Secretary at the Foreign Office, Sir Alexander Cadogan, balefully jotted in his diary: "Cabinet 11:30—pretty gloomy. Tanks galloping all over North East France."[21] One of Hitler's elite *Panzer* divisions had advanced to within fifteen miles of Dunkirk. The British Expeditionary Force and the Frenchmen with it seemed done for.

Then twelve minutes later, at 11:42 a.m., while the War Cabinet in London discussed the bloody debacle, Adolf Hitler made one of the most perplexing decisions of the war. He ordered his tanks to halt. It would turn out to be a strategic blunder of huge magnitude for which Hitler's precise reasons remain unclear to this day. Certainly there were military factors. The day before Hermann Goering had assured Hitler that his Luftwaffe on its own would eliminate the British forces, and the field commander of the spearhead tanks was happy to give his men and machines a rest. But Hitler's long-held dream of an ultimate collaboration with Britain may also have affected him at this crucial moment. On May 25, the day after the halt order, General Jeschonnek, head of the air staff and a close associate of Goering, who may have picked up hints from Hitler, remarked: "The Führer wants to spare the British a humiliating defeat."[22]

General Halder found it incredible: "Our armored and motorized forces have stopped as if paralyzed in compliance with top-level orders, and must not attack. ... These orders from the top just make no sense. ... They freeze the troops to the spot when the enemy could be cut into any time you wanted to attack."[23] Finally on May 26 Hitler rescinded the halt order. His spearhead tanks captured Boulogne and Calais and the German army closed on Dunkirk.

Hitler's adjutant, Major Gerhard Engel, noted Goering's continued assurances that the Luftwaffe was allowing no escape: "Goering reports successes at Duenkirchen harbor, says word for word: 'Only fishing boats get through; I hope the tommies are good swimmers.'"[24]

The friction between Hitler and his generals was matched by Churchill's first crisis at home. The French government, which was bound by treaty to consult with Britain on any negotiation with Germany, asked for permission to explore peace terms with Hitler. It planned to approach the Italian dictator Mussolini to act as an intermediary. At a series of meetings of the War Cabinet between May 26 and 28 the Foreign Secretary, Lord Halifax, the man who could have become prime minister, argued that Britain should agree to the request, saying that there would be no harm in seeing what kind of deal Hitler had to offer. Churchill opposed the idea but on the first day of the critical War Cabinet meetings, it seemed a majority might line up against him and side with Halifax. Only two weeks after becoming prime minister, Churchill was in real political danger.

As the argument continued on May 27, the war news grew ever grimmer. The Belgian king surrendered and the troops moving back towards Dunkirk were more exposed than ever. At the afternoon meeting of the War Cabinet Halifax continued to insist that there was nothing to be lost by approaching Mussolini to put out feelers. Churchill passionately argued that this was a slippery slope, which would not only be futile, but involve deadly danger. "We are going to fight to the end," he declared, "our prestige in Europe is very low. The only way we can get it back is by showing the world that Germany has not beaten us."[25] Halifax was infuriated. "It drives me to despair," he told Alexander Cadogan, "when he works himself up into a passion of emotion when he ought to make his brain think and reason. ... I cannot work with Winston any longer."[26] Cadogan told Halifax not to do anything silly under stress.

The next day, the argument in the War Cabinet shifted in Churchill's favor on the grounds that it was unwise to explore peace terms at this moment of weakness when there were so few counters to bargain with. At 6 p.m. Churchill met his full Cabinet. "If this long island story of ours is to end at last," he announced with great emotion and intensity, "let it end only when each one of us lies choking in his own blood upon the ground."[27] His colleagues' cheers reverberated through Westminster. An hour later the War Cabinet agreed that there would be no overture to Hitler. Churchill had survived the first real challenge to his authority; just as importantly, Halifax stayed in the government and unity was preserved.[28]

At Felsennest, Hitler, unaware of events in London, was watching with growing satisfaction as Churchill's troops scurried from the continent. "The sweat of fear comes out of all his pores," Joseph Goebbels crowed, "the great victory is waiting."[29] On May 29 Hitler took time out to tour the places where he served at the front in the First World War. At 10 p.m. the simple pleasures of the day were complicated by a cable from his ambassador in Moscow, Count von der Schulenburg, who reported that Stalin had agreed to accept Stafford Cripps as British ambassador. Schulenburg assured Hitler: "There is no reason for apprehension concerning Cripps' mission, since there is no reason to doubt the loyal attitude of the Soviet Union toward us."[30]

The Foreign Office in London agreed with that verdict, a senior civil servant, Orme Sargeant, noting: "I suspect that Stalin, who probably has a keen sense of humour, is going to make the most of the false position into which he has now manoeuvred us." Sargeant concluded that Stalin viewed Cripps as no more than a plaything whom he could use "to annoy the Germans without provoking any unpleasant measures of retaliation from them."[31]

Stalin appeared still to be more interested in Britain as a target for communist expansionism than as a potential partner. Recently declassified transcripts of phone taps by B Division, MI5's counter-espionage unit, show that a lavish Soviet espionage campaign conducted by agents under cover in the Soviet Embassy and the Russian Trade Delegation was monitored constantly by MI5.[32] Occasionally these subterranean activities surfaced in the form of high-profile arrests, such as the case of John Herbert King, a cipher clerk at the Foreign Office who was exposed as a Soviet agent in September 1939. He had been passing secret information, possibly relating to the Anglo–Soviet negotiations that preceded the Nazi–Soviet pact,[33] to his Soviet handler Andrei Gorsky.[34]

For Stalin, subversion was a serious business. In his diary, declassified in 2002, Guy Liddell, the wartime head of MI5's B Division, admitted: "There is no doubt that the Russians are better in the matter of espionage than any other country in the world."[35] Evidence to support this came from the defection in January 1940 of Walter Krivitsky, the former head of Soviet Military Intelligence in western Europe, who became the most significant defector yet from the elite of the Soviet intelligence services. Krivitsky gave tantalizing clues pointing to a network of agents embedded deep in both the British government and the intelligence services. Though he did not know their identities, he was talking about the Cambridge Five, headed by the notorious trio of Burgess, Maclean and Philby.

There was overt communist agitation too. From constant secret surveillance, including phone taps, mail intercepts and infiltration,[36] MI5 had no doubts that the Communist Party of Great Britain was "only an off-shoot" of the national party in Moscow and, as such, held a potent threat to national security.[37] MI5 was right. In his diary Georgi Dimitrov, the head of Comintern, recorded Stalin's instructions on the outbreak of war that the Communist Party of Great Britain should act as the "gravediggers at the funeral of capitalism."[38]

Churchill was an avid reader of intelligence reports, but believed he could not allow the overwhelming evidence of Soviet subversion to obstruct him in his quest to seek partners in the fight against Hitler. Later he wrote: "We were under no illusions about the Russian attitude. We nonetheless pursued a patient policy of trying to re-establish relations of a confidential character with Russia."[39] The consequences of appeasing Stalin would take years to unfold. Now, as May 1940 turned to June, the immediate crisis, the battle of France, was entering its final, fatal phase.

The greater part of the British Expeditionary Force, more than 330,000 men, accompanied by 100,000 French soldiers, had made their miraculous escape from Dunkirk. "We shall fight on the beaches, we shall fight on the landing grounds, we shall fight in the fields and in the streets, we shall fight in the hills," Churchill announced to a packed House of Commons on June 4.[40] The next day Hitler launched Nazi forces at Paris and their spearheads sped across the river Somme. French forces fought hard, their casualties exceeding even the murderous killing rate of the deadliest battles of the First World War. But they were badly led and the tactics of their generals outdated in the face of the mechanized might of the *Blitzkrieg*.

Hitler moved his headquarters to Bruly de Pesche, closer to the French–Belgian border. "Churchill is half mad," he declared to his inner circle on June 5, "He will ruin England."[41] Hitler was now realizing that Churchill was the obstacle to the peace deal he wanted, but he was sure that the British people would come to terms despite their deranged new leader. "I want to spare England," he pronounced, "an equitable peace would be the best thing here." The one proviso was that British forces "should not retain the ability to attack us."[42]

Then, on June 10, an unexpected twist seemed to give Britain and France new hope. The Italian dictator, Benito Mussolini, eager to share in the spoils of victory before the fighting was over, declared war. Hitler was infuriated at his ally's presumption: "That is the most belated declaration of war in the world. I would never have thought *Il Duce* was so primitive."[43] Churchill pithily told John Colville: "People who go to Italy to look at ruins won't have to go as far as Naples and Pompeii in future."[44] The most significant reaction came from the other side of the Atlantic.

In Charlottesville, Virginia, Roosevelt stood stiffly in his uncomfortable leg braces before a lectern at the University of Virginia. In order to conceal the paralyzing effects of the polio he had caught as a young man, the president had ordered that the metal of these primitive braces be painted black so that they would not catch the light and alert people to his disability. That evening his audience was not just those few in the auditorium but also millions around the world to whom his speech was being broadcast. The president's tone was a revelation. "The hand that held the dagger," he thundered, "has struck it into the back of its neighbor."[45] "The Boss," recalled President Roosevelt's devoted secretary Grace Tully, "was enraged."[46] Roosevelt then appeared to make an unequivocal offer of immediate practical help to Britain and France: "We will extend to the opponent of force," he announced, "all the material resources of this nation."[47]

In London Churchill and his colleagues sat up late to listen to the speech and the thrilling prospects which Roosevelt seemed to be brandishing. "We all listened to you last night and were fortified by the grand scope of your declaration," he cabled the president and then repeated his request for the loan of the destroyers. "Nothing is so important," he wrote, ending with a flourish designed to further his aim of wrapping the president into the European war: "I send you my heartfelt thanks and those of my colleagues for all you are doing and seeking to do for what we now indeed call the Common Cause."[48]

John Colville watched Churchill's swelling optimism with a dubious gaze. "Winston has sent a graphic telegram to Roosevelt, describing the impending catastrophe," he wrote in his diary, "and he seems to hope that America will come in now, at any rate as a non-belligerent ally. But can American support, in materials, be made effective in time?"[49] In Nazi HQ, the view was scathing. "Roosevelt," commented Joseph Goebbels with characteristic scorn, "has nothing left for the western powers except sympathy. And it's well known how much use that is against Stukas."[50]

On the afternoon of June 11, after the message to Roosevelt had been sent to Washington, Churchill flew over to France to meet the French Cabinet, which had now left Paris and was lodging at a chateau near Orleans in central France. He did not know that the day before, the defeatist French Commander-in-Chief, General Weygand, had told his prime minister, Paul Reynaud, that France had no choice but to seek an armistice. To any suggestion from Churchill of alternative, even guerrilla, forms of resistance, Weygand's mind was closed.

The next morning, June 12, after a further pessimistic meeting, Churchill flew back to London in his Flamingo aircraft, which was normally escorted by twelve Hurricanes. The morning was cloudy, which made it impossible for the Hurricanes to join up. Churchill took the risk of flying alone. As the Flamingo neared the Channel, the weather cleared and its passengers could see the port of Le Havre in flames eight thousand feet below. Crossing the Channel, the pilot made a sudden dive to one hundred feet above the sea and skimmed his way back to the coast. Churchill only learned later that they had passed beneath two German fighters which were attacking fishing boats. The Germans had not spotted the defenseless Flamingo.

On June 13 Churchill sent a desperate message to Roosevelt. "French have sent for me again, which means that crisis has arrived. Am just off. Anything you can say or do to help them now may make a difference."[51] Churchill's destination was Tours, the next stage of the French government's retreat that would soon end in Bordeaux. When his party arrived at Tours airport, which had been heavily bombed the previous night, there was chaos everywhere and no one to meet them. They borrowed a car and headed for the local *préfecture*. Once again they found no one of consequence. A hungry Churchill insisted on lunch and a local café was specially opened.

When Reynaud finally arrived, he made it apparent to Churchill that, while he personally would fight on, only one thing might now prevent the French Cabinet insisting on an armistice: American entry into the war, even if in the first instance this only meant sending warships over to Europe. While Churchill was in Tours, a cable arrived from Roosevelt for Reynaud repeating his offer of help: "As I have already stated to you and to Mr. Churchill, this government is doing everything in its power to make available to the Allied governments the material they so urgently require, and our efforts to do still more are being redoubled. This is so because of our faith in and our support of the ideals for which the Allies are fighting."[52]

Now it seemed to Churchill that private messages were not enough. To keep France in the fight, the president had to go public and commit America to the possibility of war. Churchill sent another transatlantic cable. "Mr. President I must tell you that it seems to me absolutely vital that this message should be published tomorrow June 14 in order that it may play the decisive part in turning the course of world history."[53]

The following morning, June 14, Churchill was awoken at first light by a phone call from Joseph Kennedy. His hope of the night before was shattered as the American ambassador told him that Roosevelt had refused to make public his letter to Reynaud. "My message ... was in no sense intended to commit and did not commit the government to military participation in support of Allied governments," the president wrote. "I am unable to agree to your request that my message be published since I believe it to be imperative that there be avoided any possible misunderstanding."[54] It was a crushing response.

The dark cloud of depression engulfing 10 Downing Street was further blackened by news from France. Hitler's troops had marched into Paris. It was the sixth capital to submit to the Nazi warlord in less than nine months.

Churchill spent the night at Chequers, the British prime minister's country residence in the Chiltern Hills 30 miles from London. John Colville recorded that "dinner began lugubriously. However champagne, brandy and cigars did their work and we soon became talkative, even garrulous."[55] After dinner Churchill paced up and down the rose garden in the summer moonlight with his son-in-law, Duncan Sandys. Colville was constantly on the telephone to London, emerging to search out Churchill among the rose bushes with updates of news. "I told him that fuller information had been received about the French attitude, which appeared to be slipping. 'Tell them,' he said, 'that if they let us have their fleet we shall never forget, but that if they surrender without consulting us, we shall never forgive. We shall blacken their name for a thousand years!' Then, half afraid I might take him seriously, he added: 'Don't, of course, do that just yet.' He was in high spirits, repeating poetry, dilating on the drama of the present situation."[56]

On June 17, the French government sued for peace. The next day Hitler met Mussolini in Munich, the two men parading before a crowd of cheering, smiling, hysterical supporters. After six weeks of *Blitzkrieg*, Hitler's new *Reich* included France, Belgium, Holland, Norway, Denmark, Poland, Austria and Czechoslovakia. "He is deeply moved and seized with emotion," noted Goebbels, "the English are still bold and declare their desire to carry on fighting alone. We'll see about that."[57]

The Italian foreign minister, Count Galeazzo Ciano, was among the party and assessed the Führer's state of mind. "Hitler makes many reservations on the desirability of dismantling the British Empire, which he considers, even today, to be an important factor in world equilibrium," he recorded in his diary. "Hitler is now like the gambler who, having made a big win, would like to cash in his chips, risking nothing more."[58] For Hitler victory had lanced a boil: Germany's defeat in the First World War had been avenged. Now, for the first time in his political life, he wanted a rest from conquest and, in line with his core instincts, peace with Britain.

While the *Blitzkrieg* was a triumph for Hitler, it was a disaster for Stalin. The long-lasting and mutually destructive war of the capitalist and fascist states, which he had so gleefully anticipated, was over in a trice. "Couldn't they have put up any resistance at all?" he complained angrily to his acolyte, Nikita Khrushchev. "Now Hitler's going to beat our brains in!"[59] As Hitler strutted in Munich, Stalin, with gritted teeth, sent his congratulations on the Wehrmacht's "splendid success." Behind the closed walls of the Kremlin he was panicking. "He was extremely nervous," Khrushchev recalled, "racing around, cursing like a cab driver. He cursed the French. He cursed the English. How could they allow Hitler to defeat them, to crush them?"[60]

Stalin's mental duel with Hitler hung in the balance. Fearing that Hitler, having won his victory in the west, might immediately be tempted by his long-held ambition of expanding to the east, he now embarked on a double strategy, going on a ten-day land grab to expand and protect his empire while also trying not to provoke Hitler. Russian troops occupied the Baltic states and Bessarabia, the northern province of Romania. These moves were allowed under the Nazi–Soviet pact. But Stalin also decided to invade another Romanian province, Bukowina, which was not assigned to him under the pact. Though he did not realize it, the Soviet leader was playing a dangerous game.

In London Churchill now stood alone against Hitler. June 18 was the 125th anniversary of the battle of Waterloo, but there was nothing to celebrate. That afternoon he made his famous "Finest Hour" speech to the House of Commons. Four hours later he repeated the speech on radio. Many listeners, including friends, criticized its delivery, thinking Churchill sounded tired or as if he had been drinking. That evening his mood was dark. "Another bloody country gone west, I'll bet," he raged at the long-suffering John Colville, as the final telegram of the day was brought. Churchill was so flustered he spilt whisky and soda all over his papers.[61] Worse was to come.

In Washington Roosevelt had watched the French surrender with dismay. He feared that Britain might go the same way and decided that, for the moment, there was little point in helping a drowning man. To the disappointment of some in his Cabinet, he refused again to loan Churchill the First World War American destroyers. "It is my belief that unless we help out the British with some destroyers it is hopeless to expect them to keep going," Roosevelt's treasury secretary, Henry Morgenthau, wrote to his boss.[62] The president was unmoved. Even a letter from King George VI, who had spent a memorable few days at Roosevelt's family house in Hyde Park, New York State, in June 1939, had no effect. Roosevelt chose to ignore the monarch's appeal that "the need is becoming greater every day if we are to carry on our solitary fight for freedom to a successful conclusion."[63]

On June 19 Colville sorrowfully noted in his diary: "President R. has turned down our demand for 40 destroyers. We need them badly."[64] This opening skirmish in his duel with Roosevelt was a shattering blow to Churchill. In reality he had deluded himself in thinking even fleetingly that Roosevelt could at that stage have made any declaration committing Americans to the prospect of war. Yet Roosevelt had made an unequivocal promise of help both privately and publicly. It should have been a warning that the president's words could not always be taken at face value.

After his immense victory, Hitler began to relax. The Wehrmacht high command warned him that peace must immediately be made with Britain or a cross-Channel invasion swiftly prepared and realized. Major Engel noted his response: "Führer is doubtful and considers Britain so weak that bigger operations on land won't be necessary after bombardment. F. remarks 'that they will give in now in any case.'"[65]

Instead of pressing on with the battle, Hitler went walkabout. At 5:30 a.m. on June 28, 1940, he stepped out of his plane at Le Bourget airport. Accompanied by his architects Albert Speer and Hermann Gielser he began a tour of Paris, his one and only visit to the occupied French capital. Beginning at L'Opéra, Hitler's tour finished at Sacré-Coeur, the perfect vantage point to view his latest prize. "It was a dream of my life to be permitted to see Paris," Hitler confided to Albert Speer as the three-hour tour came to an end. "I cannot say how happy I am to have that dream fulfilled."[66] "When we're finished in Berlin," the Führer whispered as they stood overlooking the beautiful French capital, "Paris will only be a shadow."[67] By lunchtime he had returned to field headquarters and the disconcerting news that Soviet troops had included Bukowina in their land grab. Stalin's rapacity lodged in Hitler's mind, but this was, for the moment, a time to dream of peace, not further confrontation.

On July 1, a steamy summer's day in Moscow, Sir Stafford Cripps was led from the baking streets into the inner sanctum of Soviet power, the Kremlin Palace, for his first meeting with Stalin as British ambassador. Cripps was carrying a letter from Churchill. He watched in silence as the dictator's cold, dark eyes moved dispassionately over Churchill's carefully crafted message. "Geographically our two countries lie at the opposite extremities of Europe, and from the point of view of systems of government it may be said that they stand for widely differing systems of political thought. But I trust that these facts need not prevent the relations between our two countries in the international sphere from being harmonious and mutually beneficial."

Churchill stated that "the problem before all Europe—our countries included—is how the states and peoples of Europe are going to react towards the prospect of Germany establishing a hegemony over the Continent." He declared that "the British government certainly intend to use their geographical position and their great resources" in a bid to defeat Hitler, and that he merely wanted to assure Stalin of his "readiness to discuss fully with the Soviet government any of the vast problems" created by "Germany's present attempt to pursue in Europe a methodical process by successive stages of conquest and absorption."[68] It was a subtle and exquisitely drafted appeal to Stalin to beware of Hitler and come over to Britain's side. Stalin did not bother even to reply to Churchill's letter. Instead, to show Hitler his loyalty, he reported Churchill's approach to Berlin.

Hitler now began to make his own interpretation of these two pieces of evidence, Stalin's greed in Romania and Churchill's approach. Before the war he had described to his adjutant his secretive mental processes. "Bear in mind that my brain works like a calculating machine. Each person who makes a presentation to me introduces into this calculating machine a small wheel of information. There forms a certain picture, or a number on each wheel. I press a button and there flashes into my mind the sum of all this information."[69] The Hitler calculating machine would now begin to build a conspiracy theory which would be the turning point in his duel with Stalin and have devastating consequences.

Back in London the Foreign Office quickly concluded that Cripps's first meeting with Stalin had put paid to Churchill's hopes that an alliance with Stalin could soon be forged. "Stalin has … got Sir S. Cripps exactly where he wants him," wrote Orme Sargeant, the senior official on the Russia desk, "that is to say, as a suppliant doormat holding his pathetic little peace offerings of tin in one hand and rubber in the other." Sargeant concluded that Stalin only had one use in mind for Cripps: "to be able to counter any German browbeating and nagging by pointing to Sir S. Cripps on the doormat, and by threatening to have him in and start talking with him instead of with the German ambassador."[70] But if Stalin, in meeting Cripps, had partly wished to keep Hitler in check by hinting that there was another game in town beside the Nazis, he was making a big mistake.

Hitler's priority was still to force Britain into a peace negotiation, but Churchill's obstinacy loomed ever larger. "He wants to speak to the *Reichstag* and give England a last chance," Goebbels wrote on July 2 of Hitler's latest plans. "But will she show an interest in this?" he continued uncertainly. "Churchill certainly will not. He is a fool ... if London ignores this, it will be responsible for the outcomes. These will be horrifying."[71] As well as planning this peace offer, the two men were putting in place the final arrangements for Hitler's triumphal return to Berlin. The victory parade was to be four days later on Saturday, July 6, the overture to Great Britain in a speech to the *Reichstag* the following Monday. Goebbels was correct in his assumption that Churchill would rather invite total destruction than make peace with Hitler. But neither he nor Hitler had counted on the immediacy of Churchill's defiance. Their carefully made plans were laid waste in a hail of shells just 24 hours later.

At 5:55 p.m. on July 3, 1940, at the port of Oran in French Algeria, the British navy attacked the most modern warships of its former ally, France. Churchill, who was determined to remove the French fleet from the war, had given an ultimatum to the French admiral: sail to Britain, sail to America, or scuttle your ships. At the appointed hour there was no clear response and the Royal Navy opened fire. By 6:04 p.m. 1,250 French soldiers were dead and three battleships were ablaze. It was a daring move that caused horrific destruction. Churchill told John Colville the French were now fighting with all their vigor for the first time since war broke out.

The next day Churchill went to the House of Commons to explain the attack on a nation which only two weeks before had been Britain's main ally. "The premier was visibly agitated," noted Ivan Maisky, who was watching the scene from inside the chamber. "The members listened to him with bated breath."[72] "However painful," Churchill declared, "the action we have already taken should be, in itself, sufficient to dispose once and for all of the lies and Fifth Column activities that we have the slightest intention of entering into negotiations," he thundered. "We shall prosecute the war with the utmost vigour by all the means that are open to us."[73]

Inside the Commons the response was remarkable. "When Churchill finished," Maisky explained excitedly, "there took place a scene which 'old hands' in Parliament told me, had never occurred before: all the members with one accord, in a kind of spontaneous outburst, sprang up and gave the premier a real ovation."[74] It was a message intended not just for the British people, but for the world beyond, including present enemies and potential friends, the most important among them the American president.

Roosevelt was in the White House, looking forward to a rest at Hyde Park, the scenic family estate by the Hudson River. He had declared just days before that Britain's chances of survival were merely 50-50; now he bestowed on Churchill much better odds.[75] The prime minister's bold strike at Oran impressed Roosevelt immeasurably, particularly as he had become obsessed by the possibility of the French fleet falling into Nazi hands.[76] He let the British embassy in Washington know that he approved.

On July 6 Hitler made his triumphal return to Berlin. "Overhead is a wonderful July sun. A real day of celebration," Goebbels noted in breathless awe, "the streets are strewn with flowers like a bright carpet. An unimaginable ecstasy fills the city." Thousands of people had been waiting more than six hours by the time Hitler's train pulled into the Anhalter station at 3 p.m. Goebbels enthusiastically described the mood of elation: "A roar of joy fills the station. The Führer is very moved. Tears come into his eyes. Our Führer!"[77] Cheering crowds, their enthusiasm wholly spontaneous and surpassing any of the prewar victory parades, followed Hitler along the whole of his drive to the *Reich* Chancellery.

However, in the midst of his triumph, Hitler was increasingly tormented by one overriding thought. As far as he was concerned, he had won the war. So why did the British not recognize that fact and make peace with him? Why instead were they carrying on their fight, even advertising their determination with the action at Oran? Hitler began to convince himself that there must be some external factor on which Britain—and Churchill— were relying.

A few days after the glory of Berlin General Halder recorded a major development in Hitler's thinking: "The Führer is greatly puzzled by Britain's persisting unwillingness to make peace. He sees the answer in Britain's hope in Russia."[78] Hitler was beginning to believe that Churchill was holding out because he had a secret deal in the offing with Stalin. His building conspiracy theory was standing in the way of clear decision-making. "The Führer is as indecisive as never before and doesn't know what to do or how to do it," recorded Engel.[79] Churchill gave Colville an uncannily accurate insight into his Nazi opponent's dilemma: "The PM keeps on repeating that 'Hitler must invade or fail. If he fails he is bound to go east, and fail he will.'"[80]

On July 16 Hitler finally signed Directive No. 16 for Preparations of a Landing Operation against England. "I have determined," he claimed, "to prepare a landing operation against England." This was, he stated, "since England ... still gives no recognizable signs of readiness to come to terms." Despite the hopes of his generals, rhetoric outweighed reality. The Supreme Command did not take the order seriously, and Hitler told Goering in private that he had no intention of carrying out the invasion.[81] Instead, he continued to work on one last appeal to the British to make peace.

Three days later, for the second time in a fortnight, Hitler paraded through Berlin to the sound of jackboots and the gleam of helmets. This time his destination was the Reichstag, finally to deliver the much-delayed speech on which he had been working so painstakingly. He saw Churchill, in Goebbels' words, as "a raging fool who had burned his bridges."[82] But the British people might still be open to persuasion. "Mr. Churchill," Hitler declared in a tone that was intended to convey reason rather than rant, "has repeated that he wants war. Mr. Churchill should place trust in me when as a prophet I now proclaim: a great world empire will be destroyed—a world empire which I never had the ambition to destroy, or as much as harm. Alas, I am aware that the continuation of this war will end only in the complete shattering of one of the two warring parties. Mr. Churchill may believe this to be Germany. I know it to be England. In this hour I feel compelled, standing before my conscience, to direct yet another appeal to reason in England. I see no compelling reason which could force the continuation of this war."[83] It was a prophecy of great accuracy, except in its conclusion.

"Hitler speaks simply, and, I should say also, in an unusually humane tone," observed Ciano, who had come to Berlin for the great occasion. "I believe his desire for peace is sincere."[84] When asked by a colleague whether he planned to respond, Churchill was curt. "I do not," he said, "propose to say anything in reply to Herr Hitler's speech, not being on speaking terms with him."[85] Ciano recorded: "Late in the evening, when the first cold British reactions to the speech arrive, a sense of unconcealed disappointment spreads among the Germans."[86]

That day, by pure coincidence, Franklin Roosevelt was nominated as Democratic candidate for president for an unprecedented third term. He had preferred to stay away from the party convention, wishing to be drafted as candidate rather than be seen to be campaigning for it. His acceptance speech was read out in his absence and contained a coded attack on Nazi aggression: "The fact which dominates our world is the fact of armed aggression, of successful armed aggression, aimed at the form of government, the kind of society that we in the United States have chosen and established for ourselves."[87] It was another wheel of information for Hitler's calculating machine of a mind to slot into place. He was now seeing specters across the globe.

On July 22 Hitler pieced together all these factors into an interim assessment for his generals. "The reasons for continuation of war by Britain," Hitler told them. "One: it hopes for a change in America … Two: it puts hope in Russia. Stalin is flirting with Britain to keep her in the war and tie us down."[88] Nothing could have been further from the truth. The delusion was mounting every day.

The next day Hitler went to see *Götterdämmerung* at the Bayreuth Festival. The summer before he had the time to see seven Wagner operas; this year he only saw one. Then he was excited as he prepared to invade Poland; now frustrated as his unwanted war with Britain dragged on. *Götterdämmerung* ends with the destruction of Valhalla, the mythical home of the gods. But whose destruction would Hitler bring about on earth? He retreated to the mountains of Obersalzberg. "We are waiting and waiting," Goebbels complained, "when will the Führer launch the attack on England?"[89] In London there was increasing confidence that it was not going to happen. "At the risk of being proved wrong tomorrow morning (which I don't mind)," noted Alexander Cadogan, "I do not think Hitler is going to be fool enough to attempt an invasion."[90]

On July 31, six weeks after the fall of France, Churchill wrote to Roosevelt to ask yet again for the loan of the First World War destroyers: "Mr. President, with great respect I must tell you that in the long history of the world, this is a thing to do now."[91] Circumstances had changed. The shock of Hitler's conquests had forced many Americans into a rethink about the cataclysm in Europe and the prospect of a rampant Hitler. Opinion polls showed that the number willing to help Britain, even if it meant the United States being dragged into the war, had jumped from 30 to 60 percent. Roosevelt could see that Churchill and the British intended to fight on, come what may. He viewed Churchill's request with renewed sympathy.

On that same day, as the prime minister's letter was telegraphed across the Atlantic, a momentous conference was under way at the Berghof. At 11:30 a.m. Hitler walked into the meeting room at his mountain retreat. The air was clear and bright and his sense of unwavering confidence had returned. He announced to his generals the result of weeks of agonized reflection. "Russia is the factor on which Britain is relying the most," he concluded. "Something must have happened in London. The British were completely down; now they have perked up again. With Russia smashed, Britain's last hope would be shattered. The sooner Russia is crushed the better. If we start in May 1941, we would have five months to finish the job."[92]

It was as yet only a plan, should all other means of bringing the British to heel fail. But two enormous delusions, the first that he had already won the war, the second that some secret deal was brewing between Britain and Russia, were leading Hitler down the road to catastrophe.

CHAPTER TWO

August 1, 1940–March 26, 1941

August 1, 1940, Moscow. A year after the Nazi–Soviet pact had shocked the world and one day after Adolf Hitler had planted the seeds for an invasion of Russia, Joseph Stalin offered a public riposte to anyone who doubted the longevity of his collaboration with the Nazi leader. Vyacheslav Molotov, often deployed as his mouthpiece, was dispatched to the Supreme Soviet to make a speech. "Our relations with Germany," Molotov informed the party faithful, "which were radically changed nearly a year ago, remain entirely as laid down in the Soviet–German agreement."[1] Stalin could feel a certain satisfaction. In the previous weeks he had expanded the Soviet empire by incorporating the Baltic states and two provinces of Romania, and Hitler still appeared to be on side.

At the Berghof, as the late summer sun glinted on high glacial strips, the Führer had just signed Directive No. 17. "In order to create the conditions to defeat Britain, I intend," he promised his generals, "to carry out the air and naval war against the British homeland more keenly than previously."[2] Despite his pronouncements on Russia of the day before, the key tactic remained to force the British to make peace without the dangers of a cross-Channel invasion.

Under cover of darkness a swarm of German planes headed over the Channel. Over the south coast of England the pilots steered themselves above carefully chosen targets and hundreds of bundles were ejected. As the shadowy objects plummeted to the ground Hitler's airmen made quickly for home. These were not bombs, however, but leaflets, copies of Hitler's final appeal for peace. It confirmed the view in Churchill's inner circle that the Nazis were sidestepping a direct assault. "It looks as if the military authorities are becoming more doubtful of their ability to invade us rapidly and successfully," observed John Colville as the news of this peculiar bombing raid reached No. 10.[3] It was a Friday and the prime minister was preparing for a weekend at Chequers. Even if he personally believed there would be no invasion, he wanted his nation to keep up its guard. He began work on an article for the Sunday papers warning that peaceful noises from Berlin meant nothing.

That same morning President Roosevelt received a stinging memo from his interior secretary, Harold Ickes, protesting at the United States' failure to help the British. "It seems to me that we Americans are like the householder who refuses to lend or sell his fire extinguishers to help put out the fire in the house that is right next door," Ickes complained, "although that house is all ablaze and the wind is blowing from that direction."[4] Ickes imagined, as had happened before, that the president would brush his complaint politely under the carpet; that afternoon he set out for the weekly cabinet meeting determined to press his case. What he did not know was that, in response to Churchill's repeated request for the destroyer loan, Roosevelt was having a change of heart.

"It was the general opinion, without any dissenting voice," the president recorded, "that the survival of the British Isles under German attack might very possibly depend on their getting these destroyers. It was agreed that legislation to accomplish this is necessary."[5] However, Roosevelt intended to attach strings to his offer. One was a written guarantee from Churchill that, should the Nazis appear to be on the verge of a successful invasion of Britain, the ships of the British navy "would not be sunk, but would sail for North American or British Empire ports where they would remain afloat and available."[6] "I think you will feel with me," Roosevelt replied to Ickes, "that we made real progress today."[7] Lord Lothian, the British ambassador in Washington, was approached that afternoon with details of Roosevelt's offer and he telegraphed them urgently to London. Roosevelt also declared that some kind of trade would have to be made with the British to satisfy the Republicans in the United States Congress.

Hitler had called for the intensification of the air offensive against Britain to begin on August 5, 1940; the weather stepped in and delayed the attack.

One project was stalled, but that same day he was presented with plans for the potential invasion of Russia. General Erich Marcks, who had been designated to draw up a blueprint, envisaged 147 German divisions launching an attack that would secure victory within a mere seventeen weeks.

On August 6 Churchill, after an invigorating weekend in the countryside, was examining Lord Lothian's cable and a follow-up telegram from the president. The very suggestion that the British could ever be conquered by Hitler put him into a cantankerous mood. "Winston was in a nervous and irritable frame of mind in the evening," John Colville noted. "He refuses to contemplate a promise to give Canada, and thus the US, a lien on our warships if these islands are conquered and brands any such proposal as defeatism."[8] "Pray make it clear at once," Churchill telegraphed to Lothian the next day, "that we could never agree to the slightest compromise of our full liberty of action, nor tolerate any such defeatist notion, the effect of which would be disastrous."[9]

There was a further unpalatable condition. To keep Congress sweet, the president was adamant that the loan of military hardware be given the appearance of a quid pro quo. He asked Churchill to lease a set of British naval bases in the Caribbean and Newfoundland to the United States for 99 years in return for the mothballed First World War destroyers. Churchill did not mind the Americans having the bases but felt humiliated that it should be made to appear a trade. In a transatlantic phone call with the American Attorney General, Robert Jackson, he remarked: "Empires just don't bargain." Jackson replied: "Republics do."[10]

Despite the frustrations, the door to American aid was at least opening. In Moscow the chance of any meaningful link with Russia remained frozen as Sir Stafford Cripps endured a fruitless meeting with Molotov. Stalin's foreign minister listed eight reasons why the USSR was not at that moment contemplating an alliance with Great Britain, foremost on his inventory being the territorial gains the Soviet Union had been able to accomplish with the blessing of its German allies. "Agreements with Germany have thus been of real value; Soviet interests are protected by these pacts and agreements," Molotov declared. Cripps listened in abject silence as Molotov explained that the Nazi–Soviet pact had "facilitated the adjustment of our relations with the Baltic states."[11] The inference was clear: to make any kind of progress the British government would have to recognize the new Soviet boundaries and spheres of influence.

On that Tuesday afternoon Churchill was in a foul temper, irritated by an interruption of his traditional after-lunch nap. A greater threat to his peace of mind then arrived as the weather allowed Operation "Eagle," the result of Hitler's Directive No. 17, to get under way. Some 1,485 German fighter planes flew sorties against British aircraft factories and other installations vital to the war effort. It was a dramatic show of force and a major escalation in the air raids Britain had been sporadically enduring since July. "What is the motive of these gigantic daylight raids," Colville asked anxiously, "are they reconnaissance in force, or a diversion, or just the cavalry attack before the main offensive?"[12] There was some comfort to be gleaned from what seemed at first to be a bleak afternoon. Though they were outnumbered, Fighter Command claimed it had shot down a total of 45 German aircraft for the loss of only thirteen British planes.

The next day Roosevelt finalized his destroyer offer. "The plan," noted the U.S. Treasury Secretary, Henry Morgenthau, who was among those aiding Roosevelt with the fine detail, "is that England is to give us land in Newfoundland, Bermuda, Trinidad, and some other places in exchange for the 50 destroyers. The president also mentioned giving them 20 speed boats which we once had contracted and revoked, also five long distance four-engine bombers and five long distance navy bombers."[13] Roosevelt squared Congress by showing it was a staggeringly good deal for the United States. He wrote to Senator David Walsh, a member of the Naval Affairs Committee who had initially put up substantial opposition: "For 50 ships, which are on their last legs anyway, we can get the right to put in naval and air bases in Newfoundland, Bermuda, the Bahamas, Jamaica, St Lucia, Trinidad and British Guiana."[14]

As the formal offer reached London, there was jubilation. "Roosevelt has really, I think, weighed in with destroyers," Cadogan remarked with relief.[15] At 6:30 p.m., Churchill told the War Cabinet that once the destroyer deal had been concluded, the United States would have made "a long step towards coming into the war on our side."[16] However, Roosevelt, in his letter to Senator Walsh, added an aside that would have made Churchill shiver: "I am absolutely certain that this particular deal will not get us into war and, incidentally, that we are not going into war anyway unless Germany wishes to attack us."[17]

On August 20 Churchill, unaware of Roosevelt's cautionary note, jubilantly announced the destroyer deal to the House of Commons. Colville noted his confidence that "dragging in the United States" was working: "The PM ended his speech by comparing Anglo–American cooperation (will it one day be unity?) to the Missouri River and saying, 'Let it roll on!' I drove back with him in the car and he sang 'Ole Man River' (out of tune) the whole way back to Downing Street."[18]

That day there was also celebration in the Kremlin. Stalin was informed that his arch-enemy, Leon Trotsky, had finally been tracked down and bludgeoned to death with an ice pick by a Soviet agent in Mexico. The Soviet leader was now the only surviving member of Lenin's Politburo, having spent the past two decades wiping out anyone with the potential to oppose his leadership. His position was unassailable. "The party will always be grateful to you," Stalin announced to Leonid Eitington, one of the agents responsible for Trotsky's brutal murder. "Your name will be added to history and its letters will be written in gold."[19]

Stalin's agents were also busy elsewhere. From its London headquarters the British security service, MI5, was collecting substantial evidence that the Communist Party of Great Britain was being ordered by Moscow to adopt a policy that was nothing short of treachery. "Moscow's instructions," noted Guy Liddell, the head of MI5's counter-subversion unit, "are that the imperialist war must be gradually converted into a civil war, that no steps should be taken to oppose a German landing in this country since a short period under a Nazi regime would be the quickest way of bringing about a Communist revolution."[20] Churchill was serious about intelligence and knew that Stalin was approving subversion in Britain, but he was not willing to jeopardize even the slightest prospect of an alliance with the Soviet leader by bearing down too heavily on Soviet espionage. He and his Cabinet continued to "abstain from any action which might suggest impatience, suspicion or irritation."[21]

All that mattered was fighting Hitler and on August 28, 1940, Churchill authorized a "precision" bombing raid on Berlin. The American journalist

William Shirer was in Berlin that night. "Two hundred-pound bombs landed in the street, tore off the leg of an air-raid warden standing in the entrance to his house," Shirer observed, "and killed four men and two women, who, unwisely, were watching the fireworks from a doorway."[22] Hitler "interpreted it as a calculated insult," recalled his Luftwaffe adjutant, Nicolaus von Below, "and told Goering to take counter measures."[23] While the British air raids inflicted inconsequential material damage, the psychological effect upon Hitler was immense. Standing on the podium before a sea of uniformed faces at the monumental Sportpalast arena, he promised deadly retribution. "We'll wipe out their cities!" he announced. "We'll put an end to the work of these night pirates ... we will raze their cities to the ground!"[24] He ended with a stark and vengeful declaration. "The hour will come when one of us will break, and it will not be National Socialist Germany."[25]

In London the attempted alliance with Russia rolled slowly on as the Foreign Office minister R. A. Butler met Ivan Maisky. The Soviet ambassador explained Stalin's irritation at the British refusal to recognize his country's right of sovereignty over the freshly occupied Baltic states. Butler's private response was illuminating. "Great Britain is not adopting an unreasonable or lachrymose attitude about the passing of the states," he explained to Maisky, "but a decent attitude at the funeral was surely what you would expect from this country."[26] In public Churchill took a different stand. "We do not propose to recognise any territorial changes," he announced to the House of Commons on September 5, 1940, "which take place during the war unless they take place with the free consent and goodwill of the parties concerned."[27] Churchill was as yet unwilling to sacrifice the freedom of other nations to please Stalin.

As the Battle of Britain intensified, the protection of his own country's freedom was the immediate task, and survival was still by no means certain. At 4 p.m. on September 7, 1940, three hundred German bombers arrived over the skies of London and in two waves dropped 337 tons of explosives. Maisky graphically described the scene: "There began high in the darkened sky a kind of strange and unaccustomed roar. It seemed as though a multitude of enormous birds was circling the sky, each of them giving out a protracted howling and piercing sound. At once it was frightening and revolting."[28] This was the beginning of the Blitz, nearly two months of horrifying daily air raids that pounded the British capital. Churchill's Chiefs of Staff knew the possible meaning of the onslaught. At 8:07 p.m. the code word "Cromwell" was transmitted to every military unit in Great Britain. The Nazi seaborne invasion might be launched at any hour. Yet the switch in the Luftwaffe's tactics, provoked in part by the RAF's raid on Berlin, from bombing airfields to blitzing cities was a life-saver, allowing the beleaguered Fighter Command to regroup.

The agonizing wait continued. "Still no move on the part of the Germans!" General Alan Brooke, who at this stage was in charge of home defense, noted in his diary. "Everything remains keyed up for an early invasion, and the air war goes on unabated. The coming week must remain a critical one, and it is hard to see how Hitler can now retrace his steps and stop the invasion. The suspense of waiting is very trying especially when one is familiar with the weakness of our defence!"[29] Two days later Hitler made a decision that would change the direction of the war; it would also have afforded every comfort to General Brooke had he known it.

On September 17, while Churchill was announcing casualty figures in the thousands to the House of Commons, the Führer indefinitely postponed Operation "Sealion," the invasion of Britain. "We have conquered France at the cost of 30,000 men," he told his naval adjutant, Karl von Puttkammer, "during one night of crossing we could lose many times that—and success is not certain."[30] It was a key stage in the extraordinary mental journey he was making. He continued to believe that he had in effect won the war. All that was needed was to find ways, without launching a full-scale invasion, of cornering Britain to make her realize she must come to terms with Germany. Hitler now began to look for those ways.

On September 27, 1940, Germany, Japan and Italy signed the Tripartite Pact. Count Galeazzo Ciano, the Italian foreign minister, was in Berlin and noticed a muted reaction to what Hitler intended as a message to the British of his global strength. "Even the Berlin street crowd, a comparatively small one, composed mostly of school children, cheers with regularity but without conviction," Ciano observed. "Only one thing is certain: that it will be a long war." Ciano also saw that Hitler was thrashing around for a means of resolving his dilemma with Britain. "He did not speak about the current situation," Ciano explained with some surprise, "he spoke rather of Spanish intervention. ... He proposed a meeting with the Duce at the Brenner Pass, and I immediately accepted. No more invasion of England. No more blitz destruction of England. From Hitler's statements there now appears worry about a long war. He wishes to conserve his armed power. He speaks," Ciano noted, "with less impetuousness."[31]

In London Churchill was confident that Roosevelt would read the Tripartite Pact as being directed just as much against the United States. "If anything, it is likely," he told the War Cabinet, "to accelerate the entry of the United States into the war."[32] In Washington Henry Stimson, Roosevelt's hawkish Secretary of War, hoped the pact would alert insular Americans to Hitler's ambitions: "It will be pretty useful, I think, in waking up our people to the effect that at last they have got what they have been talking about—isolation. The US isolated except for one great power and that's the British Commonwealth, and I already see signs of a realization of this among the thoughtless."[33] In Moscow too the implications of the pact hung heavily. Georgi Dimitrov, Stalin's loyal head of Comintern, noted "further expansion of the war to world war dimensions."[34]

Hitler was exploring every avenue. The ambiguity he had shown towards Britain was being replicated in a split-mindedness towards Russia. The initial plan for an invasion had been made and the process of moving troops to Finland and Romania, whose borders abutted the Soviet Union, had begun under the pretext of sending training missions to those countries. But Hitler was now more interested in enlisting Stalin to join his war against the British. On September 30 he wrote to the Soviet leader. "A letter has gone out," General Franz Halder noted, "designed to get him interested in dividing up the estate of a defunct Britain, and to induce him to join up with us. If the plan succeeds, it is believed we could go all out against Britain."[35]

While Hitler tried to line up Stalin, Churchill was using all his wiles to seduce Roosevelt. So far all he had been able to offer the president was a series of desperate pleas, but with Hitler's invasion now rendered improbable by the advance of winter, he could begin to show his lighter side. "The gent has taken off his clothes and put on his bathing suit," he cabled, "but the water is getting colder and there is an autumn nip in the air."[36] Those close to Churchill could even see him begin to relax. A few days later John Colville recorded a delightful vignette. "The PM, dressed in his blue 'siren-suit,' dined with Eden in his new dining-room at No. 10. He was in great form and amused Eden and me very much by his conversation with Nelson, the black cat, whom he chided for being afraid of the guns and unworthy of the name he bore. 'Try and remember,' he said to Nelson reprovingly, 'what those boys in the RAF are doing.'"[37]

While Churchill awaited ever-closer American involvement, Roosevelt was keeping his distance. "We are no nearer to war than we have been for six years," he told his assistant Secretary of State, Breckinridge Long, during a meeting at the White House on October 11. The presidential campaign was reaching its final weeks and Roosevelt knew that any encouragement of war could mean electoral disaster. "I am not headed for war and I am going to call the newspaper correspondents aboard my train and give a direct talk to them and emphasize the fact that we were trying to steer clear of war," he continued.[38]

The next day he went public with an unequivocal assertion. "We arm to defend ourselves," Roosevelt told his audience in Dayton, Ohio. "This nation wants to keep war away from these two continents. Because we, all of us, are determined to do everything possible to maintain peace in this hemisphere." He was at pains to reassure potential voters that the aid given to Great Britain was no more than a defensive measure. "It can no longer be disputed that the forces of evil, bent on conquest of the world, will destroy whomever and whenever they can destroy," he warned. "We know now that if we seek to appease them by withholding aid from those who stand in their way, we only hasten the day of their attack upon us."[39]

That day Churchill had retreated to the relative calm of Chequers. It was a glorious late autumn day and he was relaxing at tea, discussing with John Colville the threat posed by British fascists to the war effort and the tough new procedures being put in place to limit any subversive activities. "I much dislike locking people up and the suspension of Habeas Corpus," Churchill remarked. He also explained that "those filthy communists are really more dangerous than the fascists."[40] But he remained convinced that the fight against Hitler compelled him to keep knocking at the Soviet dictator's door.

Five days later Ivan Maisky made it clear that there was only one way by which the British had any chance of ingratiating themselves. "Believe me, Lord Halifax," he told the British Foreign Secretary, "we are tired of your good intentions, we can be convinced only by your good deeds."[41] Maisky's blandishments meant little; the main game for Stalin remained Hitler. On October 21 the German ambassador, Count von der Schulenburg, left the Kremlin clutching a letter from Molotov to the German foreign minister, Joachim von Ribbentrop. It contained Molotov's acceptance of an invitation to Berlin for talks. At 5:02 a.m. the next day it was cabled to Berlin. "The form and style leave no doubt that the letter was composed by Stalin personally," Schulenburg explained.[42] For Hitler the prospect of enticing Stalin into his axis against Britain beckoned.

The next day the British ambassador, Sir Stafford Cripps, also had an appointment at the Kremlin. He arrived to find that not only Stalin refused to see him personally, but Molotov also claimed to be otherwise engaged. It fell to Andrei Vyshinsky, the Deputy *Commissar* for Foreign Affairs, to receive him. Whether or not it was a calculated snub, the difference between the treatment of the British and German ambassadors made its point. Cripps set about explaining British proposals for a treaty with the Soviet Union. Great Britain, he announced, was prepared to give the Soviet Union prominence in the postwar peace settlement; it would promise not to form any alliances against the Soviets; and most importantly of all, it would recognize Soviet de facto control of the territorial acquisitions Stalin had made since 1939.

Thousands of miles from his masters in Whitehall, Cripps then went much further. He told Vyshinsky that the British would also recognize the legality of Soviet sovereignty over the Baltic states. The Foreign Office was furious that Cripps had overstepped his orders, but Lord Halifax, the Foreign Secretary, was blunt about the possibilities of any retraction. "We shall try, if the negotiations proceed, to get this phraseology altered," he told Churchill the following day, warning, however, "This will clearly not be easy, as if the Soviet reply is at all satisfactory and we then go back on Cripps, they will accuse us of watering down our original offer."[43] Cripps's unilateral action had placed Churchill in the extraordinary position of offering as early as October 1940 to give away the freedom of three independent nations, Lithuania, Estonia and Latvia, to Stalin.

While Churchill pursued Stalin, Hitler was traveling through Europe trying to complete his encirclement of Britain. On October 23 he arrived in *Amerika* at Hendaye on the Spanish border for a conference with the Spanish dictator, Francisco Franco. During a long lunch in his special train's luxurious saloon car Hitler attempted to induce Franco to enter the war and tighten the noose in the Mediterranean. Arrogant and overconfident, Hitler was prepared to offer only minimal territorial rewards to Franco in return for joining the fight against the British. Franco was contemptuous. "These people are intolerable," he told his foreign minister, "they want us to come into the war in exchange for nothing."[44] To Hitler's disbelief Franco declined his offer. "For the future in this war he had expected no less than brotherhood-in-arms," Gerhard Engel noted of Hitler's disappointment.[45]

The next day, in the security of a railway tunnel at Montoire in France, Hitler's frustrations were compounded as he endured another frustrating set of discussions, this time with Marshal Philippe Pétain, the aged leader of Vichy France. Hitler demanded that the Frenchman commit his army to the fight. Engel, who was present in the saloon car, noted: "Pétain was taciturn and dismissive, he gave no answer throughout, but his manner said it all."[46] The empty offer of administrative collaboration left Hitler cold. His overtures to France and Spain had failed, leaving the Führer in a state of flux. Russia was now the fulcrum. On the long journey back to his headquarters Hitler explained to Generals Franz Halder and Alfred Jodl that Russia would be in a position to attack Germany from 1942.[47] He confirmed to them that an invasion of Russia remained in the cards for 1941. But the more attractive prospect was still to bring Stalin into his fold.

Churchill's parallel attempt to lure Roosevelt was hitting the buffer of American domestic politics. On October 29, as he traveled the nation on a whistle-stop tour, Roosevelt announced the introduction of a peacetime draft. "It was a brave decision on the part of the president to let it come now," Henry Stimson enthused.[48] The next day the presidential train drew into Boston where Roosevelt was scheduled to make an important speech. As with all stops en route, a mailbag was brought aboard filled with letters from party organizers up and down the country. Though it appeared that the electorate was not against the draft, Roosevelt's party faithful advised that there was anxiety that young American men would soon be heading for the war in Europe.

A keen observer of public opinion and a politician to his fingertips, the president responded that evening. "Your boys are not going to be sent in to any foreign wars," he declared, with only the qualification that the situation might change should an attack occur on the United States.[49] Churchill had no choice but to be sanguine. "He said he hoped America would come into the war," Colville recorded, "he said he quite understood the exasperation which so many English people feel with the American attitude of criticism combined with ineffective assistance; but we must be patient and we must conceal our irritation."[50]

After the frustrations of the autumn, Hitler was now investing his final hopes in Stalin. "Führer hopes he can bring Russia into the anti-British front,"[51] General Halder recorded. It was November 1, 1940, and preparations for Molotov's upcoming visit to Berlin had begun. "The English are tough. They will hold out a little longer," Hitler told Goebbels that afternoon.[52] "The goal is clear," he explained. The British must be driven out of Europe. This would be possible as it was obvious that Stalin was not going to ally himself with Churchill. "Stalin is too clever for that." The bravado masked a certain indecision; Engel noted that Hitler was "visibly depressed ... conveying the impression that at the moment he does not know how things should proceed."[53]

Four days later Roosevelt was swept to a resounding victory in the polls. "I did not think it right for me as a foreigner to express any opinion upon American policies while the election was on," Churchill wrote in congratulation, "but now I feel you will not mind my saying that I prayed for your success and that I am truly thankful for it."[54] The next day in Berlin Goebbels dripped scorn. "After his statements Roosevelt will hardly be able to enter the war in an active capacity," he noted.[55]

In his simply furnished *dacha* in Kuntsevo just outside Moscow, Stalin was turning an apprehensive eye to the future. It was nearing 9 p.m. and his guests were preparing to leave when he took his glass in hand and announced that he wanted to speak. "History has spoiled us," he began in his Georgian burr, "people are not studying the lessons of the war with Finland, the lessons of the war with Europe. ... We are not prepared for the sort of air war being waged between Germany and England," he continued. "But I am the only one dealing with all these problems. You are squandering Lenin's legacy."[56] That war which Stalin feared would soon be racing towards him faster than he could begin to imagine.

At 11:05 a.m. on November 12, 1940, Molotov's train pulled into Berlin's Anhalter station. The defining moment in Stalin's psychological duel with Hitler was at hand. The *Commissar* for Foreign Affairs emerged into a station bedecked with flowers, swastikas and flags which for that one day displayed the hammer and sickle. Molotov, in his ubiquitous grey homburg hat and dark coat, lined up oddly against his Nazi hosts buttoned up in their shiny uniforms. A German foreign ministry official, Ernst von Weizacker, commented that the Russian delegation would make "good gangster types for a film."[57] Displaying the hammer and sickle was one thing, but the Nazis had decided that playing the *Internationale* was a step too far; German passers-by might feel compelled to join in.[58]

After a brief inspection of the guard of honor Molotov and his entourage of secret agents were swept in an open-topped Mercedes to the fabulous Schloss Bellevue hotel. The conference began with talks between Ribbentrop and Molotov. Dr Paul Schmidt was present as interpreter. Ribbentrop was charming and polite; Molotov was inscrutable. "Only at long intervals did Molotov reciprocate," Schmidt noted, "when a rather frosty smile glided over his intelligent, chess player's face. This rather short Russian with his lively eyes, behind old-fashioned pince-nez, constantly reminded me of my mathematics master."[59] Schmidt could hardly believe it when Molotov "dispensed with flowery phrases and as though he were taking a class, gently rebuked the sweeping, vague generalities of Ribbentrop."[60]

After lunch Molotov was taken for his first meeting with Hitler. The imposing surroundings of the *Reich* Chancellery, with its brass doors and imposing architecture, did nothing to dampen his stern confidence. The Führer opened proceedings with a grand oration, declaring to his guest the importance of Russo-German collaboration. He assured him that Britain was defeated and its capitulation only a matter of time. Then he offered Russia a share in the spoils of victory in return for helping to finish off the British. "It is time to think about division of the world after our victory.

Fragments of its empire spread all over the globe will be left. We must deal with this property 'without a master.'"[61]

However, Stalin was not interested in speculative carve-ups of the British Empire; he had instructed Molotov to find out from Hitler what German troops were doing in places like Romania and Finland, dangerously close to Russia's borders. Molotov launched a barrage of questions. Could the Chancellor explain what the German military mission was doing in Romania and why it was sent there without consulting the Soviet government? Why had German troops been sent to Finland? Why was such an important decision made without consulting the Soviet government? According to Molotov's account on his return to Moscow, these questions "had an effect on Hitler as a cold shower." He huddled up and looked confused. But his acting skills took over and, dramatically weaving his fingers, he threw back his head and fixed his look on the ceiling. Then he fidgeted in the armchair and said in a patter that "the German military mission was sent to Romania on the request of Antonescu's government to train the Romanian troops. As far as Finland is concerned, the German troops are not staying there for long, they are just passing this territory on their way to Norway."[62]

"No foreign visitor had ever spoken to him in this way in my presence," Schmidt noted as the *Commissar*'s insistent probing continued.[63] Hitler tried to give an overall assurance that "the Axis Pact will regulate conditions in Europe according to the natural interests of the European countries themselves and that is why Germany now approaches the Soviet Union. ... Germany plays a mediating role," he continued, "in no circumstances will Russia be faced with a *fait accompli*."[62] Reassuring Molotov that he would go further into all of his questions the following day, Hitler concluded the opening discussions, explaining: "We must now break off this discussion otherwise we might be caught in an air-raid warning."[63] That evening, Molotov continued the conversation with Ribbentrop. During it British bombers did indeed arrive overhead. Molotov asked Ribbentrop: "If England has already been defeated why are we sitting in a bunker and whose planes are bombarding Berlin?"[64]

The next day, November 13, the talks continued in the same vein. Molotov hailed upon Hitler a flurry of further questions on Finland. Hitler replied that "Germany had lived up to the agreements, which was not quite the case on the Russian side."[67] He pointed to the Russian incursion into Bukovina, stating: "It would mean a considerable concession on the part of Germany, if even a part of Bukovina were to be occupied by Russia."[68] Continuing the discussion of spheres of influence, Molotov argued that the revisions desired by Russia in Romania "were insignificant."[69] "If German–Soviet relations were to show positive results in the future, the Soviet government would have to understand that Germany was engaged in a life and death struggle," Hitler replied.[70]

Molotov continued his complaints about German troop movements in Finland and Romania. Hitler tried to side-step, but then accused Russia itself of threatening Finland. With a hint of menace Molotov warned: "The only thing we are interested in is securing peace and safety in the area. The German government should keep this in mind if it is interested in the development of the Soviet–German relations."[71] The conversations were blunt, occasionally frosty and, though Hitler did not express any anger in Molotov's presence, he kept away from the banquet held that night at the Soviet embassy.

For Hitler the Molotov visit was decisive. "The talks had shown where the Russian plans were heading," Engel noted on November 15, recording Hitler's verdict the day after Molotov's departure. "Molotov had let the cat out of the bag. Führer was really relieved. It would not even remain a marriage of convenience. Letting the Russians into Europe meant the end of central Europe. The Balkans and Finland were also dangerous flanks."[72]

Back in the Kremlin Molotov was briefing Stalin. It was clear to the Soviet dictator that a shift had occurred. "Hitler is playing a double game," Stalin pronounced. "What is the point of Hitler's expatiation on the cooperation between Germany and the Soviet Union? Is it possible that Hitler has changed his plans to attack the USSR that he declared in *Mein Kampf*? Obviously not … we must always remember this about Hitler and prepare hard to repulse the attack."[73] But Stalin believed he had time on his hands. In early December he told his generals: "We know that Hitler is intoxicated by his victories and believes that the Red Army will need at least four years to prepare for war. Obviously, four years would be more than enough for us. But, we must be ready much earlier. We will try to delay the war for another two years."[74]

Stalin's analysis was correct in all but its timescale. On December 5 Hitler met Generals Walther von Brauchitsch and Halder. Though he had not made his final decision, he was now set on war with Stalin. "The decision concerning hegemony in Europe will come in the battle against Russia," he told them and ordered an escalation in preparations for an attack in May 1941.[75]

While Stalin and Hitler drifted apart, Churchill redoubled his efforts to reel in Roosevelt. The president now had a mandate for a further four years and Churchill needed him more than ever. So far everything the British government had received from the United States had been paid for in cash or territory. Despite his brave face and words, Churchill was painfully aware of a devastating truth: the fight against Hitler was bankrupting Britain. On December 7, 1940, in one of the most carefully worded messages ever sent by one head of state to another, he pleaded for massive American aid. Within his seven-page cable was one short, stark sentence: "The moment approaches when we shall no longer be able to pay cash for shipping and other supplies."[76] The president, who was on a two-week break aboard the heavy cruiser USS *Tuscaloosa*, received the letter by seaplane two days later.

For over a week there was silence. Churchill's anxieties and frustrations simmered. For six months he had been fighting his solitary battle against Hitler; surely now, after his re-election, it was time for the president to make a real commitment. On December 17 he drafted an angry letter. "If you were to 'wash your hands of us' i.e. give us nothing," he wrote, "we cannot pay for with suitable advances, we should certainly not give in, but we should certainly not be able to beat the Nazi tyranny and gain you the time you require for your rearmament."[77] The letter remained sitting on Churchill's desk. News had come through that Roosevelt was to hold a press conference that evening.

That day Hitler too was thinking of the United States. "We must solve all continental European problems in 1941," he told General Jodl, "since the USA will be in a position to intervene from 1942 onwards."[78] Jodl knew what this meant: Hitler was about to confirm the most devastating decision of the war.

In Washington, Roosevelt geared up to present the American people with a dramatic initiative. In fact, even before Churchill had sent his plea for more aid on December 7, he had already decided to help. His problem was reconciling two apparently contradictory objectives. On the one hand he had promised Americans that their country was not going to war; on the other he believed that Hitler could not be stopped without substantial American support. On December 17 he gave the first public glimpse of his new idea: he would finance and equip the British to do the fighting and, in so doing, keep the Nazis away from the United States.

That evening he told a characteristically informal press conference in the Oval Office: "The best immediate defense of the United States is the success of Great Britain in defending itself." Then, borrowing the language with which Harold Ickes had berated him back in August, he spun a folksy story for the journalists: "Suppose my neighbor's home catches fire, and I have a length of garden hose four or five hundred feet away. If he can take my garden hose and connect it up with his hydrant, I may help him to put out his fire. Now, what do I do? I don't say to him before that operation, 'Neighbor, my garden hose cost me $15; you have to pay me $15 for it.' What is the transaction that goes on? I don't want $15—I want my garden hose back after the fire is over." Roosevelt concluded: "Now, what I am trying to do is to eliminate the dollar sign."[79] It was the first public hint of what would become known as lend-lease. Reading the president's words, Churchill tore up his exasperated cable and threw it in the trash.

The next day, December 18, 1940, Hitler issued War Directive No. 23. "The German Wehrmacht," he declared, "must be prepared, before the ending of the war against England, to crush Soviet Russia in a rapid campaign."[80] The invasion date was set for May 1941. But behind Hitler's order lay an element of uncertainty about his present, future and potential enemies. Engel noted: "I'm convinced that the Führer himself doesn't know how it will turn out. He is very concerned at the lack of clarity as regards the strength of the Russians. Hopes for an English surrender. Does not think America will enter the war."[81]

Hitler had finally made the momentous decision—a war on two fronts, the very thing he had sought to avoid when he had first made his pact with Stalin in the summer of 1939. But he had deluded himself that one front, Britain, was already won; it simply required a knockout blow against Russia for the British to understand their defeat. Hitler's line of reasoning never began to occur to Stalin. He believed that Hitler either had to beat Churchill or make a deal with him before he could think of turning against Russia. He told Politburo members: "We must cherish no illusions. Fascist Germany is clearly preparing for an attack on the Soviet Union. Why does Hitler want to make an agreement with England? Because he wants to avoid war on two fronts."[82]

Stalin was trusting Hitler to act rationally; and to fight Britain and Russia at the same time was clearly irrational. However, he failed to realize that, despite their similarities, there was one profound difference between him and Hitler which made his perfect logic irrelevant. He himself was a methodical, calculating, hard-working man; a master of detail, personally signing death lists at one extreme, and at the other keeping the tiniest details of gold production in his notebook.

Hitler by contrast was at heart an idle dreamer. He once described why he loved the mountains of Obersalzberg. "When I go to Obersalzberg I'm not drawn there merely by the beauty of the landscape. I feel myself far from petty things, my imagination is stimulated. When I study a problem elsewhere I see it less clearly. I'm submerged by the details. By night at the Berghof I often remain for hours with my eyes open contemplating from my bed mountains lit up by the moon. It's at such moments that brightness enters my mind."[83] For Hitler the big idea was never to be disrupted by small facts. Now, having decided to attack Russia for tactical reasons, his mind began to stir in ways that would begin to lead him back to the original and biggest idea of all—the ideological struggle against Jews and Bolsheviks.

On December 29, 1940, Roosevelt confirmed his investment in Britain as America's front line. From the diplomatic reception room of the White House, sitting behind a desk covered with radio microphones, he launched into his final *Fireside Chat* of 1940 with a scathing attack on Hitler's Axis. "The British people and their allies today are conducting an active war against this unholy alliance. Our own future security is greatly dependent on the outcome of that fight. Our ability to 'keep out of war' is going to be affected by that outcome ... we must be the great arsenal of democracy. For us this is an emergency as serious as war itself. We must apply ourselves to our task with the same resolution, the same sense of urgency, the same spirit of patriotism and sacrifice as we would show were we at war. ... We have furnished the British great material support and we will furnish far more in the future."[84]

Roosevelt's speech sent shock waves throughout Europe's capitals, nowhere more so than Berlin where Goebbels sensed a sea change. "The USA is sliding increasingly into war-psychosis, but will Roosevelt actually declare war?"[85] In London, this was precisely the question Churchill was now daring to ask himself. In the coming weeks, as Roosevelt appeared to move both privately and publicly to offer ever- stronger support, he began to believe that the president was on an intentional and inevitable road to war. It would turn out to be an illusion that would bring him both disappointment and great distress.

For the moment the New Year of 1941 offered unlimited hope. On January 3 Roosevelt announced in a press conference that he was sending his personal representative, Harry Hopkins, to London, "just to maintain— I suppose that is the best word for it—personal contact between me and the British government."[86] A firm believer in the power of personal diplomacy, he told Harold Ickes: "I am sending Harry Hopkins for two or three weeks so that he can talk to Churchill like an Iowa farmer."[87]

Three days later the president laid out before Congress a concrete strategy for providing the aid he had promised to the British. "I do not recommend that we make them a loan of dollars with which to pay for these weapons," he announced. "For what we send abroad, we shall be repaid within a reasonable time following the close of hostilities, in similar materials, or, at our option, in other goods of many kinds, which they can produce and which we need."[88] Roosevelt was kidding Congress; he had no intention of asking the British to repay with money or goods. Instead he had a different agenda; in his quest to create a non-imperialist world he would demand that in return the British tear down its empire's trade barriers, in the process opening up new markets for American goods.

On January 8 Hitler gathered his military leaders at the Berghof for a two-day summit. He repeated the tactical reason for the turn against Russia: "The possibility of a Russian intervention in the war is sustaining the English. Were they able to hold out and put together 40 to 50 divisions, and the USA and Russia were to help them, a very difficult situation for Germany would arise."[89] Hitler also opened a window into his more visceral motives, as he began in a very personal way to identify Stalin as the ideological enemy he must beat. Halder noted Hitler's verdict: "Stalin—intelligent and shrewd; his demands will become bigger and bigger. German victory incompatible with Russian ideology."[90]

By January 10 the Lend-Lease Bill was submitted to both the Senate and the House of Representatives. The same day Harry Hopkins arrived at 10 Downing Street for his first meeting with Churchill. He was shown into the little dining room, formerly an office used by the prime minister's secretaries, in the basement. "The prime minister," Hopkins wrote to Roosevelt that evening in a hand-written letter on Claridges notepaper, "a rotund—smiling—red faced, gentleman appeared—extended a fat but none the less convincing hand and wished me welcome to England. A short black coat—striped trousers—a clear eye and mushy voice was the impression of England's leader."[91] The two men enjoyed a simple lunch of soup, cold beef and green salad followed by cheese and port. "They were so impressed with one another," John Colville observed of the three-hour luncheon, "that their *tête-à-tête* did not break up till nearly four."[92]

Brendan Bracken, Churchill's Minister of Information, said that Hopkins was Roosevelt's confidant and "the most important American visitor to this country we had ever had ... he could influence the president more than any living man."[93] In the conversation over lunch Churchill assured Hopkins that he would open every door for him to fulfil his mission and see for himself what Britain needed. Most reassuring of all was a personal message Hopkins brought from Roosevelt. "The president is determined that we shall win the war together. Make no mistake about it. He has sent me here to tell you that by all costs and by all means, he will carry you through."[94] The pair then set off for a weekend in the country. Chequers was now considered too conspicuous a target, its long driveway a perfect marker for enemy bombers. Instead their destination was Ditchley Park, an imposing Georgian mansion in Oxfordshire donated by its Anglo-American owners as a government hideaway during the Blitz.

The next morning details of Roosevelt's proposed new legislation reached Churchill, so exciting him that he sprang out of bed far more promptly than usual. The long-suffering John Colville noted: "Very annoyed at being disturbed early by the PM. He is delighted by the new American bill which allows British warships the use of American ports and contains wide powers for the president in every sphere of assistance to us. He says this is tantamount to a declaration of war by the United States."[95] Sunday at Ditchley Park was jovial and relaxed. "The PM asked what the Americans would do when they had accumulated all the gold in the world and the other countries then decided that gold was of no value except for filling teeth. 'Well,' said Mr. Hopkins, 'we shall be able to make use of our unemployed in guarding it!'"[96]

Hopkins toured Britain and was overwhelmed by the determination he found. A week later he joined Churchill at Scapa Flow in Scotland to bid farewell to Lord Halifax, who had been appointed British ambassador in Washington in place of Lord Lothian, who had recently and unexpectedly died. During dinner in Glasgow, after a tour of naval bases, Hopkins turned to Churchill and said, "I suppose you want to know what I am going to say to President Roosevelt on my return. Well, I'm going to quote you one verse from that Book of Books in the truth of which Mr Johnston's mother and my own Scottish mother were brought up: 'Whither thou goest I will go; and where thou lodgest, I will lodge; thy people shall be my people, and thy God my God.'" He then added, very quietly, "even to the end."[97]

Churchill, never one to hide his emotions, was reduced to tears. In a sealed hand-written note dispatched to Roosevelt from Scotland Hopkins was emphatic: "The people here are amazing from Churchill down and if courage alone can win—the result will be inevitable. But they need our help desperately and I am sure you will permit nothing to stand in the way." He affirmed that "Churchill is the gov't in every sense of the word. … I cannot emphasize too strongly that he is the one and only person over here with whom you need to have a full meeting of minds."[98]

While Hopkins' warmth encouraged Churchill that Roosevelt was drawing ever nearer, his efforts to entice Joseph Stalin into a partnership were collapsing. No answer had yet been received from the Kremlin to the inducements of territorial recognition held out by Cripps two months before. "Russian suspicions lie so deep and Russian fears of German military might are so vivid and real that our task must be a formidable one," Anthony Eden, who had succeeded Halifax as Foreign Secretary, wrote to

Cripps on January 17. "In general I feel that we can only possess our souls in patience until such time as we have sufficient success in our military operations to inspire in the Soviet government some of the fear and respect which they now feel for the Germans."[99] It was stalemate.

Ten days later in Washington Anglo-American relations appeared to take a further bold step forward. On January 27 joint British–American staff talks, known as ABC-1, opened in Washington. Secretly authorized from the very top by Roosevelt, they were designed to determine "the best methods by which the armed forces of the United States and British Commonwealth, with its present allies, could defeat Germany and the powers allied with her, should the United States be compelled to resort to war."[100] Churchill was further encouraged by a visit to Britain that same day by another American, Wendell Willkie, the Republican candidate whom Roosevelt had defeated in the presidential election. Over lunch, Willkie gave Churchill a hand-written message from Roosevelt. It read: "I think this verse applies to your people as it does to us:

> Sail on, O ship of State!
> Sail on, O Union, strong and great!
> Humanity with all its fears,
> With all the hopes of future years,
> Is hanging breathless on thy fate!"[101]

The message was yet another confirmation to Churchill of the president's intentions; the obvious meaning was that he was preparing to fight side by side with him. Churchill knew that, under the United States constitution, the president could only ask for a declaration of war; Congress had to approve it. But while a vocal minority of Americans wanted to have nothing to do with Europe's war, the majority wished to help. Churchill told John Colville: "The important element is the boldness of the president. He will lead opinion and not follow it. He does not want war; but he will not shrink from war."[102]

In Berlin Hitler was gearing up for genocide. Throughout 1940 he had hardly mentioned the Jews, but on January 30, 1941, in his traditional speech marking the anniversary of the Nazis' rise to power, he repeated a chilling threat he had first made before war broke out. "If the rest of the world should be plunged into a general war because of Jewry, the whole of Jewry will have played out its role in Europe!" he declared at the Sportspalast. "They can still laugh about it today, just as they used to laugh about my prophecies. The coming months will prove that here, too, I've seen things correctly."[103]

Hitler was reinvigorated. "I've seldom seen him like this in recent time," Goebbels observed, "the Führer always impresses me afresh."[104] On February 2, 1941, Hitler told Engel: "Originally it was in my power to break the Jewish might only in Germany; but now the goal must be to destroy Jewish power in the whole of the Axis sphere of influence."[105] Two weeks later on February 17 Hitler, constantly juggling his motives, was back on his tactical track. "He is stunned by the reports on the Russian air force. A conflict is inevitable," Halder noted after that day's military conference. "Once England is finished, he would not be able to rouse the German people to a fight against Russia; consequently Russia would have to be disposed of first."[106]

That day Wendell Willkie was back in Washington briefing Roosevelt on his meeting with Churchill. The president's first question was: "Is he a drunk?"[107] In the light of all the assurances conveyed by Hopkins and the personal messages from Roosevelt himself, it was an extraordinary thing to ask. Nine months on from that Cabinet meeting of May 10, 1940, the private suspicions remained.

What Churchill did not yet understand was that nothing Roosevelt said could be taken at face value; nor, despite his surface charm and affability, how impenetrable and elusive the president really was. At this time Henry Stimson described how it was impossible to pin Roosevelt down: "His mind does not follow easily a consecutive chain of thought but he is full of stories and incidents and hops about in his discussions from suggestion to suggestion and it is very much like chasing a vagrant beam of sunshine around a vacant room."[108]

Roosevelt's lack of clarity and commitment was a deliberate cover, sometimes to keep his real intentions secret, sometimes to keep his options open; and his bonhomie was deceptive. Later Roosevelt's wife, Eleanor, would warn Churchill: "When Franklin says, yes, yes, yes, it doesn't mean he's agreeing, it means he's listening."[109] As yet Churchill, trying to build a relationship across three thousand miles of ocean via cable messages, intermediaries and transatlantic phone calls where words had to be watched for fear of German interception, realized very little of this. He could only proceed on the basis of what he saw and heard; and since the "arsenal of democracy" speech of December 29 the noises from the man in the White House had been increasingly supportive and belligerent.

Stalin's priority was to avoid signs of belligerence; nothing must be done to hasten conflict with Hitler. At the end of February 1941 General Georgy Zhukov, his newly appointed Chief of Staff, arrived at his *dacha*, accompanied by General Semyon Timoshenko. Zhukov was alarmed by intelligence reports that the Wehrmacht was eyeing up Russia.[110] "Take into consideration," Timoshenko warned before they arrived, "that he will not listen to a long lecture. All that you have told me in three hours has to be said in ten minutes."[111]

Stalin was dining with Molotov, Zhdanov, Voroshilov and others from the Politburo. As always at the *dacha*, the dinner was simple: Ukrainian borshch, kasha and stewed meat. Zhukov was brief and to the point, commenting simply that "considering the complicated military-political situation it was necessary to take urgent measures in time to remedy shortcomings in the western front."[112] Stalin was in a good mood, making jokes and drinking Khvanchkara, a light Georgian wine. He told Zhukov to proceed with planning for increased mobilization, but warned against the implementation of "wild unrealistic plans for which Russia lacked the means."[113] Stalin also intimated that he had information suggesting that the German troops massing in Poland were simply on training exercises.[114]

Hitler was planning the exact opposite, working with his generals on the final instructions for Operation "Barbarossa." On March 3, 1940, the Nazi warlord issued General Jodl with directions for the drafting of *Instructions on Special Matter Attached to Directive No. 21*. "The forthcoming invasion is more than a mere armed conflict; it is a collision between two different ideologies," Hitler instructed Jodl. "The Bolshevist-Jewish intelligentsia must be eliminated," adding that "all Bolshevist leaders or *commissars* be liquidated."[115] It was a key step on the path to genocide.

Information suggesting that Hitler was planning to attack the Soviet Union had now circulated in Moscow, London and Washington. Roosevelt's assistant Secretary of State, Adolf Berle, noted, "If my guess as to what happens is right, I think I know now how this thing is coming out. The Germans will tackle Russia, and probably will smash her. They will be smashed themselves, in the process. I think the two dictatorships are going down in one hideous mass of slime and blood and anarchy."[116]

On March 8 the Lend-Lease Bill was passed by the Senate by 60 votes to 31. Harry Hopkins telephoned Chequers in the middle of the British night to give Churchill the good news. The prime minister cabled the president: "Our blessings from the whole British Empire go out to you and the American nation for this present help in time of trouble."[117] Goebbels commented in his diary: "Certainly a great success for England, and one which was expected and counted on. Roosevelt wants to encourage England to a prolonged resistance, so that afterwards it will be easier for him to inherit everything that's left. Now in London they'll once again forget all the defeats and setbacks and cheer on Washington. But how long will it last?"[118]

Roosevelt gave his answer on March 15 with a rip-roaring speech at the annual dinner of the White House Correspondents' Association. "The big news story of this week is this," the president declared. "The world has been told that we realize the danger that confronts us and that to meet that danger our democracy has gone into action. This is the end of any attempts at appeasement in our land; the end of urging us to get along with dictators; the end of compromise with tyranny and the forces of oppression. And the urgency is now."[119] Lord Halifax, the British ambassador, was in the audience. "The general impression of it was that there was no longer any doubt that the United States were up to the neck and to the end, whatever the cost," he noted. "Certainly no such speech has ever been made by the head of a state not at war without putting it into war."[120] "Pray accept my most sincere congratulations and grateful thanks on your magnificent speech," Churchill wrote to Roosevelt the next day from Chequers, "it is a trumpet call to free men all over the world, and will play a weighty part in drawing them together."[121]

Yet, as so often with Roosevelt, words would not always relate to actions. Some close to him in Washington sensed that he was playing a double game with Churchill, doing everything to boost his morale while also keeping a certain distance. Henry Morgenthau for one sounded a note of caution. "I may be mistaken," he noted after a lunch at the White House, "but I don't think that the president has in mind to do anything very dramatic to help England at this time."[122]

Churchill could guess nothing of these private doubts in Washington. The day Roosevelt gave his speech, he was spending the weekend at Chequers with the new American ambassador, John Winant, and Roosevelt's trusted envoy Averell Harriman. The following Monday Churchill told the War Cabinet that he had been "greatly encouraged by their attitude. These two gentlemen," he explained, "were apparently longing for Germany to commit some overt act that would relieve the president of his election and pre-election declaration regarding keeping out of the war."[123]

Churchill used the occasion of the Pilgrim's Society Luncheon the next day to thank his American guests. "We are met here today under the strong impression and impact of the historic declaration made on Saturday last by the president of the United States," Churchill declared, "and where could there be a more fitting opportunity than at this gathering of the Pilgrims to greet the new American ambassador and for me to express on behalf of the British nation and empire the sense of encouragement and fortification in our resolve which has come from across the ocean in those strong, august and fateful presidential words?"[124]

Hitler was boasting at the paucity of the American threat. "The Americans have finally let the cat out of the bag," he announced on March 24, "if one wanted, that in itself could be grounds for war. I could let it come to a war immediately. But at the moment it doesn't suit my purpose. It will come to a war with the USA either way. Roosevelt and the Jewish high finance want war and have to want it, since a German victory in Europe would bring huge capital losses for American Jews in Europe."[125]

That afternoon the Führer departed for Austria. Three weeks before he had summoned the aging Regent of Yugoslavia, Prince Paul, to the Berghof, and, with all the bullying and threats perfected in previous years against Austria and Czechoslovakia, had browbeaten him into joining the Axis. On March 25 a lavish ceremony in Vienna, attended by the Yugoslav prime minister, Dragiπa Cvetkovic, set the seal on the new alliance.

Hitler could feel that he had the Balkans on his side in good time to protect his rear before the invasion of Russia. His plans were about to be hit by an unpleasant blow.

As for Churchill, he was buoyant at the prospect of his imminent rescue by the president; the coming weeks would bring a savage deflation.

CHAPTER THREE
March 27–June 21, 1941

March 27, 1941, Berlin. It was a bolt from the blue, an insufferable challenge to his authority. In his office in the *Reich* Chancellery Hitler angrily brandished the offending telegram. The nasty surprise he was reading through the spectacles kept firmly hidden from public view threatened his entire strategy in the east.

At 2 a.m. a group of high-ranking Serbian officers in the Yugoslav army, blazing with the patriotic zeal and aggressive nationalism associated with the Führer himself, had launched a lightning coup in Belgrade. Disgusted by Prince Paul's submission to the Nazis and the coerced entry of their country into the Axis, they had arrested the Regent and installed in his place his seventeen-year-old nephew, King Peter II.

Their daring operation was both humiliating and infuriating. Hitler had every reason to assume that, with Yugoslavia in the bag, he could exert an easy mastery over the Balkans without having to use force. Now he had an unwelcome diversion, but one that had to be dealt with. He immediately set about planning the destruction of the upstart regime and a ruthless punishment of the Yugoslav nation. "The Führer does not let himself be messed around in these matters," Joseph Goebbels observed.[1]

By early afternoon, Hitler had gathered together army and Luftwaffe officers. "I am determined … to make all preparations to smash Yugoslavia militarily and as a state-form," he brutally explained.[2] While the coup's leader, General Duṭan Simovic, enjoyed his first few hours at the head of the new Yugoslav government, operational orders for the invasion of Yugoslavia, Directive No. 25, were sent out by General Alfred Jodl.

In Moscow Joseph Stalin was issuing proclamations of his own. As dusk settled on the snowbound Kremlin, street lights flickering feebly on its icy cobbles, the Soviet leader, normally keen to placate Hitler, now decided to use the Yugoslav coup to send him a signal that the Balkans were just as much a Russian as a German sphere of influence. The arguments over territory during Vyacheslav Molotov's visit to Berlin back in November still rankled; it was time to remind Germany that Russia had muscle too. As soon as news of Simovic's coup reached his desk, Stalin announced official Soviet recognition of the new government in Belgrade.

Stalin's impetuous gesture was an extra irritant to Hitler, but also an extra reason to savor the surprise he had lined up for his Soviet collaborator in the early summer. Goebbels, lucid as ever, summed up the Führer's state of mind. "The problem of Yugoslavia," he noted confidently, "will not take up too much time ... the big operation then comes later: against R."[3]

In London, as Hitler planned his Balkan bloodbath and Stalin drove one further nail into his own coffin, the Yugoslav coup was a shot in the arm. Churchill was having lunch that day with John Winant before giving a speech to the Trades Union Congress. The news of an unexpected pocket of resistance in eastern Europe could only improve the appetite. "It was breaking all our hearts to see the gallant Serbian and Yugoslav people signing away their souls through weak and cowardly rulers," he told his fellow diner. "But I rejoiced when I heard ... that a revolution had taken place."[4]

Churchill used his speech as a further affirmation of the unequivocal support he now believed Roosevelt was giving him. Winant sat in the audience as guest of honor; nodding in his direction Churchill told the trade unionists that all the president's men "gave me the definite impression that they would be shot stone dead rather than see this cause let down."[5] That evening, in his second major speech of the day, he told the Conservative Association: "There is another supreme event more blessed than victories, namely, the rising of the spirit of the great American nation and its ever more intimate association with the common cause."[6] His words were not only intended to boost British spirits; they were a rallying cry to the president and the supporters of war within his entourage.

The day's events added steel to his words. "The Yugoslav nation has found its soul," he informed his evening audience.[7] In Berlin his speeches were met with anger and derision. "The old liar," wrote Goebbels, "is, of course, on his high horse." Hitler, already blanching from the Yugoslav affront, allowed himself to be goaded further by Churchill's words. "The Führer is outraged," admitted Goebbels.[8]

In the early afternoon, five hours behind London time, president Roosevelt was on the last leg of an Atlantic fishing trip aboard his favorite yacht, *Potomac*, trying to relax despite the buffeting from the choppy Atlantic waters of the Bahamas. A flying boat lumbered into view. On board was the business of Washington, D.C. As the yacht rolled in the surf the airplane circled closer, taking an age to land in the uncertain conditions. Although the United States Congress had passed the Lend-Lease Bill two weeks before, neither money nor materials could start flowing until the president signed the authorization to release the necessary funds. While Churchill was talking up the transatlantic friendship, Roosevelt was handed the papers that would release the billions of dollars necessary to keep Britain afloat. The president signed, and the pilot took to the skies again with his valuable cargo. Within hours the $7,000,000,000 appropriations Bill would pass into law.

On March 30 Hitler summoned his generals for a 2½-hour lecture in the *Reich* Chancellery. Yugoslavia was a fly to be quickly swatted; at the same time the German army would sort out the mess the Italians were making in Greece. After that the road ahead was clearer than ever. The Führer continued to express both surprise and anger at Churchill's obstinacy; it was a "mistake of the British not to take advantage of chances for peace." However, when Russia was quickly crushed, the prop upon which Churchill was relying would have disappeared, leaving Germany the dominant nation in the world. "Only the final and drastic solution of all land problems," he told his audience, "will enable us to accomplish within two years our tasks in the air and on the oceans."[9]

After the tactical analysis, it became clear that the seething hatred of "Jewish Bolshevism" was now foremost in Hitler's mind. "This is a war of extermination," he told his generals, "we must forget the concept of comradeship between soldiers."[10] Murder was in the air. General Franz Halder described that day as a "crushing denunciation of Bolshevism." "Barbarossa" was not just about land. It was, wrote Halder after the meeting, about a "clash of ideologies."[11] "Communism is a danger for our future," Hitler explained, and it needed to be totally destroyed.[12]

The billions of dollars Roosevelt had signed off for lend-lease could only help to thwart Hitler if supplies were shipped safely across the Atlantic. As Nazi U-boats cut an ever-mounting swathe through the merchant shipping upon which British survival rested, Roosevelt's more hawkish colleagues pleaded with him to allow American warships to escort the merchant convoys. It was an immediate test of how far Roosevelt was willing to go in risking confrontation with Hitler. He pulled back. Henry Morgenthau noted his words at Cabinet on April 2: "The president said that public opinion was not yet ready for the United States to convoy ships. This was his whole attitude anyway, that he seemed to be still waiting and not ready to go ahead on 'all out aid for England.'"[13] It was the first sign of back-sliding, and not the attitude of a man who intended to give his people the firm lead Churchill had come to assume.

That weekend Churchill, blissfully unaware of Roosevelt's retrenchment, was at Ditchley Park. According to John Colville, he "spent much of the weekend pacing—or rather tripping—up and down the Great Hall to the sound of the gramophone … deep in thought."[14] While the corridors rang to the tune of Strauss waltzes and brass band anthems, thoughts were germinating in the prime minister's mind. Many months ago he had sensed that Hitler would turn east; now intelligence reports confirmed it. Despite all the rebuffs from Moscow so far, he decided to write his second letter to Stalin.

He told him that a trusted agent, in fact a decrypt of Nazi Enigma messages, had informed the British of German troop movements that could only herald an invasion of the Soviet Union. On March 20, just after Hitler had initiated his pact with the now deposed Yugoslav government, thus protecting his rear in the Balkans, the Germans had begun "to move three out of the five *Panzer* Divisions from Romania to southern Poland. The moment they heard of the Serbian revolution this movement was countermanded. Your Excellency will appreciate the significance of these facts."[15]

Churchill was asking Stalin to believe that only Hitler's need to deal with the crisis in Yugoslavia was delaying the build-up of a massive German army on the Soviet border. He knew that Stalin would suspect him of engineering friction between Russia and Germany and instructed Stafford Cripps not to imply that "we ourselves required any assistance from the Soviet government or that they would be acting in any interest but their own. What we want them to realize," Churchill explained, "is that Hitler intends to attack them sooner or later. The fact that he is in conflict with us is not in itself sufficient to prevent him from doing so. It is in the Soviet interests to take every possible step to ensure that he does not settle his Balkan problem in the way that he wants."[16] It was a clever, and correct, deduction; but was there any chance of Stalin fighting Hitler for the sake of General Simovic and his friends?

In the early hours of the morning on April 6, 1941, it might have seemed so. Stalin stood beside a delegation from Simovic's new government in the malachite splendor of Catherine Hall deep in the heart of the Kremlin Palace. He bent down to sign the treaty spread out before him. Placing the pen back on the table, he beamed. Celebratory cheers broke out among the assembled ambassadors and politicians as the Soviet–Yugoslav non-aggression pact was cast in ink. Within hours the vodka-fueled congratulations in Moscow were dashed. At 5:15 a.m., with the city still sleeping, the first Nazi bombs fell on Belgrade. The Soviet warlord was defiant. "Let them come," he said, "we've got strong nerves."[17] It was all froth. Stalin had no intention of fighting.

Three days later, Berlin was subjected to the Royal Air Force's heaviest bombardment of the war so far. The opera house was flattened and Hitler forced to leave the city. Field headquarters were established aboard his special train *Amerika* at the mouth of a railway tunnel on the line to Vienna. But on April 13 his equilibrium was restored as Wehrmacht soldiers marched into the smoking ruins of Belgrade. The rejoicing became louder with the news that General Erwin Rommel, the Third *Reich*'s most charismatic commander, had encircled Tobruk in the north African desert. In Greece, the British, already routed in Africa and the Balkans, were executing a humiliating lightning retreat from Mount Olympus. Sitting aboard his train at the foot of the Alps Hitler, though he did not know it, was enjoying his final unmitigated triumph, the last of the *Blitzkrieg*.

At the same time, at the Yaroslavsky station in central Moscow, Joseph Stalin was bidding farewell to a new friend. The platform was deserted save the heavy faceless guards and their precious charge, the Japanese foreign minister, Yosuke Matsuoka. Stalin had just signed a non-aggression pact with Japan. He was thrilled with his coup and got happily tipsy; a newsreel of the signing showed him beaming with pleasure as he linked arms with Matsuoka. His rear was now protected and he could prepare for the inevitable but, as he saw it, still distant confrontation with Nazism. For Hitler, it was another nuisance; he had harbored every hope that Japan, his ally in the Tripartite Pact, would pose a continuing threat to Russia, tying down Soviet troops in Siberia.

For Stalin the overriding aim still remained to prolong the peace with Hitler by continuing his double game of combining occasional displays of firmness with friendly gestures and scrupulous observance of the Nazi–Soviet pact. As Matsuoka's train pulled out, Stalin walked over to the German military representative in Moscow, Colonel Hans Krebs. Swinging his arm over Krebs's shoulder Stalin told him: "We must remain friends and you must now do everything to that end. We will stay friends with you whatever happens."[18] Stalin's words were reported back to Berlin. Hitler was delighted: "This is marvellous and for the moment extremely useful." Goebbels noted after conversations with his leader: "It is a fine thing to have power. It seems that Stalin has no desire to make the acquaintance of our German *Panzers.*"[19]

Despite the risk of enemy bombing, Churchill was spending this weekend at Chequers in the rolling Buckinghamshire countryside hosting a dinner for the two Americans, Winant and Averell Harriman. "They must have thought it a funny party," Anthony Eden recalled, "Winston in his rompers in which he had apparently travelled from south Wales."[20] The evening had started on a gloomy note with talk of the setbacks in Libya. It ended, wrote John Colville, "in glad momentous news from the USA." While Roosevelt had balked at armed convoys, he now cabled his intention to extend the limits over which American flying boats and warships could patrol the Atlantic. The pace appeared to be quickening in the long distance roller-coaster ride with the president. The next morning, while the party prepared to motor back to London, Colville had a quiet word with Harriman. "Do you not think last night's news from the US might mean war with Germany?" Colville asked expectantly. "That's what I hope," Harriman replied.[21]

But Roosevelt's move gave only small extra protection to the shipping lanes between Britain and America and was little use against a Hitler who now controlled most of Europe and was threatening the whole of the Middle East, and India beyond.

On April 17 the last remnants of Yugoslav resistance vanished before Hitler's brutal onslaught. The Nazi dictator celebrated in style with an outdoor concert at his improvised headquarters in the foothills of the Alps. Next to the sidings of his special train the evening air was filled with the music of triumph and power.

Not one to rest on his laurels, the Führer sent orders for the most devastating attack yet on the heart of Churchill's Britain. Yugoslavia had been punished for her impudence. It was now time for the British people to pay for the bombing raids on Berlin. London woke up on the morning of April 21 to the smoking aftermath of thousands of German incendiaries unleashed by a fleet of seven hundred Luftwaffe bombers. Safely ensconced at Ditchley Park deep in the Oxfordshire countryside, Churchill mourned yet another battering to British morale. He was entering his darkest period of the war.

Nazi triumph in the Balkans, the inexorable retreat in Greece, burning buildings in Britain's cities and burning ships on the Atlantic added up to a dire prospect. Even worse, Roosevelt, in the view of several of his most senior cabinet members, was retreating on his commitment to support the British. At a quiet luncheon in Washington the Secretary of the Interior, Harold Ickes, and a Supreme Court justice, Felix Frankfurter, were venting their frustration. "I have become thoroughly concerned about the state of public opinion in this country," Ickes told Frankfurter, "and at a total loss to understand the president's failure to do something about it."[22]

They were not alone in their criticism. Twenty-four hours later more protests were audible in the offices and restaurants frequented by the great political players. "I found everybody rather discouraged by the war news," complained Henry Stimson in his diary. "The president doesn't seem to be keeping his leadership in regard to the matter."[23] Another close associate of Roosevelt, the former American ambassador to France William Bullitt, told Ickes that he also did not understand "the president's apparent inertia."[24]

Retreat in Washington was matched by the continuing freeze in Moscow. Churchill's letter had, after several delays by Cripps, who believed it would be counter-productive, finally reached Stalin. Cripps's judgment was right; Stalin was instantly suspicious, not of Hitler but of Churchill. He told his generals: "We're being threatened with the Germans, and the Germans with the Soviet Union. They're playing us off against each other."[25]

Hitler could smell Stalin's fear of battle. "Moscow wants peace," crowed the propaganda minister Joseph Goebbels, "Stalin has caught a whiff of what is cooking ... and is offering the olive branch."[26] The next day he also offered an uncannily accurate insight into Churchill's mood. "He is said to be in a very depressed state, spending the entire day smoking and drinking. This," recorded Goebbels in triumphant tones, "is the kind of enemy we need."[27]

The British prime minister was now facing up to his greatest crisis since coming to power just under a year before. On April 29 he conveyed to Roosevelt his private fear that Hitler's *Blitzkrieg* in the Balkans might lead to large parts of the Middle East falling under Nazi control. Not only were Britain's oil supplies under threat but also the link to her empire in India and beyond. "I feel Hitler may quite easily now gain vast advantages very cheaply," he confided. "We are so fully engaged that we can do little or nothing to stop his spreading himself. At this moment much hangs in the balance."[28]

Churchill's position was also being undermined by internal rumblings against his style of government. The Paymaster General, Maurice Hankey, a stalwart of British administrations since the First World War, wrote to Lord Halifax in Washington: "It is a complete dictatorship. The War Cabinet consists of a long monologue by one man. The others are just: 'yes men.'"[29] In an attempt to convince the British people of his energetic leadership, Churchill reshuffled his Cabinet. The changes were noted in Berlin with relish. "It is proof of England's bad situation," wrote Joseph Goebbels, "must be worse than all of us assume."[30]

On May 1 Churchill received Roosevelt's reply to his *cri de coeur*; and it shocked him. The president appeared not to see what he was fussing about. "Personally I am not downcast by more spread of Germany for additional large territories," he wrote. "There is little of raw materials in all of them put together—not enough to maintain nor compensate for huge occupation forces."[31] For Churchill, Roosevelt's message revealed a devastating truth.

It showed that the president simply didn't care about the Middle East, viewing it as part of the outdated empire he would prefer the British to do without. He even appeared to gain positive comfort from the thought of Hitler overreaching himself. The only thing that seemed to matter to him was supplying Britain through the Atlantic in order to keep Hitler away from America.

Sitting in his patterned dressing gown, not yet out of bed, Churchill was stuck in gloom. The remaining stack of telegrams piled up the bad news. A British destroyer had been sunk blocking the grand harbor in Malta; reinforcements for General Archibald Wavell's Operation "Tiger" in the Mediterranean had been delayed due to engine trouble; in Iraq the anti-British rebellion continued to explode. Iraqi troops had opened fire that morning on British troops "two hours before we had intended firing on them!" Churchill exclaimed to John Colville.[32]

The next day, May 2, 1941, Churchill toured the bombed city of Plymouth. In public he was keeping his chin up, but Hitler's destruction and Roosevelt's message had together pitched him to rock bottom. He prepared a searingly honest reply to Roosevelt. "The PM, in worse gloom than I have ever seen him, dictated a telegram to the president drawing a sombre picture of what a collapse in the Middle East would entail," recorded Colville. "Then he sketched ... a world in which Hitler dominated all Europe, Asia and Africa and left the US and ourselves no option but an unwilling peace."[33]

In desperation, Churchill told Roosevelt he must come to his rescue. "Mr. President. The one decisive counterweight I can see ... would be if the United States were immediately to range herself with us as a belligerent power."[34] Churchill minuted Eden: "It seems to me as if there has been a considerable recession across the Atlantic and that quite unconsciously we are being left very much to our fate."[35] It was a year since Churchill had become prime minister. And he was back at square one, on bended knee to Roosevelt begging him to join the fight, threatening disaster if he didn't. The evasiveness of the man on whom he had pinned everything was dashing all his hopes.

In Berlin, laughter echoed from the Führer's office. Hitler and Goebbels were browsing through a new book about Churchill. It reported that he drank like a fish, wore pink silk underwear and dictated messages in the bath or in his underpants. It was an accurate portrayal of the British leader's endearing eccentricities but one hardly designed to appeal to Hitler, who was terrified of being seen in a state of undress. Once the laughter had subsided, Hitler regained his composure and turned to his companion. "The British Empire is slowly disintegrating. Not much will be salvageable."[36]

Churchill and Stalin had deeper pockets of resistance than Hitler was at this point capable of imagining. Despite the transatlantic depression Churchill still did not countenance the possibility of defeat. As he began to recover from the jolt of Roosevelt's cable he told Colville that while this was the decisive moment, "it is being established not whether we shall win or lose, but whether the duration of the war will be long or short."[37] Stalin too was preparing to fight. On May 5, 1941, he told graduates of the Red Army Academy, "We must prepare for war. The enemy will be Germany."[38] But not yet, for another year at least.

In the meantime, while Russia's forces retrained and rearmed, Stalin ordered that nothing must be done to provoke a Nazi attack. His submissiveness only quickened Hitler's pulse. In Berlin, Colonel Krebs had just returned from Moscow. "Russia will do anything to avoid war," he told Hitler, who heard him out with mounting pleasure. "Russia's higher officers corps are decidedly bad," announced the Führer, "it will take Russia 20 years to reach her old level."[39] The next day, Halder outlined Hitler's plans for his war in the east to the foot soldiers of the Third *Reich*. "Troops," Halder told them, "must do their share in the ideological struggle of the eastern campaign."[40] Hitler's genocidal aspirations were filtering down through the ranks.

Driving down to Berchtesgaden on May 9, Hitler was able to believe that his opponents across the globe were mastered. Churchill was an idiot paralyzed by depression; Roosevelt too canny to fight; Stalin too feeble to resist. He told Goebbels: "Churchill is out of his depth. But what can England do? The Empire will be ruined when all this is over."[41] The next day Hitler was in for a nasty shock.

At 6 p.m. on May 10, 1941, a Messerschmitt 110D took off from the small airstrip in the pretty town of Augsburg, just north of Munich. Flying due northeast, the plane sped into the darkness. Four hours later, passing over the blacked-out cities of Britain, the Nazi aircraft, rather than stopping to unload a deadly barrage of explosives, continued northwards, eventually emerging from the clouds above the rolling Lanarkshire countryside. At Dungavel, the Scottish estate of the Duke of Hamilton, the quiet of the starless night was broken by the splutter of engines as the plane lurched towards the ground and crash-landed in a smoking heap. Having bailed out just minutes before, the pilot was discovered alive, well and with an extraordinary tale to tell.

The following day, as the Duke of Hamilton carried his strange story to Churchill at Ditchley Park, Hitler was handed a sealed envelope by the adjutant of the deputy leader of the Nazi Party, Rudolf Hess. Karl-Heinz Pintsch winced as the silence at the Berghof was suddenly broken with an almighty roar. "Bormann immediately," Hitler screeched, "where is Bormann?" He picked up the telephone. In Nuremburg, Hermann Göring answered. "Get here immediately," Hitler raged, "something dreadful has happened."[42]

At Ditchley Park a dinner party was in full swing; Churchill, fully fortified by champagne and good food, was in the best of humors. "Now come and tell us this funny story of yours," he told Hamilton. All the guests except the Secretary of State for Air, Sir Archibald Sinclair, withdrew. Churchill was informed of the bizarre events of the day before. The mystery guest who had landed in Dungavel was claiming to be Hitler's long-term associate and heir apparent, Rudolf Hess. He said he was on a top-secret peace mission authorized by the Führer himself. Not convinced of Hamilton's tale, the prime minister was determined not to allow the evening's entertainment to be interrupted. "Hess or no Hess, I am going to watch the Marx Brothers," he told the stunned Duke.[43]

After a full interrogation on May 12, Hess's identity was confirmed. Churchill, enjoying every moment, decided to sit on the story in the hope of confusing Hitler. A few hours later Germany issued a communiqué. The silence maintained by Great Britain had convinced Hitler that his worst fears were true; Hess had not crashed to his death, but was in captivity. He immediately sought to discredit Hess and his treachery. Churchill was thrilled as he listened to German claims that Hess was a "victim of hallucinations" and that his parting letter showed "in its confusion the traces of a mental derangement."[44] Hitler was rattled and embarrassed. It may have made little difference to the military struggle but it certainly raised the spirits. It also had a remarkable effect on Stalin.

"Hess's contact with the British," wrote Sergo Beria, the son of Stalin's notorious intelligence chief, "was followed by Stalin hour by hour, studied microscopically, analyzed minutely." Beria claimed that the Soviet spy at the heart of the British secret service, Kim Philby, was feeding through the latest information to Moscow even before Churchill himself was receiving it.[45] Stalin quickly jumped to a conclusion which would have devastating consequences. All along he had suspected the motives behind Churchill's letter warning him of German troop movements. Now the Hess mission confirmed all those suspicions. There could only be one explanation. Churchill's message, and intelligence reports emanating from different parts of the world, were all a conspiracy designed to trick him into launching a pre-emptive strike against Hitler.

Three days after Hess landed, Stalin addressed the central party committee. What he said was taken down verbatim by Yury Chadayev, its recently appointed secretary. Stalin first laid bare the background to the giant conspiracy he had detected. "On the one hand, Churchill sends us a personal message in which he warns us about Hitler's aggressive intentions. ... And on the other hand, the British meet Hess, who is undoubtedly Hitler's confidant, and conduct negotiations with Germany through him."[46]

Stalin argued that there was only one possible conclusion. "Apparently, when Churchill sent us his personal warning, he believed that we would 'activate' our military mechanism. Then Hitler would have a direct and fair reason to launch a preventive crusade against the Soviet Union." Stalin asked his audience: "Is Hitler ready for such a crusade?" Stalin knew that Hitler could not be: to fight a war on two fronts was the act of an irrational man; and Hitler was not that. So the policy must continue: "We must not supply reasons for Hitler to attack us. ... Let's not complicate our relations with him."[47] For the next five weeks, this deduction became a blinding article of faith as Stalin dismissed warning after warning of imminent German attack.

His generals were desperate. German forces continued to build up along the borders of the USSR. On May 12, Stalin sanctioned the calling up of 500,000 reserves, but this was a timid gesture, particularly as that day Marshal Semyon Timoshenko had told Stalin that German reconnaissance flights had been flying illegally over Soviet territory. Stalin listened impassively. "I'm not sure Hitler knows about those flights," he replied.[48]

On the other side of the world in Washington a similar conflict was being played out. Some of Roosevelt's most senior colleagues were conspiring against what they saw as the president's feebleness. On May 12 the interior secretary, Harold Ickes, organized a secret meeting with the war secretary, Henry Stimson, the Attorney-General, Robert Jackson, and the navy secretary, Frank Knox. Ickes noted in his diary: "I called this meeting to see to what extent these men might be willing to join in a written representation to the president. All of us found ourselves in complete agreement ... none of us could account for the president's failure of leadership."[49] Two days later, another senior Cabinet member, Henry Morgenthau, recorded in his diary a meeting with Harry Hopkins, the man closest to Roosevelt: "Hopkins said the president has never said so in so many words, but he thinks the president is loath to get us into this war, and he would rather follow public opinion than to lead it."[50]

At this pivotal moment, Roosevelt appeared to suffer some form of psychological crisis. Pressured by the small but still vocal minority of isolationists on one side and the hawks in his Cabinet on the other, he spent much of May 1941 in bed and rarely went to the office. He had a mild cold but was not otherwise physically ill. After visiting him in his White House bedroom, one of Roosevelt's speechwriters, Robert Sherwood, remarked to the president's secretary, Marguerite "Missy" LeHand: "The president seems in fine shape to me. He didn't cough or sneeze or even blow his nose the whole time I was there and he looked wonderfully well." Sherwood, however, had noticed that the president's usually sunny disposition was missing. "What is really the matter with him?" he asked as he followed Missy back into her office. LeHand passed it off by replying: "What he's suffering from most of all is a case of sheer exasperation."[51] Churchill's ever more desperate cables could only have added to his feelings of oppression. On May 21 he told him, "Whatever happens you may be sure we shall fight on and I am sure we can at least save ourselves, but what is the good of that?"[52]

As Churchill was sending his message, in the cold waters of the south Atlantic a German submarine closed in on its prey, a passenger ship en route to South Africa. The U-boat commander signalled a warning to the ship to stop for inspection. There was no response. Within 30 minutes it was heading for the ocean floor. There were few survivors. The sinking had a significance beyond the human tragedy. The ship, the *Robin Moor*, was American. Could this be the belligerent act, the "something dramatic," that Roosevelt needed to push his nation to war? When the news filtered through to Washington, Harry Hopkins told Roosevelt it was time to give the United States Navy full freedom to police the Atlantic, using force where it saw fit.

On May 27 Roosevelt got up from his bed to deliver a *Fireside Chat* to the nation. Several of his colleagues were hoping for a raising of the stakes against the Nazis. The day before he privately admitted that Hitler and his increasingly bloody domination of Europe was weighing heavily in his thoughts. "My recent nightmares," Roosevelt told a group of aides, "have been dominated by images of the Luftwaffe bombing New York and … being forced to shelter in a bomb proof cave until a squadron of German planes has passed over."[53] It was a rare window into the deepest fears of this most elusive of leaders.

As Americans awaited their president's speech, Churchill sat in glum silence in the cramped hall of Church House, a wartime location of the House of Commons. Brendan Bracken entered the room in a flurry of excitement holding a piece of paper. It was passed to the prime minister, who glanced at the text and leapt from his seat. "I have just received news," he announced triumphantly, "that the *Bismarck* is sunk."[54] The tension in the room was shattered by victorious cheering and clapping. Nearly a week of cat and mouse between the deadly German battleship and the Royal Navy had finally come to an end. The sinking of HMS *Hood* and the deaths of two thousand men were avenged. Returning to the Cabinet War Rooms later that day, the cheers and encouragement of his parliamentary colleagues still ringing in his ears, Churchill sat down to listen to the radio.

Sitting at his desk, Roosevelt leaned towards the microphone. "The first and fundamental fact," he told his listeners across the world, "is that what started as a European war has developed, as the Nazis always intended it should develop, into a world war for world domination." In London Churchill listened with satisfaction. "The war," Roosevelt continued, "is approaching the brink of the western hemisphere itself. It is coming very close to home." The president announced that the United States had "doubled and redoubled our vast production, increasing, month by month, our material supply of the tools of war for ourselves and for Britain."[55]

To his listeners across the Atlantic, there was an aggression in Roosevelt's words that surely meant action would this time follow. "We will not hesitate to use our armed forces to repel attack. I have tonight," he declared, "issued a proclamation that an unlimited national emergency exists and requires the strengthening of our defense to the extreme limit of our national power and authority."[56] The cautious Lord Halifax, listening at the British embassy in Washington, was encouraged. "I thought it was very good indeed," he noted. "I had hardly hoped he had gone so far, and certainly there is no drawing back now."[57]

However, some in Roosevelt's own cabinet were not so sure. "It was not the kind of speech that I hoped he would make," complained Harold Ickes. "Right at the end, when I thought that the whole thing was going to flatten out into what would inevitably have been a psychological nose-dive for the country, he did declare a total emergency. But to declare a total emergency without acts to follow it up means little."[58] "Lo and behold, the speech has been softened," judged Henry Stimson, Roosevelt's war secretary.[59] However, the next morning he found his boss in blazing form, interrogating him about delays in delivering American-built bombers to Britain. "I am anxious to cut through all of the formalities that are not legally prohibitive," the president told Stimson, "and help the British get this job done with dispatch."[60]

Was this the visionary leader edging his nation towards war; or the consummate politician continuing to do everything to stay out while arming others to do the fighting? In Berlin Goebbels delivered his verdict: "We must wait and see what he does next. In any case there is no talk of war at present. At the moment, he doesn't dare."[61] Not for the first time, Goebbels hit the nail on the head. Scanning the British and world press he concluded: "Officially, London is delighted, but the Reuters office makes no attempt to hide its deep disappointment. They had expected more." Encouraged that Roosevelt seemed no nearer to war, Goebbels turned his attentions to Russia. "Moscow is still buzzing with rumors," he noted. "Stalin seems to be gradually seeing the light. But the rest of the time he stares like a rabbit with a snake."[62] Brimming with confidence the Nazi war machine moved inexorably towards Hitler's date with destiny.

Stalin was scoffing at all the predictions, even by his own intelligence service, of what that date might be. On June 5 he told the Central Committee: "At first, our intelligence gave May 14, 15, 20 as possible dates of the attack. Now they claim it's going to be either June 15 or 22. Apparently, these dates could also be wrong. Let's instead cherish the hope that 1941 will remain peaceful." General Timoshenko was appalled by his leader's breezy complacency. "German military preparations demonstrate that the war will break out this year and very soon," Timoshenko objected. "Don't try to frighten us!" Stalin snapped. He continued to stake his life on his conspiracy theory that the democratic nations of Europe and America were ganging up on him. "England, France and America see in Germany their only hope of getting rid of Bolshevism and, therefore, help the Nazis in all possible ways in their 'crusade to the east.'" He was implacable. "We must carefully fulfil our obligations under the Soviet–German treaty," he ordered, "so that Germany will be unable to find any violations of the treaty on our part."[63]

In London, Churchill and his colleagues could not fathom Stalin's behavior. During the first two weeks in June, despite the hostile silence from Moscow, Churchill instructed the Foreign Office to continue to pass information to Stalin on the activities of Hitler's forces along the Soviet border. In the privacy of his diary, the permanent under secretary, Sir Alexander Cadogan, railed at his thankless task. "You can't do anything nowadays with any country unless you can (a) threaten (b) bribe it. Russia has (a) no fear of us *whatever* and (b) we have *nothing* to offer her. You can juggle with words and jiggle with drafts as much as you like, and you'll get nowhere."[64]

On June 12 Stalin told his generals: "I am certain that Hitler will not risk creating a second front by attacking the Soviet Union. Hitler is not such an idiot."[65] Two days later he directed a public counterblast at the interfering and troublemaking British. The official Soviet press agency, TASS, published a statement from the Kremlin to every news bureau in the world. "In the opinion of Soviet circles rumors of Germany's intention to break the pact and open an attack on the USSR are devoid of all foundations," TASS reported. "The USSR, consistently with its policy of peace, has observed and intends to observe the provisions of the Soviet–German non-aggression pact, and therefore rumors that the USSR is preparing for war with Germany are lies and provocations."[66] Stalin wanted the world, and Hitler above all, to see where his loyalties lay. It was eight days to the launch of "Barbarossa." Three million Nazi troops were gathering on his border.

On June 16, six days to go, the People's *Commissar* for State Security, Vsevolod Merkulov, was ushered in by Stalin's rotund secretary Aleksandr Poskryobyshev. Clearing his throat, Merkulov spoke carefully. Soviet agent "starshina," embedded deep in Luftwaffe headquarters, had confirmed Merkulov's worst fears. The final decision to attack the USSR had been issued by the Führer. "Tell the 'source' in the Staff of the German Air Force," Stalin screeched, "to fuck his mother!"[67] The same day Hitler told Goebbels: "That which we have spent our lives fighting, we will now annihilate. Whether right or wrong, we must win. And when we have won, who will ask about the method?"[68]

On June 18, four days to go, Stalin chaired a fiery three-hour meeting of the Red Army General Staff. Marshals Timoshenko and Georgy Zhukov implored their leader to issue a full alert to the army. Stalin moved restlessly in his chair, the anger mounting. Suddenly he leapt to his feet. "Have you come to scare us with war, or do you want a war because you're not sufficiently decorated or your rank isn't high enough?" he bellowed at Zhukov. "You have to realize that Germany will never fight Russia on her own. You must understand this." The dictator marched out of the room. A moment later, as the marshals exchanged fearful glances, Stalin stormed back in. "If you're going to provoke the Germans on the frontier by moving troops there without our permission, then heads will roll," he warned in sinister tones, "mark my words."[69] Goebbels was watching the people of Berlin walking harmlessly about in the rain, "happy people who know nothing of all our concerns and live for the day."[70]

On June 20, two days to go, Hitler summoned his favorite architect, Albert Speer, to the grand wood-paneled office in the *Reich* Chancellery. The music he had chosen as his fanfare for victory in Russia, a grandiose passage from Liszt's *Les Preludes*, swirled around the room. "You will hear that often in the future," Hitler declared as Speer entered, "how do you like it? We'll be getting our granite and marble from Russia in any quantities we want." At 2:30 a.m. Hitler made his way to bed. "Before three months have passed," Hitler announced to his entourage before retiring, "we shall witness a collapse in Russia, the like of which has never been seen in history."[71]

On Saturday, June 21, one day to go, Churchill sensed the tremors. "The PM says a German attack on Russia is certain and Russia will assuredly be defeated," recorded John Colville. "He says he will go all out to help Russia. I said that for him, the arch anti-Communist, this was bowing down in the House of Rimmon. He replied that he had only one single purpose—the destruction of Hitler—and his life was much simplified thereby. If Hitler invaded Hell he would at least make a favourable reference to the Devil!"[72]

In Berlin Hitler was content to have thrown his fate into the hands of Providence. "The Führer seems to lose his fear as the decision comes nearer," wrote Goebbels. "It is always the same with him. He relaxes visibly. All the exhaustion seems to drop away. We pace up and down in his salon for three hours. I am granted more insights into his most secret thoughts. We have no choice but to attack. This cancerous sore must be cauterized. Stalin will fall. The fortune of war will decide."[73]

In Moscow, though Stalin still refused to see it coming, it was now apparent to his closest associates that the Nazis were on their way. One of them, Georgy Dimitrov, noted in his diary: "Rumors of an impending attack are multiplying on all sides. Have to be on guard. Called Molotov this morning. Molotov: The situation is unclear. There is a major game under way."[74]

Stalin was spending the weekend at his *dacha* among the flat wheat fields and forests west of Moscow, a countryside that would soon be bloodied by the most violent war mankind had ever fought. After a grueling Politburo meeting, the Soviet dictator walked slowly into the calm silence of his bedroom.

Within minutes he was asleep. Just two hours later the silence was broken with the sounds of the telephone. "Who's calling?" the NKVD officer on duty asked grumpily. "Zhukov, Chief of Staff," came the insistent reply, "please connect me to comrade Stalin. It's urgent."[75] The time was 3:30 a.m., and the destiny of all four warlords was about to be changed forever.

CHAPTER FOUR

June 22–August 8, 1941

"Did you understand what I said, Comrade Stalin?" The telephone line fell silent. General Zhukov tried once again. "Comrade Stalin, do you understand?" The response was a mumble: "Come to the Kremlin with Timoshenko. Tell Poskrobyshev to summon all the members of the Politburo."[1] It was 4 a.m. on June 22, 1941.

On the same date that Napoleon had once invaded Russia, Hitler had now followed in his footsteps. It was, as Joseph Goebbels noted, "the greatest deployment in world history."[2] Over three million German troops were sweeping across a 930-mile stretch of the Soviet frontier. Operation "Barbarossa" had begun. German radio played Liszt's *Les Preludes*, Hitler's fanfare for victory, as Stalin's car swept through the empty streets of Moscow towards the Kremlin.

At 5:45 a.m. the Politburo, together with Generals Georgy Zhukov and Semyon Timoshenko, gathered in Stalin's office. After hearing a situation report from Timoshenko, Stalin dispatched Vyacheslav Molotov to telephone the German embassy. "The German government has declared war on us," Molotov announced when he returned to the office. "The enemy will be beaten all along the line," Stalin retorted.[3] Zhukov and Timoshenko departed with instructions from Stalin that "our armies will fall upon the enemy with all the forces and all the means at their disposal."[4]

As Georgy Dimitrov arrived in Stalin's office at 8:40 a.m.[5] Molotov, Kliment Voroshilov, Lazar Kaganovich and Georgy Malenkov were with him sitting in silence. "They attacked us without declaring any grievances," Stalin told Dimitrov, "without demanding any negotiations; they attacked us viciously, like gangsters."[6] Yury Chadayev, the Sovnarkom secretary who was taking a record of that morning's meeting, noticed that his boss "looked tired, worn out. His pockmarked face was drawn and haggard."[7] Stalin refused to speak to the nation. Molotov had to do it instead. As news of the enormous losses came in—hundreds of aircraft in 66 aerodromes destroyed in the first few hours—Stalin instructed Lavrenty Beria, the bloodthirsty head of the KGB, to take immediate action. "This is a monstrous crime," he said, "those responsible must lose their heads."[8] Beria's targets were not Germans, but Russian commanders on the front.

Behind the new front line, Hitler had gained a sense of inner peace. He had completed an extraordinary mental journey. A year before he had seen the invasion of Russia as a tactic to make Britain crumble; now the ideology with which he had set out 20 years before had once again taken pride of place. He wrote to his Italian ally, Benito Mussolini: "Let me say one more thing, Duce. Since I struggled through to this decision, I again feel spiritually free. The partnership with the Soviet Union was often very irksome to me, for in some way or other it seemed to me to be a break with my whole origin, my concepts, and my former obligations. I am happy now to be relieved of these mental agonies."[9]

In London, Churchill too was at peace. John Colville woke him at 8 a.m. with the life-saving news from Russia. Finally, he had a fighting ally against Hitler. He immediately set about preparing a public statement. "I had not the slightest doubt where our duty and our policy lay. Nor indeed what to say," he later wrote.[10] He had been waiting for rescue ever since May 1940 and imagined his savior would be Roosevelt; Hitler with his folly had beaten him to it and driven Stalin into his arms. "The Russian danger," he announced in a radio broadcast several hours later, "is therefore our danger and the danger of the United States."[11] Churchill, the arch anti-communist who had been the leading proponent of sending British troops in 1919 to fight the Bolsheviks, now joyously and unreservedly welcomed Stalin into the fold.

Over in Washington, Roosevelt had just woken up. Despite the momentous nature of events, he stayed silent. "It was extremely fortunate for us that Churchill stepped forward in this forthright manner because there was not a word from the president," complained Harold Ickes with familiar frustration. "It would be just like him to wait for some expression of public opinion instead of giving direction to that public opinion."[12] But Roosevelt's subtle mind was already in overdrive. To Churchill, the invasion showed more than ever Hitler's global ambitions; he believed that it could only compel Roosevelt to draw nearer to war. But the president was soon drawing a different conclusion. He quickly calculated that Hitler's move would get him off the hook which had been causing him such depression. Russia's forced entry into the battle could help America to continue to stay out of the war; instead the Soviet Union could be a second nation to be financed to fight Germany.

The sudden convulsion was sending chain reactions to all corners, among them the nether world of espionage. On hearing of the attack, Guy Liddell, head of MI5's counter-subversion unit, noted: "I shall be pleased and surprised if the Germans are not in Moscow within a fortnight. They may however get severely damaged in the process."[13] For men like Liddell, the recasting of international alliances brought a problem. Stalin was now an ally of Great Britain and Churchill's spy chiefs were instructed to treat her as such. The official history of F2C, the unit within MI5 that dealt with Soviet espionage, noted that the new alliance "caused the Foreign Office to lay down rigid rules restricting action permissible by the Security Service to the barest minimum."[14] The insidious burrowing of spies such as the Cambridge Five proceeded unmolested.

As 3:20 a.m. on June 23, 1941, Stalin's closest colleagues were recalled to the Kremlin. Operation "Barbarossa" had been hammering Soviet cities and military installations for 24 hours. Stalin seemed unable to absorb the scale of the devastation. His generals told him that German tanks were bearing down on Minsk, which had already been pounded with Luftwaffe bombs. "What was that you said? What's happening in Minsk?" Stalin demanded of General Nikolai Vatutin. "Have you got this right? How do you know this?" "No, Comrade Stalin, I'm not getting mixed up," Vatutin responded, "the western front has virtually collapsed."[15] "We must insist on immediate help from our allies," Stalin told the Politburo, "It is important that the Allies not only declare their intentions but provide real help."[16] However, Stalin believed that the British and Americans would not support the USSR until "they think that we are out of breath and are ready for an armistice with Germany."[17]

Later that day in London, Churchill summoned the War Cabinet. He had not sought prior consent from his colleagues before announcing in his broadcast the day before that Britain would commit itself to Russia. "It had been necessary to act quickly," he told them.[18] Churchill was filled with energy. Not only was he seeking to aid Stalin as much and as quickly as possible, he was thinking of fresh campaigns. "The PM is now toying with the idea of an armed raid on the French coast while the Germans are busy in Russia," John Colville noted, "now, he says, is the time 'to make hell while the sun shines.'"[19]

In Washington Roosevelt was consolidating his plan to finance the Russians. He had just received two memos from Oscar Cox, one of Harry Hopkins's most brilliant aides. Cox advised "there is no doubt that aid can legally be rendered to Russia under the Lend-Lease Act"[20] and stated: "Our practical choice is clear: whether or not we like Russia's internal and other policies, we will aid Russia, in our national interest, to eliminate the far more immediate danger to our security from Hitler's already partially executed plans to rule the world."[21]

The war secretary, Henry Stimson, wrote to the president imploring him also to take a more aggressive line with naval operations in the Atlantic: "This precious and unforeseen period of respite should be used to push with the utmost vigor our movements in the Atlantic theater of operations," he wrote after discussions with the American Chiefs of Staff. "They were unanimously of the feeling that such pressure on our part was the right way to help Britain, to discourage Germany, and to strengthen our own position of defense against our most imminent danger."[22] Yet Roosevelt would continue to be wary of anything that might involve Americans in hostilities.

Late on that night of June 23 Hitler arrived for the first time at his new headquarters near Rastenburg in the dark wooded countryside of eastern Prussia. The *Wolfsschanze*, or Wolf's Lair, a vast, gloomy complex of concrete bunkers, was to be the Führer's home for much of the rest of the war. The regime was strict. Situation reports were given to Hitler by Generals Alfred Jodl and Walther von Brauchitsch, followed by lunch at 2 p.m. At 5 p.m. his secretaries would be called in for coffee and cakes, after which a further situation report would be given at 6 p.m. Dinner always started promptly at 7:30 p.m. with Hitler consuming simple, vegetarian food. Baked potatoes with curd cheese were a favorite.[23]

In Berlin, despite the atmosphere of exhilaration as reports came in of sweeping victories, Goebbels sounded a note of caution: "We'll soon pull it off. We must soon pull it off. Among the people there's a somewhat depressed mood. The people want peace … every new theater of war causes concern and worry."[24] Benito Mussolini was less restrained. "I am certain," he replied to his letter from the Führer, "that the campaign against Bolshevist Russia will culminate in a dazzling victory, and that this victory will be the prologue to the total victory over the Anglo-Saxon world."[25]

Three days later German troops were continuing to enjoy unlimited success. Hitler's armies had marched 185 miles within the borders of the USSR. That same day, June 26, 1941, Roosevelt was confirming the strategic core of his new tactics. He wrote to one of his closest associates, Admiral William Leahy: "Now comes this Russian diversion. If it is more than just that it will mean the liberation of Europe from Nazi domination—and at the same time I do not think we need to worry about any possibility of Russian domination."[26] Roosevelt's benign view of Soviet intentions, which in the coming years would exert such a grip on Allied relationships, was beginning to color his actions.

Stalin was sinking into a depression. On June 28 the meeting in his office at the Kremlin finished at 12:50 a.m. Angry at the lack of information from the front, he walked out with Beria and Molotov to visit the Defense Commissariat. There was no good news. In fact there was very little news at all. The situation at the front was chaotic. Before getting in his car to travel to his *dacha* at Kuntsevo Stalin erupted. "Lenin founded our state and we've fucked it up."[27] The Soviet warlord did not return to the Kremlin for three days.[28]

"His closest associates were alarmed, to say the least," Chadayev said of this time. "We all knew that he usually summoned one official after another, with not much of an interval in between. But now the telephones were silent. We knew only that he was at the nearest *dacha*, but nobody felt bold enough to go and see him. During the days of his seclusion members of the Politburo met in Molotov's office, trying to decide what to do. According to the *dacha* staff Stalin was alive and well, but had shut himself up, away from everybody, was receiving nobody, and wasn't answering the phone."[29]

Stalin knew that he had lost the mind game with Hitler. His great conspiracy theory that the democracies were plotting to provoke him was shattered. His misreading of Hitler, the man he had viewed as a rational strategist, was total. His daughter Svetlana later suggested that "he had not guessed or foreseen that the pact of 1939, which he had considered the outcome of his own great cunning, would be broken by an enemy more cunning than himself. This was the real reason for his deep depression at the start of the war. It was his immense political miscalculation. Even after the war was over he was in the habit of repeating, 'Ech, together with the Germans we would have been invincible!'" While militarily "Barbarossa" turned the war on its head, his experience with Hitler also had a vital psychological effect on Stalin. He later remarked: "When you're trying to make a decision, NEVER put yourself into the mind of the other person because if you do, you can make a terrible mistake."[30]

At the Wolf's Lair, Hitler was in dramatic form. "In four weeks we will be in Moscow. It will be razed to the ground," he told the assembled group, including his secretary Christa Schroeder.[31] Yet he still felt the need to justify himself. According to Schroeder, her boss was "constantly emphasizing what a great danger Bolshevism was for Europe, and that if he had waited another year, it would probably have been too late."[32] "If ever the German soldier earns a laurel wreath," the Nazi warlord told his companions at the Wolf's Lair, "it'll be for this campaign."[33] Yet Hitler would be the eventual loser of his duel with Stalin. Though it seemed an inconceivable outcome in these early triumphant days, his decision to attack Russia had signed the death warrant of his own dreams of empire, and of European imperialism in general.

In London Churchill, unaware of Stalin's slump into depression, was giving instructions for precious information to be passed on to his new ally. The code-breakers at Bletchley had managed to crack the Enigma key used by Hitler's troops on the eastern front. This information, known as "Vulture," was passed on to the Soviets via a British military intelligence officer, Cecil Barclay, who was based at the British embassy in Moscow. The source of the information was not released, and details of German troop movements and orders were given to Stalin in disguised form. There was little the Soviets could do with it. The death toll that day in the battle for Minsk reached tens of thousands.

The next day, June 29, Sir Stafford Cripps, now a visitor to be welcomed at the Kremlin rather than frozen out, was presented with an enormous list by his Soviet hosts of equipment they required. It included three thousand fighter aircraft, 20,000 light aircraft guns, radar and night-fighting equipment. The Foreign Office noted that the Soviet demands were presented in "less than diplomatic language."[34] However, the Russians had no intention of giving away in return any information about the basis of their list. In London 24 hours later there was frustration. "The Russians, who are being driven back by the Germans, are showing unbelievable reticence to our military mission in Moscow," John Colville noted. "Molotov will tell us nothing beyond what is in the official communiqués. Now, in their hour of need, the Soviet government—or at any rate Molotov—is as suspicious and uncooperative as when we were negotiating a treaty in the summer of 1939."[35]

MI5 agreed that old suspicions remained. "I sense that the Russians are angling for a binding agreement as they probably fear that at some future date we may make peace at their expense," Guy Liddell noted in his secret diary.[36] Ivan Maisky wrote to his superiors at the Foreign Ministry in Moscow that the British were reluctant to discuss wider political issues because of "the position of the USA and its diehards."[37] Maisky was astutely hinting at Roosevelt's long-standing hostility towards spheres of influence in Europe and the brakes this might put on the British in coming to a long-term agreement.

In Washington old frustrations were rearing up again. While Roosevelt was planning his aid package for Russia behind closed doors, he was hesitating to go public and whip up the support of the American people. Any further commitments in the Atlantic remained off limits. Henry Stimson talked to the president on the telephone. Roosevelt explained that a new and favorable Gallup poll was due to be published. "I replied that I was glad of that," Stimson recorded, "but that I wanted to remind him again that all these polls omitted one factor which he seemed himself rather to neglect—namely, that is the power of his own leadership; that I had no fear that if he would lead, the whole country would follow." The president replied "in a rather weary and tired voice that he appreciated that but he had been feeling 'so mean' as he expressed it ... I was troubled by the fact that he seems to be without spirit."[38]

That evening in Moscow a bold initiative was under way. For 48 hours the government had been crippled. Orders could not be given without Stalin's consent. In his two-day absence, while the Wehrmacht continued to advance towards Moscow and Leningrad, the Soviet machinery of power was paralyzed. Beria devised a plan for a State Defense Committee, essentially a war cabinet, to be formed with Stalin at its head. Beria, Molotov and several of Stalin's closest colleagues decided to go to Kuntsevo and drag Stalin from his quagmire and back into active leadership.

"Why've you come?" a haggard and depressed-looking Stalin asked when they arrived at the *dacha*.[39] His colleagues explained the plan for the Defense Committee and said that they desired Stalin to lead it. All the tension knotted in Stalin's face lifted immediately. His peers had reasserted their confidence in his leadership, and the Soviet warlord's vigor and confidence returned. His colleagues knew there was a downside. "We were witness to Stalin's moments of weakness and he will never forgive us for that. Don't forget it," Beria warned.[40]

Meetings resumed at the Kremlin at 4:40 p.m. on July 1, 1941. Two days later Stalin finally addressed the nation. It was a patriotic call to arms and to join hands with Britain and America, an idea that must have puzzled many of his beleaguered listeners. "Comrades! Citizens! Fighting men of our army and navy! Brothers and sisters! I turn to you my friends," he announced in his soft, indeed unimpressive, voice, "in this national war of defense of our fatherland against the fascist oppressor. The historic speech of the British prime minister, Mr. Churchill," he continued, "regarding aid to the Soviet Union, and the declaration of the United States of its readiness to render aid to our country, can only evoke a feeling of gratitude in the hearts of the people of the Soviet Union."[41] "Historic speech made by Stalin," Georgy Dimitrov noted, "explaining the situation and calling for a merciless national war to smash the enemy."[42] Stalin in his moment of danger was choosing to invoke patriotism rather than the ideological struggle.

The fighting talk in Moscow was matched by an unshakeable confidence at Führer HQ. "It is probably no overstatement to say that the Russian campaign has been won in the space of two weeks," Franz Halder noted. Hitler announced that "as soon as the battle in the east changes from an effort to annihilate the enemy armed forces to one of paralyzing the enemy economy, our next tasks in the war against Britain will come to the foreground and require preparation."[43] The tactical reason for "Barbarossa" had not been forgotten.

Four days later in Washington the president explained his own analysis of Hitler's latest move. At a meeting in the White House with the British ambassador, he was, according to Lord Halifax, "on good form." "Hitler's attack on Russia was based on a political miscalculation as to the psychological effect it would have on the world," Roosevelt said.[44] While this discussion was taking place, Operation "Indigo" was finally launched, the American occupation of Iceland, strategically important because of its position on the northern route between the United States and Great Britain. British troops had been stationed there to deter a German attack since December 1940, but now American solders had arrived to take their place. British soldiers were released to join the battle while the Americans waited and watched.

In Moscow the next day, July 8, 1941, Stalin received his first letter from Churchill as a comrade in arms. "We are all very glad that the Russian armies are making such strong and spirited resistance to the utterly unprovoked and merciless invasion of the Nazis," Churchill wrote. "We shall do everything to help you that time, geography and our growing resources allow."[45] Stalin was unimpressed by such flowery language and vague reassurances. He wanted a formal agreement with Britain which in the first instance would allay his continuing suspicion that Churchill really wanted to stand aside while Germany and Russia destroyed each other. He told Sir Stafford Cripps, who had delivered the letter to the Kremlin, that he was "not raising the question of the establishment of spheres of influence" and wanted a general agreement that would assert: "1. Mutual help without any precision as to quantity or quality, 2. Neither country to conclude a separate peace." It would be, he stated, "dangerous to delay agreement."[46]

Hitler was in conference with his generals at the Wolf's Lair. "It is the Führer's firm decision to level Moscow and Leningrad, and make them uninhabitable," Halder recorded, "so as to relieve us of the necessity of having to feed the populations through the winter. The cities will be razed by air force. Tanks must not be used for the purpose." It must, Hitler announced, "be a national catastrophe which will deprive not only Bolshevism, but also Muscovite nationalism, of their centers."[47]

Goebbels arrived for his first visit to the Führer's new headquarters. Hitler's own rooms bore the usual hallmarks. The windows in his concrete bunker all faced north so that no sunlight would penetrate into the cold darkness. Hitler informed him that two-thirds of the Red Army had been destroyed or damaged, along with five-sixths of their tanks and aircraft. Hitler had learnt that day that in the Minsk area alone, his forces had seized 287,704 prisoners of war and nearly three thousand Soviet tanks had been destroyed in battle.[48] Goebbels recorded that Hitler and his closest colleagues believed that "the war in the east was in the main already won."[49]

That evening in London Churchill set about preparing a personal response to Stalin's demands. At the uncivilized hour of 2 a.m. he summoned a distinctly cranky Anthony Eden to discuss it. "A is having some difficulty with the PM," noted Eden's private secretary Oliver Harvey, "who likes to take all the decisions and get all the credit!"[50]

On July 10, with his troops having retreated over three hundred miles, Stalin issued a strict rebuke to his commanders along the northwestern front. "Officers who do not carry out orders, abandoning their positions like traitors and leaving the defensive ridge without orders have not yet been punished," he declared, also accusing "attacking units who have done nothing so far … it is time to put a stop to this shameful state of affairs." He ordered that the head of the NKVD, along with a member of the war council and the prosecutor, "are to go at once to forward units and deal with the cowards and traitors on the spot."[51]

While the purge was set in motion, Stalin received Churchill's reply. It contained welcome news. "I should like to assure you that we are wholly in favour of the agreed declaration you propose," Churchill wrote. "We think it should be signed as soon as we have heard from the dominions, and published to the world immediately after."[52] Churchill also informed the

Admiral of the Fleet, Sir Dudley Pound, that the British navy should send a small squadron of ships to the Arctic to operate with Soviet naval forces. "The advantage we should reap if the Russians could keep in the field and go on with the war, at any rate until the winter closes in, is measureless," he explained, "a premature peace by Russia would be a terrible disappointment to great masses of people in our country. As long as they go on, it does not matter so much where the front lies. These people have shown themselves worth backing and we must make sacrifices and take risks, even at inconvenience which I realise, to maintain their morale."[53]

The next day, as the finishing touches were applied to the Anglo-Soviet pact of mutual assistance, Roosevelt was briefing his trusted envoy Harry Hopkins, who was about to travel to London. Hopkins's notes of the meeting recorded the president's aversion to any secret deals on European territory and also his caution against Churchillian entreaties to join the battle: "Economic or territorial deals—NO. No talk of war."[54] In a note to Churchill he severely warned him off any backdoor trickery: "I refer to rumors which of course are nothing more nor less than rumors regarding trades or deals which the British government is alleged to be making with some of the occupied nations. As for example the stupid story that you have promised to set up Yugoslavia again as it formerly existed and the other story that you had promised Trieste to Yugoslavia." The president suggested that "an overall statement on your part would be useful at this time, making it clear that no post war peace commitments as to territories, populations, or economics have been given."[55]

While Churchill announced to the House of Commons the initial, limited agreement with the Soviet Union, the German High Command was making some alarming discoveries on the eastern front. "The Russian troops now, as ever, are fighting with savage determination and with enormous human sacrifices," Halder noted in his diary.[56] Despite their superiority in tactics and hardware, the Germans were facing unexpected resistance.

On July 18 Stalin outlined to Churchill the military help he wanted to distract the Germans. "It seems to me," he wrote, cutting straight to the chase, "that the military position of the Soviet Union and by the same token that of Great Britain, would improve substantially if a front were established against Hitler in the west (northern France) and the north (the

Arctic)." "The best time to open this front is now," Stalin concluded.[57] Ivan Maisky hand-delivered the letter to Churchill the next day. He quickly read it, and with a sigh said: "I quite understand Mr. Stalin, and sympathise with him deeply, but unfortunately what he asks is at present impracticable."[58]

"Churchill began a detailed justification of his statement," Maisky recalled, "I began objecting ... Churchill, however, could not be shaken." Churchill then led Maisky into the drawing room, which was full of guests. "Let me introduce you," Churchill said to Maisky, "this is Mr. Hopkins." The prime minister turned to Hopkins. "Here is Stalin," he said, "asking for the creation of a second front in France." Then, shrugging his shoulders, he went on: "We can't do it at present ... we are not strong enough."[59] Just as suspicions over imperialism would cast a shadow over Churchill's relations with Roosevelt, the second front was to become a thorny and long-lasting problem between him and Stalin.

On July 21 Stalin received Churchill's reply. "Anything sensible and effective that we can do to help will be done," Churchill promised, adding, "I beg you, however, to realise the limitations imposed upon us by our resources and geographical position."[60] Stalin read the letter at the Politburo meeting. Yury Chadayev, present as always to take the minutes, noted that Stalin was agitated. "They turned down our offer," Stalin told his colleagues. "We have never had any delusions about our allies but it is extremely important to prove to Churchill the extreme danger of the delay of the opening of the second front."[61]

That day in London Harry Hopkins and John Winant visited the Foreign Office. "They told me that Roosevelt was most eager that we should not commit ourselves to any definite frontiers for any country before the peace treaty," Eden noted. "H[opkins] said that US would come into the war and did not want to find after the event that we had all kinds of engagements of which they had never been told."[62] It was a double-edged sword. Hopkins's hints that Roosevelt was moving closer to war—if they could be trusted—were pleasing: the British government was nonetheless aware that togetherness with America was bound to curtail its freedom of action. "The spectacle of an American president talking at large on European frontiers chilled me with Wilsonian memories," Eden wrote in his diary that night.[63]

In Moscow judicial murder was on the agenda. While the Luftwaffe mounted its first air raid on the Soviet capital, a trial was taking place. Reminiscent of the terrifying show trials of the 1930s, several high-ranking Soviet commanders were standing before Vasily Ulrikh, the overweight and vicious president of the Military Collegium of the Supreme Court of the USSR, accused of "causing damage to the fighting capacity of the Red Army."[64] These men, commanders along the frontier when Operation "Barbarossa" had struck, were Stalin's scapegoats. The guilt for the chaos and destruction wrought by Hitler's invasion was placed at their feet, even though they were only obeying the Soviet leader's orders. They were all shot, among them General Dimtry Pavlov, commander of the western front, and General Aleksandr Korobkov, who was killed despite managing to remain in contact with Moscow throughout the bloody debacle. A month after the invasion the situation had improved little. "The Red Army is constantly retreating, retreating, retreating," Maisky recorded with alarm.[65]

Hitler was entertaining Marshal Slavko Kvarternik, the head of the Croatian armed forces.[66] Executions in Moscow were being mirrored by thoughts of genocide at the Wolf's Lair. Hitler told Kvarternik: "Russia has become a plague-centre for mankind. ... For if only one state tolerates a Jewish family among it, this would provide the core bacillus for a new decomposition. Where the Jews are sent to, whether to Siberia or Madagascar, is immaterial."[67] While Hitler was dreaming at this stage of simply expelling every European Jew, his generals were becoming increasingly concerned about military setbacks. "Enemy by no means finally smashed," Halder noted on July 23, "mounting German casualties."[68]

Having made the destruction of Moscow a centrepiece of his policy, Hitler was now beginning to change his mind. Halder was thoroughly irritated. "These arguments mark the beginning of the decline of our initial strategy of imaginative operations, and a willingness to throw away the opportunities offered us by the impetus of our infantry and armor," he complained on July 26. "It remains to be seen whether this radical change in strategic conception, which at first certainly will come as a surprise also to the enemy, will bring the desired success," he continued. "My representations stressing the importance of Moscow are brushed aside without any valid counterevidence."[69] Hitler admitted to his army adjutant his concern about his army's progress: "I'm not sleeping at night because of it."[70] But rather than listen to his generals, he would increasingly dictate to them.

In Washington Roosevelt was playing the armchair strategist. "The way to lick Hitler is the way I have been telling the English, but they won't listen to me," he pronounced to Morgenthau before the weekly Cabinet meeting. "I know south Germany, because I have bicycled over every foot of it when I was a child and there is a town every ten miles. I have suggested to the English again and again if they sent a hundred planes over Germany for military objectives that ten of them should bomb some of these smaller towns they have never bombed before."[71]

At Cabinet the president was in a bullish mood. After the crisis of May and the hesitations in the immediate period after "Barbarossa," he was a liberated man. He swung into action, asking Congress to supply Stalin with everything he demanded, with no strings attached, and chiding his government into action. On August 4 he launched into a 45-minute tirade at his colleagues for delays in sending equipment. Henry Morgenthau observed: "The president is in much better spirits. He is much more forceful. He said, 'I am sick and tired of hearing the Russians are going to get this or they're going to get that ... the only answer I want to hear is that it is underway.' He directed most of his fire at Stimson, who looked thoroughly miserable."[72]

Stimson made his own record of Roosevelt's unexpected reprimand: "In his outburst today the president said that we must get the Russians the arms, even if it was necessary to take them from our troops and I felt very badly about it ... he was really in a hoity toity humor and wouldn't listen to argument."[73] What Stimson failed to realize was that Roosevelt did not care about taking arms from American troops. He had no wish or intention that they should fight. That was for Russian and British soldiers to do with weapons supplied by the United States.

Churchill's belief that events in Russia would move Roosevelt closer to war had been reinforced by an invitation from the president for a face-to-face meeting. On August 4 he boarded HMS *Prince of Wales* at Scapa Flow for a transatlantic voyage through U-boat infested waters. Before sailing he confided to the Queen: "I must say I do not think our friend would have asked me to go so far for what must be a meeting of world-wide importance unless he had in mind some further forward step."[74]

On the voyage over he was in high spirits. Harry Hopkins, who had just returned to Britain from his first visit to Moscow, was also on board for the final leg of his journey home to America. Alexander Cadogan, another of the party, noted: "6 August 1941. HMS *Prince of Wales*. H.H. produced a tub of admirable caviar, given him by Joe Stalin. That, with a good young grouse, made a very good dinner. As the PM said, it was very good to have such caviar, even though it meant fighting with the Russians to get it."[75]

Two days later they all watched the new movie *That Hamilton Woman*, starring Laurence Olivier and Vivien Leigh. Cadogan recorded: "Film … quite good. PM, seeing it for fifth time, moved to tears. At the close he said 'Gentlemen, I thought this film would interest you, showing great events similar to those in which you have been taking part.' Left him and H.H. playing backgammon. H.H. ended up a winner of seven guineas."[76]

As the *Prince of Wales* neared North America with her precious cargo, Hitler was wavering about the military campaign. His ideological objectives were set but Gerhard Engel noted: "One can see clearly how undecided the Führer is with regard to the continuation of operations. His thoughts and goals are always fluctuating."[77] Walter Warlimont, an officer of the Operations Staff, complained that Hitler was becoming more removed from the realities of the front. "Although when the advance started, *Wolfschanze* was unusually close to the front," Warlimont recalled, "the loneliness of the place was hardly conducive to that sense of being in close touch with great military events."[78]

Stalin was consolidating his power and creating a new streamlined structure for his staff headquarters. They became on this day the Headquarters of the Supreme High Command with Stalin as overlord. He frequently worked sixteen- to eighteen-hour days, becoming ever more harsh and intolerant. It was normal for meetings in the Kremlin to end well into the small hours.[79] "Stalin established a round-the-clock system of work for the General Staff and personally regulated the duties of its leading personnel," explained Red Army general S. M. Shtemenko.[80]

In Placentia Bay, Newfoundland, President Roosevelt was waiting that afternoon on his ship USS *Augusta* for Churchill to arrive. His son Elliott, who later wrote an account of the momentous meeting, was with him. "The PM is coming here tomorrow because—although I doubt he'll show it—he knows that without America, England can't stay in the war," Roosevelt told Elliott, who whistled in amazement at this description of Britain's plight. "Watch and see if the PM doesn't start off by demanding that we immediately declare war against the Nazis," Roosevelt continued.[81] The president knew exactly what Churchill's hopes for the meeting were. For his part he wanted to find out whether Great Britain had "reached the absolute bottom of the barrel" in terms of manpower and supplies. "Our hearts, our national interests are with the British," Roosevelt said, but then added his strict condition that "America won't help England in this war so that she will be able to continue to ride roughshod over colonial peoples."[82]

The stage was set for the two warlords of the democratic world to face each other for the first time since that ill-starred encounter 21 years before in London.

CHAPTER FIVE

August 9–December 7, 1941

On August 9, 1941, HMS *Prince of Wales* sailed into Placentia Bay, ironically one of the British bases that Churchill had been forced to lease to the United States a year before. At 9 a.m. the prime minister, dressed in his seafarer's uniform and jaunty navy blue cap, crossed a few hundred yards of water in the ship's barge and clambered on board USS *Augusta*. It was a damp, gray morning. The president, erect on his steel legs and propping himself against a ship's railing on one side and his son Elliott on the other, welcomed him and shook his hand. Watching this historic moment, Harry Hopkins said of Churchill: "You'd have thought he was being carried up into the heavens to meet God."[1]

As Roosevelt had predicted, during the first dinner that evening in the captain's mess, Churchill immediately seized his chance to make a direct appeal to the president. Elliott described the scene: "Churchill reared back in his chair; he slewed his cigar around from cheek to cheek and always at a jaunty angle. For a time his talk was colored over with an insistent note of pleading: 'It's your only chance! You've got to come in beside us! If you don't declare war, declare war, I say, without waiting for them to strike the first blow, they'll strike it after we've gone under. You must come in if you are to survive!'"[2] Roosevelt listened carefully, occasionally rubbing his eyes, readjusting his pince-nez and doodling on the tablecloth with a burnt match. "But never," remarked Elliott, "an aye, nay or maybe, came from the Americans sitting around that smoke-filled saloon."[3]

The two men were determined to get on and the combined ships' crews, with Roosevelt and Churchill seated at the front, held a moving service on deck, with stirring renditions of "Onward, Christian Soldiers" and "Oh God, Our Help in Ages Past." But on the second evening one subject threatened to disrupt the conviviality—Roosevelt's running bugbear, empire. The Americans had been driving a hard bargain over lend-lease, insisting that in return Britain would promise to remove trade barriers with the Empire.

"The kettle began to bubble up and once or twice nearly went over," Elliott recalled. "No artificial barriers," Roosevelt insisted as he laid out his postwar blueprint, "as few favored economic agreements as possible." Churchill began to talk of the trade agreements within the British Empire. "Those agreements are a case in point," Roosevelt interrupted as Churchill's neck reddened, "it's because of them that the people of India and Africa, of all of the colonial Near East and Far East are as backward as they are." Churchill crouched forward: "Mr. President, England does not propose for a moment to lose its favoured position among the British dominions, the trade that has made England great shall continue, and under conditions prescribed by England's ministers." "You see," said Roosevelt, "it is along in here somewhere that there is likely to be some disagreement between you, Winston, and me."[4]

The argument at that stage was good-natured, twinkles in the eye taking the heat out of deep conviction. "PM and president appear to hit it off very well," Alexander Cadogan noted the next day as the two leaders set about agreeing the final wording of the Atlantic Charter, a joint Anglo-American declaration of common principles.[5] It promised to respect ideas of self-government, and eschew the use of force. The charter also stated that no territorial changes would be made without the agreement of the people of the nations involved. Churchill would later claim to Parliament that this excluded the British Empire while Stalin would insist that his adherence to the principles of the charter did not prevent the Soviet Union building up a ring of buffer zones on its borders.

That day, August 11, the Russian air force launched its first bombing raid on Berlin; it was just one of the many incidents that were unsettling Hitler's generals. "The whole situation makes it increasingly plain that we have underestimated the Russian colossus, who consistently prepared for war with that utterly ruthless determination so characteristic of totalitarian states," Franz Halder noted. "At the outset of the war, we reckoned with about 200 enemy divisions. Now we have already counted 360. These divisions indeed are not armed and equipped according to our standards, and their tactical leadership is often poor. But there they are, and if we smash a dozen of them, the Russians simply put up another dozen."[6]

The murder of the Jews in the Baltic states was taking Hitler from ideas of forced removals ever closer to the process of systematic extermination. "Vengeance is being wreaked on the Jews in the big towns," Joseph Goebbels wrote, "being slain in their masses on the streets by the self-protection organizations. What the Führer prophesied is now taking place, that if Jewry succeeded in provoking another war, it would lose its existence."[7]

Churchill left Placentia Bay full of optimism and enjoyed an uninterrupted voyage back to Scotland. On the train down to London he was in splendid form, Cadogan recording the marvels of his constitution: "18 August 1941. [On train back to London] long lunch. Winston did himself well, finishing up with a Benedictine. 10 min. later he called for a brandy. The attendant reminded him he had had Benedictine. He said: 'I know: I want some brandy to clean it up.' (Next morning I found him eating cutlets and bacon for breakfast!)"[8]

Hitler's digestion, despite the rigors of his vegetarian diet, was playing havoc. While Churchill was enjoying lunch on the train, Goebbels was visiting his boss at the Wolf's Lair. "At about midday I had my first lengthy consultation with the Führer. He is exceptionally pleasant, but unfortunately looks rather tired and unwell. That's probably due to his bout of dysentery and also to the fact that the last few weeks have affected him very badly. That's not surprising. The responsibility for a whole continent now rests on his shoulders."[9]

Hitler, still only 52, more than a decade younger than Churchill, was feeling the strain. He was also angry at what he saw as the failure of German intelligence to give accurate estimates of Russian strength, a fear he had harbored when he had first issued the directive for "Barbarossa" the previous December. "Internally and emotionally the Führer is very annoyed with himself because he has been taken in so much by the reports from the Soviet Union over the potential of the Bolsheviks," Goebbels noted. "He has suffered a lot from that. It was a major crisis."[10] However, Hitler displayed a disquieting ability to analyze his enemies. "Churchill," he told Goebbels, "only traveled to the Atlantic meeting with the intention of dragging Roosevelt into the war. But Roosevelt couldn't do as he wanted to. He has to take care too much about the domestic situation in the United States ... the USA," Hitler continued, "are not ready for war."[11]

Churchill by contrast was convinced that the president was now not just ready but willing. On August 19 he arrived back in London and told the 11:30 a.m. meeting of the War Cabinet that Roosevelt had said he would deliberately look out for an incident which would allow him to bring America into the war. "The president has said that he will wage war, but not declare it, and that he will become more and more provocative."[12]

However, chilling news was coming over the wires from the United States. Roosevelt had given a press conference on board his yacht, the USS *Potomac*, anchored just off Rockland, Maine. He told journalists: "The conferences were primarily an interchange of views relating to the present and the future—a swapping of information." When pushed further he asserted that there had been an "interchange of views, that's all. Nothing else." Asked whether the United States was any closer to war his answer was blunt. "I should say, no," he said.[13]

For Churchill, Roosevelt's words were another shattering disappointment. He cabled Harry Hopkins, the man closest to Roosevelt: "I ought to tell you that there has been a wave of depression through Cabinet and other informed circles here about president's many assurances about no commitments and no closer to war &c."[14] Churchill also wrote to his son Randolph, to whom he had first mentioned his strategy of "dragging in the United States" over a year before, that he was "deeply perplexed" about how the United States was to be brought "boldly and honourably into the war."

Despite the goodwill of the Atlantic meeting, Roosevelt's priority remained clear: to send as much aid as quickly as possible to the Russians, even at the expense of the British. "I deem it to be of paramount importance for the safety and security of America," Roosevelt wrote to Henry Stimson the next day, "that all reasonable munitions be provided for Russia, not only immediately but as long as she continues to fight the Axis powers effectively. I am convinced," he continued, "that substantial and comprehensive commitments of such character must be made to Russia by Great Britain and the United States. It is obvious that early help must be given primarily from production already provided for."[15]

Feeling let down by Roosevelt, Churchill turned his attention back to Stalin. He could see that if the president was still determined to keep his distance, his own best hope of thwarting the Nazis lay with the Soviet leader. At the end of August he gave him an assurance of his unequivocal support. "I have been searching for any way to give you help in your splendid resistance pending the long-term arrangements which we are discussing with the United States of America." Churchill went on to describe the sacrifices he was making to help Russia's struggle: "You will, I am sure, realise that fighter aircraft are the foundation of our home defence, besides which we are trying to obtain air superiority in Libya and also to provide Turkey so as to bring her in on our side. Nevertheless I could send 200 more Hurricanes, making 440 fighters in all."[16]

Despite these offerings, Churchill was far from erasing Stalin's paranoia or satisfying his unlimited appetite for aid. The Soviet leader wrote to Ivan Maisky that same day repeating his suspicions of Churchill's motives and lack of military initiative: "The crux of the matter is that the English government helps the Hitlerites by its passive temporizing policies. The Hitlerites hope to defeat their opponents one at a time—today the Russians, tomorrow the English." "What do the English want?" he asked Maisky and then answered his own question. "They want, it seems to me, our weakening. If this supposition is true, we must be guarded in relations with the English."[17] As summer gave way to autumn 1941 any hopes Churchill might have had for ever warmer and closer collaboration with his allies both to the west and east appeared to be evaporating in the seasonal mists.

Life in Hitler's "inner circle" was also joyless and remorseless, far removed from those heady days of May 1940. Christa Schroeder wrote a doleful letter to a friend. "Here on the compound we continuously come across guard posts where we have to show our passes which means you feel really confined. I think after this war I must put some effort into spending a lot of time with people who are in the midst of life," she explained. "I was walking along the fence in the compound, passing the guard post again and again, and it came to me that it is always like this wherever we are, in Berlin, on the mountain or traveling, it's always the same limited circle, the same routes. And I see this as a great danger and a big dilemma from which I am longing to break free but then when you are outside, you don't know what to do with yourself because you have to concentrate wholly on this life because there are no opportunities for a life outside this circle."[18]

Hitler's generals were in querulous mood. While Halder and his colleagues had advocated a decisive strike on Moscow, the Führer had insisted on different objectives and continually interfered. General Walther von Brauchitsch, the Commander-in-Chief, had spoken with Hitler that morning in an effort to smooth things over. "Everything is just lovely again," Halder recorded with weary sarcasm after a talk with Brauchitsch. "Of course, nothing has changed, except that we are now supposed to wait upon not only the Führer, but also the *Reich* Marshal with separate reports on the railroad situation, supply, signal communications, and ground forces replacements."[19]

Four days later in London, an awkward meeting took place at Downing Street. It was September 4 and Maisky had arrived to deliver Stalin's reply to Churchill's letter on the shipment of Hurricanes. "Churchill received me in his official room, where usually meetings of government were held. He was in evening dress, with the inevitable cigar between his teeth," Maisky recalled. "Do you bring good news?" Churchill asked in bullish manner. "I am afraid not," Maisky replied, and handed over the message.[20] The prime minister read the letter, muttering as he went along. Stalin thanked Churchill for the airplanes, but wrote: "I must say, however, that these aircraft, which it appears we shall not be able to use soon and not all at once cannot seriously change the situation on the eastern front." [21]

Cadogan was also at the meeting and noted an alarming undercurrent of mutual threat and recrimination in the conversation: "Maisky talked to Churchill and Eden in grim terms of Russia's burdens and plight. This might, he said, prove a turning point. If Russia were defeated, how could Britain win? The prime minister, sensing "an underlying air of menace in his appeal," reminded Maisky that but four months earlier the British had not known whether Russia would fight against them on Germany's side. 'Whatever happens and whatever you do, you of all people have no right to make reproaches to us.'"[22] Suspicion remained in the air. Stalin continued to believe that what Churchill really wanted was Germany and Russia to destroy each other; Churchill for his part feared that Stalin would do another deal with Hitler.

Churchill's official reply was presented to Stalin on September 6. "Although we should shrink from no exertion," he explained, "there is in fact no possibility of any British action in the west except air action, which would draw the German forces from the east before winter sets in. There is no chance whatever of a second front being formed in the Balkans without the help of Turkey."[23] "What a revolting answer!" Stalin announced to his Politburo colleagues. "Before, they have at least tried to explain why they can't open the second front, now they don't even see the point in doing so."[24]

While the epistolary argument raged between Moscow and London, a very personal tragedy was playing out in America. Roosevelt had spent the day at Hyde Park at the bedside of his ailing mother. She had suffered a stroke. At noon the next day, she died. Sara Delano Roosevelt had been a constant and formidable presence in the president's life; for a year afterwards he wore a black armband as a mark of respect. As usual, his manner was that of inscrutable reserve; he returned to Washington by train directly after the funeral.

Churchill's one remaining hope of dragging in America was the sort of incident he claimed Roosevelt had privately speculated on at Placentia Bay. The sinking of the *Lusitania* had shocked Americans in the First World War and, cruel though it might be, Churchill could only hope for a similar provocation now by U-boats in the Atlantic. The USS *Robin Moor* had been sunk in May; now in the first week in September the USS *Greer* had survived a torpedo attack and the *Steel Seafarer* had been attacked by German aircraft in the Red Sea.

On September 11 President Roosevelt used a radio broadcast to issue a stinging warning to the Nazis. "No act of violence, no act of intimidation will keep us from maintaining intact two bulwarks of American defense: first, our line of supply of materiel to the enemies of Hitler; and second, the freedom of our shipping on the high seas," Roosevelt announced to his global audience. "We have sought no shooting war with Hitler. We do not seek it now," he continued, "but when you see a rattlesnake poised to strike, you don't wait until it has struck you before you crush him."[25] Churchill listened in London as the speech was broadcast in the early hours of the morning British time. He was delighted, and wrote the next morning to a friend: "Roosevelt this morning excellent. As we used to sing at Sandhurst, 'Now we shan't be long!?'"[26] Was Roosevelt mounting his charger at last?

As Churchill wrote, the first snow began to fall on the eastern front. Hitler ordered his troops to halt outside Leningrad and decreed that the Soviet Union's second city be starved into submission. Two weeks later Stalin and the Politburo were discussing evidence that Hitler was planning to try and take Moscow. "Hitler's brains must be stuffed full of nonsense if he meddles in such an adventure!" Stalin exclaimed. Two days later an Anglo-American mission, headed by Averell Harriman and Lord Beaverbrook, arrived in Moscow to discuss aid. Stalin's mood was alternately surly and charming, a one-man routine of good cop, bad cop with which his allies would become familiar. "The paucity of your offers clearly shows," he told Harriman during one hostile session, "that you want to see the Soviet Union defeated."[27]

On the evening of October 1, there was a grand dinner at the Kremlin in honor of the foreign delegates. Stalin made his entrance at 8 p.m. Valentin Berezhkov, a Soviet interpreter and official of the Commissariat for Foreign Affairs, was there. Stalin, he noted, "was shorter than average and his sallow, pock-marked face looked almost emaciated. Instead of the shining marshal's uniform with its gold epaulettes and hero's stars, he was wearing a military style tunic which seemed to hang off his wasted frame."[28] During dinner Stalin goaded Beaverbrook about Britain's unwillingness to open a second front. "What is the good of having an army if it doesn't fight?" he said. "An army which does not fight will lose its spirit."[29]

The following day Hitler launched Operation "Typhoon," the offensive against Moscow. After weeks of wrangling with his generals the course was now set. Nazi troops were just over one hundred miles from the Soviet capital. Churchill, an avid reader of the Enigma decrypts, was aware that the assault had begun. In London on October 2, there were two things on his mind. Firstly, he was concerned lest all of the useful information gleaned from Enigma was not being sent, in disguised form of course, to Stalin. He sent an urgent minute to "C," the head of the Secret Service, MI6: "Are you warning the Russians of the developing concentration? Show me the last five messages you have sent out to our missions on the subject."[30]

Churchill was also worried that Roosevelt's desire to prioritize weapons for Russia would compromise the aid being given to Great Britain. He wrote to Harry Hopkins, whom he had come to view as the best gateway to the president: "The offers which we are making to Russia are necessary and worthwhile," but sounded a note of caution that these offers were making "grievous inroads into what is required by you for expanding your forces and by us for intensifying our war effort."[31] Churchill's problem remained that Roosevelt, despite the aggressive speech of September 11, continued to show little interest in moving those American forces any closer to war.

In Berlin the *Reich* Chancellery was gearing up for a visit from Hitler. Goebbels was relieved. He was worried about the state of German morale, particularly as Hitler had not appeared in public since the campaign against Soviet Russia was launched. At 1 p.m. on October 3 Hitler arrived in the capital. Goebbels was summoned and the two men talked together in Hitler's office. "The Führer is convinced that, if the weather remains halfway favorable, in two weeks the Soviet army will be largely destroyed," Goebbels recorded.[32] Hitler said that he considered it necessary "to reach a conclusive resolution with England, since otherwise the bloody conflict will have to be repeated again in a few years."[33] The Führer said that he doubted Stalin would ever capitulate. The short war against Russia to bring the British to heel was not quite working to plan. However, the ideological war was hastening; the Nazis executed 33,771 Jews at Babi-Yar outside Kiev.

The German people knew nothing of that and, as the two men made their way to the Sportspalast, cheering crowds lined the streets; in the grand hall itself the atmosphere was electric. Hitler blamed the war on Britain's warmongering supported by international Jewry, and to a rapturous response, declared that "I can see today that the enemy is already broken and will not rise up again."[34] Hitler left Berlin on his special train at 7 p.m., the sound of his standing ovation ringing in his ears. The news at the Wolf's Lair was also good. "The 'Typhoon' front is making cheering progress,"

Halder wrote that night, "enemy resistance has been broken on the entire front."[35]

Two weeks later, as six inches of snow settled over Hitler's Prussian headquarters, Stalin made an important decision. With Moscow nearly under siege, most government departments had been evacuated to Kuibyshev. For days Stalin had been agonizing whether he too should leave the capital. Late in the evening of October 18 he returned to his *dacha* at Kuntsevo to find his staff preparing for the move. A special train was waiting to spirit him out of Moscow. It was then that he made his decision. "No evacuation," he announced. "We'll stay here until victory."[36] He returned to the Kremlin and announced to his guards: "I'm not leaving Moscow. You'll stay here with me."[37] A special bunker was prepared for the Soviet warlord, which replicated almost exactly his office in the Kremlin. Sometimes he also slept, with only his greatcoat for bedding, in the deep halls of the Moscow metro.[38]

Despite the crisis in Moscow, British intelligence chiefs were still sure that Stalin's agents abroad were up to no good. Lord Swinton, appointed by Churchill to head the Security Executive, complained: "The Communist game is still the same, but it is being played on a much better wicket."[39]

At home Stalin made a public proclamation of his stand. "Moscow will be defended to the last," he announced. In private, the Soviet warlord was just as confident. "When you go to bed—remember how to get up!" he instructed his Politburo colleagues. "Hitler will sink in this battle as a fly in the molasses."[40] He also remained scornful of his allies' attempts to help, claiming that the Beaverbrook-Harriman mission had only "symbolic meaning." "It is clear that our allies have no intention of helping us," he snarled.[41]

The next day, with Hitler's troops just 65 miles from the Soviet capital, over half a million Soviet citizens were mobilized to dig miles of trenches and anti-tank ditches to protect their city. Churchill was keen that Roosevelt should not forget who was next on the Nazi hit list. "My dear Mr. President," he wrote, suggesting that Hitler's timetable would be "1939—Poland; 1940—France; 1941—Russia; 1942—England; 1943—? At any rate, I feel that we must be prepared to meet a supreme onslaught from March onwards."[42] Later that day, more disappointing news came from the United

States. "Many of the less violent isolationists have become reconciled to the inevitability of war," Averell Harriman wrote, "and yet, with all this trend, it is not at all clear what or when something will happen to kick us into it."[43]

Having been told that the second front was not possible, Stalin demanded that Churchill send 25–30 British divisions to the Soviet Union. It was, Churchill told Stafford Cripps, "a physical absurdity. It took eight months to build up ten divisions in France only across the channel when shipping was plentiful and U-boats few," he complained. "To put two fully armed British divisions from here into the Caucasus or north of the Caucasus would take at least three months. They would then only be a drop in the bucket."[44] Cripps, however, warned that "a drop or two in a bucket or tumbler may make a difference when a stimulant is urgently needed." He explained that the Soviets "are now obsessed with the idea that we are prepared to fight to the last drop of Russian blood as the Germans suggest in their propaganda."[45] At 5 p.m. on October 27 Churchill agreed with his War Cabinet that Stalin's demands could not be met.

The same day Roosevelt provided Churchill with a welcome distraction from the arguments with Stalin with his strongest speech of the war so far. It was Navy and "Total Defense Day." Eleven days earlier a convoy of merchant ships had encountered a U-boat "wolf pack" four hundred miles off the coast of Iceland. Five US destroyers were urgently sent to the rescue. As they arrived at nightfall, the USS *Kearny* was hit with a Nazi torpedo. Eleven sailors lost their lives. The president broadcast from the Mayflower Hotel in Washington. "The shooting has started. And history has recorded who fired the first shot," he announced. "In the long run, however, all that will matter is who fired the last shot." The United States, he explained, "has been attacked."[46] Congress agreed to his demand for amendments to the Neutrality Act that would allow U.S. merchant ships to be armed for self-defense. It was another small step but it remained far short of war.

"Deeply moved by your wonderful speech," Churchill wrote the following day before setting off to Harrow School to give a speech. The boys listened intently to their most famous alumnus. "We stood all alone a year ago," he proclaimed. "We now find ourselves in a position when I can say that we have only to persevere to conquer."[47] With his spirits lifted, Churchill also wrote to Cripps oozing scorn on Stalin's demand that British troops should be sent to fight on the eastern front. "We have done our very best to help them at the cost of deranging all our plans for rearmament," he explained robustly. "We will do anything more in our power that is sensible, but it would be silly to send two or three divisions into the heart of Russia to be cut to pieces as a symbolic sacrifice. ... They certainly have no right to reproach us," he continued, "they brought their own fate upon themselves when by their pact with Ribbentrop they let Hitler loose on Poland and so started the war."[48]

While these draining exchanges continued to and fro between Moscow and London, in the early hours of October 31 Hitler's U-boats launched their most deadly attack yet on American interests. While escorting convoy HX-156 from Halifax the USS *Reuben James* was struck by a torpedo. Of the 160-strong crew 115 members were killed, including all of the officers on board, as the ship sank into the sea off the west coast of Iceland. "I am grieved at the loss of life you have suffered with *Reuben James*," Churchill wrote two days later. "I salute the land of unending challenge."[49]

That evening while Churchill waited, hoping that the president might at last ask Congress for a declaration of war, the snow falling at Hitler's headquarters was settling deep on the ground. The Führer seemed unperturbed. With his guests that night he expounded on his grand visions for the future. "If Russia goes under in this war, Europe will stretch eastwards to the limits of Germanic colonization," he said, detailing his plans to change the place names of the territory now under his control. "The Crimea," he explained, "might be called Gothenland."[50] Goebbels had just returned from a visit to the Jewish ghetto in Vilna, Lithuania. Jews, he wrote in his diary, are "the lice of civilized mankind. They had to be somehow eradicated, otherwise they would always again play their torturing and burdensome role. The only way to cope with them is to treat them with the necessary brutality. If you spare them, you'll later be their victim."[51] There was no secret within Hitler's circle about the acceleration of murder.

While fighting talk and murderous ideology were mingling in Germany, in America the strong words of Navy Day were fading into oblivion. At a press conference on November 3 Roosevelt told reporters: "We don't want a declared war with Germany because we are acting in self-defense. To break off diplomatic relations," he continued, "won't do any good. It might be more useful to keep them the way they are."[52] It was the final hammer blow to Churchill. This most deadly incident yet had brought no further action; once again there had been rhetoric, but no move to war. Churchill had to accept that his grand strategy dreamed up eighteen months before of "dragging in the United States" had failed. Indeed Roosevelt's elusive behavior over that long period begged the question of what game he had been playing all along.

The president himself kept his cards so close to his chest that he never told a single soul, relative, crony or colleague, whether at any stage he intended to fulfil Churchill's hopes and bring America into the war as a fighting ally as opposed to a financial prop. However, it is possible to piece together the mental jigsaw. Roosevelt used words and promises, some of them misleading or exaggerated, to boost Churchill's resolve to fight on. Apart from the public speeches there were the frequent private assurances from Harry Hopkins and the poem brought by Wendell Willkie.

In addition the president used American money and industrial muscle to finance and equip Britain and then Russia; and he was willing to deploy the American navy and air force to defend the Atlantic. What this added up to was one of the most brilliantly self-interested political strategies of all time. Roosevelt was defending America and opposing Hitler, his two core aims, at almost no cost to American lives. At the same time, he ignited a massive increase in arms production which finally brought the United States out of economic depression. The extent to which he deliberately intended all this, or whether it was the result of his bobbing and weaving in the face of events, will always remain unclear. As for the one thing Churchill wanted above all—an American declaration of war—of that the evidence overwhelmingly suggests Roosevelt never had the slightest intention. Churchill's great hope had turned out to be an illusion all along. Even lend-lease had made practically no difference; it only provided 1 percent of Britain's weapons in its lonely year of 1941.

While there was stalemate across the Atlantic, the decisive theater remained Russia. Unlike Roosevelt, Stalin was trying to prove himself every inch the war leader. On November 6, to the sound of enthusiastic applause he stood on a rostrum before an audience in the Mayakovsky metro station, safe from German bombardment. "If they want a war of extermination," he declared, "they shall have one."[53] At 8 a.m. the next day, despite freezing winds and heavy snow, he lined up with the Politburo on the Lenin Mausoleum in Red Square. Ignoring the threat of Nazi bombers he had ordered a military parade. It was a showy act of defiance that saw hundreds of soldiers and T-34 tanks execute a regimented march-past across the square. "It is a gesture of strength and confidence, a gesture of contempt for the enemy," Maisky noted approvingly.[54] The Luftwaffe avoided Moscow that day, but in Minsk genocide was under way. Outside the city, twelve thousand Jews were murdered in pits.

The next day, as the killing continued and the inhabitants of Leningrad suffered their 66th day under siege, Stalin continued his testy correspondence with Churchill, bluntly stating that relations between them were "unclear." "The unclarity is due to two circumstances," he charged, "first, there is no definite understanding between our two countries concerning war aims and plans for the postwar organization of peace; secondly, there is no treaty between the USSR and Great Britain on mutual military aid in Europe against Hitler." Until this was sorted out, Stalin warned, "not only will there be no clarity in Anglo-Soviet relations, but, if we are able to speak frankly, there will be no mutual trust."[55] The letter finished with an unpleasant aside. "Even though it is a trifling matter," Stalin wrote of the military hardware being convoyed to the Soviet Union, "the tanks, guns and aircraft are so badly packed, some parts of the guns come in different ships and the aircraft are so badly crated that we get them in a damaged state."[56]

That evening, as this bitter message made the journey to Churchill's desk, Hitler was in Munich giving a speech to mark the anniversary of the beer hall *putsch* of 1923. "Never before has a giant empire been smashed and struck down in a shorter time than Soviet Russia," he pronounced. Addressing enemy claims that war would last for another year at least he told the party faithful: "The war can last as it wants. The last battalion in this field will be a German one."[57] "In his speech the Führer dismisses with irony the English fighting-talk of a coming invasion; he declares that the *Reich* is well prepared for it and that the English are invited to carry out in practice the invasion of which they have so often boasted," Goebbels wrote admiringly of the speech. "The Führer also has his final say on Roosevelt. He declares that he does not want war against the United States, but that if American warships attack

German U-boats they will be shot at."[58] Hitler was ready to take on the world.

Three days later Maisky was received in Churchill's Cabinet room at the House of Commons. The ambassador had come bearing an insulting letter from Stalin. "I followed Churchill's facial expression as he was reading the letter," Maisky noted. "It grew gloomier and gloomier." After reading the letter Churchill handed it to Anthony Eden and began to pace the room. After a period of angry conversation the prime minister erupted. "Why did Stalin need to add such a tone to our correspondence? I can't tolerate this," he exclaimed. "Who benefits from it? Neither you nor us, only Hitler! I was the one who, without any doubt, volunteered to help Russia on 22 June," Churchill raged, "who needs these debates and disagreements? We are fighting and we will keep fighting for our lives whatever happens!" Maisky prepared to leave. "It looks as if we've arrived at a first crisis in relations with our 'allies'!" Maisky wrote afterwards in his diary.[59]

While Churchill simmered, Stalin signed off on November 17 Order No. 0428. It matched his stern words in the metro: "We must deprive the German army of the opportunity to stay in our villages and towns, we must evict all the aggressors into the cold and make them freeze under the open air." In the name of the Headquarters of the Supreme Command, Stalin ordered the military on the front line to "destroy and burn all the populated areas in the rear of the German troops." If any retreat had to take place, the instructions were to "take the Soviet inhabitants with you and destroy the populated areas so that the enemy cannot use them."[60] The Soviet leader was ready to scorch his nation to defeat Hitler. He also decided to mollify Churchill, agreeing that Eden should visit Moscow to try to dispel the mutual suspicions that had built up.

Hitler was in destructive mode. Goebbels recorded that he "wants to take neither Leningrad nor Moscow, but if possible destroy both cities." He asked Hitler if he still believed in victory. "If I believed in victory in 1918, when I was a lance-corporal with no resources lying half-blind in a Pomeranian field hospital," Hitler replied, "how could I not now believe in our victory, when I have the strongest army in the world at my disposal and almost the whole of Europe at my feet?"[61] The next day, November 23, despite German troops having advanced to within 30 miles of Moscow, Halder was not so optimistic. "Despite our extraordinary performance," he noted, "we shall not be able to totally destroy the enemy this year. Given the vastness of this country and the inexhaustibleness of the people, we cannot be totally certain of success."[62]

Thousands of miles away, a new theater of war was threatening. For months the United States had enforced an oil embargo against Japan in an attempt to warn it against further expansionism. Now there were reports of Japanese moves which might be aimed at America's key asset in the Far East, the Philippines, and British possessions. "I wish I knew whether Japan was playing poker or not," Roosevelt confided in Harold Ickes. "It seemed to me that the president had not yet reached the state of mind where he is willing to be aggressive as to Japan," Ickes noted afterwards.[63]

The war was encroaching on Roosevelt's habitual optimism. Two days later, November 25, he painted a gloomy picture. The president was in a meeting with Henry Morgenthau when his wife Eleanor called. "Everything is terrible. The Russian situation is awful. Moscow is falling," he told her, "I don't think the English are going to make it in Libya. It looks very bad."[64] At the afternoon Cabinet Japan was the only item on the agenda. "The president brought up the event that we were likely to be attacked perhaps next Monday for the Japanese are notorious for making an attack without warning," Henry Stimson noted, "the question was how we should maneuver them into the position of firing the first shot without allowing too much danger to ourselves."[65] No one dreamed that the attack would be on the United States itself.

November 29, 1941, was Churchill's 67th birthday. Stalin remembered to send "hearty birthday greetings."[66] The prime minister, however, was not preoccupied with celebrations, but, like Roosevelt, with Japan and decrypts of intercepted Japanese messages, labeled "Magic" by code-breakers, which showed something was being planned. Churchill suggested to Roosevelt that he warn the Japanese there would be a mighty American backlash if they dared to attack: "It seems to me that one important method remains unused in averting war between Japan and our two countries, namely a plain declaration secret or public as may be thought best," Churchill advised carefully, "that any further act of aggression by Japan will lead immediately to the gravest consequences." Hoping that the personal touch might do the trick, Churchill signed off with a muted apology: "Forgive me, dear friend, for presuming to press such a course upon you, but I am convinced that it might make all the difference and prevent a melancholy extension of the war."[67]

The weather on the Russian front continued to worsen. "We started a month late," Hitler told his adjutant Gerhard Engel.[68] By November 30 General Halder noticed that Hitler was "in a state of extreme agitation."[69] At 1 p.m. General von Brauchitsch had to endure a nasty meeting with the boss. "The interview appears to have been more than disagreeable," Halder reported afterwards, "with the Führer doing all the talking, pouring out reproaches and abuse, and shouting orders as fast as they came into his head."[70] Goebbels recorded that Hitler was now "foreseeing the war stretching into 1943."[71]

Roosevelt, who had gone to his country retreat in Warm Springs, Georgia, for a delayed Thanksgiving holiday, returned to Washington on December 1 after only two days away. It was clear that the Japanese were preparing to strike, but neither Churchill nor Roosevelt had any idea that on this very day the Japanese high command had ordered its task force in the Pacific to head for Pearl Harbor. "I think the Japanese are doing everything they can to stall until they are ready," the president told Henry Morgenthau.[72] On his return to the White House Roosevelt was shown four documents: intercepts of Japanese messages sent from Tokyo to the embassy in Berlin. One was from the prime minister, Hideki Tojo, to the ambassador, Hiroshi Oshima, which included vital information to be passed to their German allies. "Say very secretly to them," Tojo instructed, "there is extreme danger that war may suddenly break out between the Anglo-Saxon nation and Japan through some clash of arms. This may come sooner than anyone dreams."[73]

Roosevelt asked for a copy to be put in his personal files. At noon the president had a meeting with his Secretary of State, Cordell Hull. "We both agreed," Hull recalled, "that from all the indications, a Japanese attack was in the imminent offing." They decided that, in an attempt to discover what was being planned, a last-minute plea for peace should go from Roosevelt to Emperor Hirohito. They also discussed Churchill's cable of November 30. "We felt it best," Hull noted, "to hold up any such warning until we saw what the reaction would be to the president's message to the Emperor, if he sent it."[74]

The next day, while Roosevelt wavered, Hitler flew to General Paul von Kleist's headquarters at Mariupol on the Sea of Azov. He wanted to find out for himself what had occurred during the retreat from Rostov which had taken place against his orders several days before. General Gerd von Rundstedt, once his favorite commander, had resigned over the issue, and though Hitler absolved Kleist's forces of blame, he did not reinstate von Rundstedt. The Führer was not one for public admissions of error. However, there was good news when he returned to his own headquarters. A Nazi reconnaissance battalion had advanced to within twelve miles of Moscow.

In the first week in December the SS's first mobile gas van began gassing hundreds of Jews at Chelmno, a village just over one hundred miles west of Warsaw in Nazi-occupied Poland. On December 5, as the temperatures dropped to minus 32 degrees Fahrenheit, the Soviets counterattacked outside Moscow. Four of Stalin's armies launched themselves on Hitler's exhausted and frozen armies. The German death toll on the eastern front had now reached over 85,000. From 3 p.m., in heavy snow, the Red Army began to force Hitler's troops into retreat.

On December 6, as the Soviet leader granted General Zhukov a further three armies for the thrust against Hitler, Roosevelt was preparing finally to send his message to the Japanese emperor. At 9:30 p.m. Commander Schulz interrupted a meeting between the president and Harry Hopkins in the White House study. He handed Roosevelt a Magic decrypt. The fifteen-page document was thirteen parts of a fourteen-part message from Tokyo to ambassador Kichisaburo Nomura in Washington. The president read in silence and then handed it to Hopkins. "This means war," he said. Hopkins said it was "too bad that we could not strike the first blow." Roosevelt nodded and replied: "We can't do that. We are a democracy and a peaceful people."[75] Roosevelt tried to put a call in to his naval chief, Admiral Harold Stark. He was told by the White House phone operator that Stark was at the theater. The president decided not to pull him out, fearing public alarm.[76]

At 10 a.m. the following day the last part of the decrypted message was delivered to Roosevelt. It stated: "The earnest hope of the Japanese government to adjust Japanese–American relations and to preserve and promote the peace of the Pacific through cooperation with the American government has been lost."[77] Over lunch, eaten at Roosevelt's desk in the Oval Office, Hopkins recalled that "we were talking about things far removed from the war." At 1:40 p.m. the telephone rang. It was Frank Knox, the navy secretary. Knox reported that the Commander-in-Chief of American forces in Honolulu had issued a radio warning that an air raid attack had started and "it was no drill."[78] While the president demanded confirmation of this report, over two thousand American soldiers and sailors were losing their lives in a sea of oil, blood and bullets. Pearl Harbor was ablaze and the four warlords were about to be locked in a global conflict.

CHAPTER SIX

December 7, 1941–January 16, 1942

The Oval Office, 2:28 p.m., December 7, 1941. President Roosevelt had just put down the telephone to Admiral Harold Stark. He looked up at Harry Hopkins and confirmed the devastating news: Pearl Harbor had been attacked. The details reaching Washington were still patchy, but it would later turn out that 366 Japanese fighters and bombers had sunk four battleships, including the *Arizona* in which 1,177 died. Eleven warships were also damaged or destroyed, along with a further four battleships. The final death toll would reach 2,330.

As Henry Stimson, Frank Knox, Admiral Stark and the US army chief, General George Marshall, joined Roosevelt and Hopkins for a conference at 3 p.m., news of the attack was convulsing Washington. "I think all of us believed that sooner or later we were bound to be in the war and that Japan had given us an opportunity," Hopkins revealed in his personal notes of this momentous day. "Everybody, however," he continued, "agreed that it would be a long, hard struggle. During the conference the news kept coming in, indicating more and more damage to the fleet. The president handled the calls personally."[1]

At Chequers Churchill was listening to the wireless. It was 9 p.m. and with him were Averell Harriman and John Winant. After a pedestrian broadcast summarizing events on the Russian and Libyan fronts, a few words were said of a Japanese attack on American shipping in Hawaii. "We looked at one another incredulously," Winant recalled. Churchill immediately leapt from his chair. "We shall declare war on Japan," he announced and strode out of the room. "You can't declare war on a radio announcement," Winant said as he hurried after the prime minister. It was decided, instead, that a call should be made to the White House.[2]

The telephone rang in the Oval Office and Roosevelt answered. After a brief word with Winant, Churchill came on the line. "Mr. President, what's this about Japan?" he asked. "It's quite true. They have attacked us at Pearl Harbor," the president replied, "we are all in the same boat now."[3] Roosevelt explained that he was planning to ask Congress the next day to sanction a declaration of war against Japan, and advised Churchill to wait until everything was settled before making his own announcement. Churchill agreed, stating that his declaration would "follow the president's within an hour."[4] Churchill was informed that Japan had struck not just at Pearl Harbor and the Dutch East Indies, but at Malaya as well. Despite the savage escalation in the war, Churchill retired that night to enjoy, as he later wrote, the sleep of the saved.

As midnight approached on the Continent, news of the attack reached Hitler at the Wolf's Lair in the forest near Rastenburg. He also saw reason to celebrate, a welcome antidote to the success of the recent Soviet counterattack which had filled Führer HQ with gloom. "Now it is impossible for us to lose the war," he told Walther Hewel, a foreign office liaison officer. "We now have an ally who has never been vanquished in three thousand years."[5] He telephoned Joseph Goebbels. "The Führer," Goebbels noted excitedly, "is extremely pleased at this development. ... Now this war is a world war in the truest sense of the word."[6]

In Washington Roosevelt summoned his secretary Grace Tully. "He was alone, seated before his desk on which were two or three neat piles of notes containing the information of the past two hours. The telephone was close by his hand," she recalled. "He was wearing a grey sack jacket and was lighting a cigarette as I entered the room. He took a deep drag and addressed me calmly: 'Sit down, Grace. I'm going before Congress tomorrow. I'd like to dictate my message. It will be short.'"[7] After another drag on his cigarette Roosevelt began to dictate one of the most famous speeches of his career. "He spoke incisively and slowly," Tully remembered, "carefully specifying each punctuation mark and paragraph."[8] This was interrupted at 8:30 p.m. by a Cabinet meeting. Just one hour later, hot on the heels of his Cabinet

Hitler, triumphant in the summer of 1940

Hitler with Mussolini in Munich, June 18, 1940

The first handshake. Placentia Bay, August 9, 1941

Churchill, Stalin and Harriman in Moscow, August 1942

Joseph Davies hands Roosevelt's secret letter to Stalin, May 1943

All smiles at Tehran in November 1943

Churchill's birthday in Tehran

Dinner at Yalta in February 1945

The sick man of Yalta

Stalin and Churchill at Yalta

Aging leaders at Yalta

Churchill with Eisenhower in Germany, March 25, 1945

colleagues Roosevelt received a party of Congressional leaders. "The casualties, I am sorry to say, were extremely heavy," the president explained. "The fact is that a shooting war is going on today in the Pacific and we are in it."[9]

At 12:30 p.m. the next day President Roosevelt addressed a joint session of Congress with the simplest, and strongest, speech of his presidency. "Yesterday, December 7, 1941—a date that will live in infamy—the United States of America was suddenly and deliberately attacked by naval and air forces of the Empire of Japan," he announced and went on to describe in brief but grim tones the targets of the Japanese attack. "I ask that the Congress declare," he continued, "that since the unprovoked and dastardly attack by Japan on Sunday, December 7, 1941, a state of war has existed between the United States and the Japanese Empire."[10] The British ambassador, Lord Halifax, was in the gallery. "When he said that America would fight as long as was necessary to prevent such an act of treachery as the Japanese being repeated," Halifax noted, "the whole place rose and cheered him for about three minutes. A very remarkable demonstration."[11]

An hour later both the House of Representatives and the Senate had agreed, with just one dissenting voice. The United States was at war. Yet not in the European war, for Roosevelt had made no mention of Germany. When the Assistant Secretary of State, Adolf Berle, was visited by the Hungarian representative in Washington, Berle noted that his visitor "assumed that we would shortly be at war with Germany and Italy." Berle was evasive. "I said that I could not say anything at this time," he explained.[12] Roosevelt, too, was elusive on the subject. A press release was issued stating that "Germany did all it could to push Japan into the war" because "it was the German hope that if the United States and Japan could be pushed into war that such a conflict would put an end to the lend-lease program."[13] No further announcement was made.

In London Churchill was trying to convince the War Cabinet that he should immediately go to America to be with Roosevelt. During the discussion it was suggested that the same careful attitude thus far employed towards the United States should continue. "Oh! That is the way we talked to her while we were wooing her," Churchill replied, "now that she is in the harem, we talk to her quite differently!"[14] His colleagues agreed to his plans but Churchill also had to convince Anthony Eden, who was in Scotland en route to Moscow. The Foreign Secretary was summoned by a naval officer to the telephone and Churchill passed on all the known details of the Japanese attack.

"He was quite naturally in a high state of excitement," Eden recalled. "I could not conceal my relief and did not have to try to. I felt that whatever happened now, it was merely a question of time. Before, we had believed in the end but never seen the means, now both were clear."[15] Churchill told Eden of his intentions to travel at once to the United States. "I saw the force of this, but I did not imagine we could both be away and was not sure that the Americans would want him so soon." Brushing aside Eden's concerns, Churchill told him: "The emphasis of the war has shifted: what now matters is the intentions of our two great allies. We must each go to one of them."[16]

That day, as the first T-34 tanks rolled off the production line at the Kharkov Tank Works, which had been moved to the Urals, Hitler told his adjutant, Major Gerhard Engel, that he did not believe the Russians had any more troops to push into the fight along the eastern front. "Thinks it's all bluff," Engel noted, "considers these are the last reserves from Moscow."[17] "Information provided by the army high command about the enemy is exaggerated and has been deliberately painted worse than it is," Hitler explained. "It would not be the first time that the Germans have lost their nerve at critical moments. I do not wish to hear again the word 'withdrawal.'"[18] Despite this display of confidence, Engel was concerned. "I noticed how unsettled and unsure he was," he confessed.[19] General Franz Halder remarked that even now Hitler remained wistful for deals with the British: "The Führer still hopes to come to terms with Britain at the expense of France."[20]

The next morning, December 9, Hitler left the sanctuary of his forested lair and took his special train to Berlin. At noon he met Joseph Goebbels. "The Führer is delighted at the fortunate outcome of the talks between the USA and Japan, and at the outbreak of war," the Nazi propaganda chief noted. "He knew nothing in advance about the outbreak of hostilities; it took him completely by surprise and at first he, like me, could not believe it."[21] After such a run of bad news, Goebbels was relieved to meet Hitler face to face and find him in such confident form. "Japan was right to make the first crushing blow," Hitler told him, "a boxer who saves up his blows for the fifth or sixth round can experience the same as Schmeling in his last fight with Joe Louis, namely that he is knocked out in the first round."[22]

Despite the attack on Pearl Harbor and Japan's alliance with Germany and, indeed, despite the catalog of attacks by Nazi U-boats on American ships, Roosevelt was still hesitating about any formal involvement of the United States in the war against Germany. Halifax advised Churchill that the president "still feels he has to educate up to the complete conviction of the oneness of the struggle against both Germany and Japan. I wouldn't overstate it, but," Halifax continued, "I seem to be conscious of a still lingering distinction in some quarters of the public mind between war with Japan and war with Germany."[23]

Having let Roosevelt off the hook with "Barbarossa," Hitler was about to relieve him again of a dilemma. He informed Goebbels of what would become his second cataclysmic decision following the invasion of Russia: He intended to declare war on the United States in a speech before the Reichstag scheduled for two days' time. He said that he had given orders that "any American vessel which comes within range of a torpedo tube will be sent to the bottom of the sea."[24]

In the Far East, two prized British ships were about to suffer that terrible fate at the hand of Japanese fighters. On the morning of December 10 Churchill was working in bed when the telephone rang. It was Admiral Sir Dudley Pound. "Prime Minister, I have to report to you that the *Prince of Wales* and the *Repulse* have both been sunk by the Japanese." "Are you sure it's true?" Churchill replied. "There is no doubt at all," Pound answered.[25] "In all the war I never received a more direct shock," Churchill later confessed.[26] He had dispatched the two ships to protect Singapore from Japanese attack; but the only available air cover was shore-based fighters based on the Malayan mainland. In the new technology of battle at sea, it was a fatal error. Churchill was distraught. Just five months before, he had been singing hymns at Placentia Bay with the crew of the *Prince of Wales*, almost all of whom were now dead.

Three full days after Pearl Harbor there was still no word from Washington on joining the war against Germany; Churchill was still fighting alone against Hitler in Europe and North Africa. Roosevelt was also not sure that the time was ripe for another face-to-face meeting and drafted a telegram to London suggesting that it might be wise to wait a few weeks. At 6:30 p.m. he changed his mind and cabled Churchill: "Delighted to have you here at the White House," adding at the end that his "one reservation is great personal risk to you—believe this should be given most careful consideration for the Empire need you at the helm and we need you there too."[27]

Then, at 2:18 p.m. on Thursday, December 11, 1941, the Nazi foreign minister, Joachim von Ribbentrop, summoned Morris, the American Chargé d'Affaires, to his office on Berlin's Wilhelmstrasse. Morris was handed a document. "Although Germany on her part has strictly adhered to the rule of international law in her relations with the United States of America during every period of the present war," it stated, "the government of the United States of America from initial violations of neutrality had finally proceed to open acts of war against Germany." The document concluded that Germany was breaking off diplomatic relations with the United States and declared that "in these circumstances brought about by President Roosevelt Germany too, as from today, considers herself as being in a state of war with the United States of America."[28]

Later that afternoon, before a swiftly assembled audience of the Reichstag, Hitler made his personal declaration of war. During his 90-minute-long speech he mounted an unrelenting attack on Roosevelt, claiming that the president was supported by the "entire satanic insidiousness" of the Jews and that he was determined to destroy Germany.[29] "I can only be grateful to providence that it entrusted me with the leadership in this historic struggle which, for the next 500 or 1,000 years, will be described as decisive, not only for the history of Germany but for the whole of Europe and indeed for the whole world," he announced. Now standing on the cusp of a truly world war Hitler declared that "a historic revision on a unique scale has been imposed upon us by the Creator."[30]

Despite the military setbacks in Russia, Hitler had achieved full spiritual contentment. Under his pact with Japan, he had no obligation to declare war on America, but he wanted to show that he was the master, controlling events. To the east he was fighting the racist and ideological war he had always wanted. As for Britain and America, they had never been part of the plan. But, as his attacks on both Churchill and Roosevelt had shown, it was now personal. The British people had been misled by Churchill; Roosevelt was controlled by international Jewish plutocracy. If they wished to drag their nations to destruction, so be it.

However, Hitler had made one further, vital miscalculation. According to his Luftwaffe adjutant, Nicolaus von Below, he was relying "on the hope that the conflict between the USA and Japan would keep the Americans out of the European theater."[31] This would savagely rebound on him. For eighteen months Roosevelt had stopped short of the brink; indeed there is no knowing what might have happened if Hitler had not himself declared war on America. But whatever his prevarications, the president had never doubted that Nazi Germany was enemy number one in the global struggle. He was a reluctant warlord, but now that he was committed, Hitler was his priority.

All that was now left were the formalities. At 12:30 p.m., a message for Congress from Roosevelt was delivered. He did not attend to read the note himself, which announced that "the government of Germany, pursuing its course of world conquest, declared war against the United States. The long known and the long expected has thus taken place." He asked Congress "to recognize a state of war between the United States and Germany, and between the United States and Italy."[32] "It was a pretty quiet affair compared to two days ago," Halifax noted after making the trip to Congress to observe the constitutional rites, "the result was a foregone conclusion. I remember Winston saying to me in London that he had told the president when they had met in August that he would sooner have an American declaration of war and no supplies for six months than double supplies and no declaration. It has come in a way differently to what most of us then expected."[33]

The long-drawn-out psychological duel which Churchill had been waging with Roosevelt since May 1940 had been resolved by a bolt from the blue. Whatever the circumstances, he could not hide his immense sense of relief. In a telegraph to Eden, still en route to Moscow, he wrote that "the accession of the United States makes amends for all, and with time and patience will give certain victory."[34]

A palpable release of pressure was also being felt in Berlin. Goebbels noted in his diary on December 13 that for the past few weeks Hitler had been under increasing strain. The Führer "knew that either the U-boat war was doomed to be ineffective, or that he had to make a decisive step towards war with America. Now this heavy weight has fallen from his heart."[35] Hitler rightly calculated that much would turn on the Battle of the Atlantic: "He believes that the figures for sinkings will rise rapidly. Above all he sees the tonnage problem as the decisive problem of the war at the moment. Whoever can solve this problem will probably win the war."[36]

Hitler was also accelerating the ideological struggle and the accompanying genocide. "With regard to the Jewish question the Führer is determined to make a clean sweep," Goebbels noted. "He told the Jews that if they caused another world war they would be destroyed. That was no empty promise. The world is at war, the destruction of the Jews is the necessary consequence. We must look at this question unsentimentally. We're not here to pity the Jews, we're here to pity our own German people. If the German people have sacrificed 160,000 dead in the eastern campaign, those who caused this bloody conflict must pay for it with their lives. The situation is difficult," Goebbels concluded, "but we will master it."[37] As Goebbels wrote, events on the front line were fluid. The Red Army had recaptured some four hundred villages and towns and driven German forces from the Moscow–Volga canal. On December 15 Nazi forces were repulsed from Klin on the Leningrad front.

That day Churchill was on board the *Duke of York*, bound for the United States. "I am on my way to a rendezvous with President Roosevelt to discuss our common plans. From Washington I shall cable you full information on the state of affairs," he cabled Stalin. "I cannot tell you how relieved I am to learn daily about your remarkable victories on the Russian front. I have never felt so confident of the outcome of the war."[38] That night, amid temperatures of minus 57 degrees Fahrenheit, Eden and his delegation arrived in the Soviet capital.

At seven the next evening, while Erwin Rommel's forces were being forced into a temporary retreat by General Sir Claude Auchinleck in North Africa, Eden arrived at the Kremlin. For four hours he spoke with Stalin, with Maisky and Cripps translating and taking notes. "All was friendly,"

Eden explained. "Stalin is a quiet dictator in his manner. No shouting, no gesticulation, so that it is impossible to guess his meaning, or even the subject of which he is speaking until the translation is given."[39] Stalin's enigmatic manner was not matched by his forthright demands. He handed Eden drafts of two separate treaties which showed that, even while Hitler's soldiers were knocking on Moscow's door, future Soviet territory was uppermost in his mind.

"It would be desirable to attach a secret protocol in which a general scheme for reorganizing European frontiers after the war should be outlined," he told Eden. Apart from weakening and breaking up Germany, Stalin announced that "the Soviet Union finds it imperative to restore its frontiers as they were in 1941, prior to the German attack on the USSR."[40] Stalin was insisting that the British agree to the legal incorporation into the postwar Soviet Union of everything he had grabbed as part of his devil's bargain with Hitler in August 1939: the three Baltic states, Lithuania, Estonia, and Latvia; the eastern chunk of Poland; a swathe of Finland; and the Romanian province of Bessarabia.

Hitler had returned to the Wolf's Lair. Reports from the full length of the Soviet front were painting a picture of chaos and defeats. He reluctantly agreed to a retreat on the Volkhov River. Meanwhile, Army Group South reported that "the enemy is bringing reinforcements," Army Group Center that "the enemy is feeding new forces" along the line and Army Group North that "attacks out of Leningrad have been stepped up."[41] At midnight, Hitler issued a brutal order for his military commanders battling with Stalin's armies in the east. "General withdrawal is out of the question," he instructed, "the idea of preparing rear positions is just drivelling nonsense. The only trouble at the front is that the enemy outnumbers us in soldiers. He does not have any more artillery. His soldiers," the order continued, "are not nearly as good as ours."[42]

Yet the losses continued. On December 19 Field Marshal von Brauchitsch, ill and broken by reversals on the eastern front, coupled with Hitler's refusal to see the chaos, offered his resignation. It marked a watershed in Hitler's war. Having been offered this useful scapegoat for the failures so far, he personally assumed supreme command of Germany's armed forces. "It was a successful move since it prevented the catastrophe into which a withdrawal would have degenerated," Hitler's loyal Luftwaffe adjutant, von Below, noted.[43] "Hitler would not countenance withdrawals to gain freedom of maneuver or to spare his forces," Below continued, though he did notice that his Führer's "burgeoning mistrust of the generals—a sentiment of which he was never to rid himself entirely—cramped him, since he insisted on reserving for himself even the most minor tactical decisions."[44]

The next day, Winston Churchill was busy aboard the *Duke of York*. Early that morning he had received a telegram from Auchinleck. "The relentless attack of the RAF on the enemy's retreating forces, coupled with continued pressure of our forward columns, has kept him on the run all day," the commander in Africa reported.[45] Churchill had also received a cable from Eden passing on Stalin's territorial demands. "Naturally you will not be rough with Stalin," Churchill wrote to his Foreign Secretary, but "we are bound to the United States not to enter into secret and special pacts. To approach President Roosevelt with these proposals would be to court a blank refusal, and might cause lasting trouble on both sides."[46] Churchill told Eden such questions must await "the peace conference when we have won the war" and advised him not to worry if a failure to satisfy Stalin delayed a formal agreement with Russia.[47]

Back in Moscow Eden and his colleagues believed there could be no smoothing of the edges. "Pretty clear Russians won't sign treaties if we don't recognise their 1941 frontier," Alexander Cadogan observed after the final day of talks.[48] That evening, at a grand Kremlin banquet in honor of Stalin's 62nd birthday, 36 toasts were drunk. Churchill had sent a telegram wishing him "sincere fond wishes" for his birthday; whatever the past and future turbulence in their relations, the warlords were always scrupulous in their observance of anniversarial niceties. "We drank your health and some others," Eden reported back to the prime minister. "Stalin spoke very warmly of you."[49]

Churchill's ten-day voyage came to an end the following day. From Hampton Roads he flew to Washington for his second face-to-face meeting with the president. Code-named "Arcadia," the conference got off to an amicable start. "After dinner we talked in the president's study about Vichy and North Africa, and various other matters on the Atlantic side of the world," Lord Halifax wrote in his diary that night, "complete unanimity of view and the atmosphere very good, Winston and the president getting on very well indeed together."[50]

The next day Churchill's lingering fears that, after Pearl Harbor, the Americans might feel compelled to concentrate on the Pacific were allayed when Admiral Stark and General George Marshall reiterated the outcome of the ABC-1 talks earlier in the year that the European theater of war was decisive. Churchill's mood was buoyant. Halifax described how "he pleased the press very much by getting on to a chair in order that they might see him better."[51] Churchillian bravura could not disguise the fortunes of war; on Christmas Day Hong Kong surrendered to the Japanese and in the besieged city of Leningrad some 3,700 people died. Nevertheless Churchill continued to entertain: "Found him in his coloured dressing gown in bed, preparing for his speech for the Senate tomorrow," Halifax observed, "surrounded by cigars, whiskies and sodas and secretaries!"[52]

At 12:30 p.m. on December 26 Churchill delivered his speech to a joint session of Congress. The galleries in the Senate Chamber were packed. "Winston spoke for about 35 minutes," Halifax noted, "and was much cheered."[53] "In the days to come," Churchill declared, it was his great hope that "the British and American peoples will for their own safety and for the good of all walk together side by side in majesty, in justice and in peace."[54] "Churchill made a great and moving speech," noted Harold Ickes, who a year and a half before had believed that Churchill was very unreliable when under the influence of drink. Now Ickes wrote: "I think that in such a situation as that in which we find ourselves he is the greatest orator in the world. He was greeted with great enthusiasm, hand-clapping and cheers, and he was interrupted throughout his speech by similar outbursts."[55]

The New Year opened with a declaration of the United Nations unveiled by Roosevelt and Churchill in Washington; it was signed by a rainbow of nations around the world opposed to Hitler and propounded the principles of the Atlantic Charter. Events on the battlefields augured less well. The Japanese onslaught was carving through Malaya and threatening Singapore. In the Ukraine the Germans pushed Red Army parachutists into retreat on the Kerch peninsula.

Outside Moscow Hitler stuck to his policy of no withdrawal. There was, wrote Halder, "another dramatic scene" during a conference with the Führer, who "calls in question the generals' courage to make hard decisions. The plain truth however is that with the temperature down to 30 below freezing our troops simply cannot hold out any longer."[56] "First close the breach by attacking from the adjoining sectors," ordered the new Supreme Commander, "then we can talk about moving the front back. But in every individual instance I will have to give the word for withdrawal." His generals were, in Halder's words, "at the end" of their wits.[57]

In the White House, after nearly two weeks, Churchill was very much at home. "I found the president talking to him in his bedroom," Halifax recorded with bemusement. "Max Beaverbrook and I sat on a box in the passage for a few minutes and exchanged views, Harry Hopkins floating past in pyjamas and dressing gown. Certainly the oddest ménage anybody has ever seen."[58]

The oddities multiplied. "When I was fixing up with him last night what would be a good time to come and see him in the morning, I said what about twelve o'clock," Halifax noted. "He thought this a bit late as that was about the time the president was apt to blow into his bedroom. He had two or three days before, and found Winston with nothing on at all, and he had quickly to drape himself with a towel." Churchill remarked: "He is the only head of a state I have ever received in the nude!"[59] "What a wonderful showman he is,"[60] concluded Halifax.

Forty-eight hours later in the Wolf's Lair Hitler, who was so afraid of exposing his flesh to ridicule that he had years before even stopped wearing *Lederhosen*, was in the midst of a late-night monologue. "I'm very glad I recently said all I think about Roosevelt. There's no doubt about it, he's a sick brain," the Führer declared. "There's nobody stupider than the Americans," he continued. "Churchill and Roosevelt—what impostors! One can expect utterly extravagant repercussions."[61] The diatribe against his enemies continued during his midday meeting the next day. "If things go on following this rhythm," Hitler told his guests, "in four weeks the Japanese will be in Singapore. It would be a terribly hard blow."[62] He rounded off with an attack on the US Army: "I'll never believe that an American soldier can fight like a hero."[63]

While Churchill might have preferred to devote every minute to his friend in Washington, his other ally in Moscow was demanding his attention. Eden had sent a further cable, insisting that Stalin's demands on his postwar frontiers must be addressed. "I am clear that this question is for Stalin acid test of our sincerity and unless we can meet him on it, his suspicion of ourselves and the United States government will persist," Eden warned. The nub of it was brute force. "Nothing we and the United States of America can do or say," argued the Foreign Secretary, "will affect the situation at end of war. If Russians are victorious they will be able to establish these frontiers and we shall certainly not turn them out."[64]

With Eden's promptings, and many other matters in mind, Churchill traveled south for a five-day rest in Miami, Florida. He had suffered a heart scare and needed to recuperate.[65] Some in Washington were relieved to see him go for reasons that went beyond his health; he was proving thoroughly exhausting. "I am troubled and distressed that he has taken with him for the journey General Marshall simply to have a talk with him in the plane," Henry Stimson confided in his diary. "Marshall is very busy, very overworked, and should not have been taken from his work. He will have to come back on a night train and will lose 24 hours of his precious time without getting any rest from it. It was only due to the president's urgings that he did not decline Churchill's invitation, and I think it was one of the thoughtless things which the president ought not to do."[66] Stimson remained convinced throughout most of the war that Churchill never stopped pulling the wool over the president's eyes. He underrated his boss.

In Moscow that evening Stalin was in conference with members of his Supreme Headquarters. General Boris Shaposhnikov, Chief of the General Staff, opened discussions with a short briefing detailing plans, supported by Stalin, for a new counteroffensive. "The Germans are now in a state of confusion after their defeat at Moscow," Stalin explained after Shaposhnikov finished. "They are badly prepared for winter. This is the most suitable time for launching a general offensive."[67]

General Georgy Zhukov was horrified and tried to explain that this would be an impossible task, but Stalin would not let him finish. "I have talked with Timoshenko," the Soviet dictator explained. "He is for the offensive. We must grind up the Germans more quickly so that they will not be able to attack in the spring." Stalin's Politburo cronies, Georgy Malenkov and Lavrenty Beria, offered their support. The rest of the group remained silent. "On that," Stalin declared, "if you will, we shall conclude the meeting."[68] "You argued in vain," Shaposhnikov told Zhukov once they were safely outside the leader's office, "directives have already been given to almost all army groups, and they will begin the offensive in the next few days." "Then why was our opinion solicited?" bemoaned Zhukov. "I don't know dear fellow, I don't know," replied another of Zhukov's downcast military colleagues.[69]

While in Florida, though much bathing and resting took place, a daily courier kept Churchill busy with cables and matters of war. He responded that day to Eden's request that Stalin's demands for his 1941 borders be recognized. "I could not be an advocate for a British Cabinet bent on such a course," he averred.[70] That evening, January 8, as the cable began the journey from Miami to London, Churchill telephoned his ambassador in Washington. "During our conversation I told him that I had been interested to see his very sharp reply to Anthony about Stalin's desire to have the 1941 boundaries of Russia recognised," Halifax noted in his diary. "Winston said he had been greatly surprised with Anthony, and was greatly surprised that I was not prepared over the telephone to say that I wholeheartedly agreed with Winston."[71] For the moment, while Churchill enjoyed the hospitality of the anti-imperialist president, spheres of influence in Europe were out.

Churchill returned to Washington to resume the discussions on war strategy. As British forces were beaten out of Kuala Lumpur, Roosevelt expressed his desire that American troops should be fighting Hitler on the battlefield. "We cannot wage this war in a defensive spirit," he said, "we intend to bring this battle to him on his home grounds."[72] Stimson thought that Churchill, in luring Roosevelt exclusively towards the European theater, was "taking advantage of the president's well-known shortcomings in ordinary administrative methods."[73] Churchill's colleagues on the other hand were very pleased with the progress of the Arcadia conference. "I don't think it is possible to measure the results of your time here," Halifax wrote to him as the end of the conference was in sight. "The immense usefulness of your personal contacts with FDR will remain and grow, as the field of joint action widens. I don't think you have ever done a better fortnight's work in value!"[74]

On January 14, as the situation in Singapore grew bleaker, Churchill prepared to leave Washington. Hopkins was present at the final meeting between the two heads of state: "Churchill expressed not only his warm appreciation of the way he and his associates had been treated but his confidence that great steps had been taken towards unification of the prosecution of the war." Afterward, as Churchill flew by plane from Washington to Bermuda, Hopkins and Roosevelt returned together to the White House. "The president made it perfectly clear," Hopkins noted, "that he too was very pleased with the meetings. There was no question but that he grew genuinely to like Churchill and I am sure Churchill equally liked the president."[75]

A few days later it was Roosevelt's birthday. "Many happy returns of the day," Churchill cabled, "and may your next birthday see us a long lap forward on our road ahead."[76] Roosevelt replied: "It is fun to be in the same decade with you."[77]

However, beneath the smiles, those close to Roosevelt, like his labor secretary, Frances Perkins, an important member of his inner circle, had already noticed a new steel in his soul. She recalled that "he was a changed, more potent, and dedicated personality. The terrible shock of Pearl Harbor, the destruction of his precious ships, the unknown hazards which war might bring to the people, the death of his hope of being the peacemaker and mediator of the world acted like a spiritual purge and left him cleaner, simpler, more single-minded."[78]

This change in Roosevelt would have a vital impact on his relationship with Churchill. There was no doubt of a burgeoning personal affection; but in the coming months and years it would and could not mask the political gulf that divided them. In the end Churchill lost his mental duel with Roosevelt; he failed to persuade him to bring America into the war. Japan and Hitler did that. What this meant was that Roosevelt was not fighting Churchill's war but his own, and the two men had very different long-term objectives.

Beyond the defeat of Hitler, Churchill wanted above all to preserve the British Empire; but this and all other manifestations of European imperialism were anathema to Roosevelt, who was determined to banish them from the brave new postwar world. There was a second gulf between them. Britain had initially gone to war for the freedom of Europe, specifically the independence of Poland. But as the war ground on, Churchill began to see a new threat to Europe—the man who had become the third ally in the fight against Hitler, Joseph Stalin. In late 1942 he told Anthony Eden: "It would be a measureless disaster if Russian barbarism overlaid the ancient states of Europe."[79]

Roosevelt thought otherwise. As far as he was concerned, the cause of war in the first place was the in-fighting between Europe's ancient, imperialist nations and he began to see in Stalin someone who would help him in his great cause of freeing the world of that imperialism. Also in 1942, in a conversation with the Roman Catholic Archbishop of New York, he remarked: "The European people will simply have to endure Russian domination in the hope that—in ten or 20 years—the European influence will bring the Russians to become less barbarous."[80]

These differences contained the seeds of psychological and strategic differences which would eventually bring unwelcome and unpleasant tensions, not to mention deceit and lies, to the relationship between the three ideologically very different allies who now found themselves bound together in the fight against Hitler.

As for the Führer, he now stood alone against the world. Benito Mussolini, though Hitler continued to have time for him personally, had brought nothing but trouble to the war. Japan would fight on its own terms in a separate theater. While Hitler would spend many hours reflecting on his enemies, analyzing them and above all espying the divisions between them, the only influence he could wield over them was through force of arms. His psychological battle against them was over; against his generals, having taken supreme command, it was only just beginning. As Halder grumbled in mid-January: "This kind of leadership can lead only to the annihilation of the army."[81]

CHAPTER SEVEN

January 17–June 21, 1942

At 10 a.m. on January 17, after a transatlantic flight of eighteen hours, Churchill arrived in Plymouth. Anthony Eden was also back home but still mulling over his talks in Moscow. "Russian suspicions lie so deep and Russian fears of German military might are so vivid and real that our task must be a formidable one," he wrote to Sir Stafford Cripps, who remained in Moscow as British ambassador. "In general I feel that we can only possess our souls in patience until such time as we have sufficient success in our military operations to inspire in the Soviet government some of the fear and respect which they now feel for the Germans."[1] While Stalin remained wary of his allies, the British secret services were equally suspicious of the Russians, and with good reason. "Some days ago we discovered that the transmitter which had previously been active in Kensington Palace Road was in actual fact operating from the top floor of the Soviet Consulate, Rosary Gardens," MI5's counter-intelligence chief Guy Liddell noted in his diary.[2]

On January 20 in Germany the Wannsee conference opened to draw up its cold bureaucratic blueprint for the final extermination of Europe's millions of Jews. Hitler blamed the whole conflagration on Churchill: "The Führer sees him as a complete plutocratic criminal, who must be removed if the world is ever to be at peace," Joseph Goebbels noted. Churchill was "the chief perpetrator of this war. It is because of him that the war began and must be so bitterly fought."[3] "Perhaps," Hitler told his propaganda chief, "he is no longer in peak fitness; the most recent pictures show a thinner and broken man. But we don't want to rely on that. We base our strategy on real facts."[4]

Facts seemed to be turning back Hitler's way. In a reversal of fortune in Africa Erwin Rommel's forces were advancing on Tobruk, and in the Far East the Japanese drove ever nearer to Singapore. In Washington Roosevelt's cabinet were trying to accustom themselves to their newly autocratic leader. Leo Crowley, a gifted administrator dubbed "manager par excellence" by Roosevelt, was with Henry Morgenthau. Crowley described a lunch with the president, during which Roosevelt had said: "It is up to you to go along with anything that I want at this time." Crowley was shocked: "Something has happened to the president. He has lost his touch with the people," he told Morgenthau. "This war has suddenly made him think he has got to have his own way, whatever it is."[5]

That evening, Hitler was on his favorite theme. "The Jews must pack up, disappear from Europe," he announced to his after-dinner guests. "It's natural that we should concern ourselves with the question on the European level, it's clearly not enough to expel them from Germany. We cannot allow them to retain bases of withdrawal at our doors. We want to be out of danger of all kinds of infiltration."[6] As he spoke, hundreds of Yugoslavian Jews, all women and children, were being forced to march for miles on foot through the snow to the concentration camp at Sajmiste.

The next day, January 28, 1942, Anthony Eden submitted a memorandum entitled "Policy on Russia" to the War Cabinet. He argued that for the sake of smooth relations and winning trust, there was no point in opposing Stalin's claims to the Baltic states. "If Russia is in occupation of the territory involved at the end of the war, neither we nor America will turn out. Probably, however, M. Stalin's demand is intended as an acid test to find out how far His Majesty's Government are prepared to make unpalatable concessions in order to obtain the postwar cooperation of the Soviet Union; in other words to see what value we attach to that cooperation and what sacrifice of principle we are prepared to make in order to achieve it."[7]

Eden witheringly argued that while Soviet policy might be "amoral" American policy was "exaggeratedly moral, at least where non-American interests are concerned."[8] Churchill continued to be shocked by Eden's approach, reminding him: "The 1941 frontiers of Russia were acquired by acts of aggression in shameful collusion with Hitler. The transfer of the people of the Baltic States to Soviet Russia against their will would be contrary to all the principles for which we are fighting this war. ... I know President Roosevelt holds this view as strongly as I do."[9]

The next day Rommel's troops took Benghazi. Despite military setbacks and despite his continuing resistance to territorial deals with Stalin, Churchill was determined to keep up the supply to Russia of whatever weapons could be spared. General Alan Brooke, now Chief of the Imperial General Staff, thought such generosity foolhardy. "It is quite evident that we are incurring grave danger by going on supplying tanks to Russia," he recorded in his diary after the Defence Committee meeting.[10] Churchill did not attend, sending instead his deputy, the Labour leader, Clement Attlee, in his place as chairman, "having decided beforehand," Brooke noted to his great irritation, "that he would not stop sending tanks to Russia!!"[11]

Hitler was in Berlin, standing before a huge crowd at the Sportspalast, marking the ninth anniversary of his assumption of power. "We are clear," he proclaimed, "that the war can only end either with the extermination of the Aryan peoples or the disappearance of Jewry from Europe. Nothing, whatever it may be, can throw me out of the saddle."[12] "His attack on Churchill and Roosevelt is sharp," Goebbels noted with satisfaction. "The Führer does not believe that Churchill is any longer sitting on top of the world."[13] "All the English people I received before the war broke out," Hitler told him, "agreed that Churchill was a fool."[14]

Four days later the long-running squabble about the concessions which Britain would have to make in return for the munificence of American lend-lease boiled over. British negotiators were objecting to an article in the draft agreement which stated that both parties would relinquish discriminatory trade practices. This was clearly aimed at the British system of imperial preference. Churchill had thought that it was the State Department that was backing this clause, not Roosevelt himself. He was about to be disabused. "I am convinced that further delay in concluding this agreement will be harmful to your interests and ours," wrote the president. "I am likewise convinced that the present draft is not only fair and equitable but it meets the apprehension which some of your colleagues have felt."[15]

Churchill drafted a furious response, even allowing himself a dig at Roosevelt's wavering before Pearl Harbor: "I consider situation is completely altered by entry of the United States into the war. This makes us no longer a combatant receiving help from a generous sympathiser, but two comrades fighting for life side by side. In this connection it must be remembered that for a large part of 27 months we carried on the struggle single-handed, and that had we failed the full malice of the axis powers, whose real intention can now be so clearly seen, would have fallen upon the United States." He argued with a cutting edge of bitterness that "lend-lease goods ... ought not to be a cause of the judgment of our future cooperation in the economic rebuilding of the world."[16] Wisely Churchill sat on his emotional words and in the coming months allowed the agreement, largely unaltered, to be signed. It was one small sign of a changing world.

On February 8 five thousand Japanese troops landed on Singapore Island from the neighboring Johore Straits. It was a gloomy day for Hitler too, as his trusted armaments minister, Dr Fritz Todt, was killed in an air crash just after taking off from the Wolf's Lair. Goebbels, meanwhile, was scathing of Churchill and Roosevelt's relationship. "Anglo-American cooperation is the big theme of the Anglo-Saxon press. There seem to be problems in every quarter. This is because in the much-lauded democracies no one knows who is supposed to give the orders and who is supposed to obey," he crowed, "here too the personal vanities and rivalries between Churchill and Roosevelt must play a large part."[17]

On February 15 disaster struck the British Empire. At noon London time Singapore surrendered. The Gibraltar of the east had been lost to the Japanese and over sixteen thousand British prisoners captured. For Churchill, Goebbels noted with glee, this military defeat "has weakened his position very much."[18]

Churchill looked to his allies for comfort. "We must remember that we are no longer alone," he assured the British people in a radio broadcast later that day. "We are in the midst of great company. Three-quarters of the human race are now moving with us," he declared. "So far we have not failed. We shall not fail now, let us move forward steadfastly together into the storm and through the storm."[19] Goebbels was unimpressed. "He is like a doctor who prophesies that his patient will die and who, every time the patient's condition worsens, smugly explains that, after all, he prophesied it."[20]

Over in Berlin, before an audience of 10,000 trainee SS officers Hitler was full of confidence and enthusiasm. He told these fledgling cadres of the Third *Reich* to "stem the Red tide and save civilization."[21] "I am attempting to create a world power out of the German *Reich*," he shouted to wild applause in the Sportspalast in Berlin.[22]

Ivan Maisky observed that events seemed to be getting on top of Britain's great leader. "I was in Parliament. Churchill spoke about the fall of Singapore. He did not look well, and was irritable, ready to take offense and stubborn," Maisky judged from the Gallery on February 17. "The members were critical and wrought-up. They received Churchill badly, and reacted badly to his statement. I have never seen anything like it before," he noted, "Churchill is making it increasingly harder for even his friends to support the government. At every step he insists: 'I answer for it all.'" "If Churchill continues to be stubborn, it may topple over his head," Maisky warned.[23]

The next day there was comfort from Roosevelt. "I realize how fully the fall of Singapore has affected you," he wrote.[24] In his reply Churchill did nothing to conceal the intense pressure he was feeling. "I am most grateful to you for your warm hearted telegram," he confided, "I do not like these days of personal stress and I have found it difficult to keep my eye on the ball. We are however in the fullest accord in all main things."[25] Churchill reshuffled his Cabinet in an attempt to impose his authority, but he was at a low ebb.

The wearying debates over the Soviets were not helping. The Foreign Office offered subtle, psychological advice. "It is essential to treat the Russians as though we thought that they were reasonable human beings. But as they are not, in fact, reasonable human beings, but dominated by an almost insane suspicion, we have to combine this treatment with infinite patience."[26] Roosevelt, as Churchill had predicted, was proving sticky at the prospect of any deals. Lord Halifax relayed the president's view that the present direction of the negotiations was "difficult to reconcile with the Atlantic Charter, and that it was premature to attempt detailed treatment of the problem." Roosevelt, who held his own personal diplomatic skills in the highest regard, was also causing irritation by suggesting that he could quickly wrap up a deal with Maksim Litvinov, the Soviet Ambassador in Washington. Halifax tartly commented: "It was with us and not with the Americans that Stalin wished to sign a treaty."[27]

There were further troubles for Churchill. He found himself standing before the House of Commons deflecting calls for his resignation as Minister of Defence. "However tempting it may be to some, when trouble lies ahead, to step aside adroitly and put someone else up to take the blows, the heavy and repeated blows—which are coming, I do not intend," he stated, "to adopt that cowardly course."[28] His health was also causing concern. "Brendan (Bracken) talked to me," Eden noted in his diary on February 27, "he was much troubled. It seems ... that the heart will affect his circulation and perhaps even his speech, that there may be something in the nature of a 'blackout.'"[29]

On March 7 Churchill bit the bullet on Russia. The mounting disasters in the war in the Far East, the U-boat scourge in the Atlantic, and the change of fortune in the Middle East combined to force him into an about-turn. Everything seemed to depend on Stalin; and his old worries that the Soviet leader might once again be tempted to do a deal with Hitler if his new allies did not satisfy him had resurfaced. He wrote to Roosevelt that the Baltic states could be sacrificed to keep Stalin on side. "The increasing gravity of the war has led me to feel that the principles of the Atlantic Charter ought not to be construed so as to deny to Russia the frontiers she occupied when Germany attacked her. ... I hope therefore that you will be able to give us a free hand to sign the treaty which Stalin desires as soon as possible," he appealed. "Everything portends an immense renewal of the German invasion of Russia in the spring and there is very little we can do to help the only country that is heavily engaged with the German armies."[30]

That same day, as the *Tirpitz* sailed from Trondheim to cause havoc to the Allied convoys heading through Arctic waters to Murmansk, Sir Stafford Cripps gave an interview to the *Daily Mail* which was reprinted in *Life* magazine, offering a benign view of Soviet ambitions. "To protect Leningrad it is essential that the Russians should control the Gulf of Finland and the Baltic coast," Cripps explained. "The Soviet government has no intention, and of this I am certain, to demand anything more in the way of territorial aggrandisement." Cripps stated that he was certain "that the Russians do not want to interfere with the internal affairs of other countries," and that the Soviets were "the only people of Europe who have been able to meet the blitz tactics of Hitler with success."[31]

In Washington Halifax was "rather impressed by Winston's sharp change of front on Russia. ... Having called Anthony every name from a dog to a pig for suggesting composition with Stalin, he now goes all out for it himself."[32] The British ambassador was immediately summoned to the White House to discuss Churchill's volte-face. Halifax recorded that he found the president "very sticky" and worried about "his own public opinion, the general morality, effect on Poles, and all the rest of it. He continues to remain quite confident that if he could see Stalin he could settle it in five minutes."[33]

It turned out that Roosevelt's real concern was not over coming to an accommodation with Stalin, but over doing it in a public treaty. Halifax recorded that he showed himself just as willing as Churchill to sacrifice the Baltic states, but preferred to do it more furtively: "His mind is already moving along the only remaining line, i.e. of saying to Stalin that we all recognise his need for security, that to put anything on paper now is impossible and would lead to dangerous explosive opinion here, that future of Baltic States clearly depends upon Russian military progress, and that neither United States nor Great Britain would or could turn them out. Why then should Stalin worry?"[34] As early as March 1942 Churchill, and Roosevelt, had shown themselves willing to give away the future freedom of three independent nations to keep Stalin sweet.

For Roosevelt the priority remained the sending of supplies to Russia, and he was privately accusing the British of not doing enough. On March 11 he told Morgenthau: "I do not want to be in the same position as the English. The English promised the Russians two divisions, they failed. They promised them help with the Caucasus. They failed. Every promise the English have made to the Russians, they have fallen down on. ... Nothing would be worse than to have the Russians collapse. I would rather lose New Zealand, Australia or anything else."[35]

Debates over convoys to Russia occupied much of the correspondence between the three Allied warlords. Stalin always wanted more; Roosevelt chided the British to send more; Churchill reminded him that the losses of ships, men and weapons on the Arctic route were unsustainable.

Arguments over the second front also rumbled ever louder. On March 14 Maisky traveled to Chequers to deliver Stalin's latest letter. The Soviet ambassador was received by Eden and taken to see Churchill, who, wearing his blue siren-suit, pored over the Soviet leader's barbs. "I feel entirely confident that the combined efforts of our troops," Stalin had written, "will culminate in crushing the enemy and that the year 1942 will see a decisive turn on the anti-Hitler front."[36] Churchill shrugged his shoulders. "I don't see how 1942 can become a decisive year," he said. Maisky noticed "a slight note of irritation" in Churchill's voice. He then subjected Maisky to "a long lecture" on Britain's inability to fulfil all Soviet demands, namely the creation of a second front, in 1942.[37] Instead he would offer Stalin a great bombing offensive on German industrial targets to take the weight off the Red Army.

It needed little to stoke Stalin's suspicions of his allies. On March 16 he met a group of soldiers who had just returned from the front. Yury Chadayev was present and noticed his boss's furrowed brow. Stalin looked round at the men and puffed on his pipe. "We should always be on alert with our allies," he told his visitors. "We continue getting intelligence demonstrating that after his defeat near Moscow, Hitler expressed his intention to sign a separate peace with England and America. We are also aware," Stalin continued, "that the British ruling circles continue their behind-the-scenes efforts to make an agreement with Germany." "Stalin," Chadayev noted, "reminded them of Hess's appearance in England and of the suspicious negotiations with him."[38] The old conspiracy theory gripped as strongly as ever.

Roosevelt was agitated by what he saw as the mess in Britain's relations with the Soviet Union. Two days later he offered Churchill a disparaging verdict: "I know you will not mind my being brutally frank when I tell you that I think I can personally handle Stalin better than either your Foreign Office or my State Department. Stalin hates the guts of all your top people. He thinks he likes me better, and I hope he will continue to do so." Presidential vanity was mitigated by the personal touch. "I know," Roosevelt added, "you will keep up your optimism and your grand driving force, but I know you will not mind if I tell you that you ought to take a leaf out of my notebook. Once a month I go to Hyde Park, crawl into a hole and pull the hole in after me. I am called on the telephone only if something of really great importance occurs. I wish you would try it, and I wish you would lay a few bricks or paint another picture."[39] It was a lot of advice in one mouthful and it also contained a warning. The president, even if he was viewed by the British as a johnny-come-lately into the war, had no intention of sitting on the sideline while Stalin and Churchill rearranged Europe.

In the dark heart of that battered continent the first deportations of Jews to Auschwitz were under way. "The Jews are now being deported to the east. A fairly barbaric procedure, not to be described in any greater detail is being used here, and not much more remains of the Jews themselves," Goebbels noted with grim satisfaction. "In general, it can probably be established that 60 percent of them must be liquidated, while only 40 percent can be put to work. A judgment is being carried out on the Jews which is barbaric, but fully deserved. It's a life and death struggle between the Aryan race and the Jewish bacillus. Here, too, the Führer is the unswerving champion and spokesman of an unswerving solution."[40] While Hitler carefully avoided putting his own name to any written program of extermination, Goebbels' record was proof that the will and the orders came from the very top.

In April 1942 Churchill and Roosevelt had their first real row. Churchill, even though he had made the Raj one of the defining causes of his political career, had allowed negotiations to go ahead with Indian nationalists, mainly to ensure India's loyalty in the war. When the talks broke down, Roosevelt blamed Churchill: "The feeling is almost universally held here that the deadlock has been caused by the unwillingness of the British government to concede to the Indians the right of self-government." Roosevelt insisted on his right to interfere: "I feel I must place this issue before you very frankly and I know you will understand my reasons for so doing."[41]

Churchill felt no such understanding. He was enraged by what he saw as Roosevelt's meddling; according to Harry Hopkins, who happened to be staying in Downing Street at the time, "the string of cuss words lasted two hours into the night."[42] He drafted a furious reply: "I am greatly concerned to receive your message because I am sure that I could not be responsible for a policy which would throw the whole sub-continent of India into utter confusion while the Japanese invader is at its gates."[43] Churchill told

Roosevelt that he would resign over India if he was pushed too far: "I should personally make no objection at all to retiring into private life, and I have explained this to Harry just now, but I have no doubt whatever that Cabinet and Parliament would be strongly averse from reopening the Indian constitutional issue in this way at this juncture. Far from helping the defence of India, it would make our task impossible."[44]

As was often his custom when tempestuous messages had been written, Churchill sat on the cable. The next day he reconsidered and sent a more carefully worded response. "You know the weight which I attach to everything you say to me, but I did not feel I could take responsibility for the defence of India if everything has again to be thrown into the melting pot at this critical juncture," he explained. "Anything like a serious difference between you and me would break my heart and surely deeply injure both our countries at the height of this terrible struggle."[45] From that point Roosevelt, on Hopkins's advice, laid off Churchill on India. However, he had no intention of being thwarted in his long-term ambition of creating a non-imperialist world.

Despite the personal camaraderie forged in Washington, a range of issues continued to invite niggles. General George Marshall led a delegation to London to argue for a second front invasion of France in 1942; his consistently held view was to follow the shortest line to Berlin. However, American troops were not yet bloodied in battle and the British were disinclined to throw their own limited forces into ill-thought-out and premature slaughter against the German defenses on the French coast.

After meeting Marshall on April 14 Brooke noted: "Marshall has started the European offensive plan and is going 100 percent all out on it! It is a clever move which fits in well with present political opinion and the desire to help Russia. It is also popular with military men who are fretting for an offensive policy. But," Brooke explained, "and this is a very large 'but,' his plan does not go beyond just landing on the far coast!! Whether we are to play baccarat or chemin de fer at Le Touquet, or possibly bathe at Paris Plage is not stipulated! I asked him this afternoon—do we go east, south or west after landing? He had not begun to think of it!!"[46]

The one consolation in this time of tetchiness was the news that Stalin had agreed to send Vyacheslav Molotov to London in May to iron out the tortuous

Anglo-Russian treaty. The Soviet leader was also encouraged by prospects which Roosevelt, despite British wariness, was holding out of a second front in the summer.

From his frozen Prussian headquarters, Hitler too was planning new offensives. "The Führer," Joseph Goebbels recorded on April 17, "has ordered that ... retaliatory air attacks should be resumed against English towns, mainly those which are undefended. In the long run we can no longer permit the shameless terrorizing of German towns to go unanswered." He boasted that the previous night's attack on Sunderland was "a small foretaste of what is to come."[47] On this day the siege of Leningrad reached its 250th agonizing day.

On April 25, while the town of Rostock recovered from a devastating Allied bombing raid, Hitler and Goebbels had a long conversation after lunch in the *Reich* Chancellery. "The Führer," Goebbels noted with relief, "judges the situation on the eastern front to be quite positive, thank God. With winter past, the strongest and most pressing concerns are over." "They have nothing to eat, they live from hand to mouth, the people are fed on bread and pickles," Hitler said of conditions behind Russian lines, "the soldiers' equipment and arms are also apparently at the lowest level. There are plenty of proven examples of widespread cannibalism not only in the Bolshevik army, but also among the Russian civil population. I have never looked forward to Spring so fervently," he announced. "The Führer doesn't want to see any more snow this year," Goebbels noted. "Snow has become physically repugnant to him, which I can quite understand."[48] Winter in Obersalzberg was never quite the same again.

While the ordinary people of Russia suffered, Georgy Dimitrov, the leader of Stalin's Communist International, continued to think of world revolution. "Aviation engineer Afanasiev (back from America) gave me an account of his impressions and observations of the United States. Overall conclusion," Dimitrov recorded, "enormous possibilities for revolutionary movements against trusts and magnates."[49] In Berlin Hitler celebrated the Luftwaffe's raid on Bath in revenge for Rostock. "It must have been much more extensive than the English air raid on Rostock," reported Goebbels. "I will now repeat these raids night after night until the English lose their desire to carry out terrorist attacks," Hitler told him.[50]

In May 1942 the British negotiations with Russia came to a head. On May 20 Stalin's foreign minister, Molotov, dashingly clad in his flying gear, landed at RAF Tealing in Scotland—the first visit to Britain by a top Bolshevik since the revolution. After parading for photographers, he nipped back into the plane to change into his business suit and then took the train down to London. Stalin had given Molotov an extensive shopping list of territory that Britain must agree to as part of the postwar Soviet Union. "Molotov immediately pressed his maximum demands," noted Averell Harriman, who was keeping an eye on the negotiations for Roosevelt, "British recognition of Soviet claims on eastern Poland and Rumania as well as the Baltic States."[51]

The same day Stalin received a telegram from Churchill intended to reassure him of continuing practical support. "A convoy of 35 ships left yesterday with instructions to make its way to you," Churchill reported.[52] He pleaded with the Soviet leader to send his long-range bombers to knock out enemy airfields within range of the Arctic during the week the convoy would be sailing through its most hazardous waters. "I know you will do all in your power. If we are in bad luck and the convoy suffers very heavy losses," Churchill warned, "then the only thing we can do will be to hold up the further sailing of convoys until we have greater sea space when the ice recedes northwards in July."[53]

At 11:30 a.m. on May 21 Molotov arrived at 10 Downing Street. While Churchill had conceded that Stalin could have the Baltic states, he was unwilling to allow further territorial concessions, particularly in Poland. "Russians as wooden as ever," noted Alexander Cadogan. "We discussed Treaties. Their attitude is: 'We have made large concession in agreeing to leave Polish frontier for later settlement. What concession do you make?' They ignore that we have made the great concession about the Baltic States! No conclusion."[54]

Despite the sacrifice Churchill was making by sending such a substantial Arctic convoy, Stalin's mistrust of his British ally had not waned. "Yes, the question of the opening of the second front is still in the air," he told his Politburo colleagues over lunch in the Kremlin, "our allies are still doing nothing in this direction. Obviously, we do not cherish any illusions about it. The Allies won't do anything about it this year. Apparently, the British dislike of socialism slows down the process. Yes, I am sure that's the point." Settling down and puffing on his pipe the dictator continued: "You are right about Churchill's dislike of us. This was the case before the war and remains so today. It would be strange if Churchill treats us differently."[55]

While Stalin was analyzing Churchill, Hitler was giving Goebbels his verdict on Stalin. "The Führer is clear on the fact that in the Soviet Union— in contrast to England and the USA—we have an opponent who possesses an ideology. He recognizes in Stalin a man of importance, who towers above the democratic figureheads of the Anglo-Saxon powers."[56] Hitler saw himself irrevocably locked in the ultimate contest of the totalitarians: "It is a world struggle on a huge scale, which we must win if the *Reich* is not to be destroyed," he told Goebbels. "The Soviet struggle against us is a struggle to destruction. This war cannot be compared to any war in the past. Then it was a question of victory or defeat; now it is a matter of triumph or ruin."[57] As for Roosevelt, he declared: "The US will lose their interest in this war when they have plundered and feasted on the English empire as much as they can."[58]

The talks in London were at a standstill. Then German forces launched their summer offensive on the eastern front. Soon three Soviet armies were being smashed at the battle of Kharkov. Stalin's priorities instantly changed. Military help from the British and Americans suddenly assumed far more importance than pieces of paper about future territory, which would look after itself. He cabled Molotov: "We have received the draft treaty Eden handed you. ... It lacks the question of the security of frontiers, but this is not bad perhaps, for it gives us a free hand. The question of frontiers," he stated, "or to be more exact, of guarantees for the security of our frontiers at one or another section of our country, will be decided by force."[59]

Molotov told the astonished British that Russia was dropping all mentions of territory; instead the treaty became a general agreement of friendship for 20 years. "Russians last night agreed our treaty. Much of the morning taken up by the Russians trying to slip in various amendments," Cadogan noted, "but none of them were vicious. Cabinet at 1 ... Winston relieved and delighted, and bouquets were heaped on A (Eden)!" "Many toasts and many speeches," Brooke noted after the signing ceremony had been concluded, "somehow the whole affair gave me the creeps and made me feel that humanity has still many centuries to live through before universal peace can be found."[60]

Molotov immediately flew off to Washington in the hope of securing from Roosevelt a commitment to the launching of the second front later in the summer. He was not to be disappointed. On June 1, 1942, talks between the globetrotting Russian and the president were concluded. Roosevelt gave his permission for a public communiqué to be released which stated that "in the course of the conversations full understanding was reached with regards to the urgent tasks of creating a second front in Europe in 1942."[61] Roosevelt cabled Churchill: "Molotov's visit is, I think, a real success because we have got on a personal footing of candor and as good friendship as can be acquired through an interpreter. ... I have a very strong feeling that the Russian position is precarious and may grow steadily worse during the coming weeks. Therefore," he explained, "I am more than ever anxious that BOLERO [the code name for the cross-Channel attack] proceed to definite action beginning in August and continuing so long as the weather holds in 1942."[62]

In London there was horror at Roosevelt's unilateral announcement of an operation which would at this early stage have to be carried out largely by British troops. Within a few days Molotov was back in Britain for a stopover before flying home to Moscow. "Molotov returned to London," Eden noted in his diary, "bringing an explosive message with him."[63] At midday on June 9 the Cabinet gathered for what Eden described as a "sticky" meeting. Churchill dined that night with Molotov and Maisky. "Long talk after dinner, mainly explanation by W. of second front problems," Eden reported, noting that he thought it had done "much good. At least it helped to increase confidence."[64]

Churchill knew that he could not publicly countermand Roosevelt's statement and instead gave Molotov a private *aide-mémoire* explaining that "it was not yet possible to say whether the plan for a landing on the Continent was feasible that year. We could therefore give no promise."[65] At 9 p.m. in London on June 10 the final farewells were exchanged at Downing Street. "Toasts were drunk and farewell speeches made. All very friendly," recorded Eden.[66] The next day Molotov headed home.

At the same time, over on the Continent, Hitler was talking with Goebbels and the Finnish president. "Leningrad and Moscow must disappear completely," he declared. England's situation, meanwhile, was "hopeless. This great empire has chosen its own destruction and that is what it will therefore endure. It might take a long time, but it will be the end. The USA will probably inherit whatever remains. As the grave digger of the English empire Churchill has chosen this path, and England must pay for it."[67]

Churchill, who had become thoroughly alarmed by the president's off-the-cuff strategic announcements, decided to fly to the United States to hammer out a clear plan. On the morning of June 18 he and his party neared their destination. "Had long morning in bed as the clock was going back and breakfast was not available till 11 a.m. (about 8 a.m. real time)," Brooke recorded. "Still flying over blankets of cloud till about 12:30 when we found the sea again and shortly afterwards flew over a large convoy of some 35 ships. PM in tremendous form and enjoying himself like a schoolboy! As we waited to embark he was singing a little song to himself 'We're here because we're here.'"[68]

The prime minister landed at 8 p.m., but was not met by President Roosevelt, who had escaped to Hyde Park for a short break. "Winston," recorded Halifax, who greeted him at the airport, "was rather put out at the president being away, and inclined to be annoyed that he hadn't been diverted to New York … he got into a better temper when he had had some champagne," Halifax noted. "He certainly is the most extraordinary man; immensely great qualities, with some of the defects that sometimes attach to them. I couldn't live that life for long!"[69]

The next day the two warlords of democracy were together again. "It was a fascinating lunch. One could only watch these two men talking," noted Daisy Suckley, "they were both in fine form, rested and playing on and with each other. There seemed to be real friendship and understanding between F.D.R. and Churchill. F.D.R.'s manner was easy and intimate—His face humorous, or very serious, according to the subject of conversation, and entirely natural. Not a trace of having to guard his words or expressions, just the opposite of his manner at the press conference, when he is an actor on a stage—and a player on an instrument, at the same time."[70]

This was the honeymoon period and adversity brought the two men closer together than ever. On June 21, 1942, as Stalin's counteroffensive was failing across the entire length of the eastern front, news of a parallel setback in north Africa arrived at the White House. Roosevelt handed Churchill a telegram that had just been delivered to the Oval Office. Moments later, before Churchill had a chance to react, another pink slip of paper was delivered into his hands. Churchill's face bowed; Rommel's troops had secured a crushing victory over the British 8th Army in Tobruk. Without hesitation Roosevelt asked: "What can we do to help?" "Sherman tanks," Churchill replied, "as many as can be shipped immediately to the Middle East."[71] Within hours Roosevelt and General Marshall ordered the dispatch of three hundred Shermans to Egypt.

Thousands of miles away in the Wolf's Lair, Hitler was triumphant. "The English public's extraordinary shock at the fall of Tobruk will be a mark of crisis for Churchill," he announced gleefully to Goebbels. "Churchill is in a very precarious situation and effectively has run away to Washington."[72] The Führer celebrated by ordering that Rommel be promoted to Field Marshal. His confidence was unbounded. It seemed that north Africa would soon be his and, to top it all, Soviet resistance on the eastern front continued to crumble.

For the three Allied warlords there was a war to be won. Over the next year the bickering over empire and postwar territory that had sometimes soured relationships would be put to one side in the pursuit of victory. The arguments between Roosevelt and Churchill would be over military strategy; at the same time Stalin would find himself locked in a decisive duel of arms with Hitler as they headed towards bloody collision in Stalingrad.

CHAPTER EIGHT

June 22–August 19, 1942

News of the Tobruk disaster spread across Washington. Churchill's traveling doctor, Sir Charles Wilson, was at the British embassy with Lord Halifax. "That is bad, and very surprising," the ambassador remarked, "certainly Rommel moves quickly." He judged it important that Churchill did not stay too long in the United States: "He certainly will not make the mistake he made in January of overlooking feeling at home."[1]

Rommel took 30,000 prisoners. Roosevelt was under no illusions about the power of Hitler's armies. That day Daisy Suckley had one of her intimate conversations with the president and noted his verdict in her diary: "F. told Sir John Dill [the senior British military officer in Washington] the trouble with the British is that they think they can beat the Germans if they have an equal number of men, tanks etc. F. says that is not so—the Germans are better trained, better generaled."[2] "You can never discipline an Englishman or an American as you can a German," Roosevelt told Daisy. "I asked where the blame lies for the present situation in Egypt," Daisy continued. "Partly Churchill, mostly the bad generals," Roosevelt replied.[3]

Overall, Daisy recorded, "F. was depressed over the situation. If Egypt is taken, it means Arabia, Syria, Afghanistan, etc., i.e. the Japs and Germans control everything across from the Atlantic to the Pacific—that means all the oil wells, etc. of those regions—a bleak prospect for the United Nations."[4] Roosevelt had come a long way since May the year before when he appeared happy to wave goodbye to large parts of the Middle East.

The next day, the aftershock of defeat was still rippling through Washington. "I was very sorry for Churchill. He was evidently staggered by the blow of Tobruk and showed it in his speech and manner, although he bore up bravely," Henry Stimson noted. Churchill did not disagree with Roosevelt's harsh verdict on British fighting qualities: "He did not attempt to excuse it because of overwhelming numbers or anything of that sort but he said it was just plain bad leadership; that Rommel had out-generaled them and out-fought them and had supplied his troops with better weapons."[5] On the behavior of his own leader Stimson was not so generous. In the immediate aftermath Roosevelt plucked from the air the idea of sending an instant task force to protect a line from Alexandria to Iran. "Altogether it was a very unhappy meeting for me," wrote Stimson. "The president was in his most irresponsible mood, he was talking of a most critical situation and in the presence of the head of another government with the frivolity and lack of responsibility of a child."[6]

Over in Hitler's headquarters the jubilant mood showed no sign of abating. "Tobruk proves to be a great victory," General Franz Halder recorded, "Rommel has become a field marshal."[7] At noon Hitler was holding court. "Rommel's efficiency, of course, is unquestionable," he declared. "From the very beginning of the present offensive, he foretold with almost photographic accuracy the advance to the coast and the attack on Tobruk."[8]

At lunchtime Churchill read reports in American newspapers predicting that the fall of his government was likely to come hot on the heels of this latest military defeat. Late that night he telephoned his Foreign Secretary. It was 5 a.m. in London. A sleepy Anthony Eden answered the call and was able to reassure him: "I told him that I had heard not one word of this. Of course there was much grief. No doubt there would be blame for the government, but so far nothing had happened to shake us."[9]

The next day, June 23, the Nazis' euthanasia program reached a sickening crescendo. While the first Polish patients from mental institutions were packed off to Auschwitz, Hitler was gloating over victory with Joseph Goebbels: "The English public's extraordinary shock at the fall of Tobruk will be a mark of crisis for Churchill," Hitler foretold, "even with the English, who are politically notoriously stupid, you can't do whatever you want. Churchill is in a very precarious situation, and effectively has run away to Washington."[10] That day a BBC radio broadcast from London informed its listeners that 700,000 Jews had been murdered by the Nazis. Hitler's advancing troops launched an attack on Rostov-on-Don.

On June 27, as convoy PQ17 sailed with its precious cargo of weapons to Archangel in the frozen north of the USSR, Churchill landed back in Great Britain. It was 5 p.m. The prime minister was greeted with another setback, this time on the domestic front. As soon as he had boarded his train, codenamed "Dives," he was told that his government had been defeated in the recent Maldon by-election.

Later that evening Hitler was engaged in one of his late-night monologues, suggesting the real reason why Churchill spent eight days with Roosevelt in the United States. "When two people are in general agreement, decisions are swiftly taken. My own conference with the Duce never lasted more than an hour and a half, the rest of the time being devoted to ceremonies of various kinds," he told his guests. "It is easy, therefore, by comparison to imagine how enormous their difficulties must appear. To harness to a common purpose a coalition composed of Great Britain, the United States, Russia and China demands little short of a miracle."[11]

As so often, Hitler's analysis of his opponents hit the mark; yet, despite the enormous obstacles and Stalin's continuing suspicions and grievances, the three Allied warlords knew that their survival depended on keeping their military alliance intact. The miracle had to be achieved. Stalin's military strategy was clear-cut: first to halt Hitler, then to drive him back to Berlin. For Roosevelt and Churchill it was less obvious and remained unresolved even after Churchill's long stay in Washington.

The American Chiefs of Staff still wanted to establish a cross-Channel bridgehead; Churchill and his chiefs remained convinced that it was folly. Roosevelt listened to the arguments from both sides, veering between an operation against France and an idea he and Churchill had discussed back in January of invading Morocco and Algeria in northwest Africa. These two countries were part of the French Empire and still controlled by the collaborationist Vichy government of Marshal Philippe Pétain. However, there was a hope that, once the French local civilian and military administration saw American and British troops landing in their tens of thousands, they might join up with the Allies.

While the cables continued to flow between London and Washington, Operation "Blue," a massive German offensive between Taganrog on the Black Sea and Kursk, was launched. "Hitler found himself faced for the first time with the full import of the new responsibilities which he had arrogated to himself as Commander-in-Chief of the Army: that of directing great army formations in an extremely perilous offensive operation," General Walter Warlimont of the OKW Operations Staff recalled. "Now he really had to get on top of the job which he hitherto had to leave to the 'experts'; now he had to ensure that his airy-fairy thoughts fitted the hard facts of life."[12]

Three days later, German forces overran the last of the fortresses of Sevastopol, doggedly and bravely defended by the Soviets for months. As thousands of Soviet prisoners were rounded up, Churchill was in the House of Commons for the beginning of a two-day vote of censure debate. A small minority of MPs were calling for the prime minister to be replaced.

At noon Hitler, delighted with the reports from Crimea, expatiated on one of his favorite topics: the menace presented by Franklin D. Roosevelt. The president, Hitler announced, "who both in his handling of political issues and in his general attitude behaves like a tortuous, pettifogging Jew, himself boasted recently that he had 'noble' Jewish blood in his veins. Such examples," Hitler pronounced, "should open the eyes of all reasonable people and be a warning of the menace half-castes can be."[13]

The next afternoon, July 2, 1942, Winston Churchill faced his parliamentary colleagues and defended his position as leader of the national government and Commander-in-Chief of the British war effort. "A complete record exists of all the directions I have given, the inquiries I have made, and the telegrams I have drafted. I shall be perfectly content to be judged by them," Churchill announced. He concluded that a victory for his government in this vote would ensure "a cheer will go up from every friend of Britain and every faithful servant of our cause, and the death knell of disappointment will ring in the ears of the tyrants we are striving to overthrow."[14] The vote of no confidence was beaten by 475 votes to 25; it was overwhelming but short of unanimous.

In these times of adversity, Roosevelt remained a comforting supporter. "Good for you," he telegraphed when the news reached Washington.[15] Hitler's entourage was less generous. "What else can the English do but support him?" Goebbels wrote in his diary. "Churchill is in fact the only person who can deal with the United States and above all with Roosevelt; moreover, the English have no one to replace him."[16]

The Russian front was becoming critical. Soviet generals were ever more concerned with the strength and success of Hitler's Operation "Blue." "By the night of July 2, the situation in the Voronezh direction sharply deteriorated," Georgy Zhukov recalled, "the defenses at the junction of the Bryansk and the southwestern fronts were ruptured to a depth of up to 80 kilometers. The front's reserves in this sector were drawn into battle. There was now an imminent danger of the enemy's shock forces breaking through to the River Don and capturing Voronezh."[17] Twenty-four hours later, however, Hitler and his generals were expressing concern that their advance was not rapid enough. Halder noted: "The enemy knows our operational plans. Danger that the Russians can avoid destruction."[18]

In London Ivan Maisky was surveying events of the past few days. Voronezh had fallen. "A heavy week! Things at the front are very serious," he noted. "It is quite obvious that the Germans are heading for Stalingrad. For the time being one cannot close one's eyes to the fact that at present we are face to face with a deadly danger to our country, to the revolution, to the whole future of humanity."[19] Maisky was not the only one who was feeling jumpy. That evening Halifax had dinner with Eden and Churchill: "Winston sat and talked at the dinner table until quarter to one, and he struck me as being rather edgy and nervy, exaggerating minor difficulties with the press or the House of Commons, complaining that he had not sufficient power, and generally, as I thought, exhibiting symptoms of nervous fatigue," Halifax wrote in his secret diary. "I hope I am wrong. I can't conceive how anyone can live that life and retain reasonable sanity."[20]

The problems were compounded by the disaster of convoy PQ17, which had been ordered to scatter in the face of a concerted German attack. On July 14 its remains arrived in Archangel. Of the original 33 ships that set sail, only eight had survived. Four of those arrived in Archangel; the others were stuck precariously in the Arctic ice. For Churchill, this could mean only one thing. He cabled President Roosevelt at 3:25 p.m.: "We therefore advise against running PQ18."[21] It was a sound decision but a sure way of angering Stalin.

The arguments over strategy were coming to a head. The American chiefs sent a memorandum containing a veiled threat that, if the British refused to launch a cross-Channel operation, they would prefer to concentrate their forces in the Pacific. On July 15 Halifax visited Churchill and found him agitated: "Winston's own description of it was: 'Just because the Americans can't have a massacre in France this year, they want to sulk and bathe in the Pacific.'"[22]

Roosevelt was unimpressed by his own chiefs' attitude and insisted that Hitler remained the prime target. The president, Stimson reported of a meeting that day, "did not like the manner of the memorandum in regard to the Pacific, saying that it was a little like 'taking up your dishes and going away.'"[23] The next day, July 16, an American delegation headed by General George Marshall and Harry Hopkins flew to London, carrying instructions from Roosevelt on his strategic priorities. "Defeat of Germany means the defeat of Japan, probably without firing a shot or losing a life," he explained.[24]

As the first two thousand Dutch Jews were deported to Auschwitz, Hitler moved nearer to the front line. The bunker complex in the forests of Rastenburg was replaced by a new lair near Vinnitsa in the Ukraine, codenamed Werewolf. However, it turned out not to suit the Führer. "Hitler did not feel well here," Nicolaus von Below recalled, "he found the heat oppressive and the place was plagued by flies and mosquitoes."[25] This swampy complex was to be Hitler's home for three and a half months. Heinrich Himmler was his first important visitor. They discussed the necessity of securing the oil wells of the Caucasus; their gateway, Stalingrad, must be captured.

In Moscow Stalin had just finished dinner. Aleksandr Poskryobyshev, his rotund assistant, delivered a transcript of a German radio broadcast from the General Staff central intelligence department claiming this had already happened. "Stalingrad has been taken by brilliant German forces," it had announced, "Russia has been cut into two parts, north and south, and will soon collapse in her death throes."[26] Stalin immediately dictated a telegram to his military and civilian commanders in the area, Andrei

Yeremenko and Nikita Khrushchev. "Report some sense about what is happening in Stalingrad," he demanded, "is it true Stalingrad has been captured by the Germans? Give a straight and truthful answer. I await your immediate reply."[27] In fact the bitter fighting in Stalingrad was far from over; one of the most dreadful and iconic battles of the eastern front was just warming up.

It was hardly an opportune moment to tell the Soviet leader that, for the moment, Arctic convoys were suspended; but, two days later on July 18, Churchill took up his pen to explain that the strength of enemy battle squadrons and shore-based aircraft in the most exposed parts of the Arctic run was too great. Churchill, seared by the experience of the *Prince of Wales* and *Repulse* off the coast of Singapore, added that it was too great to risk the British Home Fleet in protecting the convoys: "If one or two of our very few most powerful types were to be lost or even seriously damaged while the *Tirpitz* and her consorts, soon to be joined by the *Scharnhorst*, remained in action, the whole command of the Atlantic would be lost," Churchill wrote carefully. "It is therefore with the greatest regret that we have reached the conclusion that to attempt to run the next convoy, PQ18, would bring no benefit to you and would involve a dead loss to the common cause."[28]

At 12:30 p.m. Alexander Cadogan handed over the telegram to Maisky at the Foreign Office. "He had been prepared for it," Cadogan noted, "so didn't take it too badly."[29] The next day, Sunday, July 19, Maisky wrote in his diary that he believed that "our allies left us to the mercy of fate in the most critical moment for us. This is a very unpleasant truth. But there is no point in denying it," he continued, "we must remember this and take it into account in all our future plans."[30]

Harry Hopkins, along with Marshall and the head of the American Navy, Admiral Ernest King, had arrived in Britain. "Churchill," Hopkins wrote to the president, "is pretty restless and quite unhappy that we did not go to see him in the first place."[31] The bad mood did not last long, however, and Hopkins reported happily that "all of this was cleared up over the weekend and he is now in the best of spirits."[32]

On Monday morning, July 20, the British chiefs met their American counterparts. "After lunch at 3 p.m. we ... had long argument with them," Alan Brooke complained, "found both of them still hankering after an attack across Channel this year to take pressure off Russia. They failed to realise that such an action could only lead to the loss of some six divisions without achieving any results!"[33]

Three days later Maisky visited Churchill to deliver Stalin's reply on the halting of Arctic convoys. "You know, of course, that the Soviet Union is suffering far greater losses," Stalin wrote, "be that as it may, I never imagined that the British government would deny us delivery of war materials precisely now, when the Soviet Union is badly in need of them in view of the grave situation on the Soviet–German front."[34] Stalin finished by stating that he hoped Churchill would "not take it amiss that I have seen fit to give you my frank and honest opinion."[35] "Stalin's reply produced the impression I expected," Maisky observed. "Churchill was both depressed and offended. His pride was deeply touched, in particular by Stalin's accusation of not fulfilling the obligations."[36]

As before, when Stalin censured him, Churchill reminded Maisky that it was only a year since Britain was standing alone in the face of Stalin's collaboration with Hitler. Meanwhile the police were informing the Home Office and MI5 that "the Communist Party of Great Britain has instructed leading officials when addressing 'closed' meetings to emphasise the dangers to which the USSR is exposed and that Britain cannot rely upon the Union to win the war for Europe."[37]

The Germans reoccupied Rostov-on-Don that day, but rather than take the advice of his generals Hitler issued Directive No. 45. It ordered a continuation of Operation "Blue"—now renamed "Operation Braunschweig." According to Hitler's directive, in just three weeks "the broad goals set for the southern flank of the eastern front have essentially been achieved."[38] The next strategic priority was the Caucasus and the valuable Black Sea oil fields. At the Werewolf Hitler ranted at his generals' caution. "He explodes in a fit of insane rage and hurls the gravest reproaches against the General Staff," Halder noted. "This chronic tendency to underrate enemy capabilities is gradually assuming grotesque proportions and develops into a positive danger. This so-called leadership is characterized by a pathological reacting to the impressions of the moment and a total lack of any understanding of the command machinery and its possibilities."[39]

Six days later, July 28, while German troops crossed the river Don near Rostov and entered the town of Bataisk, Stalin issued the infamous Order No. 227. "Not one more step backwards!" it instructed. "We will no longer tolerate officers and *commissars*, political personnel, units and detachments abandoning their battle positions of their own free will," it warned, stating that "panic-mongers and cowards must be destroyed on the spot."[40] In Moscow Georgy Dimitrov was discussing with Vyacheslav Molotov their British and American allies. "The English are hardly likely to open a second front this year. But they must be pressured," the two men agreed. "The English and the Americans evidently intend to wage war against Hitler, but they would like to do so by our hand. There are enemies, after all, in the Admiralty and other English bodies who want to wreck the cause of aid for us."[41]

Twenty-four hours later, in the sweltering wooden huts of the Werewolf, an argument was raging. Walter Warlimont described it as a "stormy briefing conference."[42] The military situation on the Stalingrad front was dire. "A wild battle is raging in sixth army sector inside the Don bend west of Stalingrad," Halder noted, "we do not have yet an accurate picture of its development. Sixth army's striking power is paralyzed by ammunition and fuel supply difficulties." Alfred Jodl announced that the "fate of the Caucasus will be decided at Stalingrad." Reversing a Headquarters order of the previous week, forces were diverted from Army Group A to Army Group B south of the Don.[43]

The British ambassador in Moscow, Sir Archibald Clark Kerr, had cabled Eden pleading that an "early visit of Winston to Joe" be engineered as soon as possible.[44] "Took the telegram to Winston and he jumped at it," Eden recorded.[45] Churchill knew that, however difficult and awkward it might be, it was best to deliver disappointing news in person. After weeks of transatlantic debate, Roosevelt was now leaning towards the option of invading north Africa rather than launching the cross-Channel operation Churchill had so long opposed. It would be yet another blow to the Soviet leader to add to the postponement of convoys.

After delivering the telegram, Eden had enjoyed a relaxing dinner and retired to bed when suddenly, at midnight, a call came through from

Churchill. Eden was summoned. "Found him with Chiefs of Staff," Eden recalled wearily, "discussed draft of messages to Joe and Roosevelt and at 1 a.m. sent for Maisky to give him former."[46] When Maisky arrived at Downing Street he found Churchill sitting at a table in his siren-suit with Eden next to him. "Both looked tired, but excited," Maisky recalled.[47] Churchill handed the Soviet ambassador his draft letter for Stalin. "Here," he said, "read it and tell us if you think it is any good."[48] Maisky quickly read the draft. "It is very, very good," he replied.[49] "It was great indeed," Maisky confided in his diary when he returned to the embassy, "a meeting between Stalin and Churchill could lead to serious consequences."[50]

The following day, July 31, Churchill's telegram to Stalin was dispatched. "I am willing, if you invite me, to come myself to meet you in Astrakhan, the Caucasus, or similar convenient meeting place," he wrote, "we could then survey the war together and take decisions hand-in-hand. I could then tell you plans we have made with President Roosevelt for offensive action in 1942."[51] Stalin immediately confirmed the invitation but insisted that Churchill must go to Moscow "since the members of the government, the General Staff and myself cannot be away at this moment of bitter fighting against the German."[52]

Just before midnight on August 1, as Churchill was preparing to take off from RAF Lyneham, news came through from Washington confirming the invasion of north Africa, Operation "Torch," for later in the autumn. The attack on mainland France was postponed for at least a year. Churchill steeled himself to tell Stalin. He boarded his unheated and uncomfortable American Liberator aircraft *Commando* for the long trip to Moscow via Gibraltar and Cairo, where he would drop in on his generals. Later he wrote that the journey to Russia was like carrying a "large lump of ice to the North Pole."[53]

By August 4 Churchill was in Cairo. The British embassy was stuffy and hot, but the prime minister's room was air-conditioned. En route to meet one ally, he asked the advice of the other: "I should greatly like to have your aid and countenance in my talks with Joe," he wrote to Roosevelt, "would you be able to let Averell come with me? I feel that things would be easier if we all seemed to be together. I have a somewhat raw job."[54] Averell Harriman was assigned to accompany Churchill, who was, according to his doctor, in good heart. "No longer is he compelled to deal with great events by correspondence," Sir Charles Wilson noted, "he is 'the man on the spot.' Twice he has said this to me. A great feeling of elation stokes the marvellous machine, which seems quite impervious to fatigue."[55]

That day Hitler was reminiscing about the First World War, where he had cut his teeth as a lowly infantryman. "The soldier has boundless affection for the ground on which he has shed his blood," he said, "if we could arrange the transport, we should have a million people pouring into France to revisit the scenes of their former struggle."[56] In Stalingrad Zhukov was impressing on his soldiers the severity of the present struggle. "In order to warn detachments against retreating and to combat cowardice and panic-mongering, the first line of every assault battalion was followed by a tank carrying officers specially picked by the army war councils," he reported to Stalin.[57]

At the Werewolf Hitler received Field Marshal Günther von Kluge, commander of Army Group Center. "The heat of the Ukrainian summer was stifling," Warlimont observed, and the atmosphere was "explosive."[58] Von Kluge pleaded for two extra armored divisions—nine and eleven—to be deployed against the strong Soviet counterattack in the Rzhev region. Hitler as usual was interested only in advancing. "He mulishly insisted," Warlimont recalled, "that the two divisions must be used offensively to iron out the Ssuchinitschi salient which was left over from the winter crisis, maintaining that this would provide a jumping off point for the subsequent drive on Moscow. Von Kluge was furious. 'You, my Führer, therefore assume responsibility for this' and he stalked out of the room."[59]

While Churchill completed the last leg of his journey to Moscow via Tehran, in London MI5 was exposing a hotbed of clandestine activity ultimately overseen by the very man the prime minister was about to meet. Guy Liddell, Britain's MI5 counter-intelligence chief, was reflecting on the recent arrest of a Soviet secret agent, a certain Oliver Green. Green had photographed and passed to his Soviet handlers British intelligence summaries. His activities had only come to light after he was caught forging petrol coupons. Liddell noted that "Green is of course a Communist and has been known to us for some considerable time. He got fifteen months for forging coupons and now tells us that he did so in order that he could use his car to make contact with his agents. Ideologically he is a curious character and not altogether unlikeable."[60]

At 5 p.m. on August 12, 1942, Churchill landed in Moscow after the final 10½-hour overnight stretch on his stripped-out Liberator. General Shaposhnikov, Chief of the Soviet General Staff, and Molotov were waiting on the turf. Several handshakes later, flanked by Averell Harriman, Churchill delivered a characteristic rallying cry. "We are determined," he declaimed, "that whatever our sufferings, whatever our toils, we will continue hand in hand like comrades and brothers until every vestige of the Nazi regime has been beaten into the ground."[61] He was then whisked to villa number seven, his home for the duration of his stay. "Everything," Churchill later recalled of his quarters, "was prepared with totalitarian lavishness." The prime minister marveled at the long table and sideboards groaning "with every delicacy and stimulant that supreme power can command."[62] There were blazing electric lights and, most importantly, plenty of hot water. Churchill immediately demanded a bath, for which he longed "after the length and the heat of the journey."[63]

At 7 p.m. Churchill was taken to the Kremlin for his first meeting with Joseph Stalin. The drive from villa number seven took 30 minutes. "Churchill's agitation was clearly betrayed by his fidgetiness," the Soviet interpreter, Valentin Berezhkov, recalled. "He said there was simply no limit to his joy at being in the heroic city of Moscow. Stalin, by contrast, was very restrained. His face was impassive, as if for him this was a routine meeting."[64] The Soviet leader invited the British delegation to sit down and planted himself in an armchair at the head of the table, with Churchill to his right. The table was spread with cigarettes of various varieties, bottles of water and drinking glasses. In Stalin's place was a carefully chosen assortment of colored pencils which he would gather into a bunch and roll across his palm, apparently as a sort of exercise for his withered hand.[65]

Churchill opened the conversation by enquiring about the current state of the Soviet front with Germany. "I think," Stalin replied, "that Hitler has pumped all he can out of Europe. But we are determined to hold Stalingrad. The Red Army is preparing to launch a major attack north of Moscow in order to draw Nazis away from southern fronts."[66] "Churchill became noticeably gloomier," Berezhkov noticed. It was time for the prime minister to make his confession on the postponement of the second front invasion of France. "The British and American governments did not feel themselves able to undertake a major operation in September," he explained carefully to his Soviet host, "which was the only month in which the weather was to be counted."[67]

Stalin told Churchill that they clearly had different views of war. "A man who was not prepared to take risks could not win a war," he said. "Churchill was forced to agree in principle, but argued that it was senseless to sacrifice troops that would be needed so badly next summer," Berezhkov reported.[68] Stalin disagreed but acknowledged that there was nothing he could do to make the British government change its mind.

Then, taking a sheet of paper from the pile on the table in front of him, Churchill began to outline his alternative strategy. Firstly, he said, the British and Americans would drive the Nazis out of Africa with Operation "Torch." Then he sketched a crocodile in the shape of Europe, with its jaws opened towards Great Britain. The hard snout, he explained, was the heavily defended coast of France. Rather than invade there, he wanted to attack Hitler in what he called "the soft underbelly of Europe," the Adriatic and the Balkans. Stalin questioned him curtly but politely. At 10:40 p.m., a full three hours and 40 minutes later, this first encounter came to a close.

Churchill believed he was making progress and wrote confidently to Roosevelt the next day about the ebb and flow of the meeting: "This all ended cordially and I expect I shall establish a solid and sincere relationship with this man and convince him of our ardent desire to get into battle heavily and speedily to the best advantage."[69] "He knows the worst," Churchill wrote to his cabinet colleagues in London, "and we parted in an atmosphere of goodwill."[70]

Stalin liked to work at night, as did Churchill. The second meeting was scheduled for 11 p.m. Churchill's optimism of the morning was crushed as Stalin's mood now changed from reserved politeness to formal hostility. He opened the meeting by handing Churchill an *aide-mémoire* which was immediately translated and accused the British of reneging on their commitment to the second front. "It will be readily understood that the British government's refusal to open a second front in Europe in 1942 delivers a blow in morale to the Soviet people, which had hoped that the second front would be opened, complicates the position of the Red Army and injures the plans of the Soviet High Command."[71] Churchill said that he would reply in writing but warned Stalin that "we have made up our minds upon the course to be pursued and that reproaches were vain."[72]

Stalin became vicious. He accused the British not just of breaking promises but of cowardice. "You British are afraid of fighting. You should not think the Germans are supermen. You will have to fight sooner or later. You cannot win a war without fighting."[73] According to Averell Harriman, Stalin was "really insulting." Churchill reacted with eloquent fury. "I have come round Europe in the midst of my troubles—yes, Mr. Stalin, I have my troubles as well as you—hoping to meet the hand of comradeship; and I am bitterly disappointed, I have not that hand."[74] For the next five minutes Churchill spoke, according to one of the American delegation, "in the most lucid, dramatic, forceful way I have ever heard anybody speak," so much so that both interpreters failed to take notes. Only Alexander Cadogan had noted the prime minister's words. "Have you told him this?" Churchill asked angrily of the interpreter. Cadogan eventually began to try and read out his notes, but Stalin raised his hand and began to laugh. "Your words are not important," he said, "what is vital is the spirit."[75]

General Brooke, who had arrived a day late, accompanied Churchill to this meeting and was not taken in by Stalin's parting compliment. "It was very interesting meeting him, and I was much impressed by his astuteness, and his crafty cleverness. He is a realist, with little flattery about him, and not looking for much flattery either," Brooke noted. "The two leaders, Churchill and Stalin, are poles apart as human beings, and I cannot see a friendship between them such as exists between Roosevelt and Winston. Stalin is a realist if ever there was one, facts only count with him, plans, hypothesis, future possibilities mean little to him. Winston, on the other hand, never seems anxious to face an unpleasantness until forced to do so. He appealed to sentiments in Stalin which do not I think exist there."[76]

Churchill was shocked by Stalin's behavior and, on the way back to villa number seven, told his staff that he would leave Moscow the next morning. Cadogan was surprised by the depth of his reaction: "He was like a bull in the ring maddened by the pricks of the picadors. He declared that he really did not know what he was supposed to be doing here."[77]

The next day Stalin, in his good cop, bad cop routine, sent over an invitation for dinner at the Kremlin. Churchill put aside the emotion of the night before and accepted. At 9 p.m. he found himself guest of honor at a grand banquet in the sumptuous Catherine Hall in the Kremlin Palace. "From the beginning vodka flowed freely and one's glass kept being filled up. The tables groaned under every description of hors d'oeuvres and fish etc," Brooke reported.[78] Within five minutes an unending series of toasts was proposed, which "went on continuously." As the dinner progressed Stalin "was quite lively, walking around the table to click glasses with various people he was proposing the health of. He is an outstanding man, that there is no doubt about, but not an attractive one," Brooke judged. "He has got an unpleasantly cold, crafty, dead face, and whenever I look at him I can imagine his sending off people to their doom without ever turning a hair."[79]

Churchill had begun the evening puffing nervously on his cigar and "frequently resorted to cognac" according to Berezhkov.[80] However, as the evening progressed he, like Stalin, livened up, the one sore point being the Soviet leader's choice of toasts. "The only foreigner Stalin honored was President Roosevelt," Berezhkov recalled. "Churchill was plainly offended, but swallowed the pill in silence."[81] Despite that, the dinner appeared to make amends for the contretemps of the day before.

During the dinner Churchill referred to Stalin as "a peasant whom he could handle."[82] Air Marshal Arthur Tedder, one of the British delegation, was instantly alarmed as he was sure that microphones were planted everywhere in the Kremlin. "*Méfiez-vous*," he scribbled on a menu-card and passed it to Churchill. Later, when the party returned to the British quarters, the prime minister was warned that bugs were all around. At this he addressed the walls very loudly: "We will soon deal with that. The Russians, I have been told, are not human beings at all. They are lower in the scale of nature than the orangutan. Now then, let them take that down and translate it into Russian."[83]

Churchill spent the fourth and final night *à deux* with Stalin. At 5:30 a.m. on August 16 he boarded his plane for Tehran, the first leg of the return to London. "PM was somewhat late and no wonder!" Brooke exclaimed. "He went to see Stalin for final visit at 7 p.m. and remained with him till 3 a.m.!! He had no time for bed and after a bath came straight to the aerodrome. He arrived with Molotov. The band played the 'International,' 'God save the

King,' and the 'Star Spangled Banner'; during which period we all stood to attention and saluted!"[84]

On his return to London, a city ravaged by Hitler's bombers, Churchill consoled himself with the thought that he had at least forged a personal relationship with the man who was now bearing the brunt of the fight against the Nazi leader. "On the whole I am definitely encouraged by my visit to Moscow," he wrote to Roosevelt. "I am sure that the disappointing news I brought could not have been imparted except by me personally without leading to really serious drifting apart. It was my duty to go. Now they know the worst, and having made their protest are entirely friendly."[85]

In Germany Joseph Goebbels was making his own acerbic assessment of the Allied *tête-à-tête*. "They are trying to make a world sensation out of it, and since the published communiqué contains no substance, probably because the conference didn't reach any tangible resolutions, they are trying to create an impression through bombastically reported details," he noted. The evil genius of Nazi propaganda sneered: "In the whole of British history an English prime minister has never been treated more degradingly."[86]

CHAPTER NINE

August 19, 1942–April 9, 1943

The Channel, August 19, 1942. As dawn broke five thousand troops, mainly Canadian with some British, were preparing for a daring raid. Operation "Jubilee" was meant to lay the groundwork for the cross-Channel invasion proper envisaged for the following year. It was a fiasco. Over one thousand men lost their lives during the 65-mile crossing to the French port of Dieppe and in the bloody battles that ensued. Nearly two thousand prisoners were taken and an assortment of Allied military hardware was left abandoned for the Germans to examine. The Germans lost 345 men; four were taken prisoner and brought back to Great Britain, the operation's only prize.

As the battles raged into the night, Churchill slept aboard a converted army ambulance in Cairo. He awoke full of energy at 6 a.m. on August 20 and bathed in the sea. It was a brief moment of pleasure before the bad news came through. While he carried on with an inspection of British forces at Alam Halfa, Hitler and Goebbels were discussing the events of the previous night. "The Führer is firmly convinced that the British prime minister instigated the western venture under direct pressure from Stalin," noted Goebbels.[1]

The interpretation made sense; was Dieppe a sop to Stalin's clamor for a second front? Thoughts of the two men aroused one of Hitler's favorite themes, the contrast in his enemies. "Compared with Churchill, Stalin is a gigantic figure," he remarked. "Churchill has nothing to show for his life's work except a few books and clever speeches in parliament. Stalin on the other hand has without doubt—leaving aside the question of what principle he was serving—reorganized a state of 170 million people and prepared it for a massive armed conflict." Hitler concluded with the different punishments he would inflict upon his opponents at the final day of judgment: "If Stalin ever fell into my hands, I would probably spare him and perhaps exile him to some spa; Churchill and Roosevelt would be hanged."[2]

Four days later, August 24, Clementine and Randolph Churchill waited to greet the prime minister as he landed at Lyneham aerodrome after his historic and exhausting expedition. That day Hitler's fourteenth *Panzer* Corps began advancing on the strategically important Stalingrad tractor works. As the city exploded into another vicious round of fighting, an argument was brewing at Hitler's steamy HQ. At the midday conference Franz Halder suggested that the Ninth Army, fighting in Rzhev, should be permitted to withdraw and regroup along a shorter line. "You always come here with the same proposal, that of withdrawal," Hitler exclaimed. "I expect commanders to be as tough as the fighting troops."[3]

"I am tough enough, my Führer," Halder replied in raised tones, "but out there brave men and young officers are falling in thousands simply because their commanders are not allowed to make the only reasonable decision and have their hands tied behind their backs."[4] "Hitler recoiled," Walther Warlimont observed, and "fixed Halder with a long malevolent stare."[5] In a hoarse and furious voice he replied: "Colonel-General Halder, how dare you use language like that to me! Do you think you can teach me what a man at the front is thinking? What do you know about what goes on at the front?" With his gaze still fixed, Hitler continued yelling: "I won't stand for that! It's outrageous!"[6]

By August 27 things had not improved. Gerhard Engel reported that, whenever bad news arrived from the eastern front, Hitler "gets angrier with every sentence."[7] In London milder arguments were intruding. Churchill was worried at American proposals to dilute Operation "Torch," both in terms of the number of troops and its physical breadth. "A bold, audacious bid for a bloodless victory at the outset may win a very great prize," he cabled Roosevelt. "I feel that a note must be struck now of irrevocable decision and superhuman energy to execute it."[8]

In Moscow Stalin was enjoying more civilized and harmonious relations with his generals than his aggravated German adversary. General Georgy

Zhukov had been summoned to the Kremlin. Over tea and sandwiches in Stalin's office, he was informed that he was to be promoted to Deputy Supreme Commander-in-Chief. Stalin told him that General Kirill Moskalenko's First Guards Army, the 66th Army and the 24th Army were all being sent to reinforce Stalingrad. "You prepare everything for Moskalenko's army to strike a counterblow on September 2 and under its cover marshal the 24th and 66th armies in the forming up positions," Stalin instructed. "Rush these two armies into action immediately, otherwise we'll lose Stalingrad."[9] Zhukov was under no illusions about the importance of his mission. "With the fall of Stalingrad the enemy command would be able to cut off the south of the country from the center," he recalled. "The Supreme Command was sending to Stalingrad all that it was possible to send."[10]

In the north African desert the conflict was also reaching the boiling point. Erwin Rommel, for the moment Hitler's favored general, had launched his new offensive. Cairo was the goal, but the British knew of his plans through Enigma decrypts. Three German fuel ships had been sunk as a result. "Rommel has begun the attack for which we have been preparing," Churchill cabled to both Stalin and Roosevelt, "an important battle may now be fought."[11] This time the British were prepared.

From his Vinnitsa headquarters, Hitler informed Halder of his plans for Stalingrad. "The entire male population must be eliminated, since Stalingrad with its one million uniformly communist inhabitants is extremely dangerous."[12] Later that evening the Führer was full of bile, talking of his British enemy. "Churchill's visit to Moscow has done him a lot of harm, not only in the eyes of the Labour Party but also in those of the Conservatives," he announced. "It was the most futile stupidity he could have committed, and on his return he was greeted with a most marked frigidity. He has pleased no one."[13]

On the morning of September 4 Allied plans for Operation "Torch" were confirmed. "I am directing all preparations to proceed," Roosevelt cabled to London. "We should settle this whole thing with finality at once."[14] Churchill replied the next day. "We agree to the military layout as you propose it," he wrote. "Hurrah!" Roosevelt responded immediately.[15] With equal gusto Churchill sealed this cheery series of cables. "Okay," he replied, "full blast."[16] The main invasion was to take place at Casablanca and Oran, with a supporting attack at Algiers. Churchill had wanted a larger landing at Algiers in order to be able to drive more quickly into Tunisia and Rommel's rear; but, though there had been compromises, he was satisfied with the scale and thrust of the final plan.

On September 7 tempers at Hitler's headquarters were fraying. That evening General Alfred Jodl returned for a meeting at Stalino with the commander of the Caucasus front, Field Marshal Wilhelm List. Jodl had only bad news. He explained that List was now unable to push the Soviets into retreat over the mountains and the only option left was a final attempt to advance on the Caspian Sea and Grozny. Hitler flew into a rage, but Jodl stood his ground and a shouting match ensued. Eventually Hitler stalked out of the hut refusing to shake Jodl's hand. "I'll be glad when I can take off this detestable uniform and trample on it," he confided to one of his adjutants before he retired that night.[17]

The row reverberated through the coming days. Warlimont, who had missed the argument, was keenly aware of the aftermath. "The entire existence and work of the headquarters seemed paralyzed. Hitler shut himself up in his sunless blockhouse and apparently only left it after dark," he recalled.[18] Conferences, which had once taken place in the Map Room, now only occurred in Hitler's own hut. "The atmosphere was glacial."[19] During the *Blitzkrieg* and the dizzying success of the campaign against France Hitler had shared his meals in the mess at headquarters. That would never happen again. He also ordered that a dozen typists be sent from the Reichstag to take minutes at every military discussion so that his words could never again be twisted. On arrival the typists took an oath of allegiance to Hitler himself. "The mood here is terrible," Engel complained. "The Führer can see no end in sight in Russia, since none of the goals of summer 1942 have been reached."[20] Two days later Hitler sacked the beleaguered List.

In Washington Henry Morgenthau visited the White House and asked Roosevelt if he saw any "rosy spots" in the current situation. "No, but I don't see any very dark spots either," he replied. "I have said all along that if the Russians can hold on until the fifteenth we are all right, and I think they are going to."[21] Roosevelt could not yet know how events were swinging the Allies' way.

On September 13, just 24 hours after Field Marshal Friedrich Paulus had visited Hitler at the Werewolf to discuss the situation in Stalingrad, Stalin summoned his own Stalingrad commanders to the Kremlin. At 10 p.m. Zhukov was welcomed into the leader's office. Even while shaking hands Stalin launched into an angry attack on his allies: "While thousands of Soviet people are giving their lives in the struggle against fascism, Churchill is bargaining over a score of Hurricanes. And these Hurricanes of his are junk. Our pilots do not like them."[22] Zhukov and General Aleksandr Vasilevsky presented to Stalin a bold plan for a counterattack against German forces on the Stalingrad front that would require reinforcements and 45 days' preparation. "We must think this plan over again and estimate our resources," Stalin replied, "our main task is to hold Stalingrad."[23]

The crisis was taking its toll. On September 22 Stalin's faithful stenographer, Yury Chadayev, noticed that his boss had grown "thin, his stooped shoulders emphasized how tired he was."[24] At a meeting that day Stalin reported the progress of the current counterattacks. It was a bleak picture, and neither Roosevelt nor Churchill, much to Stalin's continuing ire, seemed to offer any respite. "Our allies understand that we desperately need the second front," Stalin complained, "but they keep ignoring our demands both about opening the second front and about increasing their help to us."[25] Later he offered a Marxist economic interpretation: "Here we can clearly see the predatory character of their monopolies. The only thing they are interested in is to get maximum profit at the expense of quality."[26]

Further evidence to stoke his suspicions surfaced in London that day. Churchill was writing to President Roosevelt. With preparations for Operation "Torch" steaming ahead at full throttle, there were no ships left to provide an escort for the next Arctic convoy, PQ18. "The time has therefore come," the prime minister explained, "to tell Stalin ... that there will be no more PQs till the end of the year, i.e. January."[27] Churchill was under no illusion about the way in which this news would be received in Moscow. "This," he told Roosevelt, was "a formidable moment in Anglo–American–Soviet relations and you and I must be united in any statement made about convoys."[28]

The following day, September 23, German troops fought their way to the center of Stalingrad. The bitter house-to-house combat ground on. On

September 24 Hitler lashed out at the military conference. His ideology and his will were not to be challenged any longer. General Halder was sacked. "After situation conference, farewell by the Führer," Halder noted in his final diary entry, "my nerves are worn out; also his nerves are no longer fresh. We must part." Hitler was determined that the army must now be fully politicized: "Necessity for educating the General Staff in fanatical faith in The Idea."[29] "Hitler," noted Warlimont, "now prepared to follow quite different principles in his command of the army."[30] The Wehrmacht was to be an ideological tool.

A week later Hitler returned to Berlin to present Rommel with his ceremonial baton, a prize for the victories of the summer. It was, noted Hitler's Luftwaffe adjutant, Nicolaus von Below, "a heartfelt reunion."[31] Goebbels was in attendance. "The Führer remains convinced that the Bolsheviks are nearly finished, and he may be right," he noted afterwards. Hitler emphasized that "he could never be made to yield. Our eventual success is certain if we stay on course."[32] It was perhaps the last occasion when Hitler truly believed that victory was possible.

On his return to his headquarters later that night Hitler learned that several Germans had been taken prisoner and had their hands tied behind their backs after a British raid on the Channel island of Sark. He immediately ordered that the prisoners recently captured at Dieppe be manacled as a gesture of revenge.

While Hitler sweated, Churchill's closest colleagues were worrying about the prime minister's health. Anthony Eden had spoken with Max Beaverbrook. "Max described him as 'bowed' and not the man he was," Eden noted. "Brendan also said that W was very 'low' yesterday when Max saw him. I told him that his powers of recuperation were very great and I was not worried," Eden concluded.[33] What Churchill needed was a victory; not just for his own peace of mind but to prove his mettle to his allies.

On October 19, two months after the visit to Moscow, Stalin sent an extraordinary message to Ivan Maisky in London which showed that Churchill was deluding himself in believing that he had made inroads with the Soviet dictator. "We all here in Moscow get the impression that Churchill is aiming at the ultimate defeat of the USSR, in order for them to come to some agreement with Hitler's Germany or Bruning's at the expense of our country," Stalin wrote. "If one does not assume so, it is difficult to explain Churchill's actions in dealing with the following matters: the second front in Europe; arms deliveries for the USSR, which are progressively being cut down, despite growth of production in England," he continued.[34] Stalin even accused Churchill of keeping Rudolf Hess in reserve as a negotiating tool.[35]

At 8 p.m. London time on October 23 the deserts of north Africa exploded with General Bernard Montgomery's massive offensive along a 40-mile front. He had over 150,000 Allied soldiers at his disposal, along with five hundred fighter aircraft and hundreds of pieces of artillery. Hitler's commander, General Georg Stumme, promptly died of a heart attack. Rommel was recalled to take over. "It may be the turning point of the war," Alan Brooke wrote as he waited for news in London, "or it may mean nothing. If it fails I don't quite know how I shall bear it."[36]

On November 1, as British forces drove back the *Afrika Korps*, Hitler refused to see the writing on the wall. "There was not the smallest recognition," Warlimont recalled, "least of all on the part of Hitler himself, that the war had now definitely turned against Germany, although this was clear to all the world."[37] Three days later the British victory at El Alamein was assured. Twenty-four hours earlier Hitler had ordered that Rommel "not yield a step," unaware that his favorite general had only 24 tanks left and had already begun to retreat. Now he was forced to approve the withdrawal. He immediately saw the political consequences of the change in military fortune: "It would be wrong to think," he told a surprised Goebbels, "that we can expect any hope of an internal disintegration in England."[38] "The Führer is very agitated," Goebbels confided in his diary, "and hardly dares to look at the north African theater of war which is now largely overshadowing even the events in Stalingrad and the Caucasus."[39]

While this black mood descended over Führer Headquarters, Churchill was celebrating. A telegram from General Harold Alexander, the overall commander in north Africa, stated that more than nine thousand enemy prisoners had been captured and hundreds of Italian and German tanks lay in smoking heaps in the desert. "I want to ring the bells all over England," he replied to Alexander, "for the first time this war."[40]

171

Four days later, November 8, the Americans and British launched Operation "Torch." 107,000 men, assisted by 370 merchant ships and 300 warships, landed on beaches along the coast of French north Africa. Though there was some initial resistance from Vichyite French forces, particularly by shore batteries in Casablanca, it became clear within hours that opposition to the landings was dying away and they would proceed unopposed. The American commander on the spot, General Mark Clark, began immediate negotiations with the senior French military and civilian leaders in the region.

As the Allied armada arrived, Hitler was traveling to Munich to give a speech to the party to celebrate the anniversary of the 1923 beer hall *putsch*. An urgent message was brought to him en route informing him of the "Torch" landings. Engel was surprised by his low-key response. "Perhaps we should have given them more incentive," he simply said of the Vichy French.[41] He gave orders for the defense of Tunis and his train continued to Munich.

Over in London, Churchill was thinking of his son, Randolph, who was among the British troops fighting at Algiers. "Well here we are," he wrote to his father at 10 a.m., "safe and sound in the anchorage to the west of Algiers."[42] The prime minister then had lunch with the Free French leader, General Charles de Gaulle. At Roosevelt's insistence, de Gaulle had been kept in the dark about the invasion; the American view was that he could only get in the way of the deal they were hoping to make with the former Vichy collaborators. Churchill, who had a tempestuous relationship with de Gaulle but never ceased to admire him, had felt guilty and expected a prickly conversation. However, de Gaulle behaved immaculately and told Churchill that he wished the landings well.

Back in Munich Hitler gave his evening speech to the party faithful. "We are facing the same opponents whom we have had before," he declared, "the international Jew … the half-Jew Roosevelt, and his Jewish brain trust, to the Jewry of purest water in Marxist-Bolshevik Russia. We shall not fall. Consequently others must fall."[43]

Two days later the Allies were in control of 1,300 miles of the north African coast. At the Mansion House in London Churchill was giving a speech at the Lord Mayor's luncheon. "I have never promised anything but blood, tears, toil and sweat," he proclaimed. "Now, however, we have a new experience. We have victory—a remarkable and definite victory. The bright gleam has caught the helmets of our soldiers, and warmed and cheered all our hearts." He ended with a note of caution, warning his audience: "Now this is not the end. It is not even the beginning of the end. But it is, perhaps, the end of the beginning."[44] The next day Hitler ordered German forces to occupy all of France.

The Americans and British began to squeeze Rommel's forces in Africa from both east and west. It was the first taste of battle for American ground troops in the war against Hitler. Their inexperience and the caution of their commanders meant that it would take a further five months of slog through the winter mud of Tunisia before they drove the Germans from the African continent. But the odds were overwhelmingly in the Allies' favor and the final outcome was never in doubt. Stalingrad was very different; it still hung on a knife-edge.

As the river Volga began to freeze over, making the evacuation of wounded soldiers near impossible, Zhukov inspected the state of the Red Army in the Stalingrad region. He cabled Stalin: "Supplies and delivery of munitions poor. Yeremenko must have immediately 100 tons of anti-freeze without which advance of the mechanized units impossible." Zhukov concluded that the 51st and 57th armies "require winter wear and ammunition urgently."[45]

Two days later, November 13, Hitler was in Obersalzberg. Nicolaus von Below had not spoken privately with him for some time. "He was depressed," Below observed, "the western powers—the USA and Britain—had begun to take an active role. He judged this to be a very serious development." From his mountaintop hideaway Hitler was now surrounded on all sides by bloody battlegrounds. Below noted that Hitler "hoped there were no new surprises in store on the eastern front, although he suspected that there would be a new Russian offensive at the start of winter."[46]

Hitler's fears were well founded. While he and Below talked, Zhukov arrived at the Kremlin to discuss plans. Stalin, sensing the change in the balance of the war, was in a cheerful mood. Though supplies were somewhat slow in coming, Zhukov estimated that within a week preparations for the counteroffensive would be complete. Operations on the southwestern front would begin on November 19, and along the Stalingrad front 24 hours later. "Stalin listened attentively," Zhukov recalled, "by the way he smoked his pipe, smoothed his moustaches and never intervened even once, we could see that he was pleased."[47] Stalin had at last learned to take advice from his generals, unlike Hitler, whose meddling and final assumption of supreme military command had been the root of so much disaster.

By November 24 Hitler was back at the Wolf's Lair, which he had reverted to in place of the Werewolf. Paulus, the commander of the sixth army in Stalingrad, had now been completely encircled by the Soviet counteroffensive launched four days before. With the temperatures dropping as rapidly as his fuel supply he sought permission to attempt a break-out. Hitler refused. Below noted Hitler's confidence that Paulus and the sixth army could be supplied by air and that the general "would eventually be in a position to fight his way out of the pocket."[48]

While Hitler was sealing the fate of nearly a quarter of a million of his soldiers, Churchill was thinking of future campaigns. Once north Africa was won, he wanted to push on towards Italy and the "soft underbelly" of Europe. But, at this stage, his anxiety to support Stalin was propelling him to argue that the second front invasion of France must also take place in 1943. It was now the Americans, once so keen for it to happen in the summer of 1942 when the task force was to be mainly British, who appeared to be dragging their feet; the War Department in Washington was refusing to assist in the build-up of forces beyond 427,000 men, far too few in Churchill's view. He wrote to Roosevelt suggesting a top-level meeting to hurry things up.

Three days later, November 27, in the crisp autumn air the president and his confidante, Daisy Suckley, were enjoying a picnic at Top Cottage, the simple house Roosevelt had designed for himself on the grounds of his Hyde Park estate. Over a lunch of hot buttered toast, cold turkey and salad they had what Daisy described in her diary as a "momentous" conversation.[49]

Roosevelt had agreed with Churchill's request for a summit and wanted to include Stalin; he was hoping that they could all meet up in Khartoum.

"The thought of F. taking that trip frightens me," Daisy noted, "I know I shall do some good old-fashioned praying while he's gone!" As well as agreeing military strategy, Roosevelt wanted to set about reordering the postwar world. "The reason for the trip," he told Daisy, "is that there is a growing demand for a definite statement about our intentions after the war."[50] At the top of Roosevelt's agenda was an end to European-style imperialism. Daisy noted the president's plans: "self-determination to be worked out for colonies over a period of years, in the way it was done for the Philippines. I wonder how the Empire owners will take to it," Daisy asked herself.[51]

Roosevelt also explained his idea for an international police force of four great nations, the United States, the Soviet Union, Great Britain and China, which would ensure that war could never break out again. All other nations would have to disarm while these four benevolent policemen oversaw the new peace. "I think Stalin will understand my plan better than Churchill," Roosevelt told Daisy.[52] Indeed the president already saw the prime minister as the chief obstacle. Six months before he had told a State Department official: "We will have more trouble with Great Britain after the war than we are having with Germany now."[53]

Over in London Churchill was celebrating his 68th birthday. At the 5:30 p.m. meeting of the War Cabinet he read to his colleagues a message he had received from Stalin three days before agreeing to the proposed conference and expressing thanks for the resumption of Arctic convoys which Churchill had now ordered. This, Churchill explained, "made it all the more incumbent upon us to start a second front in Europe in 1943."[54]

Five days later Stalin changed his mind, saying that he could not leave Moscow "even for a single day as it is just now that the major operations of our winter campaign are getting under way, nor will they be relaxed in January."[55] He followed up with a further message to both his allies stating that the strategic issue was simple and hardly required discussion: "I feel confident that no time is being wasted, that the promise to open a second front in Europe, which you, Mr. President, and Mr. Churchill gave for 1942 or the spring of 1943 at the latest will be kept."[56]

By New Year's Eve 1942 the force of British, American and Russian arms was turning the war on its head. The three warlords were thinking of the future, both military and political; but the decisive battle of Stalingrad was still to reach its conclusion. Hitler had rejected a second plea by Paulus to attempt a break-out of the deadly encirclement by Soviet troops. In Moscow Stalin was now confident. Yury Chadayev noted the great enthusiasm with which he spoke to his colleagues. "Hitler turned out to be too short-sighted!" he exclaimed. "Our people celebrate the New Year in victorious mood and the German nation celebrates it with fear—the lowest of all the human feelings!"[57]

Hitler opened 1943 by offering his nation victory or destruction; there was to be no compromise. "In his address to the German people he states with great clarity that in this war it is a question of the existence or non-existence of the whole German people," Goebbels noted, "the Führer declares that the old society is on the point of collapse, and that we can therefore look to the future calmly and trust in victory. War must be waged with extreme fanaticism."[58]

The previous night a spectacular Allied air raid had devastated Düsseldorf. "The English air raids have had the effect that in this war the German people have finally learned to hate," Goebbels concluded.[59] However, some of those who lived with the Führer day to day noticed a chill creeping in. "I had the impression that Hitler knew that a war against both the Russians and the Americans—a war on two fronts," Below recalled, "could not be won."[60]

On January 7 Goebbels described the dire prospects faced by the sixth army. "At the end of the day about 240,000 men are encircled there, and we have the greatest difficulties imaginable in providing them with essential munitions and food," he observed. "There are no more teams of horses, since they've been slaughtered and devoured. They have nothing more for heating: the last railway sleepers have all been burnt. Reinforcements cannot be sent because the nearest German fighting unit is 120 to 150 km distant from Stalingrad."[61] The next day the Soviet General Konstantin Rossokovsky sent von Paulus surrender terms. They were turned down.

At the White House, after dinner, Daisy Suckley and Roosevelt discussed the president's impending trip to north Africa. Dates for the conference, albeit without Stalin, had finally been agreed and Churchill and Roosevelt were now set to meet in Casablanca. "I think F. has mixed feelings about it—the adventure of it—seeing all he will see, etc. On the other hand it is a long trip, with definite risks—but one can't and mustn't think of that," Daisy noted. "He is going because he feels he must go."[62] In Moscow Stalin was discussing his allies with Molotov. "The only thing they do is talk, nothing else," Molotov said. "You're right, all talk and no action,"[63] replied Stalin. The next day, as Roosevelt departed from Washington, the Soviet leader remarked: "He is very generous with his promises, but in reality, encouraging us, he only misleads the Soviet Union."[64]

Hours later General Rossokovsky ordered the beginning of Operation "Ring," the bombardment of the encircled German troops of the sixth army at Stalingrad. Outside Leningrad, Operation "Spark" was launched. Soviet troops, from behind German lines, finally carved a pathway through to the city, the first signs of relief to a siege that had brought starvation and death to thousands upon thousands of Soviet civilians. The corridor was a perilous but symbolic supply route, a shaft of light for those clinging on to life.

On January 14 Roosevelt, codename "Admiral Q," arrived in Casablanca after a short stopover in the British colony of Gambia. He described in a letter to Daisy Suckley his arrival on the USS *Memphis* at its capital, Bathurst: "Went ashore at 7 a.m., a drive through the tiny town to the airport 22 miles out. A paved but very bumpy road, through crowds of semi-dressed natives—thatched huts—great poverty and emaciation—on the whole I am glad the U.S. is not a great Colonial power," he quipped.[65]

Churchill had already reached Casablanca and over the coming ten days the two men and their military staffs coordinated the next stage of the war. The American chiefs wanted to make the cross-Channel invasion of France the priority, though the slow progress through Tunisia meant that it was unlikely to begin until August or September. Churchill had by now swung back in favor of putting the "soft underbelly" strategy ahead of everything else. He believed that he was winning the battle of strategies and cabled his colleagues in London: "President Roosevelt is strongly in favour of the Mediterranean being given prime place."[66] The conference agreed that, when Africa was clear of Germans, the next step would be Sicily, Operation "Husky," with the second front against France following behind at an unspecified date. The only dilemma was how to tell Stalin.

On January 22, as Roosevelt and Churchill prepared for their final session, Hitler rejected a desperate plea from Paulus in Stalingrad for permission to surrender. Goebbels was at Führer HQ for a brief visit: "The Führer describes the situation in Stalingrad, which is positively desperate. There are still about 200,000 men encircled, and there is not the slightest hope that we can send relief," Goebbels noted, "with sunken eyes they stare total elimination in the face."[67] Hitler put all the blame on his allies: "They simply did not want to fight, and at the first Russian advance, as soon as they came within sight of a tank, they either dropped their weapons and ran off, or raised their hands in surrender."[68] Their conversation was interrupted by a telephone call with the latest news. "It is very serious. The Bolsheviks have broken six kilometers into the German line. Our troops are no longer capable of putting up any resistance; they are so physically broken by hunger and cold that they can no longer fight," Goebbels reported.[69]

Two days later, January 24, Roosevelt concluded the Casablanca conference with a statement allowing his enemies no quarter: "The elimination of German, Japanese and Italian war power means the unconditional surrender by Germany, Italy and Japan."[70] "Wherever you look, there are nothing but defeats," Goebbels noted the same day.[71]

A week later, on January 31, 1943, the tide of the war turned for good. In Moscow, protected from the freezing January winds inside his Kremlin apartments, Stalin read the text of a newsflash. As his eyes moved over the page a broad grin spread across his pock-marked face. Paulus had surrendered to Soviet troops at Stalingrad. "After this war," Hitler told Goebbels, "there will be no victors and vanquished, but only the survivors and the dead." "That evening Hitler seemed a tired old man," his secretary, Traudl Junge, recalled. "I don't remember what we talked about, but a dismal image has stayed in my memory, rather like visiting a bleak graveyard in the November rain."[72]

Churchill was stopping off to review British forces in Cyprus. "Winston was grand," wrote the commanding officer of the Fourth Hussars to his wife just after the prime minister had left. "He radiated confidence and made a most stirring speech to the troops."[73] Churchill no longer had to make bold promises that Britain would survive the Nazi onslaught. With

Stalingrad won he knew that victory was certain. "This is indeed a wonderful achievement," he cabled Stalin as soon as he landed in Cairo later that day.[74]

In Washington Roosevelt read through two telegrams from Moscow. One reported that tens of thousands of Nazi prisoners had been taken at Stalingrad. The other contained a familiar rumble of anger about the vagueness on the second front. "Assuming that your decisions on Germany are designed to defeat her by opening a second front in Europe in 1943," Stalin wrote, "I should be grateful if you would inform me of the concrete operations planned and of their timing."[75] American troops were still bogged down in the Tunisian mud; the prospects of mounting a cross-Channel invasion in 1943 were receding even beyond the autumn. There was dissension in the air.

At noon the following day, as the final remnants of the sixth army walked into Soviet captivity, Hitler was at his daily military conference discussing the disaster. "The Führer is deeply depressed, seeks errors and omissions everywhere," Engel noted.[76] Hitler said his men should have "shot it out using their last bullet on themselves. When you think that a woman's got sufficient pride just because someone's made a few insulting comments to go and lock herself in and shoot herself right off, then I've got no respect for a soldier who's afraid to do that but would rather be taken prisoner." As for Paulus, Hitler said: "That's the last field marshal I promote in this war."[77]

A few days later Hitler summoned a gathering of *Reichsleiter* and *Gauleiter*. He told them: "The Soviet power which faces us in the east is without parallel in the whole world. One would have to look to events far back in history to find any kind of comparison, perhaps to the attacks of Genghis Khan or of Attila the Hun." However, there was one powerful beacon of light, the contradictions within the enemy coalition: "Arguments between England and the USA are growing to ever larger dimensions," he assured his audience. "The Axis powers know what they want and have no profound political differences of interest, whereas in the enemy camp this is not at all the case. One can scarcely conceive of greater differences than those between England and the USA, or between England and the USA on the one side and the Soviet Union on the other."[78]

Then, on April 9, 1943, a grisly discovery in the forests of Katyn in eastern Poland ignited a process which would put enormous strain on the differences within his opponents which Hitler had identified as his secret weapon.

Deep in the Polish sector which the Russians had occupied during the Nazi–Soviet Pact, the Germans stumbled across a series of mass graves. The bodies of over 20,000 Polish officers and political prisoners taken into captivity during the Russian occupation would eventually be dug from the ground. Most of the victims had been shot in the head at close range. The Germans claimed that the massacres had been carried out by Stalin's NKVD in the spring of 1940. Goebbels' propaganda machine immediately seized on one of its biggest opportunities of the war. "I ensure that the Polish mass graves are visited by neutral journalists from Berlin. I also make sure Polish intellectuals are taken there," Goebbels noted. "They should be made to see with their own eyes what awaits them if they are ever actually granted their oft-cherished wish, that the Germans would be beaten by the Bolsheviks."[79]

The discovery not only made world headlines; it would bring into sharp relief the very different shape of the postwar world that each of the three Allied warlords had in their sights.

CHAPTER TEN

April 13–September 7, 1943

On April 13, 1943, the Germans, in a flurry of anti-Soviet propaganda, announced their ghastly find at Katyn. While he launched his propaganda strike, Hitler was also planning his next assault on Soviet forces, Operation "Citadel," a massive attack on the Red Army centered around the Kursk salient. It was intended to put the setback of Stalingrad into the shade. "This attack is of decisive importance," Hitler announced in an order of April 15. "It must be a quick and conclusive success. The victory of Kursk must shine like a beacon to the world."[1]

The Katyn revelations were soon spreading their poison among Hitler's opponents. Moscow immediately denied any responsibility and pointed the finger at the Nazis. The London-based Polish government in exile, the government for which Britain had first gone to war in 1939, was sure that the Russians were guilty. After Operation "Barbarossa," the London Poles had swallowed their bitterness at the Nazi–Soviet pact and signed a friendship treaty with the Soviet Union for the sake of Allied unity against Hitler. Since then, they had frequently asked the Russians, including Stalin himself, what had happened to the 20,000 Polish officers and political prisoners who had gone missing while the pact was in place. The answers were never satisfactory, Stalin airily suggesting that they would turn up in due course. Now they had—murdered.

At 1:30 p.m. on April 15, General Wladyslaw Sikorski, the prime minister of the Polish government in exile, and Count Edward Raczynski, the Polish ambassador in London, arrived at 10 Downing Street for lunch with Churchill and Sir Alexander Cadogan. Churchill understood their anger but warned them not to do or say anything that might provoke Stalin. He knew that the long-term future of Poland depended on building a relationship with its powerful Russian neighbor; the London Poles must steel themselves to get along with Stalin, however distasteful that might be. Even so, Churchill was under no illusions that the Soviets were almost certainly responsible for the murders. "Alas," he admitted to Sikorski and Raczynski, "the German revelations are probably true. The Bolsheviks can be very cruel."[2]

The next day, acting counter to the advice Churchill had dispensed, Sikorski issued a public protest about the Katyn massacre and made it clear that the London Poles believed the Soviet government was to blame. He demanded an investigation by the International Red Cross.

Stalin, far from being embarrassed by the revelations, now smelled opportunity. Even though he had signed a friendship treaty with Sikorski, he thoroughly disliked his government, which was determined to restore Poland's freedom and independence. Instead Stalin wanted any future Polish government to be subservient to Russia. Five days later, April 21, he wrote identical angry letters to his allies, Churchill and Roosevelt: "The anti-Soviet slander campaign, launched by the German fascists in connection with the Polish officers whom they themselves murdered in the Smolensk area, in German-occupied territory, was immediately seized upon by the Sikorski government and is being fanned in every way by the Polish official press." Stalin then stated that relations between Moscow and the London Poles were finished: "These circumstances compel the Soviet government to consider that the present Polish government, having descended to collusion with the Hitler government, has, in practice, severed its relations of alliance with the USSR and adopted a hostile attitude to the Soviet Union."[3]

Churchill found himself caught between his loyalty to the London Poles and his wish to preserve good relations with Stalin. He told the Soviet leader that Britain would vigorously oppose any "investigation" by the International Red Cross or any other body in any territory under German authority. "Such investigation would be a fraud, and its conclusions reached by terrorism," Churchill wrote.[4] He also pleaded with Stalin not to break with the London Poles as this could only help Hitler: "German propaganda has produced this story precisely in order to make a rift in the ranks of the United Nations."[5]

Stalin was unyielding; the unexpected turn of events was suiting his purposes too well. On May 4 he wrote to Churchill reiterating the break in relations: "Since the Poles continued their anti-Soviet smear campaign without any opposition in London, the patience of the Soviet government could not have been expected to be infinite."[6] That day, while Hitler was in Munich finalizing the details of Operation "Citadel," Churchill set off from London for Washington. Little could he have imagined that the shock of Katyn was being followed by a deceitful maneuver at the White House that was taking place behind his back.

Roosevelt had sensed the tension Katyn was creating with Stalin. He had also seen that the victory at Stalingrad had changed the whole nature of the war. Victory was certain; only its timing was in doubt. In these changed circumstances he secretly decided it was time that he, rather than Churchill, became the prime mover in the relationship with the Soviet leader.

From the moment Russia had been forced into war by Hitler's invasion, Roosevelt had instinctively understood that he and Stalin would emerge as the two leaders of the two future powers upon whom long-term peace would depend. He also knew that culturally and politically they were a world apart. He himself was an American patrician, brought up in luxury and educated at Harvard; Stalin a cobbler's son, beaten by his father, his university the prison cells where he and his fellow revolutionaries had drawn up their blueprint for the future. In the 1930s Roosevelt was the optimistic face of America's new deal; Stalin the paranoid orchestrator of Russia's terror.

Despite these differences Roosevelt believed that it was possible to persuade Stalin, by using the carrot not the stick, to adopt a more democratic view of the world. He had once put it like this: "I think if I give Stalin everything I possibly can, and ask nothing from him in return, *noblesse oblige*, he won't try to annex anything and will work with me for a world of peace and democracy."[7] Roosevelt also believed that he, an American progressive, rather than anyone tainted by old-fashioned European imperialism, such as Churchill, was the man to do it.

On May 5, 1943, while Churchill was sailing across the Atlantic in the

Queen Mary, Roosevelt wrote Stalin a private letter asking him for a one-to-one meeting in which he intended to apply what he considered to be his unique personal charms to the Soviet dictator. "I want to get away from the difficulties of large staff conferences or the red tape of diplomatic conversations. Therefore, the simplest and most practical method that I can think of would be an informal and completely simple visit for a few days between you and me," he proposed. The only problem was where to meet: "Africa is almost out of the question in summer and Khartoum is British territory. Iceland I do not like because for both you and me it involves rather risky flights and, in addition, would make it, quite frankly, difficult not to invite Prime Minister Churchill at the same time. Therefore, I suggest that we could meet either on your side or my side of the Bering Straits. Such a point would be about three days from Washington and I think about two days from Moscow if the weather is good. That means that you could always get back to Moscow in two days in an emergency."[8] Churchill was to be cut out.

So special was this letter that Roosevelt charged Joseph Davies, who had been his ambassador to the Soviet Union in the 1930s, with the task of flying to Moscow and delivering it personally to Stalin by hand. Before Davies left Roosevelt told him: "Three is a crowd and we can arrange for the Big Three to get together thereafter. Churchill will understand. I will take care of that."[9]

Five days later in Berlin, hours after the remnants of Erwin Rommel's army finally submitted to the Allies in Tunisia, Hitler was talking with Joseph Goebbels. It was May 10, 1943, three years since that shattering day when Churchill had become British prime minister and Hitler had unleashed his *Blitzkrieg*. "The Führer enthuses about the times we will have when the war is finally over. He is looking forward to nothing more than exchanging his gray suit for a brown one, being able to visit the theater and cinema again," Goebbels noted after their talk. Hitler told him he dreamt of having nothing more to do with generals: "All generals lie. All generals are disloyal. All generals are against the national socialists, all generals are reactionary." Goebbels came away with a certain relief that Hitler's charms would not be lost to everyone in his circle: "From all this I can conclude that the Führer's long isolation in the HQ has not in any way made him misanthropic. He just doesn't want to see any more generals, that's all."[10]

While the two Nazis talked, in Washington some of Roosevelt's colleagues were awaiting Churchill's arrival with their customary suspicion. As always military strategy was at the top of the agenda and Henry Stimson and the American chiefs were determined that the second front invasion of France remained the priority. Stimson was having his customary doubts about the constancy and resolve of the president: "I fear it will be the same story over again. The man from London will arrive with a program of further expansion in the eastern Mediterranean and will have his way with our Chief," he complained, "and the careful and deliberate plans of our staff will be overridden."[11]

The next day Churchill arrived in the United States on the *Queen Mary*. As he traveled to the White House, Joseph Davies was landing in Moscow. Roosevelt's reception of the prime minister was as warm as ever. "Churchill arrived," Stimson grumbled, "with a huge military party, evidently equipped for war on us, determined to get his own way. I dread his eloquent and vigorous presentation of cases that are themselves unstable and dramatic rather than military." The conference, codenamed Trident, was under way.[12]

Roosevelt and Churchill spent a happy weekend at Shangri-La, the president's retreat in Maryland (now called Camp David). Not a word of the private letter to Stalin was breathed. By May 15 they were back in Washington debating strategy and agreeing on the wholesale bombing of German cities. Suddenly extraordinary news came from Moscow: Stalin had announced that the Comintern, the international wing of his regime that had for years agitated among the Communist parties abroad for world revolution, was to be dissolved. Churchill and Roosevelt publicly welcomed the gesture, although the British secret services, MI5 and MI6, judged that it meant very little. "Soviet espionage continued at least until 1943 and almost certainly throughout the war," was their later verdict, even if "the Russian Embassy was meticulously correct in its public behaviour."[13]

Four days later, May 19, the grand chamber of the United States Congress fell silent as Churchill rose to speak. "Any discord or lassitude among the Allies will give Germany and Japan the power to confront us with new and hideous facts," he warned. "We have surmounted many serious dangers but there is one grave danger which will go along with us at the end; that is the dragging out of the war at enormous expense, until the democracies are tired or bored or split."[14] Roosevelt was the first to applaud. In Moscow Joseph Davies stepped out of the brilliant May sunshine and into the long, dark corridors of the Kremlin. The letter was handed over to Stalin.

At Obersalzberg the Führer contemplated recent events. Allied forces had smashed his troops in Tunis, Allied air attacks were devastating the Ruhr, his health was not good and Goebbels had reported that residents of the Ruhr were angry that the regime was not protecting them. To top it all, he had been forced to postpone Operation "Citadel." Even so speculation on arguments among his enemies provided its usual comfort. "There is a tug of war going on between Churchill and Roosevelt," he told Goebbels. "Obviously Churchill favors the European war over the east Asia war, whereas Roosevelt would prefer things the other way around."[15]

For once Hitler was wrong. At the evening meeting at the White House, Churchill and Roosevelt agreed a date for the second front. The invasion of France, now codenamed "Roundhammer," was set for May 1, 1944.

At 1:19 p.m. the next day a tense meeting opened at the Berghof. Hitler and his Supreme Command had gathered to discuss Italy, which was now under threat as the Allies headed towards Sicily. "A certain section in that country has consistently sabotaged this war from the beginning," he told his generals.[16]

On May 26 the conference in Washington ended with an act of trust. Churchill cabled London details of a final conversation with Roosevelt: "Tube Alloys. Conversation with the president entirely satisfactory."[17] Britain and America had agreed to share information on the war's greatest secret, the development of the atom bomb. Later that morning Churchill left Washington for Newfoundland on the first leg of his journey home to London.

While the prime minister settled back and reflected on a friendly and productive conference, Stalin's reply to Roosevelt's private letter arrived in Washington. "As I do not know how events will develop on the Soviet–German front in June, I shall not be able to leave Moscow during that month," Stalin wrote. "I therefore suggest holding the meeting in July or August."[18] Stalin had taken the bait. Roosevelt was moving towards center stage. The next day he gave Stimson an example of how he was now getting the better of the prime minister: "Churchill had acted like a spoiled boy the last morning when he refused to give up on one of the points—Sardinia," Roosevelt explained to his war secretary. "He persisted and persisted." The president said that he finally had to tell Churchill that he "wasn't interested in the matter" and that "he had better shut up."[19]

Despite Stalin's satisfactory reply, Roosevelt's secret plan was about to hit a snag. On June 4 he and Churchill finally steeled themselves to give Stalin the embarrassing news that the cross-Channel invasion had been postponed until May 1944. A week later came Stalin's predictably furious reply. "Now, in May 1943, you and Mr. Churchill have decided to postpone the Anglo-American invasion of Western Europe until the spring of 1944. In other words, the opening of the second front in western Europe, previously postponed from 1942 till 1943, is now being put off again," Stalin railed. He concluded with chilling formality that the Soviet government could not agree with the decision as it "was adopted without its participation and without any attempt at a joint discussion of this highly important matter and which may gravely affect the subsequent course of the war."[20]

Churchill, who was working that day at Downing Street, was worried by Stalin's hostile reaction. By now he had also had gotten wind of Roosevelt's secret letter to the Soviet leader, though he did not know what was in it. The next day he tried to flush Roosevelt out: "All this makes me anxious to know anything you care to tell me about your letter sent to him by Mr. Davis [sic] and the answer which has been received from him," Churchill wrote. "I will of course come anywhere you wish to a rendezvous and I am practising every day with my pistol to make head against the mosquitoes. Nevertheless, I once again beg you to consider Scapa Flow, which is safe, secret and quite agreeable in July and August."[21] Churchill still had no idea that he was to be excluded.

Hitler, who was spending these early summer days at the Berghof, was increasingly preoccupied with the Allied threat to Italy. On June 14 Nicolaus von Below returned to his Führer's side. While Churchill and his wife, Clementine, paid one of their few wartime visits to Chartwell, their home in Kent, Hitler and Below strolled near the Berghof. "He spoke primarily of his fears about Italy. He judged the American moves as very weighty and said that our forces were insufficient," Below recalled. "If the Luftwaffe did not succeed in driving off the American landings in Sicily then he had no hope for the entire Italian peninsula."[22]

Three days later an incident in London showed that Stalin's reining- in of international communist activities was a sham. Douglas Springhall, National Organiser of the Communist Party of Great Britain, was arrested and charged with spying for the Soviet Union. He was ordered to face a public trial. The Foreign Office was horrified at the thought of such a spectacle at a time when relations with Soviet Russia were "pretty tricky."[23] Guy Liddell recorded in his diary the contradictions of wartime coalitions: "Unfortunately the law is somewhat inadequate in the case of a man who is spying on behalf of an ally. It seems unlikely that Springhall will get more than 9 months to 2 years."[24] Springhall's subsequent confession led to further arrests, including one Captain Ormend Uren of the Special Operations Executive. As a precaution MI5 set about preparing a list of all Communist Party members employed by the government.

On Thursday, June 24 Roosevelt decided he had to come clean. Churchill was hosting a small dinner party at Downing Street; the guest of honor was Averell Harriman, the president's special envoy, who had just returned from the United States. At midnight the other guests departed. It was then that Harriman, trying to use every ounce of his considerable charm and tact to assuage the blow, dropped Roosevelt's bombshell. He explained that the president was in the process of setting up a meeting with Stalin, to which Churchill would not be invited. Roosevelt believed that there would be "great value" in a more intimate meeting with the Soviet leader which would be more comparable to Churchill's own trip to Moscow the previous summer rather than a full-scale summit. Harriman added that there was a great difference between British and American public opinion; a "three-cornered meeting on British soil," which Churchill had hoped to arrange, would give the impression that the British had been "the broker in the transaction" and this was something the Americans needed to avoid.[25]

"I have never had a better opportunity to be direct and frank," Harriman reported to Roosevelt afterwards. "It is obvious that he accepted the sincerity of my statements even though he did not always agree with them."[26] However, Harriman clearly saw that Churchill was hurt. "There is no doubt in my mind as to his sincere desire and determination to back you up in anything that you finally decide to do," he warned the president, "although I must emphasize his disappointment if he is not present."[27]

In fact, Churchill was devastated. Despite the late hour, he immediately summoned Anthony Eden to No. 10 as soon as Harriman had departed. "Found him considerably upset by a message from F.D.R. that his projected meeting will be *à deux*," Eden recorded.[28] The wound was not just the deceit perpetrated by the ally he took to be a friend but who now turned out to have kept him in the dark for six full weeks; there was something much bigger at stake, the blow to British power. Churchill could see that Roosevelt, in trying to hijack the relationship with Stalin, was taking the first steps to an American–Russian partnership which would determine the future world. The next day, June 25, controlling his emotions as best he could, he wrote one of the most important letters of his life.

First he disputed the implication that what Roosevelt was proposing had any similarities to his own visit to Moscow: "Averell told me last night of your wish for a meeting with U. J. in Alaska *à deux*. The whole world is expecting and all our side are desiring a meeting of the three great powers at which not only the political chiefs, but the military staffs would be present in order to plan the future war moves and, of course, search for the foundations of postwar settlement. It would seem a pity to draw U. J. 7,000 miles from Moscow for anything less than this." Then Churchill hinted at the depth of the personal betrayal: "You must excuse me expressing myself with all the frankness that our friendship and the gravity of the issue warrant. I do not underrate the use that enemy propaganda would make of a meeting between the heads of Soviet Russia and the United States at this juncture with the British Commonwealth and Empire excluded. It would be serious and vexatious, and many would be bewildered and alarmed thereby."[29]

While Churchill and Roosevelt were enduring the first real crisis of their friendship, the row with Stalin over the second front was smoldering on. Churchill had written to explain the sense behind its postponement while also sympathizing with Stalin's disappointment. On the same day he was forced to swallow Roosevelt's bitter pill, he received a vituperative and threatening message from the Soviet leader: "You say that you 'quite understand' my disappointment," wrote Stalin. "I must tell you that the point here is not just the disappointment of the Soviet government, but the preservation of its confidence in its allies, a confidence which is being subjected to severe stress. It goes without saying that the Soviet government cannot put up with such disregard of the most vital Soviet interests in the war against the common enemy."[30]

Two days later, Churchill privately remarked: "I am getting rather tired of these repeated scoldings considering that they have never been actuated by anything but cold-blooded self-interest and total disdain of our lives and fortunes."[31] He replied, for once putting tact to one side: "Although until 22 June 1941 we British were left alone to face the worst that Nazi Germany could do to us, I instantly began aiding Soviet Russia to the best of our limited means from the moment that she was herself attacked by Hitler. I am satisfied that I have done everything in human power to help you. Therefore the reproaches which you now cast upon your western allies leave me unmoved."[32]

Hitler was still at the Berghof, telling Goebbels of the new weapon which would transform the war: "The Führer is expecting great things from the bombardment of the English mother country, especially of London, by rocket guns launched from the channel coast," Goebbels said, referring to the V1 and V2 rockets which were being developed. "This weapon will be in use in the last quarter of this year. So we just have to have some patience."[33] Hitler knew that he needed his wonder weapon as so much else was going wrong. "It is very unfortunate that at the same time as the air war rages against us with undiminished intensity, our U-boats are condemned to inactivity," he told Goebbels, "the conjunction of events appears almost fateful. The old saying is true, troubles seldom come singly."[34]

On June 28 Churchill received Roosevelt's reply to his heartfelt letter of four days before. It was a flat lie. "I did not suggest to U. J. that we meet alone but he told Davies that he assumed (a) that we would meet alone and (b) that he agreed that we should not bring staffs to what would be a preliminary meeting," Roosevelt wrote. He then tried to smooth over the edges: "Of course, you and I are completely frank in matters of this kind and I agree with you that later in the autumn we should most definitely have a full dress meeting with the Russians. That is why I think of a visit with Stalin as a preparatory talk on what you rightly call a lower level."[35]

Churchill could see that there had been an irrevocable shift in the balance of his relationship with the president. However, it was the relationship in which he had invested all his hopes and he had no intention of changing course now. After the war he once told John Colville: "No lover ever studied every whim of his mistress as I did those of President Roosevelt."[36] He realized that it would do no good to go on feeling betrayed. What mattered now was to win the president back, and he saw an opportunity. With great adroitness he replied the same day, suggesting that the proposed meeting à deux might be a brilliant idea after all as a means of defusing Stalin's anger over the second front: "If you and Uncle J. can fix a meeting together I should no longer deprecate it. On the contrary in view of his attitude I think it important that this contact should be established."[37] Though the wound lingered within, Churchill had neatly placed himself in line with the president while subtly reminding him that Stalin remained the outsider.

Beyond the unpleasant letters, Stalin had also withdrawn the Soviet ambassadors from both Washington and London to Moscow and replaced them with virtual unknowns. He appeared to be registering his protest in a very public manner. Churchill was puzzled by the vehemence with which Stalin was insisting on the invasion of France and opposing extended Allied operations in the Mediterranean. He discussed it with Averell Harriman, who reported back to Roosevelt on July 5: "Churchill's only explanation is that Stalin wants us to become involved in western Europe to avoid our entry in the Balkans."[38] Churchill had begun to suspect Stalin of using military strategy to keep the Americans and British away from what the Soviet leader was eyeing up as his postwar domain.

That day such political speculations were interrupted by the thunder of battle. At 1:10 a.m. on July 5, 1943, the eastern front exploded in one of the most dramatic confrontations of the war so far. Yet this sudden barrage along the Kursk salient was not the beginnings of Operation "Citadel" that Hitler had confirmed just four days before from the Wolf's Lair; the artillery bombardment was a pre-emptive Russian strike on the Germans. The British had been feeding Moscow information, based on Enigma decrypts, of every detail of the planned German attack. Russian firepower and the brainpower of the codebreakers at Bletchley Park had succeeded in striking a stunning blow against Hitler's forces. Two hours after the Russian bombardment had begun, the Germans launched a premature and more stunted version of Operation "Citadel." By 4 a.m. a brutal fight for Kursk was raging. It was to become the biggest tank battle in history.

In Gibraltar that day a Liberator aircraft was shot down while taking off. All on board were killed, among them the leader of the London Poles, General Sikorski. The dreadful news soon reached the Foreign Office. Cadogan was preparing to wind down for the evening when the telephone rang. "This is a great blow," he noted, "there's no-one to take his place."[39]

The coming weeks brought mounting reverses for Hitler. On July 24, 1943, while still resident at his concrete bunker in the forests of Rastenberg, he was told that a meeting of the Fascist Grand Council in Rome had stripped Benito Mussolini of his powers. They requested that King Victor Emmanuel assume command of the armed forces. On the eastern front, the battle of Kursk was ending in burning *Panzers* and defeat. Stalin spent that afternoon rejoicing in the success of his armies. "Eternal glory to the heroes who fell on the battlefield in the struggle for the liberty and honor of our Motherland," he announced merrily to Generals Alexei Antonov and Sergei Shtemenko when they visited him at his Kremlin office.[40] So full of confidence was he that he did not even ask to be given the usual summary report of military events.[41]

Just 24 hours later Mussolini's overthrow was confirmed. Marshal Pietro Badoglio had taken over control of the Italian government and Mussolini was arrested. "Hitler swore. He was furious about the secession of Italy and Mussolini's mishap," Traudl Junge noted, "he was monosyllabic and absent-minded." "So Mussolini is weaker than I thought," he raged, "I was giving him my personal support, and now he's fallen. But we could never rely on the Italians, and I think we'll win the victory better alone than with such irresponsible allies. They've cost us more in prestige and real setbacks than any success they brought us was worth."[42] At the evening briefing Hitler was "yelling for revenge and retribution."[43] It was 9:30 p.m. "We must be clear," he screeched, "it's pure treachery!"[44]

While Hitler fumed, Goebbels was becoming increasingly disturbed about growing discontent among the German people. "The correspondence I've received has caused me considerable concern. The letters contain much criticism. More than half of them are anonymous," Goebbels noted, "above all they ask why the Führer has not visited the areas affected by air raids, why Göring is nowhere to be seen, and above all why the Führer doesn't speak to the German people to explain the present situation. I consider it essential for the Führer to do this," Goebbels continued.[45]

Churchill was watching a film with his wife and daughters at Chequers. The evening's entertainment was interrupted by a telephone call from the BBC Monitoring Service. He was informed of events in Italy. The film was stopped immediately, the lights were turned on in the Long Gallery and the prime minister announced the good news.[46]

On August 8 Churchill was traveling from Britain to Canada for a further meeting with Roosevelt, the first since that happy conference in May when deceit was still to be revealed. That day Stalin, despite the promise he had sent via Joseph Davies, finally turned down the president's proposal for the meeting *à deux*. He gave as his reason the pressures of war: "I hope you will appreciate that in these circumstances I cannot start on a distant journey. I am very sorry about this, but circumstances, as you know, are stronger than people, and so we must bow to them."[47] However, when Churchill arrived in Quebec two days later, there was a further letter waiting from the Soviet leader agreeing the importance of a meeting at some future date to thrash out strategy. Once again he apologized for his inability to travel: "I am, unfortunately, unable to lose touch with the front even for one week."[48] Since Stalin hardly ever visited the front, disliking the sound and smell of battle, it was difficult to tell what was true and what was bluff.

For Churchill the priority now was to repair any residual fissures in his relationship with Roosevelt. On the evening of his arrival in Quebec, he discussed the president with the Canadian prime minister, Mackenzie King. King noted Churchill's reasons for wanting a long stay with Roosevelt: "I can do more with the president by not pressing too hard at once. He is a fine fellow. Very strong in his views, but he comes around." King also noted how much Churchill believed the future depended on the personal transatlantic relationship: "More important than anything else was keeping the president's goodwill. He said that he really is the one friend that we have, and we must keep in as close touch as we can with him."[49]

That same day, Hitler let Goebbels into a secret plan he had concocted. "In the strictest confidence, and one to one, the Führer tells me what his real intentions are with regard to Italy in the event of an emergency," Goebbels noted excitedly. "He intends to arrest the King, take Badoglio and his entire rabble into custody, free Il Duce and give him and fascism the opportu nity to get back in the saddle and form a strong regime." Hitler said that he would attack London with "unprecedented force" in the coming months. He then demonstrated again his respect for his one-time ally and present enemy, Joseph Stalin. "He sees him as a true genius of the Asian continent," Goebbels recorded. However, peace with Stalin remained impossible. "What we want, Stalin needs, and what Stalin will not give up, we need," Hitler said. "At all events the eastern front itself must be brought back under control, no matter what it costs."[50]

Three days later Churchill had crossed the Canadian border to spend a few days alone with Roosevelt at Hyde Park. The sylvan late summer setting overlooking the broad reach of the Hudson was a tranquil backdrop to dispel the hiccups of the summer and reinvigorate friendship. Churchill took every advantage of the opportunity to play the suitor. Daisy Suckley noted her impression: "Churchill adores the P., loves him, as a man, looks up to him, defers to him, leans on him." Roosevelt meanwhile was "relaxed and seemingly cheerful in the midst of the deepest problems." Churchill, she wrote, "is a strange looking little man. Fat and round, his clothes bunched up on him, practically no hair on his head, he wore a huge ten-gallon hat."[51]

The difficulties of coalition could not be made to vanish into the late summer haze. Churchill gave Roosevelt a Foreign Office analysis of the Katyn massacre. It made for unsettling reading, arguing that the accumulation of evidence threw "serious doubt on Russian disclaimers of responsibility for the massacre. We have in fact perforce used the good name of England like the murderers used the little conifers to cover up a massacre; and, in view of the immense importance of an appearance of Allied unity and of the heroic resistance of Russia to Germany, few will think that any other course would have been wise or right."[52] As would be proved decades later, Stalin's secret police were guilty. For the sake of beating Hitler, silence had to be observed.

The combination of the Katyn revelation and his suspicions over Stalin's motives on military strategy were provoking in Churchill some discomforting reflections. Up until now both he and Roosevelt had handled the Soviet leader with kid gloves, but Churchill was becoming split-minded. On one side, he believed that he, as one great man, could deal with Stalin, another great man, by face-to-face diplomacy. On the other, Katyn and Stalin's threatening messages had reawakened all his old fears of the Bolsheviks. A nightmare was forming: that Stalin was at the head of a Russian colossus which would dictate military strategy in such a way that it would devour much of Europe and create a new, totalitarian empire before the British and Americans could get there.

On August 14, the Quebec Conference—codenamed "Quadrant"—got under way. Its main purpose was to finalize British and American military plans for the coming year. The Americans insisted that the invasion of France, set for May 1, 1944, should have priority over everything else. Churchill, however, wanted equal weight to be given to his alternative strategy, essentially the "soft underbelly" idea he had drawn for Stalin the year before.

The Allies were only three weeks away from invading mainland Italy. Churchill argued that they should also be seeking to recapture Nazi-held Greek islands in the eastern Mediterranean like Rhodes and Leros. This, he believed, would enable pressure to be put on Turkey to enter the war on the Allies' side. There was then the potential for driving towards Germany through the Balkans and the northern Adriatic.

Churchill knew that his alternative strategy, if it worked, could also have the political effect of allowing the British and Americans into the Balkans and much of eastern Europe before the Russians. After the war, in his memoirs, he denied that at this stage, when Hitler was still far from beaten, he, in the same way as he suspected Stalin, was trying to bend Allied military strategy to his political purposes. In Churchill's case these were to keep Communism out of as much of Europe as possible and protect British interests in the eastern Mediterranean. Certainly at Quebec he argued for his alternative strategy on purely military grounds. Indeed he knew it would be fatal to suggest to Roosevelt that they should try to beat the Russians to the Balkans and eastern Europe for political reasons. To the president that would smack of the sort of European imperialism he was determined to get rid of.

At dinner on August 24, however, the last night of the conference, one chance remark revealed Churchill's inner thoughts. He and Roosevelt had received that day an angry letter from Stalin complaining about the surrender terms for Italy and the fact that he had not been kept fully informed. "The prime minister and the president were particularly annoyed because they had attempted to keep him fully informed," Averell Harriman noted. After dinner Harriman and Churchill continued talking. Churchill confessed to Harriman that he foresaw "bloody consequences in the future." "Stalin is an unnatural man," he said, "there will be grave troubles."[53]

In the end Churchill did not get his way at Quebec. It was agreed that the invasion of France in May 1944, now codenamed Operation "Overlord," held sway above everything else. The invasion of Italy would still go ahead and other operations in the Mediterranean could be mounted, but only on condition that they did not detract from the build-up of forces and equipment for the cross-Channel invasion. There was an element of fudge in the agreement which contained the seeds of almighty rows ahead.

On September 1, Winston Churchill was still encamped in the White House. Roosevelt had been run ragged by his attentive visitor. "I'm nearly dead," he told his Secretary for Labor, Frances Perkins. "I have to talk to the PM all night, and he gets bright ideas in the middle of the night and comes pattering down the hall to my bedroom in his bare feet."[54] The ideas were often good, Roosevelt admitted, "but I have to have my sleep."[55] The suitor could at times become over-amorous. However, news came that day to cheer everyone up: the new Italian government had agreed to surrender to the Allies.

The only problem was that British and American troops had not yet arrived in the Italian mainland to accept that surrender and occupy the country. Two days later, September 3, the invasion at last began. At 4 a.m. General Bernard Montgomery led his troops across the Straits of Messina and landed at Reggio Calabria. The Germans prepared to move south to push the British and Americans back into the sea; a brutal and bloody slog lay ahead.

Another war was also re-emerging: the mind war of the three warlords, who remained united against Hitler but at increasing risk from the rifts that lay within.

CHAPTER ELEVEN

September 8–November 28, 1943

Adolf Hitler stepped out on to the runway near the Wolf's Lair. The air was cold and darkness was closing in on the surrounding forest. He had just returned from Army Group South's headquarters at Zaporozhye. His trip that morning was the last time that he would set foot in territory captured from the Soviet Union. It was September 8, 1943 and the atmosphere at his headquarters was ominous. Reports had drifted in, confirmed by a broadcast on the BBC, of the capitulation of the Italian army. Angry and anxious in equal measure, the Führer ordered a top-level crisis meeting.

As Hitler contemplated late into the night his lone fight against the Allied warlords, Roosevelt was struggling to stay awake. The dinner plates had just been cleared away and the president had retreated to his bedroom in the White House. Seated opposite him was Churchill, still on his apparently interminable visit, happily puffing away on a cigar and talking enthusiastically about the victorious path that lay ahead. "The PM's sleeping arrangements have now become quite promiscuous," Alexander Cadogan recorded. "He talks with the president till 2 a.m. and consequently spends a large part of the day hurling himself violently in and out of bed, bathing at unsuitable moments and rushing up and down corridors in his dressing-gown." Late in the evening a telegram was delivered to the presidential suite; the main wave of Allied troops was landing at Salerno.

Churchill's excitement was Vesuvian. He was investing a huge amount in the Italian campaign; if the British and Americans could race up Italy, the door to Germany might swing open. Yet as the prime minister continued with his energetic discussion of victory, MI5 reported that communist agitators—controlled directly from Moscow—were planning a huge protest against him on his return to London. The counter-intelligence chief, Guy Liddell, noted in his diary that "steps are being taken to meet this situation" but evidence of Soviet-inspired espionage and political agitation continued to mount.[1]

As Churchill kept a tight grip on his precious American ally, Stalin was preparing to send a telegram to Washington. "The time suggested by the prime minister for the meeting of our three representatives—early October—would be suitable," he wrote, "as to the place, I suggest Moscow."[2] A three-power conference of foreign ministers was confirmed, to be followed by a meeting of the Big Three themselves, though the date and place were left open. Certainly for this initial gathering Stalin had no intention that it should be anywhere but his own capital; he also knew that the tremendous Russian achievements in battle would leave his allies little option but to comply.

Two days later, September 10, Joseph Goebbels was at Führer HQ with the express purpose of encouraging Hitler to make a broadcast to the nation. As soon as the Führer rose, he called his propaganda chief to his quarters for talks. "Once again it's clear that in times of crisis the Führer excels himself physically, spiritually and mentally," Goebbels recorded. "He has had scarcely two hours sleep, but looks as if he's just got back from holiday." Hitler spoke of the "rotten" business in Italy. "The resistance offered by the Italian troops is largely symbolic," he judged, "the Italians do not want to fight and are glad when they can give up their weapons, even better when they can sell them."[3]

Goebbels, like many others in Germany, was wondering if there was any way out of the two-front war that seemed to be so rapidly closing in. "Can we do anything about Stalin in the long or short term?" he asked. Hitler shook his head. "In general the Führer is of the opinion that we could rather do business with the English than with the Soviets," he noted. "He says that at a certain point the English will see reason." However, Hitler conceded that "the crisis in the enemy camp is not yet ripe for us to exploit." Goebbels was uncomfortably aware, as he confided to his diary, of the precarious state of the *Reich*: "Germany has never won a war on two fronts; in the long run we will not be strong enough for it in this case."[4] He did, however, succeed in what he came for. Hitler agreed to speak to the nation. The speech was mainly a diatribe against the treachery that had been perpetrated against Mussolini, on whom he bestowed much praise and support.[5]

While German troops moved in to occupy Rome, Churchill's Foreign Secretary, Anthony Eden, was in London. Eden was feeling low. "Felt depressed and not very well all day, partly, I think, because of exasperating difficulty of trying to do business with Winston over the Atlantic," he noted. Eden was particularly annoyed that Roosevelt had agreed "with alacrity" to Moscow being the venue for the foreign secretaries' conference, to which he would be the British representative. "I am most anxious for good relations with US," Eden wrote, "but I don't like subservience to them and I am sure that this only lays up trouble for us in the future. We are giving the impression, which they are only too ready by nature to endorse, that militarily all the achievements are theirs and W., by prolonging his stay in Washington, strengthens that impression."[6]

On September 12 Churchill, accompanied by Clementine and his youngest daughter Mary, dropped in at Hyde Park en route from Washington to Halifax, Nova Scotia, the departure point for the final leg of their journey home. It was the Churchills' 35th wedding anniversary and an enjoyable occasion for all. Roosevelt accompanied them to their train. "It was a beautiful moonlit night," Daisy Suckley wrote. "God bless you," Churchill said, leaning into Roosevelt's car. "I'll be over with you, next spring," Roosevelt replied before the prime minister boarded.[7] It was a promise the president never kept; not once during the entire course of the most celebrated transatlantic relationship in history did he ever visit Britain.

That day Hitler's forces engineered a dramatic coup, Operation "Oak." A group of 90 German commandos, led by Otto Skorzeny, landed by glider in the Abruzzi mountains. They fought off an Italian force nearly triple their size and made off in the night with their prize: Benito Mussolini. The deposed Italian leader, having been held under arrest by forces loyal to the King, was then spirited away to Germany and to the Wolf's Lair.

As Mussolini was flown into Hitler's embrace and Churchill's train lumbered through the night towards Halifax, Lord Moran, who was traveling with him, was thinking back on the news of the day. The Allied landings in Salerno "did not prove to be a walk-over," he wrote, "the Germans had launched a strong counter-attack and the situation was very uncertain." "These things always seem to happen," Churchill told him, "when I am with the president." "Poor Winston," Moran recorded, "he had been so anxious to convince Roosevelt that the invasion of Italy would yield a bountiful harvest at no great cost." In these early hours of the landings, the outcome remained uncertain.

The next day, Churchill woke in a foul mood. "The PM is as irritable as if he had a big speech hanging over him. I have never seen him more on edge during a battle," Moran noted, "three 'bloodys' bespattered his conversation and twice, when I was with him, he lost his temper with his servant, shouting at him in a painful way."[8] Churchill was worried that General Harold Alexander, the overall commander, was not achieving the agreed foothold in Italy. "Has any news come in?" he demanded continually throughout the morning. The reports, however, were not good. "There is a dreadful hint," Moran recorded, "that we might be driven into the sea."[9]

Churchill set about his correspondence. "Ask for anything you want," he cabled Alexander, "and I will make allocation of necessary supplies, with highest priority irrespective of every other consideration."[10] Churchill also sent a thank-you note to the president, his ill temper vanishing in the warmth of the amicable relations he was working so hard to preserve. "My dear Franklin," he wrote, "we have all greatly enjoyed this trip, and I cannot tell you what a pleasure it has been to me, to Clemmie and to Mary to receive your charming hospitality at the White House and at Hyde Park. You know how I treasure the friendship with which you have honoured me and how profoundly I feel that we might together do something really fine and lasting for our two countries and, through them, for the future of all."[11] In the coming weeks that friendship would collide with huge strategic and political differences.

On September 20 Churchill arrived back in London to hear mixed news of the progress of the war in the Mediterranean. After the Italian surrender, small British task forces had tried to take control of Greek islands in the Aegean which had been held by Italian garrisons. In Kos, Leros and Samos they had, for the moment, succeeded; but German forces had clung on to

Rhodes, which was a vital stepping stone in Churchill's alternative strategy. It was a bad blow; he continued to believe that if the Allies could capture and hold Rhodes, it would send a signal to Turkey, which lay just a few miles of water away, that it was safe to enter the war. With Turkey on-side, and the Greek islands in the Aegean and eastern Mediterranean acting as forward bases, the gateway to the Balkans, eastern Europe and Germany itself would be open.

Churchill had been away from home for nearly six weeks, a long time to leave his nation without a leader. He awoke the following day in what his doctor described as "high spirits" and set off for the House of Commons where he was due to give an account of his recent trip and of developments in the campaign against Hitler.[12] He was above all keen to rebut suggestions that the protracted negotiations over surrender terms with the Italian government had led to a pointless delay in the Salerno landings and allowed the Nazis to regroup and inflict large loss of life.

"This criticism is as ill founded in fact as it is wounding to those who are bereaved," he told his parliamentary colleagues.[13] Churchill also claimed that he had been assured in America that "the war was being well managed."[14] The speech lasted two and a half hours, with an hour-long lunch break in the middle, and was well received. Even his doubters in America had good words to say. Henry Stimson and his wife Mabel read the text and were impressed. "It is a fine presentation," Stimson noted, "he is rapidly getting to the position where he speaks as an historian for both sides of the Atlantic on the revelation of current strategy and results."[15]

While Churchill robustly fought his corner, Hitler was retreating into depression. Benito Mussolini had been staying at the Wolf's Lair for nine days since his dramatic rescue. "I've never seen the Führer so disappointed in Mussolini as today. The Führer realizes now that Italy was not a great power, is not a great power now and will never be a great power. As a people and as a nation Italy has given up," Goebbels noted. The eastern front too, was providing much to worry about. "The troops [Stalin] is currently sending into the field are in very bad shape and are very badly armed. However, there are so many of them that our troops find it hard to hold firm against them," Goebbels recorded. He asked Hitler if he had considered negotiating with Churchill, or whether on principle he would refuse. "In politics, in questions of personality, there are no principles," Hitler replied, "negotiations with Churchill would be fruitless, since he is too deeply entangled in contradictory opinions, and moreover he listens to hatred rather than to reason." Hitler explained that he would more readily negotiate with Stalin, but this would not be fruitful either as the Soviet leader would never agree to Hitler's demands in the east. "We have to settle with one side or the other," Goebbels told him, "the *Reich* has never won a war on two fronts. So we have to see some way of getting out of this two-front war."[16]

In Washington, six days after loading Churchill with praise for his speech to Parliament, Henry Stimson was fuming at him. Despite the Quebec agreement, Churchill appeared to be pursuing his own agenda in the Aegean and eastern Mediterranean. Kos had been recaptured by the Nazis and the British contingent in Leros was under threat. The prime minister had unilaterally sent in forces to recover the position and try to wrest control of the whole of the Dodecanese.

The Americans believed that this was both drawing off forces from Italy and endangering the build-up for the invasion of France. "They have begun an attack on the Dodecanese over in the Aegean Sea and as usual have done it without having the sufficient force," Stimson noted. Churchill had tried to persuade Roosevelt to send General George Marshall to meet him in the Mediterranean where, Stimson drily recorded, he was "evidently hoping he could bull the thing through when he got there. The president I am very glad to see stood up finely against it and turned the prime minister down flat on the subject of drawing any more upon our supplies in Italy." Stimson wrote with pleasure: "The prime minister had to yield. He did it with a bad grace and with almost a childish squawk but he yielded and the lesson will be salutary."[17] Stimson's final judgment was wrong; Churchill had no intention of giving up.

While being rebuffed by his ally to the west, Churchill was coming under pressure from his other to the east to restart Arctic convoys. That day he wrote to Roosevelt: "I hope something may be possible between now and OVERLORD." That day the *Tirpitz*, the Nazi warship that had been menacing Allied shipping, was crippled by six British midget submarines. The decision to resume convoys was made easier.

Soviet agitation for more help from its allies persisted in both London and Washington. On October 5 John Winant, the American ambassador in London, was reflecting on public statements by the Soviet ambassador to the United States, Konstantin Umansky. These, Winant believed, were part of a scheme, orchestrated by the Soviet Foreign Propaganda Bureau, to whip up pro-Soviet popular opinion in Britain and the United States and therefore "prod" them to undertake policy and action demanded by the USSR.

Winant had recently been to Moscow to help make the arrangements for the forthcoming conference of foreign ministers and had met Stalin. He gave Roosevelt an assessment of the man and his methods: "The Slavic mind does not understand us any more perhaps than we understand them and they do not seem to realize that their relations with us, both now and in the future cannot be built on a sound basis with this type of devious method." Winant told the president: "From my personal talk with Stalin I am convinced that he wants above all to be on a basis of intimacy and frank interchanges with you. On the other hand it should be borne in mind that Stalin does not pretend to understand the ways of our democracies."[18]

Later that day at the White House Roosevelt was looking forward to the meeting with Stalin and Churchill which was being planned for a few weeks after the Moscow conference. He knew that the boundaries and independent status of Poland and the Baltic states were to feature heavily. Roosevelt intended, he explained, to appeal to the Soviet leader "on the grounds of high morality."[19]

Churchill was in a vile mood. Despite his failure to win support from Roosevelt, he was persisting in his campaign for an operation to take Rhodes from the Nazis. The overall Allied commander in the Mediterranean, General Dwight Eisenhower, had sent a telegram in which he refused to countenance further operations against Rhodes, judging it a waste of time and resources: "I consider any material diversion highly prejudicial to the success of Italian operations," he wrote. He implied that Churchill was trying to drag the Allies into a theater of war which would prove a pointless drain: "These operations will probably assume the aspect of a major bitter battle."[20]

Churchill was livid. That afternoon he took it out on his War Cabinet colleagues, making an extraordinary series of statements which brought his ulterior motives into question. Anthony Eden described what happened to his private secretary, Oliver Harvey, who made an instant record in his diary: "The PM spoke for three hours. He talked great nonsense and A.E. was furious. The PM kept saying such things as 'We mustn't weaken Germany too much—we may need her against Russia.'" The Cabinet colleagues were horrified at all this.[21]

Three days later Churchill was still beating the drum for a Rhodes operation. He wrote to Roosevelt: "I am sure that the omission to take Rhodes at this stage and the ignoring of the whole position in the eastern Mediterranean would constitute a cardinal error in strategy." He then pleaded with him for a face-to-face meeting to allow him to argue his case: "I am convinced also that if we were round the table together that this operation could be fitted in to our plan without detriment either to the advance in Italy of which as you know I have always been an advocate, or to the build-up of OVERLORD which I am prepared faithfully to support."[22]

Rhodes was now an obsession. "I am slowly becoming convinced that in his age Winston is becoming less and less balanced! I can control him no more," General Alan Brooke noted. Brooke supported operations in the eastern Mediterranean on purely military grounds. He believed it was a sound tactic for stretching and weakening German forces. While it might lead to the breakthrough to Churchill's "soft underbelly," it would certainly have the long-term effect of diminishing German defenses in western Europe when "Overlord" was launched. However, Churchill's Chief of Staff could not understand why his boss was behaving in such a fanatical way: "He has worked himself into a frenzy of excitement about the Rhodes attack, has magnified its importance so that he can no longer see anything else and has set his heart on capturing this one island even at the expense of endangering his relations with the president and with the Americans." Brooke wearily concluded: "The whole thing is sheer madness, and he is placing himself quite unnecessarily in a very false position! The Americans are already desperately suspicious of him, and this will make matters far worse."[23]

Roosevelt replied firmly, and negatively, to Churchill's telegram 24 hours later. The president also brusquely rejected his suggestion that they get together in north Africa immediately to discuss strategy. "This would be in effect another meeting of the Combined Chiefs of Staff, necessarily involving only a partial representative and in which I cannot participate," Roosevelt wrote. "Frankly, I am not in sympathy with this procedure under the circumstances."[24] The message was crystal clear. Despite it, Churchill had no intention of giving up.

The long-running arguments over Arctic convoys rumbled on. Churchill had offered to sail four convoys via the northern route between November and February. However, aware by now of Stalin's displays of anger when previous commitments had been shelved for sound military reasons, he had taken the precaution of making it clear this could not be construed as a "contract or bargain."

On October 13 an unpleasant letter came back from Moscow to the Foreign Office in London: "I must say I cannot agree to this approach to the matter," Stalin wrote. "The British government's deliveries of munitions and other war cargoes to the USSR cannot be treated other than as an obligation assumed by the British government, in accordance with the terms of a special agreement between our two countries, in relation to the USSR, which for more than two years has borne the tremendous burden of the struggle against Hitler Germany."[25]

Cadogan read the letter and sat on it for 48 hours. At 10:30 a.m. on October 15, he presented it to the prime minister, who was still in bed. "I warned him, before he read it, that he'd lose his temper," Cadogan recorded, "so the result wasn't so bad." Churchill "snorted." "I'll stop convoys," he stated. The Foreign Office believed it was time to take a stand against Stalin's harrying and heavy-handed tactics; it was decided, with Churchill's consent, that the letter should be returned to the Soviet ambassador in London "unread." No reply would be given. "The Soviet machine," Churchill explained to Roosevelt, "is quite convinced that it can get everything by bullying, and I am sure it is a matter of some importance to show that this is not necessarily always true."[26] However, firm stands against Stalin were hardly what Roosevelt was planning with his proposed appeal to Stalin's "higher morality."

Three days later, October 18, the Conference of Foreign Ministers opened in Moscow. Stalin's letter had been returned to Fyodor Gusev, Ivan Maisky's replacement as ambassador in London. "We must, on occasions, treat Stalin rough, and he's well in the wrong on this occasion," Cadogan reasoned, "poor A. is to settle the matter in Moscow."[27] Eden deduced that Stalin simply enjoyed playing the game over convoys and knew full well that his allies were now seriously engaged in the battles against Hitler: "He, of course, understands to the full our contribution to the war; it is a danger to the future that his people don't and now the Americans are making claims to a share in the bomber offensive which is by no means justified, but further dims our glory."

Eden described the unnerving contrasts in his host's appearance: "Joe was friendly enough to me personally, even jovial. But he still has that disconcerting habit of not looking at one as he speaks or shakes hands, a meeting with him would be in all respects a creepy, even a sinister experience if it weren't for his readiness to laugh, when his whole face creases and his little eyes open."[28]

Back in London Churchill was still fighting the battle of strategies: "We received note from PM wishing to swing round the strategy back to the Mediterranean at the expense of the cross-Channel operation," Brooke noted after a meeting with the Chiefs of Staff. "I am in many ways entirely with him, but God knows where that may lead us to as regards clashes with Americans."[29]

A week later Churchill was still at it. Eden had cabled from Moscow that Stalin was continuing to insist his allies must concentrate only on the invasion of France and that the Mediterranean was an irrelevance. Moran recorded Churchill's furious reaction. "When I called at No. 10 this morning I found the PM glowering over a telegram from Eden. His face was glum, his jaw set, misgivings filled his mind. 'Stalin seems obsessed by this bloody second front,' Churchill fumed, 'I can be obstinate too.' 'Damn the fellow,' he muttered angrily."

On October 27 Churchill again pressed Roosevelt for an immediate meeting: "I regard our right to sit together on the movements of our own two forces as fundamental and vital. Hitherto, we have prospered wonderfully, but I now feel that the year 1944 is loaded with danger. Great differences may develop between us and we may take the wrong turning," Churchill warned. As so often, he slipped in some emotional blackmail: "The only hope is the intimacy and friendship which has been established between us and between our high staffs. If that were broken, I should despair of the immediate future."[30] Roosevelt was unimpressed; he was beginning to show that, in his eyes, personal friendship had no place in matters of strategy or politics.

That same day Goebbels was engaged in a fruitful conversation. "Thank God, the Führer is once again in excellent health. It appears to me that the more critical the situation, the stronger and more self-confidently the Führer faces up to it. There is not the slightest sign of weakness in his demeanor," Goebbels noted with relief. "We begin at once with the eastern front. It's a rotten business there at the moment. Even so, the Führer is convinced that he will get it under control."[31]

Goebbels then moved the discussion on to the question which remained dominant: how to disentangle Germany from the war on two fronts. "At present the Führer inclines more to the Soviets, whereas I tend towards the English. Both have advantages and disadvantages," Goebbels reported, claiming that there were whispers in the air: "Secret approaches have been made to us from both sides: from England via a major industrialist and from the Soviets via Ankara and via the Japanese. So far the Führer has not agreed to either of the two attempts at contact, since he considers that we should not get involved in talks when things are going so badly."[32]

"If one were to rank our opponents," Hitler said, "I would say that the United States would be first to lose interest in the European war. The Americans are war-weary, and moreover they have absolutely no inner sympathy for the war in Europe." His admiration for the Soviet leader was increasing all the time. He was, the Führer declared, "the only opponent worth taking seriously."[33]

Over in America anger was mounting against Churchill. He had sent to the Moscow conference a copy of a pessimistic summary by General Alexander of the situation in Italy, which suggested that weapons and manpower, which would otherwise be held in reserve for "Overlord," needed to be thrown at the Italian campaign. This, Churchill argued, might mean a delay in the invasion of France. However, he had failed to include a more optimistic addendum by

Eisenhower which disputed Alexander's assessment. Stimson was furious. "Jerusalem!" he exclaimed, "this made me so angry because … Stalin would not have the counter-comment of Eisenhower. This shows how determined Churchill is with all his lip service to stick a knife into the back of 'Overlord' and I feel more bitterly about it than I ever have before," the American war secretary concluded.[34]

In Moscow, Anthony Eden and his team were just as angry. "The PM is untameable. He cannot leave well alone and he loathes the Russians," Oliver Harvey noted. "He would torpedo A.E.'s conference light-heartedly."[35] Churchill had become isolated within and without his own government.

The next day Stimson discussed Churchill's latest sally with Roosevelt: "The president … intervened to tell me what his views were in regard to the Balkans. He said he could not think of touching the Balkans unless the Russians got to a position in their invasion of Germany where they wanted us to join and act side by side with them." If part of Churchill's motive was to beat Stalin to the Balkans, Roosevelt was going to have nothing to do with it.

In London an MI5 report on the numbers of Communist Party members with access to potentially sensitive information was sent to the War Cabinet. There were "57 known Communists who had access to secret information, in some cases to information of the highest secrecy."[36] These included three personnel on the Anglo-US atomic project, 23 employees of the Ministry of Supply, and eighteen in the army.[37] Every government department, MI5, MI6 and SOE, the Special Operations Executive, was compromised. In a minute to the prime minister, the chairman of the Security Executive, Duff Cooper, advised Churchill that it would be a relatively simple matter to arrange the transfer of all known communists from sensitive and secret government work. "As at present advised, I agree with this," Churchill minuted in reply, and asked the Home Secretary, Herbert Morrison, to investigate.[38]

While Churchill glowered at Chequers and Stalin hosted a sumptuous banquet for his foreign guests on the evening of October 30, Roosevelt was preparing for the long-awaited conference of the Big Three. "He is preparing for a Long Trip—Hopes he won't have to go to Teheran, which is full of disease, and involves a flight over the mountains of up to 15,000 ft. He dreads both things for himself and his whole party," Daisy Suckley noted. However, Tehran it was to be. After an endless stream of intercontinental cables in which the American and Russian leaders horse-traded about who could afford to be further away from their home, Stalin emerged the winner. He would go to Tehran, just a short hop over the Soviet border, and no further.

Daisy Suckley recorded the president's view that Stalin's stickiness was, at root, a display of machismo. "The P. thinks Stalin may be suffering from a sort of inferiority complex, whether for himself or for his country, because he is being so very difficult about this meeting with F.D.R. and is insisting on F.D.R. going most of the way. F.D.R. feels the meeting is of paramount importance and he must make it happen, regardless of the cost to himself," Daisy recorded.[39] There were others gearing up for Tehran. "Urgently need bullet proof glass to complete job," a secret service agent wrote to the head of White House security, as the car that would transport the president through the streets of Tehran was made ready.[40]

On November 4 Roosevelt made it clearer than ever that he was not going to give an inch on strategy to Churchill. Stimson had lunch at the White House and found the president in resolute form. "He volunteered a strong expression of satisfaction with the fact that we had given a sharp rebuff to the attempt to divert forces from Italy to the Aegean," Stimson noted. "He pointed out that the Aegean enterprise, even if successful, got nowhere." Roosevelt then told Stimson of the plans for the Tehran conference. "He gave me a little the impression that he was going to make this journey mainly to realize the psychological benefits which would come from such a meeting," Stimson noted afterward, "rather than the solution of any concrete special problems."[41] Roosevelt was going on his long trip with one overriding mission: to make friends with Stalin.

Two days later, Averell Harriman, who was now the American ambassador in Moscow, sent Roosevelt an optimistic report on the foreign ministers' conference. He believed the Russians had clearly decided that they were going to work with the United States and Great Britain on current and postwar problems; the conference "strengthened their tentative decision." There was a caveat: "The Soviets accepted the explanation of our military plans but our whole permanent relations depend in a large measure on their satisfaction in the future with our military operations," Harriman judged. "It is impossible to over-emphasize the importance they place strategically on the initiation of the so-called second front next spring."

Harriman also noted that "although Soviet territorial questions were never raised at the conference, it can only be inferred that the Soviet government expects to stand firmly on the position they have already taken in regard to their 1941 frontiers. I believe they have the impression that this has been tacitly accepted by the British. The fact that we did not bring up the issue may have given them the impression that we would not raise serious objection in the future." The main problem was Poland, both its future borders and its future type of government. Once again, Harriman believed there was room for hope: "They gave us no indication during the conference that they were interested in the extension of the Soviet system. … I take this with some reservation, particularly if it proves to be the only way they can get the kind of relationships they demand from their western border states."[42]

Harriman's injection of caution was wise. At the conference, Stalin had pulled off a tactical master stroke. He had been angered by the unwillingness of the Americans and British to involve the Soviet Union in the surrender negotiations in Italy and the terms of subsequent occupation. He now turned that to his advantage by winning agreement from his allies that all liberated territories would be administered by the occupying power. He told his closest associates: "Now the fate of Europe is settled. We shall do as we like, with the Allies' consent."[43]

Stalin's victories were bringing those days ever nearer. While Harriman was sending his report to the White House, the Soviet leader received a heartening cable from General Georgy Zhukov. "We are delighted to report that the task set by you to liberate our beautiful city of Kiev, capital of Ukraine, has been accomplished," it read.[44]

The next day, November 7, a verdict on the Moscow conference was being given in London. MI5's Guy Liddell had lunch with a security service colleague who had been in the British delegation. "I asked him about the attitude of Russia towards the Polish question," Liddell noted. "This was the one matter on which they had been somewhat sticky," his colleague replied. "He thinks quite definitely that the Russians will occupy the whole of the Baltic States, eastern Poland and Bessarabia," Liddell recorded.

That evening in the Soviet capital, Vyacheslav Molotov hosted a lavish party to celebrate the unveiling of the new Soviet national anthem. "The whole party," noted the journalist Alexander Werth, "sparkled with jewels, furs, gold braid and celebrities." It had "something of that wild and irresponsible extravagance which one usually associates with pre-revolution Moscow." The dress code was white tie and tails, reminiscent of the grand days of the tsars, rather than the austere court of the Bolsheviks. Molotov wore a new uniform trimmed with gold braid that reminded the American diplomat Charles "Chip" Bohlen of Hitler's SS.[45] Was this symbolic of a new imperialism?

Twenty-four hours later, November 8, Hitler was in Munich to give his annual speech to Nazi Party veterans, marking the anniversary of the beer hall *putsch* that had put Hitler on the political map in 1923. "As usual he spoke very frankly to this circle," Nicolaus von Below recorded, "mentioning the extraordinary severity of the fighting in Russia and the impressive achievements of our soldiers there." Hitler also mentioned the "bestial bombing raids" being perpetrated by Allied planes. "This war may last as long as it will, but Germany will never capitulate," Hitler defiantly proclaimed. "The help of Providence was certain and would send us to victory," Below noted. Hitler then traveled to the Berghof for a week's break from the encroaching wave of troubles. "One noticed how relaxed he was in the old familiar private atmosphere," Below recalled.[46]

The next day in London, the Home Secretary, Herbert Morrison, responded in detail to the MI5 report on communists in government employment. Morrison agreed with the recommendations of the Security Service, explaining to the War Cabinet that the leakage of secret information by Communist Party members and Soviet sympathizers was a real danger, and could not be brushed aside simply because the USSR was now an ally of Great Britain. He suggested, as had been recommended in the MI5 report in October, that all communists should be moved from sensitive work and that a public statement should be made.

Churchill's adviser on intelligence matters, Sir Desmond Morton, thought that the spies were going too far. "MI5 tends to see dangerous men too freely and to lack knowledge of the world and sense of perspective," he advised the prime minister. Churchill refused to allow any public statement and ruled that MI5 would be responsible for informing government departments when it became clear that known communists were in their employ.[47] A monitoring committee was set up but hardly ever used.[48] It made no difference to long-term sleepers like Guy Burgess, Kim Philby and Donald Maclean.

With the Tehran conference approaching Churchill was desperate to have some time alone with the president and the American Chiefs of Staff to settle on joint policy before the meetings with Stalin. What he still wanted was another chance to argue for his alternative strategy. He and Roosevelt had planned to stop in Cairo to meet the Chinese leader, Chiang Kai-shek. Churchill asked for an Anglo-American strategy meeting to be added to the schedule. Once again, Roosevelt snubbed him: "In regard to Cairo, I have held all along—as I know you have, that it would be a terrible mistake if U. J. thought we had ganged up on him on military action," Roosevelt wrote. The events of the early summer were repeating themselves; Churchill was being cut out. The next day, November 12, he left for Malta in a grim mood.

On November 13 Roosevelt himself sailed from the United States for the Mediterranean. "This will be another Odyssey," Roosevelt wrote in a handwritten account of his trip he kept for Daisy Suckley, "much further afield and afloat than the hardy Trojan whose name I used at Croton when I was competing for school prizes. But it too will be filled with surprises. We are off shore," he continued, "escorted by destroyers and planes—very luxurious on the *Iowa* which with her sister-ship the *NY* are the largest battleships in the world."[49]

The president's journey contained its own drama. On the second afternoon at sea he had been escorted in his wheelchair from the lunch table to the deck just outside his mess for what was meant to be a routine anti-aircraft drill. Suddenly, from the bridge, Harry Hopkins heard an officer shouting: "This ain't no drill!" "It's the real thing," another officer yelled to the presidential party from two decks above, "it's the real thing!" Roosevelt refused to go inside and Harry Hopkins leaned over the starboard side just in time to see the deadly wake of a torpedo rocketing past just 600 meters from the *Iowa*. This was no attack by a German submarine; it was a torpedo launched by mistake from one of the destroyers acting as escort for the president. "Can you imagine our own escort torpedoing an American battleship—the newest and biggest—with the president of the United States aboard," a shocked but relieved Hopkins exclaimed. "In view of the fact that there were 20 army officers aboard, I doubt if the navy will ever hear the last of it," he noted.[50]

In Malta, Churchill was cheered through the streets by the local people; but amid the acclamation, he was angrier than ever. Leros had been recaptured by the Germans. He blamed it on the United States' refusal to supply enough resources and immediately convened a conference with his traveling Chiefs of Staff. A bad cold was not helping his temper; he remained in bed throughout and lashed out at his allies: "PM gave long tirade on evils of Americans and of our losses in the Aegean and Dalmatian coast. He was not at his best," Brooke recorded.

Churchill's disproportionate attachment to operations in the eastern Mediterranean was provoking speculation on his motives. Brooke thought that there was an element of envy in the face of increasing American domination in resources and manpower. "He hated having to give up the position of the dominant partner which we had held at the start," Brooke recalled. "As a result he became inclined at times to put up strategic proposals which he knew were unsound purely to spite the Americans. He was in fact aiming at 'cutting off his nose to spite his face.'" There was also, Brooke believed, a desire in the back of his mind "to form a purely British theatre when the laurels would be all ours. Austria or the Balkans seemed to attract him for such a front."[51]

Henry Stimson thought that there was a different force at work. Over in Washington two days later, Lord Halifax met the American war secretary to discuss the undercurrent of feeling about the British attitude to Operation "Overlord": "I asked him point blank whether I was right in feeling there was a good deal of suspicion on the American side as to our real intention to do the cross-Channel business," Halifax noted. Stimson agreed. He said that "he had been much shocked by Winston having said to him last July something about what great fighters the Germans were, when they were holding up Montgomery in Sicily, and how he visualized them doing the same thing when we landed in northern France, and sometimes imagined 50,000 corpses in the Channel."[52]

Beyond Churchill's fear of slaughter on the beaches and his wish for a purely British triumph, was there also the political motive of thwarting a land grab by Stalin? Certainly Churchill's perception back in August of "grave troubles" ahead, and his outburst at Cabinet that Germany might be needed in the future to stop the Soviet Union, proved that communist expansionism was in his mind. The coming weeks would show that these fears were growing.

On November 22, after a night flight from Oran, Roosevelt arrived in Cairo, where Churchill was now encamped after the brief stay in Malta. The two allies drove that afternoon to marvel at the pyramids at Giza "and my old friend the Sphinx," Roosevelt wrote in his handwritten journal. While the two men dined at Roosevelt's villa with Chiang Kai-shek and his formidable wife, Meiling, a devastating Allied bombing raid struck Berlin. Hitler was in a fury as reports filtered through to the Wolf's Lair.

Back in London, Churchill's wife, Clementine, had heard reports of his foul mood. The next day she wrote him a careful and loving letter sympathizing with the cold he had been suffering and the unhappiness the loss of Leros had brought. Above all she reminded him that, when history looked back, "your vision and your piercing energy coupled with your patience and magnanimity will all be part of your greatness," she continued, "so don't allow yourself to be made angry—I often think of your saying, that the only worse thing than allies is not having allies!"[53] As had happened before, Churchill's anger was cooled by her clever words. In Cairo, face to face with the president, the warmth and admiration welled up again. "I love that man," he told his daughter Sara.[54]

Personal affection made no difference to Roosevelt. He still refused to discuss strategy ahead of the meeting with Stalin and, with a hint of cruelty, teased Churchill about empire-building. On November 25, during a Thanksgiving lunch hosted by the president, the subject reared its divisive head. "The prime minister had to endure much with a good grace, including explanations from the president of other powers' higher morality," Cadogan recorded. "Winston, you have 400 years of acquisitive instinct in your blood and you just don't understand how a country might not want to acquire land somewhere if they can get it. A new period has opened in the world's history," Roosevelt warned his ally, "and you will have to adjust yourself to it."[55] It was said teasingly but threw Churchill into despair. He told Harold Macmillan, the British minister in north Africa: "Germany is finished, though it may take some time to clean up the mess. The real problem is Russia. I *can't* get the Americans to see it."[56]

Lord Moran also noticed that day that problems were brewing. "Harry [Hopkins] thinks that the PM is trying to get out of his commitments," Moran noted, referring to "Overlord." "Sure, we are preparing for a battle at Tehran," Hopkins had threatened, "you will find us lining up with the Russians." "What I find so shocking is that to the Americans the PM is the villain of the piece," Moran reflected. "They are far more sceptical of him than they are of Stalin."[57]

Later that day Eden found Churchill deflated. He remarked that Roosevelt was "a charming country gentlemen," but that "business methods were almost non-existent." Churchill complained that he "had to play the role of courtier and seize opportunities when they arose." "I am amazed at the patience with which he does this," Eden noted. Over dinner Eden explained to Roosevelt that the question of Poland's borders should be clearly agreed with Stalin in Tehran. "If nothing was settled," he warned, "Soviet Russia would gain, because the chances were that her troops would be the first to reach German territory."[58] The Red Army was bearing down at an alarming rate. Hours after Eden made his prediction, it took Gomel, just four hundred miles from Hitler's headquarters.

On November 27, 1943, the British and Soviet delegations arrived in Tehran. Roosevelt flew in the next day and the conference was under way. It was a huge moment of the war as the three Allied warlords, three giant egos all with their own agendas, met face to face for the first time.

CHAPTER TWELVE

November 28, 1943–June 5, 1944

Tehran began with a mystery which endures to this day. While he was conducting his pre-conference survey of security arrangements, the supervising secret service agent who had traveled ahead from the White House, Mike Reilly, was told an amazing story by his Soviet counterpart, General Artilov. Apparently the Germans had parachuted in a team of agents, who were now hiding in the mountains north of the Iranian capital. The implication was that an assassination plot against the Allied warlords was afoot.

Roosevelt arrived in Tehran on November 28, a day after Churchill and Stalin had installed themselves. "Now my friends in the NKVD told me that they had captured some of the parachutists," Reilly recalled. It was claimed that 38 Nazis had been dropped. Among them were "at least six German paratroopers loose in the vicinity with a radio transmitter." The NKVD suggested that, for his own safety, Roosevelt should be moved from the isolated American legation to the Soviet embassy, which was in the heart of the city and heavily walled. The president agreed.

"The Russians made the Boss very comfortable," Reilly recalled. "All of us were wryly amused by the servants in our part of the Russian Embassy. Everywhere you went you would see a brute of a man in a lackey's white coat busily polishing immaculate glass or dusting dustless furniture. As their arms swung to dust or polish, the clear, cold outline of a Luger automatic could be seen on every hip. They were NKVD boys, of course. In fact, there were about 3,000 on hand for the meeting."[1]

While Roosevelt rested in the well-protected comfort of his new quarters, Stalin summoned the NKVD agents in charge and gave them a particular duty he would like them to perform. One of those agents was Sergo Beria, the son of the NKVD chief, Lavrenty Beria. "How's your mother?" Stalin asked when Sergo arrived. With the pleasantries over, Stalin moved straight to business. "I have had you brought here, along with some other young men who have never had dealings with foreigners, because I want to entrust you with a mission that is delicate and morally reprehensible," Stalin explained. "You are going to listen to the conversations that Roosevelt will have with Churchill, with the other British, and with his own circle. I must know everything in detail, be aware of all shades of meaning. I am asking you for all that because it is now that the question of the second front will be settled. I know that Churchill is against it. It is important that the Americans support us in this matter."[2] The NKVD checked that the bugs in their embassy were working. Whether there really was a Nazi assassination plot remains unproven.

Churchill had asked Roosevelt yet again for a private meeting before the three-way talks began; he was turned down. Instead at 3 p.m. on November 28 the president was awaiting the meeting *à deux* which he had first tried to set up six months before with his secret letter to Moscow. Now, at last, it was about to happen—without Churchill in the way. Word was sent that Stalin was on his way over. "I'll talk to him in the sitting room, Mike," Roosevelt explained to Reilly. "Stall him a second while I get ready." When Stalin entered Roosevelt was sitting calmly and waiting. Both men smiled and shook hands. "It's good to see you, Marshal," said Roosevelt. "He and the Boss got down to the baffling business of carrying on a conversation through interpreters while the NKVD boys and I exchanged long, rude stares," recalled Reilly.

Roosevelt tried to curry favor with Stalin by raising the matter of Churchill's beloved British Empire. After all, were not the two of them the vanguard of a new world without old-fashioned European imperialism, in which peace and freedom would come to all nations? They agreed that India should be free of the British, but that its future should not be raised at Tehran, "because it was," Stalin observed, "a sore point with Churchill." "At some future date," the president replied, "I would like to talk with you further about India." The best solution, he explained, would be "reform from the bottom, somewhat on the Soviet line."[3] Roosevelt's interpreter, Chip Bohlen, astounded by the novel idea that Bolshevik power sprang from "the bottom," could hardly believe what he was being asked to translate.

Churchill heard of this little *tête-à-tête* and the mist descended. Averell Harriman was warned that "storm signals were flying in the British legation." He went over to see "whether there was any need to calm the waters." He found Churchill "in a grumbling but whimsical mood." "He said that he was glad to obey orders," Harriman reported, "but that he had a right to be chairman of the meeting because of his age, because his name began with C and because of the historical importance of the British Empire which he represented. He waived all these claims but he would insist on one thing, which was that he should be allowed to give a dinner party on the 30th, which was his 69th birthday." Churchill then announced "that he would get thoroughly drunk and be prepared to leave the following day."[4]

At 4 p.m. the three warlords sat down together face to face for the first time since their alliance had been forged some two and a half years before. Military strategy was at the top of the list. Roosevelt reaffirmed the Quebec decision that the cross-Channel invasion would definitely occur the following year, 1944, and that the first possible date would be May 1. He then raised, with no pretense at impartiality, Churchill's desire to put more muscle into Italy and the eastern Mediteranean: "If we undertake large-scale operations in the Mediterranean," the president declared, "the expedition across the Channel will have to be postponed for two or three months." He then ingenuously turned to Stalin: "That is why we should like to have the advice of our Soviet colleagues on the matter."

Stalin took his cue and laid into Churchill's alternative strategy: "We Russians thought that the Italian theater was important only to the extent of ensuring free navigation of Allied shipping in the Mediterranean Sea," he pronounced. "It is of no significance in the sense of further operations against Germany." The only operation that mattered, Stalin added, was to be the cross-Channel invasion of France. "In my opinion," he told his allies, "it would be better to make Operation 'Overlord' the basis of all operations in 1944." Churchill had come to Tehran to argue for the postponement of

"Overlord" and concentration on the Mediterranean. As early as round one, even though the argument would continue to be waged over the next two days, the contest was over.[5]

That evening Roosevelt hosted a banquet for Churchill and Stalin. "It was very jolly," Roosevelt recalled in his handwritten journal of the conference.[6] "The bourbon flowed like vodka and F.D.R. was every bit as canny as the Marshal in the business of handling the endless stream of toasts," Reilly noted. "Of course, His Britannic Majesty's First Minister could easily drink toast for toast with any given battalion of Russians."[7]

The next day, November 29, the respective Chiefs of Staff wrestled with strategy. Stalin's military crony, General Kliment Voroshilov, argued along the same lines as his boss: "Overlord" must take preference above all else. "In vain I argued that by closing operations in the Mediterranean German forces would be free to proceed to other theatres!" General Alan Brooke recorded. "Our friend Voroshilov refused to see any of these arguments, having been evidently briefed by Stalin who no doubt had also been prompted by Averell Harriman." Brooke noted that, for the Americans, Admiral William Leahy, Roosevelt's Chief of Staff, "said nothing" and George Marshall only "stressed the importance that the Americans had always attached to cross-Channel operations."[8] The British team left greatly frustrated at 1:30 p.m. Churchill had made one last attempt to persuade Roosevelt to sit down and have an Anglo-American discussion. For one last time, Roosevelt refused. According to Harriman, he thought it might offend Stalin.

Two hours later the three delegations gathered at the Soviet embassy for a ceremony. Churchill and Roosevelt presented Stalin with the Sword of Stalingrad to commemorate the Red Army's famous victory. Amid the bands, national anthems and photographers, Stalin kissed the sword and handed it to Voroshilov, who promptly dropped it straight out of his scabbard onto the floor; a scene carefully omitted from the official film of the event. "Finally it was handed over to commander of Russian Guard of Honour and marched off securely," Brooke wryly noted.[9]

The Big Three then settled down for another three-hour session. Brooke viewed it as "bad from beginning to end. Winston was not good and Roosevelt even worse." It was clear that "Overlord" was now set in stone for May 1, 1944. The only question was what supporting operation there should be. Churchill argued for an extension of the campaign in the eastern Mediterranean and through northern Italy, assuming the Allies had reached there by the time of "Overlord." The alternative was a supporting invasion of southern France, codenamed Operation "Anvil." Roosevelt offered Stalin the choice: "Our directive should stipulate, in conformity with the desires of the Russians, an invasion in the south of France," Stalin instantly replied. "The operations in the Mediterranean of which Churchill speaks are merely diversionary."

Stalin then made clear his distrust of Churchill: "I should like to know whether the British believe in Operation 'Overlord' or simply speak of it to reassure the Russians."[10] For Churchill and his chiefs, who thought that Operation "Anvil" was pointless, the session was a disaster. Brooke noted angrily: "I feel more like entering a lunatic asylum or a nursing home than continuing with my present job. I am absolutely disgusted with the politicians' methods of waging the war!! Why will they imagine that they are experts at a job they know nothing about! It is lamentable to listen to them! May God help us in the future prosecution of this war, we have every hope to making an unholy mess of it and of being defeated yet!"[11]

At dinner that night the atmosphere darkened yet further. Stalin, the host for the evening, spent much of the evening mocking his British ally. One barb reminded Churchill of how he had once wanted to fight the Bolsheviks: "I can't understand you at all; in 1919 you were so keen to fight; and now you don't seem to be!" he exclaimed. "What has happened? Is it the result of advancing age? How many divisions have you got in contact with the enemy? What is happening to all those two million men you have got in India?"

Then, in an exchange of banter on what to do with the enemy, Stalin announced: "50,000 Germans must be killed. Their General Staff must go." Churchill leapt from his seat and began pacing. "I will not be a party to any butchery in cold blood," he replied, his faced flushed with anger. "50,000 must be shot," Stalin declared again. "I would rather be taken out now than so disgrace my country," Churchill retorted. Roosevelt tried to calm proceedings by pretending it was all a joke. "I have a compromise to propose," he interjected, "not 50,000, but only 49,000 should be shot." After the frustrations of the day, Churchill had mislaid his sense of humor and stormed out of the room. Stalin followed after him, laughing and trying to explain the joke. "You are pro-German," he told him as they walked back into the room together, "the devil is a communist, and my friend God is a conservative." Finally, the two men made amends, the conversation ending in "a convivial embrace."[12]

The patching up was just a veneer. Lord Moran found Churchill in a slump of depresssion when he later visited his room. It was well after midnight. Whisky in hand, his eyes "popping," Churchill revealed his great fears for the future: "I believe man might destroy man and wipe out civilisation. Europe would be desolate and I may be held responsible." Lord Moran recorded Churchill's agony: "Until he came here, the PM could not bring himself to believe that, face-to-face with Stalin, the democracies would take different courses. Now he sees he cannot rely on the president's support. What matters more, he realises that the Russians see this too. Stalin will be able to do as he pleases. Will he become a menace to the free world, another Hitler? The PM is appalled by his own impotence."[13]

By the third morning of the conference, November 30, Roosevelt believed that he still had not really "connected" with Stalin. Later he told his labor secretary, Frances Perkins, how he finally got through. Once again the unfortunate Churchill was the whipping boy. "On my way to the conference room that morning," the president related, "we caught up with Winston and I had just a moment to say to him, 'Winston, I hope you won't be sore at me for what I am going to do.' Winston shifted his cigar and grunted. I must say he behaved very decently afterward. I began almost as soon as we went into the conference room. I talked privately with Stalin. I didn't say anything I hadn't said before, but it appeared quite chummy and confidential, enough so that the other Russians joined us to listen. Still no smile. Then I said, lifting my hand to cover a whisper (which of course had to be interpreted), 'Winston is cranky this morning, he got up on the wrong side of the bed.' A vague smile passed over Stalin's eyes, and I decided I was on the right track. As soon as I sat down at the conference table I began to tease Churchill about his Britishness, about John Bull, about his cigars, about his habits. Winston got red and scowled, and the more he did so, the more Stalin smiled. Finally Stalin broke into a deep, hearty guffaw, and for the first time in three days I saw the light. The ice was broken and we talked like men and brothers."

Churchill's birthday, his 69th, fell the same day. Despite losing the strategic argument and his depression of the night, he was, as so often, quick to bounce back and make the best of things. He hosted a splendid dinner and Roosevelt gave him a valuable Kashan bowl with a note: "With my affection, may we be together for many years."[14] An enormous ice cream birthday cake was brought in. The waiter, absorbed in Stalin's speech, managed to tip the huge confection over the Russian interpreter. Brooke recounted: "The unfortunate Berejkov was at that moment standing up translating a speech for Stalin and he came in for the full blast! He was splashed from his head to his feet, but I suppose it was more than his life was worth to stop interpreting! In any case he carried on manfully whilst I sent for towels and with the help of the Persian waiters proceeded to mop him down. To this day I can still see large lumps of white ice cream sitting on his shoes, and melting over the edges and through the lace holes!"

Tehran demonstrated again Churchill's split-mindedness towards Stalin. His defeat in the strategic argument, which effectively meant that the way was now open for the Soviets to win the Balkans and eastern Europe, had reawakened the vision of the communist colossus trampling over Europe. However, at other times in this gathering of great men, Churchill continued to believe that he could cut deals with the Soviet leader.

As always, a key issue was Poland. Churchill secretly agreed, without telling the London Poles, that the Soviet Union should have the part of eastern Poland it had gained under the Nazi–Soviet pact. Poland would be compensated with land from Germany. This frontier was broadly equivalent, though in places more advantageous to the Russians, to the so-called "Curzon" line, named after the British Foreign Secretary of the time, which the British had supported in 1919 as the border after Poland had won its independence from Russia at the end of the First World War. However in the Russo-Polish war that followed, the Poles had won substantial further territory which they considered to be a rightful part of their nation.

When Poland came up for discussion, one observer recorded that Roosevelt had said: "I don't care two hoots about Poland. Wake me up when we talk about Germany!" The truth was that the president wanted no overt part in any secret deal on territory. The next year, 1944, would be presidential election year. He intended to stand again and had no wish to upset the large Polish constituency in the United States by the possible discovery of any involvement in giving away their land. The same went for the Baltic states of Lithuania, Latvia and Estonia, which Churchill privately confirmed to Stalin should become part of the postwar Soviet Union. Once again, Roosevelt kept his distance but let it be known that he would not stand in the way.

On that day, as the Allied warlords finalized their agreements, Joseph Goebbels and Hitler continued to find consolation in their opponents. "The enemy has not had a significant military victory except on the Eastern front," Hitler said. "The English and Americans can't get things moving in Italy and are suffering the bloodiest losses there. Roosevelt must naturally take care to turn the war round before the election campaign starts up again."[15]

After their momentous encounter, the Big Three went their separate ways; Stalin to Moscow, Churchill to Cairo, and Roosevelt to Washington. As news of the conference filtered through to the various capital cities, it was soon clear that, inside Roosevelt's government, Stalin was the hero.

"I thank the Lord that Stalin was there. In my opinion, he saved the day," Henry Stimson noted in his diary on December 5: "he was direct and strong and he brushed away the diversionary attempts of the prime minister with a vigor which rejoiced my soul." As always, Stimson believed that on strategic matters the president was putty in the prime minister's hands: "Up to the time of his arrival, our side was at a disadvantage because of the president's rather haphazard grasp of the situation. But when Stalin came in with his General Voroshilov, they completely changed the situation and took the offensive for 'Overlord,'" he concluded happily.[16]

Tehran had created an extraordinary dynamic. Roosevelt and Stalin, in complete agreement, were now the dominant partners, Churchill isolated in feeble opposition. His misfortune multiplied as he had a severe bout of pneumonia after his arrival back in Cairo.

In Washington, on December 18, Roosevelt recounted his diplomatic triumphs to Stimson. "He said that when he first met Churchill at these meetings he was surprised at the change in him. He seemed unwell, was peevish and had prejudices against people in a way that was quite unusual to him," Stimson noted of Roosevelt's account. "He tried to reopen 'Overlord' and the eastern Mediterranean matters, like the Dodecanese and Rhodes, and finally concentrated on Turkey. The president said that he himself had fought hard for 'Overlord' and with the aid of Stalin finally won out." "I have thus brought 'Overlord' back to you safe and sound," Roosevelt told Stimson with pride.[17]

One week later, December 27, as Churchill flew to Marrakech for a much-needed recharge of the batteries, both physical and mental, Hitler was deep in conference with Colonel-General Kurt Zeitzler. The military situation in the east was grim with the Red Army bearing down on Hitler's own headquarters. "We are going to have a difficult time," Hitler admitted, thinking primarily of the battle in the Crimea and his fear that Turkey might soon enter the war. "There is going to be a major crisis. We shall not be able to save anything," he said, "the consequences will be catastrophic." Yet the Führer had not lost his sense of purpose. "I am a man who has personally built up and led perhaps the greatest organization on earth," he announced, "and I am still leading it."[18]

Roosevelt was continuing to assess his days with Stalin. "You know, I really think the Russians will go along with me about having no spheres of influence," he told Frances Perkins. "He felt himself on good terms with Marshal Stalin," she noted, "he liked him and found him extremely interesting."[19] Apart from the personal connection which he believed he had made, Roosevelt had come to an important conclusion. Tehran had persuaded him that Stalin was fundamentally a practical man with whom he could do business. For his part, Stalin had played Roosevelt impeccably; at all times he behaved respectfully towards him, in marked contrast to the rudeness he often displayed to Churchill.

On New Year's Day 1944, as troops and weapons began to mass in southern England for "Overlord," Hitler warned the German people: "The year 1944 will make tough and severe demands of all Germans." However, he managed a show of optimism: "The course of the war, in all its enormity, will reach its critical point during this year. We are fully confident that we will successfully surmount it."[20] Within 24 hours, as Allied planes pounded Berlin, the Red Army advanced to within 30 miles of the 1939 Polish border.

On January 4 General Mannstein took a deep breath, walked into Hitler's office, and laid out the crisis facing Army Group South in the Crimea. His troops were on the verge of being separated from Army Group Center and he pleaded with Hitler to allow an evacuation of the Dnieper bend. The Führer immediately rejected Mannstein's impassioned entreaty. "There are so many disagreements on the enemy side," he told him, "that the coalition is bound to fall apart one day."[21]

In Moscow that day Stalin received news that Russian troops had now crossed the Polish frontier. "Russians are doing wonders," noted Alexander Cadogan, "but that presents us with some problems!"[22] In his villa in Marrakech, Churchill was having similar thoughts, but he drafted a letter to the Soviet leader congratulating him on the Red Army's success, and assuring him that everything was now going "full blast" for "Overlord."[23] These final words were written with gritted teeth, for he had just been informed that some of the ships promised for the upcoming Anzio landings in southern Italy were to be held back for the invasion of France.

Sitting opposite Roosevelt for dinner at the White House that evening was his dearly loved daughter, Anna. In an effort to recreate the warm intimacy of his early White House days, she had moved in with her father. There were also signs that his health was deteriorating; she was there to keep a watchful eye.

With the strategic arguments that dominated the final months of 1943 now apparently resolved, the trickiest problem on Churchill's plate was Poland. He had made his secret deal with Stalin on the eastern Polish border, though differences remained between them on some of the territorial details. However, he had not told the London Poles; instead his tactic was to strong-arm them into accepting this new border, with the compensation of extra German territory to the west, without admitting that he had already done the deed in private. The situation was further complicated by the continuing rupture in relations between the London Poles and Stalin which had followed the discovery of the Katyn massacre. As it was now clear that the Red Army was going to occupy Poland come what may, Churchill believed the London Poles should accept that he had won them the best deal possible. He hoped that a resumption of relations between Moscow and the London Poles would then follow.

On January 7, while still convalescing in Marrakech, Churchill cabled Anthony Eden with his justification: "I rather contemplate telling the world that we declared war for Poland and that the Polish nation shall have a proper land to live in. But we have never undertaken to defend existing Polish frontiers. ... Russia, after two wars which have cost her between 20 and 30 millions of Russian lives, has a right to the inexpungeable security of her western frontiers." Churchill intended effectively to blackmail the Polish government in exile in London into accepting his solution: "I do not think we should give them the slightest hope of further help or recognition unless they cordially support the decisions which we and our Soviet ally have reached." The prime minister concluded that the Poles would be "silly" to assume that "we are going to begin a new war with Russia for the sake of the Polish eastern frontier."[24] It was a recipe for bitter dispute; while Churchill thought the proposed new border reasonable, the London Poles simply saw it as theft of their land and continued to believe that Stalin would never allow Polish freedom and independence.

As Churchill wrote from Marrakech, the threat of an Allied invasion was exercising Hitler's generals. Alfred Jodl had just returned from a visit to the coast of northern France. "How *is* the air defense against the invasion to be carried out?" he noted in his diary on January 10. "Major action against the enemy air forces is not possible," he wrote, "fighters can carry out minor attacks against shipping and possible targets at sea. We must not accept a battle with the enemy air force."[25] Hitler, on the other hand, was contemplating some satisfying news. A special court, sitting in the northern Italian town of Verona, now under Nazi occupation, had condemned to death members of the Grand Fascist Council, who had been party to deposing Mussolini. They were shot 24 hours later, among them Count Galeazzo Ciano, Mussolini's son-in-law, and a once frequent visitor to Berlin and the Berghof.[26]

The Red Army continued its unassailable march, launching a successful offensive in the Leningrad region; the Allies were stuck at Monte Cassino. In the new post-Tehran realities of the Big Three's alliance, Churchill was finding reasons to justify giving Stalin the territory in the Baltic states and Poland that he had demanded as long ago as December 1941. On January 16 he wrote to Eden: "Undoubtedly my own feelings have changed in the two years that have passed since the topic was first raised during your first visit to Moscow. The tremendous victories of the Russian armies, the deep-seated changes which have taken place in the character of the Russian states and government, the new confidence which has grown in our hearts towards Stalin," he explained, "have all had their effect. Most of all is the fact that the Russians may very soon be in physical possession of these territories, and it is absolutely certain that we should never attempt to turn them out." Churchill was searching every angle to justify what he inwardly knew was thoroughly dubious. He concluded that the Russian claim with regards to their western borders "in no way exceeds former Tsarist boundaries. In fact, in some parts it falls notably short of them."[27] He had traveled some distance from his first reaction two years before that Stalin's demands were "contrary to all the principles for which we are fighting this war and would dishonour our cause."

On January 20 Churchill was back in London, trying to broker a deal between the London Poles and Stalin. "The problem is a hard one and the Soviet government are ungracious bargainers," noted John Colville. "Negotiations proceeding on basis of the Curzon line."[28] "I felt sorry for them, poor things," Eden wrote of the Polish delegation after they had departed, "the outlook darkens for them."[29] Averell Harriman, the American ambassador in Moscow, agreed. He wrote to Churchill that same day: "The Russian bear is demanding much and yet biting the hands that are feeding him." "I agree with your political comment but he is biting others at the same time too," Churchill replied,[30] referring to the Red Army's relentless pursuit of Hitler.

However, Soviet shenanigans and Stalin's bristling hostility towards the London Poles, whom he still had no political interest in reconciling, began to wear as much on Churchill's patience as the obduracy of the London Poles themselves. One extraordinary Russian caper was an article in *Pravda* suggesting hush-hush negotiations between Joachim von Ribbentrop and certain British officials in the Pyrenees.

However ludicrous the story, Churchill felt obliged to knock it on the head, writing to Stalin on January 24: "I am sure you know that I would never negotiate with the Germans separately and that we tell you every overture they make as you have told us." He then offered the Soviet leader a salutary reminder: "We never thought of making a separate peace even in the year when we were all alone and could easily have made one without serious loss to the British Empire and largely at your expense. Why should we think of it now, when our triple fortunes are marching forward to victory?"[31]

That evening at Cabinet Churchill, fully recovered from his pneumonia, was "in great form." He discussed the latest Soviet outrage and commented: "Trying to maintain good relations with a communist is like wooing a crocodile. You do not know whether to tickle it under the chin or to beat it on the head. When it opens its mouth you cannot tell whether it is trying to smile, or preparing to eat you up."[32] As the prime minister repaired at 8:15 p.m. for dinner with General Brooke, Hitler had just issued a proclamation for his troops in Italy: they were to hold the line at all costs.

The Wehrmacht had managed to recapture Castelforte and Monte Rotondo from the British, though the casualties were high. The next day, in conversation with Goebbels, Hitler said that the Italian situation was "extremely positive." Feverishly loyal as he was, even Goebbels had to concede the Führer was being "too optimistic." Determined and deluded in equal measure, Hitler painted just as positive a picture of the eastern front. "The situation in the east is by and large consolidated," he remarked, "admittedly we can't win any bouquets there at the moment, but there is no crisis anticipated." The consolation, as so often, was the belief that "differences between the English and Americans on the one hand and the Soviets on the other are now out in the open. It is astonishing that Stalin can behave so arrogantly when his hand is so poor. The Führer really can't understand it. If he was in that position he would soft-soap them more."[33]

Two days later, January 27, the siege of Leningrad was finally at an end. The bitter suffering of the remaining inhabitants, who had survived bombings, starvation, cannibalism and unimaginable hardship, was now over. The city had been trapped for nearly nine hundred days. At the Berghof, before an audience of one hundred or so of his military commanders, Hitler gave a speech. "In the last contingency, if I as Supreme Leader should be deserted at any time I must ultimately expect to be surrounded by the entire officer corps with swords drawn for my protection just as every field marshal, every commanding general, every divisional leader and every regimental commander expects that his subordinate will stand by him likewise in the critical hour," he warned in what Nicolaus von Below described as a "moment of drama." "So it will be, Mein Führer!" Mannstein declared in response. "That is fine," Hitler continued, "if that will be so, then it will never be possible to lose this war."[34]

Hitler's routine was becoming ever more closeted and remote. He shared spartan meals with fewer people, exercised rarely and spent nearly all of the first half of 1944 shut away in the camouflaged Berghof or the concrete bunkers of the Wolf's Lair. In February, the scene around him became ever more paranoid. According to Below, an assassination plot had been drawn to Hitler's attention by his press officer. An article in a Swedish newspaper claimed that a German army staff officer was conspiring to shoot Hitler with a pistol. "Hitler sent for me, showing me the cutting and told me to do everything I could to prevent such an attempt being made," Below reported. Hitler demanded that all visitors be under constant observation when in his presence or at HQ, and that all "heavy file cases" should be watched.[35] Hitler's bunker at the Wolf's Lair was fortified with more layers of concrete.

On February 2 Churchill wrote to Stalin, confirming the concessions he was forcing on the London Poles: "I said that although we had gone to war for the sake of Poland we had not gone for any particular frontier line but for the existence of a strong, free, independent Poland which Marshall Stalin declared himself as supporting. I advised them to accept the Curzon Line as a basis for discussions."[36] "This, as it seems to me, is putting all the aces (including the Ace of Trumps) in Joe's hand," Cadogan noted.[37]

The next day Averell Harriman met Stalin at the Kremlin to convey Roosevelt's hope that some way would soon be found to settle the dispute with the London Poles. Stalin immediately reached for his briefcase and handed Harriman an old copy of an underground Polish newspaper printed some six months before. The headline read: "Hitler and Stalin—Two Faces of the Same Evil." "It is difficult to deal with people who could publish such a paper," Stalin told Harriman. "The Poles liked to think," he continued, that "Russians were good fighters but fools. They thought they could let the Russians carry the burden of the fighting and then step in at the end to share the spoils. But the Poles would find out who were the fools."[38] He said that those anti-Soviet elements would have to be removed before a deal could be done. That day he gave the same message to the British ambassador, Sir Archibald Clark Kerr; the Polish government in exile would have to be "reconstructed."[39] The truth was that, whatever the London Poles conceded, Stalin had no interest in resuming relations with a potential government that would insist on Poland's independence.

Trouble with Stalin was compounded by a shock at home. On February 18 Lord Hartington, a major in the Coldstream Guards who was standing for Churchill's government in the West Derbyshire by-election, was beaten by the Independent Labour candidate. Eden tried to console the Prime Minster by explaining that it was "little worse than mosquito bite. W looked tired and 'knocked about,'" he wrote in his diary, "he said that in '40 one could put up with anything because one felt one had the country being one. Now the people were not united etc."[40]

The sea of woes now included a series of devastating bombing raids by the Luftwaffe over London, the worst since the Blitz. On February 20, while Stalin's NKVD chief, Lavrenty Beria, arrived in Grozny to begin mass deportations of people of nationalities considered disloyal, one of those German air raids struck at the very heart of government. "We have just had a stick of bombs around 10 Downing Street and there are no more windows," Churchill wrote to Roosevelt the next morning, "Clemmie and I were at Chequers and luckily all the servants were in the shelter. Four persons killed outside."[41]

In Moscow Stalin was growing tired of being badgered about the Poles. "Again the Poles," he "growled" at Harriman. "Is that the most important question?" Harriman asked Stalin for his suggested solution with the London Poles, who were now led by Stanislaw Mikolajczyk, the mild-mannered leader of the Peasant Party. "While the Red Army is liberating Poland," Stalin replied, "Mikolajczyk's government will have changed, or another government will have emerged in Poland."[42] The Soviet leader's implication was clear; he would impose whatever government suited him.

That day Hitler had retreated to the Berghof, where he was discussing a familiar theme with Goebbels. "In both England and America a political crisis of the first order is taking place," noted Goebbels. "But it needs time to ripen. The crisis has become inflamed over the question of Bolshevism.

Stalin has held a gun to the heads of both Churchill and Roosevelt."[43]

The attempt to broker an agreement between Stalin and the London Poles was now hitting the buffers of its inherent contradictions. "Two months of our efforts at negotiation were greeted by Marshal Stalin with a message to the prime minister on March 3 which was discourteous in tone and abrupt in its misrepresentation of Polish claims," Eden noted angrily. Stalin's attitude was awakening dark suspicions within the man who, two years before, had argued for conceding the Soviet leader's territorial demands. "I don't like even to refer to the possibility that we should break with Polish government in London," Eden now noted, "but over and above all this, Soviet attitude on this business raises most disquieting thoughts. Is Soviet regime one which will ever cooperate with the west?"[44]

On March 7 Churchill wrote sadly to Stalin: "Force can achieve much but force supported by the goodwill of the world can achieve more. I earnestly hope that you will not close the door finally to a working arrangement with the Poles which will help the common cause during the war and give you all you require at the peace." He then regretfully explained that, should Stalin be unable to resume relations with the London Poles, the British government would itself have no choice but to continue its recognition of them "as the government of the ally for whom we declared war upon Hitler." His conclusion was heartfelt: "All my hopes for the future of the world are based upon the friendship and cooperation of the western democracies and Soviet Russia."[45]

As the message made its way to the Kremlin, Beria reported to Stalin that 500,000 Chechens and Ingush had been removed from their homes and deported.[46] The forward march of Russian forces continued to batter German resistance. Vinnitsa, once home to Hitler's swampy Werewolf headquarters, was captured by Soviet troops on March 20.

The next day Churchill wrote again to Stalin explaining that he would soon be making a public statement explaining that his attempts to forge an understanding between Poland and the Soviet Union had failed. He said that until the end of the war he would continue to recognize the Polish government in London and that any territorial agreements would now have to wait until the peace conference. "In the meantime we can recognise no forcible transferences of territory," Churchill concluded. The prime minister had gone far in trying to coerce the Poles into an agreement, but he would not sign up to their emasculation.

On March 23 Stalin sent an ill-tempered reply: "I was struck by the fact that both your messages bristle with threats against the Soviet Union. I should like to call your attention to this circumstance because threats as a method are not only out of place in relations between Allies, but also harmful, for they may lead to opposite results," he warned. "To be sure you are free to make any statement you like in the House of Commons—that is your business. But should you make a statement of this nature I shall consider that you have committed an unjust and unfriendly act in relation to the Soviet Union. In your message you express the hope that the breakdown over the Polish question will not affect our cooperation in other spheres. As far as I am concerned, I have been, and still am, for cooperation. But I fear that the method of intimidation and defamation, if continued, will not benefit our cooperation."[47] The rhetoric was a cover; the outcome suited Stalin nicely. While claiming the moral high ground, he could congratulate himself that his troops were entering Poland with no Soviet obligation to the only legitimate Polish government, which continued to sit powerlessly hundreds of miles away from the action.

While the Soviet leader grew in global strength, a personal crisis was facing the president. On March 27, after an examination at the Bethesda Naval Hospital, he was discovered to be suffering from hypertension and congestive heart failure. A severe reduction in smoking and a strict diet were prescribed. His illness was kept secret.

Six days later Hitler issued an order for counterattacks in the east. It stated that the Russian offensive to the south of the front had passed its climax. "The time is now ripe finally to bring the Russian advance to a halt."[48] Far from crumbling and weakening, the Red Army had crossed the Prut River. This river line, the Soviets stated, "represents the state border between the USSR and Romania." Not only was this announcement a bloody riposte to Hitler's order; it also demonstrated that Stalin was rubber-stamping the Soviet Union's postwar border with Romania. "The significance of this announcement was plain," Harriman recalled, "all of Bessarabia and the province of Bukovina, seized by the Red Army in June 1940, were already being treated as Soviet territory."[49]

As the Red Army began yet another victorious push into German-occupied territory, this time in Crimea, Churchill was finally turning his attention to the dangers posed to the British body politic by communist agents. "We are purging all our secret establishments of Communists," he told Cadogan on April 13, "because we know they owe no allegiance to us or our cause and will always betray secrets to the Soviets, even while we are working together."[50] As he wrote, the Russians were storming Sevastopol.

On April 20, at the Berghof, Hitler celebrated his 55th birthday. Under Goebbels' direction, Berlin was festooned with banners; the Berlin Philarmonia played a special concert; and the party gathered to celebrate their great leader's historic career.[51] Hitler, however, according to his Luftwaffe adjutant, "was not in the mood for festivities."[52] Before his usual military briefing at noon, he accepted the congratulations of the household staff at the Berghof, and then sat quietly in a corner opening his presents. With the necessary pleasantries over, he retired to spend the rest of the day in gloomy discussions with Zeitzler, Hermann Göring and Karl Dönitz.[53]

A week later disaster struck off the south coast of England. In the early hours of the morning of April 28 a flotilla of eight Allied landing craft lined up near Slapton Sands when suddenly, out of the darkness, nine German torpedo boats launched a devastating attack. Three of the craft were hit, one immediately bursting into flames. Hundreds of bodies were soon floating in the water. A total of 749 sailors and soldiers were eventually recorded as dead and missing. This was no major operation; it was a training exercise gone horribly wrong. Operation "Tiger" should have been a routine practice for the upcoming cross-Channel invasion. The German torpedo boats had chanced on their prey. For Churchill, it was a savage warning of his long-held fears for "Overlord."

At a garden party at 10 Downing Street on May 4 Averell Harriman was cornered by the prime minister. "He made me listen to a fifteen-minute fight talk," Harriman recalled, "on how badly the British had been treated by the Soviet government beginning with the Ribbentrop treaty, during the period when Britain stood alone, the insults that had been hurled at him by Stalin consistently, and his determination that the Soviets should not destroy freedom in Poland, for which country Britain had gone to war. He asked,"

Harriman continued, "that I present his attitude to the president and asked for the president's support in this policy 'even if only after he is re-elected to office.'"[54] At the same time in Washington, Henry Morgenthau recorded in his diary: "The Roosevelt–Stalin axis is gaining strength and the Roosevelt–Churchill axis is losing strength in about equal ratio." Churchill's pleas were falling on distant ears.

As D-Day, the second front he had opposed for so long, drew near, Churchill was a disappointed man. The Italian campaign had been disappointing; American and British troops, ground down in a long, brutal slog in the south of Italy, had not even reached Rome. The alternative strategy in the Mediterranean seemed a spent force. "He looked very old and very tired," Brooke noted after dinner with the prime minister on May 7. "He said Roosevelt was not well and no longer the man he had been; this, he said, also applied to himself. He said he could still always sleep well, eat well and especially drink well! But that he no longer jumped out of bed the way he used to, and felt as if he would be quite content to spend the whole day in bed. I have never yet heard him admit that he was beginning to fail."[55]

Churchill was missing Roosevelt. He tried to persuade him to come to Britain, as the president had promised the previous autumn. "There is a very good place in London which would give you perfect safety and comfort. I greatly desire to see you again. It is six months since we met," he wrote on May 25. Two days later Roosevelt turned him down, saying that a full staff meeting was not necessary.

It was the personal contact Churchill was missing. The next day, he tried again: "I still think that a short visit is, above all things, desirable for the Staffs and above all for you, but any time after D + 14 might be convenient to you, and would be received with rejoicing by us." He concluded with an appeal to friendship: "Doctor Churchill informs you that a sea voyage in one of your great new battleships would do you no end of good."[56] Roosevelt's reply combined the personal touch with a businesslike reiteration of his refusal: "I should like very much to accept Dr. Churchill's advice to make a sea voyage in your direction and I hope to do so at a later date. Condition here will not permit it shortly after D plus fourteen as suggested by you."[57] "The honeymoon stage between the president and the prime minister is over, and the normal difficulties and divergences, inseparable from staid married life, are beginning to develop," Harold Macmillan observed.[58]

At last on June 4 came the first good news for what seemed months. At 7:15 p.m. Rome fell. Allied troops marched into Piazza Venezia and paraded through the Italian capital. Churchill was ecstatic. "How magnificently your troops have fought!" he cabled Roosevelt. "I hear that relations are admirable between our armies in every rank there, and here certainly it is an absolute brotherhood."[59]

On June 5, General Eisenhower made the most important decision of his life. That day the English weather was stormy, but his meteorologists told him that there should be a clear window for the invasion to take place the next day. "OK. We'll go," he ordered.[60] Convinced that the Allies would not attack at low tide or under a full moon, Field Marshal Erwin Rommel left his French headquarters at Le Roche Guyon to return home for his wife's birthday. As Rommel drove to Germany, an awesome force of five thousand ships and over 150,000 men prepared for the biggest amphibious operation in history.

That evening the Allies watched, and waited. The tension in the United States and Great Britain was palpable. "Tonight is the eve of the great occasion," Henry Stimson noted from Washington, "Churchill has for a long time been strongly against it although he is strongly for it now. And the president had wobbled all over the lot at different times, although he is firmly for it now." Churchill dined alone with Clementine. "Do you realise," he said to her, "that by the time you wake up in the morning 20,000 men may have been killed?"

Hitler too was up late that night. After talking with Goebbels in the tea-house at the Berghof he spent the evening with a small coterie of close companions watching a newsreel and talking by the fire. "All in all," Goebbels noted, "the mood is like old times."[61] At 2 a.m., as Hitler finally retired, British and American paratroopers began landing under cover of darkness across the Channel in France. "Overlord" had begun—the end of the war was finally in sight; but the long-running strategic argument between Churchill and Roosevelt had one violent kick left in the tail.

CHAPTER THIRTEEN
June 6–August 24, 1944

Tuesday, June 6, 1944, 6:30 a.m. The invasion of France was under way, with far fewer immediate casualties than Churchill had ever imagined possible. "How I wish I could be with you to see our war machine in operations!" Roosevelt wrote, belying his repeated refusals of Churchill's pleas for him to visit Britain.

By 10 a.m. Hitler had been awoken with the news. Skeptical that the landings were the invasion proper, he did not immediately stir himself. Erwin Rommel, by contrast, scrambled back at top speed from his home in Germany where he had gone just 24 hours before for his wife's birthday celebrations. At the Berghof, Hitler "still seemed convinced that the invasion force could be thrown back into the sea," Nicolaus von Below recalled, "despite the enemy's air superiority and the huge amounts of material coming ashore unchecked."[1] Paralyzed by Hitler's decision to centralize command of the precious *Panzer* divisions in France, the German counteroffensive did not get under way until the afternoon.

In Washington Roosevelt warned against over-optimism. "You don't just walk into Berlin," he told that day's press conference; "the sooner this country realizes that, the better."[2] In private, however, he was energetic in his praise of the "brilliant success" of the Normandy landings. He was intrigued by the artificial "Mulberry harbours," one of the British inventions playing a vital role in the operation. "You know," Roosevelt said to Frances Perkins, "that was Churchill's idea. Just one of those brilliant ideas that he has. He has a hundred a day and about four of them are good," the president continued. "When he was visiting me in Hyde Park he saw all those boats from the last war tied up in the Hudson River and in one of his great bursts of imagination he said, 'By George, we could take those ships and others like them that are good for nothing and sink them offshore to protect the landings.' The military and naval authorities were startled out of a year's growth. But Winnie was right. Great fellow that Churchill, if you can keep up with him."[3] Though the president felt increasingly exhausted by Churchill, the admiration remained; but he would never allow it to interfere with politics or his own priorities.

In the Berghof Hitler was pontificating to Joseph Goebbels. "Even the loss of Rome has not depressed him at all," the propaganda chief reported in his diary on June 6, "he is rightly convinced that it is not a decisive action. The decisive point will be in the west. I'm glad the Führer sees things so realistically and clearly. If he were ever to lose heart it would have a devastating effect on those around him and indirectly also on the entire German people." Indeed, Hitler was seeing advantages in his enemies' advance: "Above all any further Soviet military successes would be devastating for the western enemy side," he pronounced. "He considers England to be lost, and is therefore determined, if he gets the slightest opportunity, to deal the death blow," Goebbels noted; "how he will achieve this, I fail to see at present."[4]

By nightfall over 155,000 Allied troops had landed. Despite the horrific bloodbath on Omaha beach, the operation had been a success. The Allies finally had a toehold in France, and they were not going to let go.

Four days later there was another of those signs of friction among his enemies with which Hitler so comforted himself. Churchill, having been thwarted of any chance of beating Stalin to the Balkans, was now trying to ensure that, at the very least, Britain would retain postwar influence in Greece, which lay close to British imperial possessions in Cyprus and the Middle East. He had suggested to Roosevelt that, because there had been "disquieting signs of a possible divergence" between Britain and Russia in the region, he should agree with Stalin that the British would "take the lead" in Greek affairs while the Soviets would do the same in Romania.[5]

Roosevelt immediately detected the whiff of imperial rivalries. He replied that, while he understood that the militarily responsible power in any region would necessarily make decisions "required by military events," he was opposed to any agreements that would cause those decisions to go any further. "In our opinion," he wrote after talks with the State Department, "this would certainly result in the persistence of differences between you and the Soviets and in the division of the Balkan region into spheres of influence."[6]

Churchill replied with a certain impatience the following day. "I am very much concerned," he protested, "if everybody is to consult everybody else about everything before it is taken."[7] As a compromise, Churchill proposed that his suggested division of authority should have a three-month trial. Roosevelt agreed, but not without one final warning that "we must be careful to make it clear that we are not establishing any postwar sphere of influence."[8]

While Churchill attempted to engage in precisely that exercise, he suddenly saw a last-minute opportunity to revive his alternative military strategy in the Mediterranean, which had seemed dead and buried by the decisions at Tehran. The row that followed would be the bitterest and most vituperative in his entire relationship with the president.

After the fall of Rome, most of the British and American troops in Italy were supposed to be switching to the invasion of southern France, Operation "Anvil," which Stalin had insisted on and was scheduled for mid-August. But British commanders in Italy, led by General Henry Maitland-Wilson—"Jumbo" as the portly officer was known—and supported by the British Chiefs of Staff in London, now suggested a break-out via Trieste and Ljubljana into the Balkans and central Europe. They believed that this was a far more exciting military option than the invasion of southern France. As for Churchill, it was the very thing he had always wanted his alternative strategy to achieve for both military and political reasons.

When the British presented their idea, the American overall Allied commander, General Dwight Eisenhower, would have no truck with it. Witheringly, he cabled Roosevelt on June 20: "Wandering off overland via Trieste and Ljubljana repeat Ljubljana is to indulge in conjecture to an unwarranted degree at the present time."[9]

The American war secretary, Henry Stimson, who had for so long suspected Churchill's strategic obsessions, was predictably annoyed. "I found from the log that a message had come from General Wilson in the Mediterranean in which he renews the old British attempt to switch the next operation in the Mediterranean to the Balkans and possibly Hungary," Stimson noted on June 21. "It is interesting to see how the deep national cleavage still persists. The British with their empire interest are anxious to throw our next blow into the eastern Mediterranean just as they were a year ago ... furthermore by going into the eastern Mediterranean we would run the risk of coming into rivalry with Russia."[10] Rivalry with Russia, indeed beating Stalin to the Balkans, and as much of eastern Europe as possible, was precisely what Churchill had in mind.

While storm clouds gathered over the transatlantic Allies, their bombing raids over Berlin persuaded Goebbels, who, in addition to his propaganda duties, was responsible for the capital, to implore Hitler to go all out for "Total War" and announce it to the German people. He would not agree. "The Führer does not regard the crisis as sufficiently serious and compelling that it could persuade him to pull out all the stops,"[11] Goebbels noted with disappointment. "England will be totally destroyed in this war. As indeed she deserves," Hitler told him, "how this destruction will be brought about, it is as yet too early to judge."[12] The main hope would be an "arrangement" with the Soviet Union, but, as Goebbels concluded, "the Führer would prefer not to go into that, given the present war situation."[13]

On the eastern front that morning Stalin was unleashing his massive summer offensive, Operation "Bagration." More than a million and a half troops, aided by nearly three thousand tanks and six thousand planes, were falling upon the Germans along a front that stretched for hundreds of miles. It was the anniversary of the Nazis' own invasion of Soviet territory two years before. Hitler ordered "that every square meter of territory was to be defended to the last."[14]

That day Hitler also addressed senior officers at the Platterhof in Obersalzburg. Though he was now ready to admit that the Allies would not be pushed back into the stormy waters of the Channel, he hoped that a breach within his opponents could still save Germany's chances of victory. "He did not deny the gravity of the situation," Below noted of the speech, "but expressed to this discriminating circle the hope and belief that the breach would leave the German *Reich* free to carry on the struggle."[15] Below recorded that Hitler's audience that afternoon were convinced: "His listeners departed confident, their belief in Hitler reinforced."[16]

Back in the west, lines between Washington and London were buzzing. Roosevelt was complaining that he had effectively been stitched up by Churchill over the deal with the Russians on Greece and Romania. "I think I should tell you frankly that we are disturbed that your people took this matter up with us only after it had been put up to the Russians and they had inquired whether we were agreeable," Roosevelt wrote, tactfully laying the blame on British officials, rather than the prime minister himself.

Churchill decided to take it personally. The next day, June 23, he replied: "I cannot admit that I have done anything wrong in this matter. It would not be possible for three people in different parts of the world to work together effectively if no one of them may make any suggestions to either of the others without simultaneously keeping the third informed. ... I hope to have your confidence and help within the spheres of action in which initiative is assigned to us."[17]

Five days later on June 28, the parallel argument over the British proposal to break out via Trieste and Ljubljana as against the American wish to stick to the invasion of southern France, which was being waged between the British and American Chiefs of Staff, drew the two heads of government into head-to-head combat and a mortal battle of letters. Churchill made a direct appeal to Roosevelt: "The deadlock between our Chiefs of Staff raises serious issues. Our first wish is to help General Eisenhower in the most speedy and effective manner. But, we do not think this necessarily involves the complete ruin of all our great affairs in the Mediterranean, and we take it hard that this should be demanded of us," he complained. "I most earnestly beg you to examine this matter in detail for yourself. I think the tone of the United States Chiefs of Staff is arbitrary and, certainly, I see no prospect of agreement on the present lines."[18]

Roosevelt would have none of it. "On balance I find I must completely concur in the stand of the US Chiefs of Staff," he replied that same day. "General Wilson's proposal for continued use of practically all the Mediterranean resources to advance into northern Italy and from there to the northeast is not acceptable to me, and I really believe we should consolidate our operations and not scatter them. It seems to me that nothing can be worse at this time than a dead-lock in the Combined Staffs as to future course of action. You and I must prevent this and I think we should support the views of the Supreme Allied Commander," Roosevelt warned. "He is definitely for ANVIL and wants action in the field by August 30, preferably earlier."[19]

Churchill, however, would not let the matter rest. His Chiefs of Staff were convinced that there were not sufficient resources to launch the "Anvil" operation, and that it would only harm the campaign in Italy. The prime minister bombarded his American ally with two more telegrams before the day was out. "At the present stage of the war in Europe, our overall strategic concept should be the engagement of the enemy on the largest scale with the greatest violence and continuity. In this way only shall we bring about an early collapse," Churchill insisted. He then laid into the invasion of southern France: "We are therefore left with the Toulon–Marseilles operation. The more I have thought about this, the more bleak and sterile it appears. ... General Wilson conceives it possible that, on this plan, he and General Alexander could have possession of Trieste by the end of September."[20] He concluded: "Let us resolve not to wreck one great campaign for the sake of winning the other. Both can be won."

As if that was not enough for one day, Churchill then fired off his second telegram.[21] "A meeting will have to be arranged unless agreement can be reached by correspondence," he wrote. "I agree with you that a deadlock on fundamental questions of strategy would be a cruel injury to our soldiers, who are now fighting so vehemently side by side. For this reason a careful and patient discussion is indispensable and not an overriding decision by either side."[22]

While Roosevelt waded through the torrent of words from his British ally, Daisy Suckley was musing on how the world's burdens were falling on his shoulders. "The more I think of this, the more extraordinary and wonderful it becomes, and the more imperative it is for the P. to continue his work of trying to make a better world," Daisy wrote. The president had informed her that that he hoped to arrange a meeting of the four great powers: the United States, the Soviet Union, China and Great Britain. "I think that Stalin, Chiang and I can bring Brother Churchill around," he told Daisy, laughing gently. "F.D.R. with his honesty, his vision and his charm, welding together completely incompatible and otherwise suspicious elements," Daisy concluded.[23]

The next day, June 29, Roosevelt took up the epistolary cudgels and admitted to Churchill that, behind all the military arguments, he had one overriding reason why the invasion of southern France must go ahead: "I am mindful of our agreement with Stalin as to an operation against the south of France and his frequently expressed views favoring such an operation and classifying all others in the Mediterranean of lesser importance to the principal objective of the European campaign," he wrote. "Since the agreement was made at Teheran to mount an ANVIL, I cannot accept, without consultation with Stalin, any course of action which abandons this operation."[24] He then injected a piece of his own emotional blackmail: "At Tehran we agreed upon a definite plan of attack. That plan has gone well so far. Nothing has occurred to require any change. Now that we are fully involved in our major blow, history will never forgive us if we lose precious time and lives in indecision and debate. My dear friend, I beg you let us go ahead with our plan." Finally there was the matter of American domestic politics: "For purely political considerations over here I would never survive even a slight setback in OVERLORD if it were known that fairly large forces had been diverted to the Balkans."[25]

Churchill was enraged. Yet again the specter of Stalin was dictating events. The next day, June 30, he drafted the strongest words he had ever written to the president. "I cannot exaggerate the seriousness of this issue. The whole campaign in Italy is being ruined." Now came his own blackmail; a threat to resign over the issue: "If my departure from the scene would ease matters, by tendering my resignation to the King, I would gladly make this contribution, but I fear that the demand of the public to know the reasons would do great injury to the fighting troops in the Mediterranean." The crowning glory was an unrivaled example of Churchillian diatribe, normally reserved for his enemies rather than his allies: "But no one contemplated that everything that was hopeful in the Mediterranean should be flung on one side, like the rind of an orange, in order that some minor benefice might come to help the theatre of your command."[26]

So strong was the language that Churchill, having drafted it, sat on the cable. That night at 10 p.m. he met his military chiefs. He had ordered his planes to be put on standby. "So we may be flying off to Washington before we are much older, but I doubt it," Alan Brooke noted before heading off to the meeting. "I think Winston will realise there is nothing more to be gained by argument."[27] Churchill spat rage, but his Chiefs of Staff convinced him that the cable needed to be revised. "In the end we got him to agree to our outlook which is: 'All right, if you insist on being damned fools, sooner than falling out with you, which would be fatal, we shall be damned fools with you, and we shall see that we perform the role of damned fools damned well!'"[28]

A new telegram was drafted and despatched the following morning, July 1. Churchill reluctantly conceded to his American ally but told Roosevelt the decision was "the first major strategic and political error for which we two have to be responsible." It was the first time Churchill had admitted to Roosevelt his ulterior, political motive for the Mediterranean strategy. And as for consulting Stalin, what would be the point? As Churchill put it, with pained understatement: "on a long-term political view, Stalin might prefer that the British and the Americans do their share in France in the very hard fighting that is to come, and that east, middle and southern Europe should fall naturally into his control."[29]

Churchill had been crushed by American political and military strength; no other episode in the war brought home so clearly how power had shifted in the transatlantic alliance. "I wanted you to know how deeply the prime minister has felt the differences that have ended in his accepting your decision," John Winant wrote to Roosevelt from London two days later on July 3. "I have never seen him as badly shaken. He believed completely in the program he was supporting, it was only his great friendship for you, the personal consideration you showed him in your exchange of messages, the knowledge of the greater contribution we were making in the campaign and a recognition that time was pressing that prevented continued resistance on his part and aided in his forwarding a directive to General Wilson."[30] Winant was making a noble attempt to paper over the cracks. Personal friendship had nothing to do with Churchill's surrender; he had simply been outmuscled.

Over in Obersalzburg Hitler's "inner circle" was feeling gloomy. "Life would have been good but for the feeling that we were sitting on a powder

Churchill at his desk

Churchill on board

Churchill with his wife
Clementine on the beach

Churchill alone on deck

Churchill with Roosevelt in Washington

All happy together

Roosevelt, the secretive president
Roosevelt, the man of bonhomie

Left, Stalin in Moscow
Below, Voroshilov,
Stalin and Molotov

Stalin the emperor

Hitler planning

Hitler in the mountains

Hitler with Eva Braun and below, at the Wolf's Lair

keg," Traudl Junge recalled, "our secret nervousness kept spreading. Among his guests, Hitler was trying to show his confidence and certainty of victory by making light conversation to the ladies, walking to the tea-house, and playing records and telling stories by the fire in the evening. But I thought he sometimes sat there ... looking old and tired, his mind elsewhere."[31]

In his Hyde Park estate Roosevelt was more relaxed and confident than ever. He spent a lazy day with Daisy Suckley enjoying the peace and good weather. Daisy was full of praise for her president. "I told the P. that his relations with Stalin are one of the great triumphs of his career, and only the future can tell how much that relationship is going to count in rebuilding our shattered world. Before they met, there was doubt and suspicion on Stalin's part, and also, probably, on the P.'s. Now, there is the basis for talking, for working things out together." Roosevelt smiled in response, telling his closest confidante that he would keep his fingers crossed.[32]

In London, over lunch with Lord Halifax, Churchill was still brooding. "The PM," Halifax explained, "struck me as being older but on the whole on good form. He was greatly hurt by the reluctance of the American Chiefs of Staff to concur in his strategical ideas. I think the truth is that before they were in the war and in the early days they were in the war, they accepted his advice pretty blindly and now they are feeling their weight and strength," Halifax concluded.[33]

Three days later the anger saw no sign of abating. At 10 p.m. on July 6 Churchill chaired a stormy meeting. Brooke was present and recorded the most violently vituperative behaviour yet displayed by the prime minister: "We had a frightful meeting with Winston which lasted till 2 a.m.!! It was quite the worst we have had with him. He was very tired as a result of his speech in the House concerning the flying bombs, he had tried to recuperate with drink. As a result he was in a maudlin, bad tempered, drunken mood, ready to take offence at anything, suspicious of everybody, and in a highly vindictive mood against the Americans."[34]

Stalin was basking in triumph. On July 9 Zhukov, who was on a brief visit to Moscow, was called to the summer house, arriving promptly at 2 p.m. Having just received some excellent reports of events on the Baltic and Byelorussian front, Stalin, Zhukov noted, was in good humor. "I haven't breakfasted yet," Stalin told his guest, "let's go to the dining room." Zhukov had eaten, but did not refuse the invitation. The conversation turned straightaway to military strategy. "From the precise manner in which Stalin expressed his ideas one could see that he had given much thought to all these matters," Zhukov recorded. "Although he believed that we were strong enough to finish off Nazi Germany single-handed, Stalin sincerely welcomed the opening of the second front in Europe."

As for Hitler, "he is like a gambler staking his last coin," Stalin judged. Vyacheslav Molotov, who joined the conference later in the day, added that the Nazi leader would probably try to come to terms with Britain and the United States. "You are right," Stalin replied, "but Roosevelt and Churchill will not agree to a deal with Hitler. They will seek their political aims in Germany by setting up an obedient government, not through collusion with the Nazis who have lost all the trust of the people."[35] Stalin had not shed the perennial suspicion that Churchill would do a deal with Germany, but he had at least moderated his view on how it might come about.

Ten days later Churchill was still firing distant cannons over "Anvil." Having achieved nothing with his emotional cables to Roosevelt, he turned to Harry Hopkins, someone who, he believed, could be guaranteed to gain the president's attention. "I greatly needed to say some things through you which are of great importance," he wrote to Hopkins on July 19, "as you know none of us here is convinced about ANVIL strategy but we have submitted under protest to the decision of the United States Chiefs of Staff even in a theatre where we have been accorded the right to nominate the Supreme Commander." Churchill believed that the postwar world was heading for chaos, as the pink map of the British imperium was smudged by a jumble of exploding color: "Our affairs are getting into a most tangled condition. We have to deal with the affairs of a dozen states, some of which have several civil wars brewing and anyhow are split from top to bottom." Yet the great powers, he said, were failing to act in concert, each one of them approaching "the topic from a different angle and in a different mood."[36]

The next day, July 20, 1944, at Hitler's headquarters deep in the forest the calm of the summer day was shattered by an almighty explosion. It was 12:45 p.m. Smoke and fire billowed from the broken windows of the

Führer bunker. Hitler had just survived the most audacious attempt yet on his life. By the time his anxious secretaries and adjutants had rushed to the scene, he was sitting calmly in the anteroom, his hair standing on end. He greeted them with a broad grin. "Well, ladies," he said, "everything turned out all right again. Yet more proof that fate has chosen me for my mission." His eyes flashed with a vigor that his inner circle had not seen for many years. "This war must be won or Europe will be lost to Bolshevism. And I shall make sure that no one else can keep me from victory or do away with me. I am the only one who sees the danger and the only one who can stop it."[37]

While his Cabinet in London debated whether or not the reports of an assassination attempt were merely a stunt by Goebbels, Churchill was touring Cherbourg. Only three weeks after the first Allied soldier had set foot on French soil, it was deemed safe for the prime minister to travel inland. Churchill was flushed with exhilaration. In between meeting the troops he was shown an unfinished flying bomb site that had been trained on Bristol. The Nazis had been stopped just in time.

In Moscow Stalin was tightening his grip on Poland's future. The first step was the establishment of a provisional government friendly to Moscow. On this day the final preparations were being made for the "Lublin Committee" to install itself as that body in newly "liberated" Poland. Russian troops were now less than one hundred kilometers from the very headquarters which had exploded with Claus von Stauffenberg's bomb that afternoon.

In San Diego Roosevelt was sitting in the observation carriage of the presidential train. The Democratic Party's Convention, which had opened in Chicago the day before, was nominating him as their presidential candidate for an unprecedented fourth term. This came as no surprise, but Roosevelt was gracious nonetheless. That day Hopkins discussed Churchill's letter with him; its impact was zero. The prime minister's last gasp attempt to thwart Stalin physically in eastern Europe and the Balkans had fizzled out. Now it would be up to Roosevelt to pursue his long-held conviction that Stalin could be won round to act as the United States' key partner in forging a new and peaceful world of free nations policed by benign great powers.

Three days later, July 23, Goebbels was relieved to find his Führer in good shape. "He meets me on the way from his bunker. My first greeting with him is quite moving," Goebbels confided in his diary, "I am most deeply touched to see him in front of me so safe and sound." "After the attempt took place, I first made sure I was still in possession of my head, my eyes, my arms and my legs," Hitler recounted. "The Führer is furious with the generals, especially those from the General Staff," noted Goebbels. "He is determined to make a bloody example of them, and root out a freemason's lodge which has always been ill-disposed to us and was only waiting for the moment when in the *Reich*'s critical hour it could stab us in the back."[38] As Goebbels wrote, the Red Army, having crossed the river Bug just hours before, reached the outskirts of Lublin.

Two days later, July 25, the Soviet advance into Poland, as well as the installation of the so-called Lublin Committee, was causing concern in London. "It is of the utmost importance that we do not desert the orthodox Polish government," Churchill wrote to Roosevelt that day, explaining that Anthony Eden would be announcing in the Commons that British support for the émigré government in London was to be abandoned under no circumstances.

The British had persuaded the leader of the London Poles, Stanistaw Mikolajczyk, to fly to Moscow, knowing full well that they were dispatching an unarmed man into the lion's den. "Anything you say to U.J. that will induce him to give Mikolajczyk a good welcome and realise the importance of founding a united Polish government," Churchill continued, "will be invaluable. The great hope is fusion of some kind between the Poles relying on Russia and Poles relying on USA and GB. We are sure that U.J. will be much influenced by your view of these things."[39] Churchill had once been on bended knee to Roosevelt to bring him into the war; now he was again the supplicant, knowing his own powerlessness and placing the future freedom of Poland in the president's hands.

The omens were bleak. "Mikolajczyk did agree to take his courage in both hands and start for Moscow tomorrow night. This in spite of the Soviets having this afternoon announced their intention to negotiate with Polish National Council," Alexander Cadogan noted. He believed that the London Poles had hardly helped their cause after putting out "one of their recurrent and ridiculous 'declarations' stigmatising the Council as 'usurpers.' I like and respect M., but by Heaven what a mess they've made of their case!" he complained.[40] Eden also despaired of the London Poles' refusal to allow Stalin any benefit of the doubt: "Their refrain being that since Stalin had chosen Communist govt. for Poland what was the use and my refrain being that since Stalin was prepared to receive it would be unforgivable to miss this, probably the last chance."[41]

Goebbels observed these public negotiations with a mercilessly accurate eye: "The Polish government-in-exile in London and also the English government will be left out in the cold. But this was predictable; only an idiot could think that Stalin would act any differently than he has in fact acted."[42] The day after Eden had given his speech to the House of Commons declaring British support for the London Poles, Goebbels returned to the theme in his diary: "Eden declares in the Commons that the English will not be able to recognize the Polish National Soviet. Stalin won't care a fig about that," he noted with scorn. "He has the power and the troops, and the English have only words and oaths."[43] One totalitarian saw straight through the other.

That same day, as Mikolajczyk flew to Moscow, Churchill wrote a careful letter to his Soviet ally. "It would be a great pity and even a disaster if the western democracies find themselves recognising one body of Poles and you recognising another," he wrote soberly. "It would lead to constant friction and might even hamper the great business which we have to do the wide world over."[44]

Stalin's reply the following day was an unexpected and pleasing surprise. For the first time he sounded a genuinely conciliatory note: "I understand the importance of the Polish question for the common cause of the Allies," he wrote, "and for this very reason I am prepared to give assistance to all Poles and to mediate in the attainment of an agreement between them." He added that "Soviet troops have done and are continuing to do all in their power to accelerate the liberation of Poland from the German invaders." Churchill was delighted; forwarding the message to Roosevelt, he said it was the "best yet from U.J."[45]

Poland was about to become the first real test of Roosevelt's policy of "giving" to Stalin. There was nothing physically to stop the Soviet leader imposing whatever government he wanted, but this latest message gave real cause for hope. Roosevelt could see it as a vindication that his tactics were working. Just a few weeks before, he had given an unequivocal assurance to Mikolajczyk, who had flown to Washington to see him: "Don't worry. Stalin doesn't intend to take freedom from you. He wouldn't dare to do that because he knows the United States government stands solidly behind you. I shall see to it that your country does not come out of this war injured."[46] Mikolajczyk had not forgotten those words and wrote to the president on the eve of his departure from London to Russia: "I trust that you, Mr. President, and the United States government will lend your further friendly assistance and support at this moment, all important for Poland."[47]

Events in Poland were about to test both Stalin's sincerity and Roosevelt's strength of purpose. The Red Army was now less than fifteen miles from Warsaw, having reached the river Vistula. On August 1, 1944, the Polish National Underground Army in Warsaw, knowing that the Russians were close, rose up against the Nazis. The fortunes of the Polish Underground, which was loyal to the Polish government in London, were dependent on the Russian forces just a few miles away to help. Its future was in Stalin's hands.

Two days later, Warsaw was descending into a bloodbath. The Nazis were bringing in massive firepower to carry out a ferocious assault on the city's population, soldiers and civilians alike. The Underground was brutally determined to win. As the fighting raged, Mikolajczyk met Stalin in Moscow. "Warsaw will be free any day," he told him. "God grant that it be so," Stalin replied, but did not dwell long on pleasantries before turning to an interrogation of his guest. "What kind of army is it—without artillery, tanks, air force? They do not even have enough hand weapons. In modern war this is nothing," he said. "I hear that the Polish government instructed these units to chase the Germans out of Warsaw, I don't understand how they can do it. They don't have sufficient strength for that."

Mikolajczyk asked Stalin if the Soviets would assist the Underground in its defense of the city by supplying desperately needed arms and ammunition. "We will not permit any action behind our lines," Stalin replied bluntly. He then deployed some political blackmail: "For this reason you have to reach an understanding with the Lublin Committee. We are supporting them. If you don't do it, then nothing will come out of our talk. We cannot tolerate two governments."[48]

The next day, August 4, Roosevelt received a disturbing memorandum from the State Department concerning the activities of the NKVD, Stalin's secret police, in areas of Poland already liberated by Russian troops. Attached was a letter from the Commander of Polish forces in Warsaw. "The Soviet authorities are arresting the officers in command and the Staffs of the Polish National (Underground) Army. The same fate undoubtedly awaits the leaders of the Polish Underground Civilian Administration. Please do your best to save these people from liquidation by the NKVD," the letter pleaded. "It is urgent to inform the British and American governments about this activity tending at the extermination of the Polish Underground Organisation."[49]

While the Polish Underground's warning was being studied in Washington, Churchill was once again being consumed by the recurring nightmare of the Bolshevik colossus. When Lord Moran visited the prime minister in his bedroom that morning he found him hot with anxiety. Moran offered some words of comfort, suggesting that "victory was following victory" and that the war was nearly at an end. Churchill exploded: "Good God, can't you see that the Russians are spreading across Europe like a tide," he thundered, "they have invaded Poland, and there is nothing to prevent them from marching into Turkey and Greece!" Moran recorded that he was still seething about Operation "Dragoon," calling it "sheer folly." "If only those ten divisions could have been landed in the Balkans," he told Moran, "but the Americans would not listen."[50]

On August 10, an ultimatum was issued by the Germans that all civilians who remained in the city of Warsaw would be massacred. Two days later, more than a week into the rising, nothing was yet being done to aid the beleaguered Polish Underground. The Russian forces on the Vistula had been temporarily held up by vigorous German resistance, but their commander, General Konstantin Rossokovsky, had now told Moscow that he was ready to cross the river and head for Warsaw. Zhukov, the Commander-in-Chief, was also in favor of an advance.

Because of Soviet secrecy, there is no documentation of Stalin's motives during the next few days; they can only be deduced from his actions. He could see that the fiercely independent Polish Underground, which would resist any future Soviet puppet government, was both distracting Nazi forces and at the same time being killed off by them. He also knew that Warsaw was a tough military target. His first decision was to order Rossokovsky to continue his halt on the Vistula and not to help the Warsaw Poles.

Mikolajczyk appealed to Roosevelt for help: "Some scores of thousands of half-armed Polish soldiers of the home force are in this struggle and are defying single-handed between two and three strongly armed Nazi divisions with strong air support and tanks. I appeal to you to order the United States Air Force in the European Theatre to give immediate support to the Warsaw garrison by dropping ammunition and arms. To delay offering help to Warsaw spells disaster." Mikolajczyk concluded with a call to action that seemed unanswerable: "The people of Poland could never understand why the Warsaw uprising should fail at the present moment when the common cause of the United Nations is championed by unexampled strength and military power." In Washington, Edward Stettinius, the Under Secretary of State, added a covering note: "If it is militarily feasible, I feel that we have moral and other obligations to do what we can to help get aid to the Polish underground in full battle against the Nazis."[51]

That day, while Roosevelt prevaricated, Churchill entered the fray. "I have seen a distressing message from the Poles in Warsaw, who after ten days are still fighting against considerable German forces which have cut the city into three," he wrote to Stalin. "They implore machine guns and ammunition. Can you not give them some further help?"[52] For four days, Stalin sat on Churchill's letter and considered his next move.

On August 15 the Allies landed 94,000 men and some 11,000 vehicles on the beaches of southern France between Toulon and Cannes. In the run-up the operation had been renamed "Dragoon," instead of "Anvil." Militarily it achieved its purpose, reinforcing the Allied push through France.

As the Allies waded ashore, the situation in Warsaw was worsening steadily. In Moscow, Averell Harriman had informed Molotov that the United States Chiefs of Staff wanted immediate Soviet approval to begin a shuttle mission of American bombers to drop arms to the Warsaw

Underground. He explained that, because the flight from Britain or northern Italy was so long, the air drop's success depended on the planes being able to fly just beyond Warsaw into Russian-occupied territory to refuel for the return journey. Harriman, along with the British ambassador, Archibald Clark Kerr, received the Soviet reply in a meeting that afternoon with Molotov's deputy, Andrei Vyshinsky. He curtly declared that the Soviets "could not go along" with this project and that the "action in Warsaw into which the Warsaw population had been drawn was a purely adventurist affair and the Soviet government could not lend its hand to it."

Harriman immediately conveyed the Russian answer to Roosevelt. After further reflection, he sent a second letter to the president before the day was out. "I am for the first time since coming to Moscow gravely concerned by the attitude of the Soviet government," he cautioned. "If the position of the Soviet government is correctly reflected by Vyshinsky, its refusal is based on ruthless political consideration—not on denial that resistance exists nor on operational difficulties."[53]

Twenty-four hours later Stalin confirmed in a letter to Churchill that the Soviet line was coming from the very top. "After probing more deeply into the Warsaw affair, I have come to the conclusion that the Warsaw action is a reckless and fearful gamble, taking a heavy toll of the population," he pronounced.[54] On or around that day, while one Russian army waited on the Vistula, Stalin ordered another to head for the Romanian capital, Bucharest.

On August 18 Churchill prodded Roosevelt to join him in a protest to Stalin about the Soviet refusal to allow refueling facilities. This, he wrote, "added to their own complete neglect to fly in supplies when only a few score of miles away, constitutes an episode of profound and far reaching gravity." Roosevelt agreed to a polite request: "We are thinking of world opinion if anti-Nazis in Warsaw are in effect abandoned. We believe that all three of us should do the utmost to save as many of the patriots as possible," said the joint message. "We hope that you will drop immediate supplies and munitions to the patriot Poles in Warsaw, or will you agree to help our planes in doing it very quickly?"[55]

At noon the next day Henry Morgenthau arrived at the White House. Warsaw was not on the agenda, but Great Britain and Germany. Morgenthau told the president that in a recent meeting in London, the prime minister had informed him that England "was broke." "What does he mean by that?" Roosevelt asked. "Yes, England really is broke," Morgenthau replied. "That seemed to surprise the president, and he kept coming back to it," the treasury secretary noted. "This is very interesting. I had no idea that England was broke. I will go over there and make a couple of talks and take over the British Empire," Roosevelt quipped. Talk then turned to Germany. "We have got to be tough with Germany and I mean the German people, not just the Nazis," the president explained, "you either have to castrate the German people or you have got to treat them in such a manner so they can't just go on reproducing people who want to continue the way they have in the past."[56]

As Stalin continued to withhold help from the Warsaw Poles, Eleanor Roosevelt was writing a short letter to her husband with her own interpretation of the reasons for the difficult relationship between Churchill and the Soviet leader. With her letter she attached two paragraphs of a memo Churchill had written in September 1919 about British military operations against the Bolsheviks: "It is a delusion to suppose that all this year we have been fighting the battles of the anti-Bolshevik Russians. On the contrary, they have been fighting ours: and this truth will become painfully apparent from the moment that they are exterminated and the Bolshevik armies are supreme over the whole vast territories of the Russian empire." Eleanor told her husband: "It is not surprising if Mr. Stalin is slow to forget!"[57]

On August 22 Stalin viciously turned down the joint Roosevelt–Churchill appeal to help. "Sooner or later the truth about the handful of power-seeking criminals who launched the Warsaw adventure will out," he wrote. "Those elements, playing on the credulity of the inhabitants of Warsaw, exposed practically unarmed people to German guns, armor and aircraft." Stalin brazenly lied that "Soviet troops, who of late have had to face renewed German counterattacks, are doing all they can to repulse the Hitlerite sallies and go over to a new large scale offensive near Warsaw."[58]

Churchill, who was in Sienna on a tour of the Italian front, was appalled. He forwarded to Roosevelt an eyewitness account of the horrors in Warsaw. "The Germans are continuing ... their ruthless terror methods. In many cases they have burnt whole streets of houses and shot all the men belonging to them and turned the women and children out on to the street where battles are taking place ... the dead are buried in backyards and squares."[59]

At Hyde Park by the Hudson, Daisy Suckley wheeled Roosevelt over to Top Cottage in the early evening sun of late summer. They spent a couple of hours talking together on the porch enjoying the peace and quiet. "He is not going to England," Daisy noted, "has decided that as Stalin can't leave Russia now, it would not be politically wise for F.D.R., the Head of the State, to take such a trip to visit W.S.C., the Head of the Govt. They will meet in Quebec, as the last time, about Sept 9 or 10."[60] The unwillingness to visit Britain persisted.

The next day, August 24, Roosevelt slammed the door shut on the Warsaw Poles. He cabled Churchill: "Thank you for the information in regard to the appalling situation of the Poles in Warsaw and the inhuman behavior of the Nazis. I do not see that we can take any additional steps at the present time that promise results. Stalin's reply of August 23 to our joint message about the Warsaw Poles is far from encouraging to our wishes to assist."[61] The president was not going to annoy Stalin any more.

That day, Paris was liberated from the Nazis. The French underground had also risen against their occupiers when they knew that the Allies were drawing near. In Paris the British and Americans diverted troops to help their fight. In Warsaw the tragedy ground on.

CHAPTER FOURTEEN

August 24, 1944–February 3, 1945

The Wolf's Lair, August 24, 1944. In the Führer bunker deep in the east Prussian forests Goebbels and Hitler talked late into the night. "I will never surrender," Hitler declared. "Now that you have agreed total warfare can become reality, it is a matter of concentrating on victory alone," Goebbels replied.[1] Apparently unshaken by events in Paris, Hitler gave one final verdict before he retired: "Churchill is in a very tragic position. He knows that the English Empire is lost, that he is hopelessly powerless in the face of the Soviets and the Americans."[2] Even if self-delusion colored so much of his thinking, there were times when the Nazi warlord could be uncannily accurate.

Hours later, as morning came on August 25, Paris prepared for a victory parade. The German General, Dietrich von Choltitz, who had disobeyed Hitler's order to scorch the city to the ground, signed the formal act of surrender at police headquarters. The streets would soon be erupting with joy.

Hundreds of miles away, at General Harold Alexander's headquarters near Sienna in Italy, Churchill was sitting at a makeshift desk, cigar in hand, contemplating a half-written cable to Roosevelt. Despite the triumphant march being planned by General Charles de Gaulle in Paris and the successes his troops were at last enjoying in Italy, celebration was not in his mind. His eyes were turned upon Warsaw and Stalin's latest refusal to help the Polish Underground. He was not even allowing the refueling facilities which British and American planes needed to drop supplies to the insurgents. Churchill beseeched the president to put pressure on Stalin.[3]

For Stalin, events were turning out satisfactorily. The Nazis and the Polish Underground in Warsaw were engaged in a bloody, mutually destructive fight. The Red Army was advancing into Estonia and Romania. The creation of a new Soviet empire in eastern Europe was proceeding without interruption or objection from his allies.

Roosevelt's first meeting of the day was with his treasury secretary. Henry Morgenthau was shocked when the president entered the room. He seemed to be wasting away. Roosevelt may have looked tired and gaunt, but he greeted Morgenthau with his customary ebullience. They quickly set about business. Stalin was first on the agenda. "There are two kinds of people," Morgenthau said to Roosevelt, "one like Eden who believes we must cooperate with Russia and that we must trust the Russians for the peace of the world; and there is the school, which is illustrated by the remark of Mr. Churchill who said, 'what are we going to have between the white snows of Russia and the white cliffs of Dover?'" The president turned to Morgenthau. "That's very well put," he said with a smile, "I belong to the same school as Eden."[4]

Just a few hours later Churchill's telegram, asking that they make a second joint request to Stalin for the use of Russian-held airfields, arrived on his desk. Roosevelt was unmoved. The next day, he replied with a slap in the face. "I do not consider it advantageous to the long-range general war prospect for me to join with you in the proposed message to U.J."[5] Nothing must be allowed to cause unpleasantness with the Soviet leader.

On August 30 Stalin's forces entered Bucharest and headed for Bulgaria. While his troops lingered outside Warsaw, the rest of eastern Europe was falling smoothly into his hands.

The next day, while Churchill, feeling under the weather, worked from his bed, Hitler gave a defiant speech to his generals. "We will under all circumstances carry on the struggle until, as Frederick the Great said, one of our damaged opponents is tired of fighting any longer, and until we get a peace which secures the existence of the German nation for the next 50 or 100 years and which, above all, does not defile our honor a second time, as happened in 1918."[6] As he spoke, American troops were less than sixty miles from the German border in the west. As for the eastern front, Hitler was as vitriolic as ever. "He swore revenge and fanned the flames of hatred," Traudl Junge noted. "They're not human beings any more, they're animals from the steppes of Asia, and the war I am waging against them is a war for the dignity of European mankind," Hitler proclaimed. "No price is too high for victory. We have to be hard and fight with all the means at our disposal."[7]

On September 4, though still confined to his bed in the annex at 10 Downing Street, Churchill summoned his Cabinet. He did not, Anthony Eden noted with concern, "look at all well."[8] Nevertheless, he was full of determination and made it clear that he would not give up on Warsaw. "The War Cabinet are deeply disturbed at the position in Warsaw and at the far-reaching effect on future relations with Russia of Stalin's refusal of airfield facilities," he wrote to Roosevelt. "Seeing how much is in jeopardy we beg that you will again consider the big stakes involved."[9] He also forwarded a telegram he had sent off that day to Stalin: "The War Cabinet wishes the Soviet government to know that public opinion in this country is deeply moved by the events in Warsaw and by the terrible sufferings of the Poles there. … Our people cannot understand why no material help has been sent from outside to the Poles in Warsaw."[10]

The next day, as Churchill prepared to leave London for his upcoming conference in Canada with Roosevelt, a cable arrived from Washington. The president had found a new reason for not pressing Stalin: "I am informed by my office of Military Intelligence that the fighting Poles have departed from Warsaw and that the Germans are now in full control … the problem of relief for the Poles in Warsaw has therefore unfortunately been solved by delay and by German action and there now appears to be nothing we can do to assist them."[11]

This was quite untrue; the Warsaw Poles were still fighting hard and would struggle on for weeks. The report had been passed on to Roosevelt unchecked by his Chief of Staff, Admiral William Leahy. For the president it was a godsend, allowing him to wriggle off his hook. There was little incentive to corroborate it. The dreadful events in Warsaw hung heavily over the British Cabinet that day. "It is a black cloud in an otherwise azure sky," John Colville noted.[12]

Churchill sailed that night from the Clyde aboard the *Queen Mary*. As he crossed the Atlantic, there was time to reflect on the arguments of recent weeks, above all the invasion of southern France which he had failed to prevent. "The PM says that after all he will not 'beat up' the Americans about DRAGOON," Colville noted from on board ship the next day, September 6. "He will suggest that the controversy be left to history and adds that he intends to be one of the historians." Churchill intended now to focus on battles that he could win, not those he might lose: "One of his major tenets was this," noted Colville: "We did not enter this war for any gain, but neither did we propose to lose anything through it."[13]

Three days later, September 9, there was an apparent volte-face in Moscow. Stalin, who could see that his inaction over the Warsaw rising was becoming a visible embarrassment, announced that he was now willing to cooperate in the dropping of supplies over the beleaguered city of Warsaw. Twenty-four hours later the British were gearing into action. "Decided we must seize this," Eden noted, "tho' I fear it is too late to help Warsaw much."[14]

As Churchill, on board the *Queen Mary*, arrived at noon at Halifax, Nova Scotia, the full text of Stalin's statement, forwarded by Averell Harriman from Moscow, reached the president. It put the onus on the Allies for what Stalin still implied was a pointless exercise: "If you are so firmly convinced, however, of the efficacy of this form of assistance and if you insist that the Soviet Command organize jointly with the Americans and the British such aid, the Soviet government is prepared to agree to it. It will be necessary, however, to render this aid in accordance with a prearranged plan." The statement implied that the British had been partly to blame for not informing the Soviets in advance of the rising; it also contained a reference to the iniquities of the Poles in daring to lay blame on the Russians for the Katyn massacre. In an accompanying assessment, Harriman judged that it was "an extremely shrewd statement for the record."

Two days later, September 11, as Churchill's train headed towards Quebec, Harriman reflected further on Soviet behavior over Warsaw. He believed that Stalin's ruthless duplicity required a reappraisal of Roosevelt's policy of "giving." He cabled the president's closest associate, Harry Hopkins, in the White House: "There is every indication the Soviet Union will become a 'world bully' wherever their interests are involved unless we take issue with the present policy."[15] Harriman wanted a face-to-face meeting to persuade Roosevelt that he must take a harder line towards Stalin.

The president had no intention of changing tack. When Churchill's train pulled into Quebec, he was at the station awaiting the prime minister in his car. The second Quebec conference, codenamed "Octagon," was soon in full swing. Many things were discussed, but Warsaw was never mentioned. Roosevelt had other matters on his mind. He was campaigning to be re-elected president for a fourth term, but he was carrying the secret of the congestive heart disease that his doctors had diagnosed six months before.

Though his illness was kept under wraps, the physical decline was obvious. At Quebec, Daisy Suckley compared the president and the prime minister. "The PM looks better to me, because he is not so florid and not so fat as he was," Daisy observed, "the Pres. on the other hand worries me. He gets so awfully tired, and has no chance of rest. This campaign will wear him still further."[16] The Canadian prime minister, Mackenzie King, agreed. "It seemed to me, looking at the president, that he had failed very much since I last saw him. He looks distinctly older and worn. I confess I was just a little bit shocked at his appearance," he noted in his diary. "He is genuinely tired and weary. He has lost much weight—30 pounds I should think. He looks much thinner in the face. It is quite drawn and his eyes quite weary. Churchill, on the other hand ... looked as fresh as a baby. He seemed to enjoy a chance again to take some Scotch as well as a couple of brandies."[17]

After driving together to the Citadel, the venue for the conference, Roosevelt, Churchill and King discussed their enigmatic Russian ally: "Stalin had sent some message today which gave both him (Churchill) and the president much satisfaction," King noted. "He had been very rude in some messages." The president explained that he liked Stalin "despite all his rudeness."[18]

On September 12, as the Quebec discussions began in earnest, German forces surrendered at Le Havre. As always when they were together, Churchill and Roosevelt bubbled happily along though both were inclined privately to complain about the frequency with which each recounted the same stories to the other. On the whole, Quebec was also harmonious in its debates on politics and strategy, although Roosevelt's sensitive nose detected one trace of covert British imperialism. Churchill was keen to carve out a role for the Royal Navy in the offensive against Japan and offered the services of the British fleet after the defeat of Hitler. Roosevelt was not convinced that his motives were entirely altruistic. "All they want is Singapore back," he told Morgenthau.[19]

The one controversial decision at Quebec was over the treatment of Germany after the war. Roosevelt had adopted Morgenthau's view that the Germans deserved tough punishment; he tabled a radical proposal for the complete dismemberment and deindustrialization of their nation. Despite his initial concerns about dismantling the fabric of the German economy, Churchill was persuaded that the British could easily take advantage by moving into markets which had previously been dominated by German interests. The Morgenthau Plan was signed by Roosevelt and Churchill on September 15: it would later be shelved.

Phase two of the Lend-Lease Agreement was also signed that day. "Churchill was quite emotional about this agreement, and at one time he had tears in his eyes," Morgenthau noted. "When the thing was finally signed, he told the president how grateful he was, thanked him most effusively, and said that this was something they were doing for both countries."[20] Churchill was thrilled with the way "Octagon" had developed. Mackenzie King recorded his verdict: "This conference had been a love-feast ... everything had gone splendidly. No difficulties at all."[21] Churchill's colleagues were not so convinced. "The tragedy is that the Americans, whilst admiring him as a man, have little opinion of him as a strategist, they are intensely suspicious of him," Alan Brooke noted.[22]

Hitler's health was deteriorating rapidly. He was complaining, his private physician, Thedor Morell, reported, "of dizziness, throbbing head, and return of the tremor in his legs, particularly the left, and hands." As events spiraled out of his control, the Führer was "greatly agitated" and his blood pressure was fluctuating accordingly. His ankles were swollen; confirmation for Morell of his fear that Hitler was suffering from a cardiac condition.[23] This did not prevent the Führer announcing the very next day his intention to launch a massive offensive against the Allies in Ardennes. General Heinz Guderian tried to argue that the situation on the eastern front would simply not allow a successful offensive of this kind. Alfred Jodl was also cautious; Hitler would not listen.

The next day, September 17, Roosevelt had arrived home in Hyde Park. Completely exhausted, he telephoned Daisy Suckley. "It was a good conference; much was accomplished," he said, but explained that all he wanted to do now was "sleep all the time."[24] This had not gone unnoticed amongst the British party. Churchill and Clementine had traveled on to stay for a few days at Hyde Park. She wrote to their daughter, Mary, that the president "with all his genius does not—indeed cannot (partly because of his health and partly because of his make-up)—function round the clock, like your father. I should not think that his mind was pinpointed on the war for more than four hours a day, which is not really enough when one is a supreme war lord."[25]

Despite his ill health, Roosevelt was determined to continue as president, convinced that he, better than anyone else, could bring a lasting peace to the world. The key to that remained his policy of converting Stalin; and he continued to see evidence that it was working.

On September 24 he received two encouraging dispatches from Averell Harriman in Moscow. "The British ambassador and I had the most satisfactory talk with Stalin this evening," Harriman wrote. "For the first time Stalin spoke with sympathy for the insurgents. He said that the Red Army was in contact with each of the groups by radio and by men going back and forth. It was now understood why the insurrection had started prematurely. The Germans had threatened to deport all of the male population from Warsaw and it became necessary for the men to fight. They had no choice as they faced death either way."[26] Harriman, whose perception of Stalin had been altered so dramatically by his conduct over Warsaw, was impressed by this new, gentler, face: "Stalin showed understanding and concern for the Poles in Warsaw and none of his previous vindictiveness."[27]

By now the Warsaw rising was in its death throes. Was this display of goodwill genuine, or was Stalin being cynically opportunistic? Once again, there are no documents by which to be sure of his motives; actions and decisions are the only evidence. The simple fact was that the Nazis had effectively destroyed the Polish Underground. With the deed done, magnanimity came free.

Hitler's health was continuing to deteriorate, not helped by some disturbing news brought that day by Heinrich Himmler. According to documents that had just been discovered, it appeared that, as far back as

1938 and 1939, important figures within Hitler's regime, including Wilhelm Canaris and Ludwig Beck, had been plotting his overthrow and assassination. There was also evidence that details of German operational plans had been leaked "continuously" to the Allies in 1940. "Hitler reacted to these reports with a breakdown in health," Nicolaus Below recalled, "he complained of severe stomach and intestinal colic ... Hitler languished in bed for several days until resuming work, very slowly, at the beginning of October."[28]

Back in London that day Churchill, despite Stalin's surface change of heart over Warsaw, was again feeling pessimistic. "Stalin will get what he wants. The Americans have seen to that," he told Lord Moran as he got into bed that evening. Soon he was too agitated to remain in bed, leaping up and pacing the room. "The advance of the Red Army has taken possession of his mind," Moran observed. Churchill told Moran that, once Stalin's forces were in a country, it would be impossible to remove them. British and American forces in Italy were simply too weak "to keep them in check" and "he might have to get his way with Stalin by other means. ... All might be well," he explained to Moran, "if he could win Stalin's friendship."[29]

On October 2 the Warsaw rising was over. The Underground commander, General Tadensz Bór-Komorowski, surrendered to the Nazis. It is estimated that around 125,000 fighters and civilians lost their lives. One of the last broadcasts, heard in London, said: "May God, who is just, pass judgment on the terrible injustice suffered by the Polish nation, and may He punish accordingly all those who are guilty."[30]

The Warsaw tragedy had an important impact on the three Allied warlords. For Roosevelt, Stalin's change of heart confirmed his view that, by a process of generosity and gentle persuasion, it was possible to win the Soviet leader's collaboration in creating the kind of world America was fighting for, albeit that there were bound to be compromises along the way. A few days before, he had written to Churchill, expressing his firm conviction that the Soviet Union should, and could, become "a fully accepted and equal member of any association of the great powers formed for the purpose of preventing international war." He then used a telling turn of phrase to describe how he saw signs of progress in Soviet deportment: "It should be possible to accomplish this by adjusting our differences through compromise by all the parties concerned and this ought to tide things over for a few years until the child learns how to toddle."[31]

Stalin, for his part, could conclude that, even when he behaved badly, Roosevelt would not confront him. However, he was also beginning to understand the importance, for appearances' sake, of making gestures to show that he was listening to Roosevelt and willing to bend to him.

Churchill drew a more straightforward lesson: if physical confrontation over eastern Europe was out, the only option for protecting British interests in the eastern Mediterranean, not to mention keeping some of eastern Europe free of Bolshevism, was to do a deal with Stalin. He planned to do precisely that and arranged to visit Moscow in October.

Roosevelt was wary of Churchill's schemes. On October 4 he cabled Stalin, politely warning him against making any commitments with Churchill behind his back: "You, naturally, understand that in this global war there is literally no question, political or military, in which the United States is not interested," the president explained, adding that he was "firmly convinced that the three of us, and only the three of us, can find the solution to the still unresolved questions. In this sense, while appreciating the prime minister's desire for a meeting, I prefer to regard your forthcoming talks with Churchill as preliminary to a meeting of all three of us."[32]

In a covering letter to Averell Harriman he was even more explicit. "Quite frankly," he wrote, "I can tell you, but only for you and not to be communicated under any circumstances to the British or the Russians, that I would have preferred very much to have the next conference between the three of us for the very reasons stated to Marshal Stalin."[33] Stalin made a show of puzzlement at this sign of discord within his allies. "I am somewhat embarrassed by your message," he replied. "I had supposed that Mr. Churchill was coming to Moscow in accordance with agreement reached with you at Quebec."[34]

Roosevelt had rightly suspected that Churchill was up to his old imperialist tricks. The prime minister was met by Harriman when he landed in Moscow at noon on October 9. He told him that he would welcome his presence at some of the upcoming meetings; however, there were some he would prefer him not to attend so that he could be *à deux* with

Stalin. "My guess is, although it is not entirely clear how it will work out, that he will have most of his important talks with Stalin alone as will Eden with Molotov," Harriman wrote to Roosevelt.[35] In Washington Hopkins revealed to Lord Halifax that "the president had not altogether liked Winston going off to Moscow, feeling that he might find himself pushed somewhat into a back seat."[36]

Back in Moscow, Churchill arrived for his evening conference with Stalin and immediately cut to the chase. After agreeing that the British would push the Polish government in exile to adopt a more compliant attitude towards Soviet demands, he then suggested that a contract should be drawn up regarding those recently liberated countries in which the Soviet Union and the British had "particular interest." Top of his agenda was Greece. Romania, he said, he was not worried about: that was very much "a Russian affair." But Greece was "different" as "Britain must be the leading Mediterranean power." He hoped that Stalin would concur and suggested that "it was better to express these things in diplomatic terms and not use the phrase 'spheres of influence' because the Americans might be shocked." As long as there was an understanding between the two of them, he could explain everything to Roosevelt.[37]

"Let us settle our affairs in the Balkans," Churchill then suggested. "Your armies are in Rumania and Bulgaria. We have interests, missions, and agents there. Don't let us get at cross-purposes in small ways." He proposed that Russia should have 90 percent predominance in Rumania and Bulgaria, Britain 90 percent in Greece, and 50–50 in Yugoslavia and Hungary.

While Stalin's translator explained the proposition, Churchill drew out what he called his "naughty document," in which he had scribbled down the list of countries with the percentages of control listed beside. Stalin looked over the scrap of paper, took out his blue pencil and ticked it. "Might it not be thought rather cynical if it seemed we had disposed of these issues, so fateful to millions of people, in such an offhand manner?" Churchill said. "Let us burn the paper." "No," Stalin replied, "you keep it."[38]

Poland was not on the list; Churchill drew back from deciding the fate of its millions of people who had suffered so viciously from both Nazi and Soviet tyranny. Instead it was agreed that Stanisław Mikolajczyk should fly to Moscow for further talks. When the Polish delegation arrived it found Churchill as immovable as Stalin on the postwar borders of Poland. "Unless you accept the frontier you are out of business forever," Churchill warned Mikolajczyk. "The Russians will sweep through your country and your people will be liquidated. You are on the verge of annihilation."[39] In his defense, Churchill could argue that he was still trying to win the Poles the best deal possible; but to have any chance of preserving the independence of their nation, they had to concede part of it to Stalin.

Though he was excluded from the crucial meeting, Harriman reported to Roosevelt the next day, October 10, that "a recognition of a sphere of influence of Russia and Britain" had occurred with regard to the Balkans.[40] Though the naughty document remained secret, Roosevelt knew the broad thrust of the deal. Yet, despite Churchill's warning to Stalin that the Americans might be "shocked," the president was not particularly perturbed, although his State Department thoroughly disapproved. What mattered to him was that Churchill was now trying to seek compromises with Stalin rather than confrontation.

Stalin was on his best behavior throughout Churchill's visit. Among his other murderous talents, he had always possessed the ability to charm; and now that the Soviet leader's collaboration was his only hope, Churchill began to paint him in warmer colors, writing home to Clementine on October 13: "I have had very nice talks with the Old Bear. I like him the more I see him. (Now they respect us here and I am sure they wish to work with us.) I have to keep the president in touch and this is the delicate side."[41]

Averell Harriman reported back the general bonhomie to Roosevelt two days later: "Stalin was in high mood yesterday. He paid Churchill an unusual and significant compliment by attending the ballet and Red Army concert at the Opera House." Churchill was in his element. "Let me tell you what a great pleasure it has been to me to find ourselves talking on the difficult and often unavoidably painful topics of state policy with so much ease and mutual understanding," he wrote to Stalin on October 17.[42] Two days later Churchill prepared to leave. Much to his delight, Stalin paid him the unexpected and unprecedented compliment of accompanying him to the airport, waving goodbye with his handkerchief as the plane taxied down the runway.[43]

The Wolf's Lair was not a happy place. After a period of ill health Nicolaus von Below returned there on October 24. "The Führerbunker had become a colossus of concrete with walls seven meters thick," Below recalled, "three other bunkers had been similarly clad. The former wooden structures had 60cm splinter protection."[44] Below was briefed with the latest updates: "In east Prussia the Russians were at Goldap. We had just won back Gumbinnen, where the Soviets had been raping and murdering the female population." Below met Hitler at noon and was warmly welcomed back into the fold. "It was relatively quiet on both major fronts and Hitler had had time to scheme the Ardennes offensive. Everything seemed to revolve around this operation."[45]

On his return to London, Churchill, after the rarefied atmosphere of Moscow, was suffering a morose reaction. According to Moran, "he seemed to realise that he had got nothing out of Stalin and that Poland had been left in the grip of Russia." He was also exhausted. "He seems torn between two lines of action," Moran noted. "At one moment he will plead with the president for a common front against Communism and the next he will make a bid for Stalin's friendship. Sometimes the two policies alternate with bewildering rapidity."[46]

Americans were gearing up to vote. Harriman, who returned briefly to Washington in late October, found the city in the grip of "election fever." Roosevelt explained to his Moscow ambassador that until the election was over he felt "helpless to do anything constructive" about the Polish question. Harriman was troubled: "He consistently shows very little interest in eastern European matters except as they affect sentiment in America."[47] Harriman was increasingly convinced that Roosevelt's faith in his ability to influence Stalin was wrong-headed: "He has no conception of the determination of the Russians to settle matters in which they consider that they have a vital interest in their own manner, on their own terms. The president stills feels he can persuade Stalin to alter his point of view on many matters that, I am satisfied, Stalin will never agree to."[48]

The Big Three were trying to arrange a second face-to-face meeting, but Stalin was displaying the same self-regard about the location as he had at the first. Roosevelt cabled Churchill: "He states that if our meeting on the Soviet Black Sea Coast is acceptable he considers it an extremely desirable plan. His doctors to whose opinion he must give consideration do not wish him to make any 'big trips.'" Roosevelt, a man who could not walk, was being asked to make another exhausting trip to the Soviet leader's doorstep. It was a sacrifice he felt he must make: "I do think it important that we three should meet in the near future,"[49] he told Churchill.

Churchill wanted the summit to take place in London. He replied that, in the event of Stalin not coming, "I earnestly hope you will pay your long-promised and deferred visit to Great Britain and then visit your armies in France."[50] Such a visit was assuming a huge political and emotional importance in Churchill's mind.

Two days later, November 7, Roosevelt celebrated his fourth win at the polls. Churchill sent his congratulations: "It is an indescribable relief to me that our comradeship will continue and will help to bring the world out of misery." He also enclosed a copy of the message of congratulations he had sent to Roosevelt after his election victory back in November 1940. It had always dismayed and puzzled him that Roosevelt had never acknowledged it; indeed, he had wondered if it had gone astray. On that score Roosevelt cleared up the matter: "Thank you for your friendly message and for your repetition of the 1940 message which I certainly had not forgotten," he replied two days later. Quite why he had not bothered to reply four years before has never been satisfactorily explained.[51]

Ten days later, November 17, Goebbels was observing Churchill's discomfiture, which had now come into the open, over the continuing failure of either of the other Big Three to pay court to him in Britain. "Churchill has been put on the spot in the Commons for continually traveling to the USA or the Soviet Union, while no important statesman ever considers it necessary to come to England," he crowed. "They call upon him to arrange for the next meeting with Stalin and Roosevelt to be in London. Of course that's easier said than done. ... The English are playing the great power which they no longer are in reality."[52]

After the pleasantries of electoral congratulations, a marked coolness began to enter Roosevelt's correspondence with Churchill. Partly this was due to authorship. Roosevelt's cables were always drafted by his staff, but he would often add the personal touch. Now he left more and more to those around him, most notably his brusque Chief of Staff, Admiral William Leahy, who was no lover of the British. Less than two weeks after the re-election Eden noted: "Three bad messages from FDR ... I am told that Leahy now has the ear. Whatever the reason the result is a bad augury for the new regime."[53] It was also to do with Roosevelt's own priorities. What mattered now was his vision of the postwar world in which he often saw Churchill more as an obstacle than a help. Previously, both men had tried to dilute any outbreaks of formal frostiness in their correspondence by frequent applications of the personal touch. Roosevelt was now too tired, or too fed up, to bother with it.

On November 20 Hitler left the Wolf's Lair; he was never to return. In his last days at his forested bunker he cast a bleak eye at the future. "We were at the end of this great struggle," Below recalled, "and there remained for Hitler only the question of his personal destiny." His Luftwaffe adjutant remembered Hitler saying several times that the war was lost. The one shaft of hope, noted assiduously by Goebbels, remained the chance that the alliance opposing him would crumble into internal conflict. "At present it is definitely in Stalin's interest to let the war in the west drag on as long as possible," Goebbels wrote on November 23, "the longer he and the Anglo-Americans are at each other's throats, the better his chances post-war."[54]

Two days later in London, November 25, yet another nasty telegram arrived from Washington. "Unpleasant message from FDR during day about civil aviation. He seems to specialise in these things just now," Eden noted bitterly.[55] John Colville, who was present when the American ambassador, John Winant, delivered the telegram to Churchill, was disgusted: "It was pure blackmail, threatening that if we did not give way to certain unreasonable American demands, their attitude about Lease-Lend supplies would change. Winant was shame-faced about presenting it and didn't want to stay to lunch, but the PM said that even a declaration of war should not prevent them having a good lunch."

Three days later Churchill replied in wounded terms to the threat from the White House: "It is my earnest hope that you will not bring on this air discussion the prospect of our suffering less generous treatment on Lend-Lease than we had expected from the Quebec discussions." He then attempted to show the president how absurd it was to think that the British could somehow stand in the way of the United States in the realities of the emerging postwar world: "You will have the greatest navy in the world. You will have,

I hope, the greatest air force. You will have the greatest trade. You have all the gold. But these things do not oppress my mind with fear because I am sure the American people under your reacclaimed leadership will not give themselves over to vainglorious ambitions, and that justice and fair play will be the lights that guide them."[56]

The president had traveled the day before to Warm Springs, his country retreat in Georgia, for Thanksgiving. On November 29 he received a reminder from Winant: "Tomorrow is the prime minister's birthday. You will remember that we were with him at Tehran a year ago."[57] Roosevelt did his duty, and duly dispatched a friendly note. "Ever so many happy returns of the day," he wrote, "I shall never forget the party with you and U.J. a year ago and we must have more of them that are even better."[58] In previous years, either the White House staff had done the prodding or Roosevelt had remembered himself.

Hitler's mind was consumed with thoughts of his planned new attack in the west. On December 2 he spoke at length with Goebbels. "Thank God the enemy haven't noticed the slightest thing, so that we can count on a considerable moment of surprise," he noted. "The Führer urgently asks me to keep completely secret the information he is giving me. Only a few people have been put in the picture about his plans." Hitler explained that the offensive would be launched in the first half of December, and that there was plenty of firepower available to smash the Allies. "The Führer has hoarded up everything for this big push so that, with a little luck, we will not encounter any insuperable difficulties … this strike could perhaps even be the turning point of the war."[59]

In early December Churchill found himself the target of another scolding from Washington. In Greece, the country he believed so vital to British interests, the local communist factions, EAM and ELAS, were waging a guerrilla campaign to take over power in the vacuum left by the Nazis' retreat. British forces were trying to keep control to ensure that a pro-Western government would emerge. Churchill had cabled General Ronald Scobie, the British commander in Athens, ordering him to destroy "all EAM ELAS bands approaching the city." Scobie was instructed "to act as if you were in a conquered city where a local rebellion is in progress."[60] His cable was somehow leaked in Washington, causing a furor. This was accompanied by another spat, in which Churchill was castigated for trying to interfere with the composition of the new Italian government. On December 5 the State Department issued what amounted to a public reprimand of the prime minister, accusing the British of trying to exert undue influence in other nations.

Churchill was incredulous. He worked late into the night in the annex at 10 Downing Street dictating two angry telegrams to the president. "I was much astonished at the acerbity of the State Department's communiqué to the public, and I shall do my best in my reply to avoid imitating it," he wrote. Above all he found it contemptible that he should be under the hammer for fostering democracy in Greece while no criticism had ever been made of Stalin's bullying or the Russian imposition of communist puppets in eastern Europe: "I am sure such things have never been said by the State Department about Russia even when very harsh communications have been received and harsher deeds done," he told Roosevelt.[61] "I deplore any offense which the press release ... may have given you personally," Roosevelt replied that same day, though he made it abundantly clear that he supported the content of the press release.

At the same time, Stalin was manipulating facts to harden his political grip of Poland. He wrote a stinging telegram to Churchill with a series of untrue allegations against the Polish government in exile: "We cannot tolerate terrorists, instigated by the Polish émigrés, assassinating our people in Poland and waging a criminal struggle against the Soviet forces liberating Poland." His motive was to build up an unanswerable case for Moscow's poodles in Warsaw: "I think that our task now is to support the National Committee in Lublin and all who want to cooperate and are capable of cooperating with it."[62]

Hitler was on the move, traveling by train to a new headquarters near Bad Nauheim, from where he would be able to observe his much-anticipated offensive in the Ardennes. Albert Speer had rebuilt and refurbished a "fine old castle" for the Führer, but Hitler told him that he would "never set foot in it." Speer was instructed "to build barracks and bunkers in the nearby woods."[63] At the new headquarters, named *Adlerhorst*, the "Eagle's Eyrie," Hitler briefed his commanders: "I have striven from the beginning to conduct the war wherever possible offensively. Wars are finally decided through the recognition by one side or the other that the war as such can no longer be won. To get the enemy to realize this is the most important task."[64] It was to be a fight to the death: "Whatever the enemy does he can never reckon with capitulation, never, never. That is the decisive point."[65]

Three days later, December 16, Operation "Autumn Mist" was launched. Some 200,000 Nazi troops were thrown into battle. The Allies were unprepared, and for over a week the Germans advanced. With the skies thick with cloud, Allied bombers were unable to exercise their air superiority to stop them.

While Hitler made what would turn out to be his final show of strength, the president's frailty was alarming those close to him. "I had quite a talk with Anna about her father's health," Daisy Suckley wrote after a visit to the White House on December 19. "It is a very difficult problem, and I am entirely convinced that he can not keep up the present rate—he will kill himself if he tries, and he won't be so very useful to the world then."[66]

At 1 a.m. the next day Goebbels was roused by a telephone call from Hitler, who was monitoring his troops' advance from his forward HQ. "The Führer is very pleased that the enemy has no idea of the extent of our offensive," Goebbels explained, "they still think it's a matter of an advance by three or four divisions, whilst in reality ten times that number have been deployed." The Führer's confidence and optimism was a great relief. "When he speaks one can immediately see his inner excitement and joy," Goebbels noted.[67]

For Churchill, the crisis was Greece. Much to the consternation of his wife, Clementine, he left Chequers on December 24 and flew to Athens to try to bang together the heads of the warring Greek factions. Kirk, the American representative in the Greek capital, reported that Churchill was "clearly deeply disturbed over the situation here ... but is also determined to persist in military operations until Athens and its surroundings are cleared." When Kirk asked him on Boxing Day if he had any message he wanted passed on to the president, Churchill said: "Tell him that I hope he can help us in some way. We want nothing from Greece. We don't want her airfields or her harbours—only a fair share of her trade. We don't want her islands. We've got Cyprus anyhow. We came in here by agreement with our allies to chase the Germans out and then found that we had to fight to keep people here in Athens from being massacred. Now if we can do that properly—and we will—all we want is to get out of this damned place."[68] Churchill was at pains to convey that his Christmas wishes did not include imperial dreams.

That day, Roosevelt received a disturbing cable from Moscow. Stalin wrote that he was about to recognize the puppet Lublin Committee as the provisional government of Poland, cutting out the London Poles. After his usual assurance that the Soviet Union "has a stake in strengthening a pro-ally and democratic Poland" came the sting of reality: "The Polish problem is inseparable from that of the security of the Soviet Union."[69]

The next day, as Churchill traveled from Greece to Italy, Hitler, in his secluded headquarters in the forests near Bad Neuheim, was expounding to his generals his new plan to regain control of Alsace and Lorraine, territory lost to Germany after the First World War. "This concept was based on no true strategic appreciation and the resources required were even less likely to be available than they had been for the Ardennes offensive," Walter Warlimont recalled, but this did not stop Hitler reporting the new strategy in "glowing terms."[70] "I do not need to explain to you again how much depends on it," he told his commanders. "There may be some who in secret will object, saying: 'Yes but will it come off?' Gentlemen," Hitler continued, "the same objection was raised to me in 1939. I was told both verbally and in writing that the thing could not be done; that it was impossible. Even in the winter of 1940, I was told: that cannot be done."[71] However, there was more of hope than strategy in his conclusion: "In the last analysis I am counting on the fact that the German soldier knows what he is fighting for."[72] Hitler understood that it was total victory or total destruction. "We'll not capitulate. Never," he told von Below: "We can go down, but we'll take the world with us."[73]

Roosevelt could see that Poland was becoming the one potentially divisive issue between him and Stalin. On New Year's Eve, he sent an uncharacteristically strong reply to the Soviet leader's cable: "I must tell you that I am disturbed and deeply disappointed by your message of December 27 regarding Poland." The president pleaded for a month's postponement of recognition of the Lublin Committee as the provisional government. Stalin quickly replied that this would be impossible as the Presidium of the Supreme Soviet of the USSR had already made the decision. It was a *fait accompli*; this time Stalin did not bother with even a nod in Roosevelt's direction.

By January 1945 the world had been consumed in its bloodiest ever conflict for over five years. The New Year would see not just the endgame on the battlefield but also in the private war of the warlords. Hitler's world was dissolving in the face of his enemies' advance, but he would not give up. "Do you believe, mein Führer, that we can still win the war?" Christa Schroeder asked her boss. "We have to," Hitler replied.[74] The Ardennes offensive had failed, fatally weakening German defenses. As the British and Americans lined up on Germany's border to the west, the Red Army was charging in to the east. Railways had been smashed by the retreating Germans; the Russian advance was dependent on the movement of supplies by trucks, mostly American Studebakers, provided by lend-lease. Roosevelt's generosity was hastening the advance of Stalin's forces.

On January 3 Churchill's great hope that Roosevelt would finally visit Britain was dashed. As in the first, Stalin had won the battle of venues for the second meeting of the Big Three. It would be held at Yalta in the Crimea. "In considering itinerary of visit to Black Sea, it has developed much to my regret that because of my extended absence from Washington it is necessary for me to postpone my projected visit to the United Kingdom until a later date," Roosevelt wrote. Churchill made no effort to conceal his distress. "We are very sorry indeed you will not come to our shores on this journey," he replied.

There was little confidence in London that much would be achieved by the upcoming conference. Eden noted: "I am much worried that the whole business will be chaotic and nothing worth while settled, Stalin being the only one of the three who has a clear view of what he wants and is a tough negotiator. PM is all emotion in these matters, FDR vague and jealous of others."[75]

A week later, January 10, with snow thick on the ground, Churchill was in bed in a rotten mood, not helped by suspicions of Roosevelt's lack of application and stamina. "He is disgusted that the president should want to spend only five or six days at the coming meeting between 'the big three,'"

Colville noted, "and says that even the Almighty required seven to settle the world. (An inaccuracy which was quickly pointed out to him. Viz. Genesis I.)."[76]

A week later Sir Alexander Cadogan was recording events in the east with a mixture of celebration and regret. "Russian news marvellous— they're tearing the guts out of the Germans. Warsaw has fallen," he recorded in his diary. However, the victims were the London Poles. "What must be the feelings of poor Edward [Raczynski] and his friends at hearing the Polish anthems broadcast! It's no triumph for them, and they won't get back. What a tragedy!"[77]

Hitler had returned from the Eagle's Eyrie to Berlin. "He realized it was the beginning of the end," Below recalled.[78] Apart from one visit to the front, he never left the German capital again. On this day, January 17, he went into "a paroxysm of rage," having learnt that his troops had been evacuated from Warsaw without his consent.[79] "He completely lost any comprehension of or interest in the frightful general situation," General Guderian recalled. "He could think of nothing but the misfortune of losing Warsaw."[80] Hitler told Guderian: "It is not you I am after, but the General Staff. It is intolerable to me that a group of intellectuals should presume to press their views on their superiors. But such is the General Staff system and that system I intend to smash." On January 21 he issued an order that every decision from "an operational movement" to the surrendering of a position was to be reported directly to him "in good time" before any action was taken. "In future I shall impose draconian punishment on any attempt at concealment, whether deliberate or arising from carelessness or oversight," he announced.[81]

While Hitler spluttered, the three Allied warlords prepared, with mixed feelings, to converge on Yalta; their agenda the future of the world. As Daisy Suckley noted in her diary on January 22, the last thing the president needed was to be away from home. "The P doesn't relish this trip at all—thinks it will be very wearing, and feels that he will have to be so much on the alert, in his conversations with Uncle Joe and W.S.C. The conversations will last interminably and will involve very complicated questions." Roosevelt boarded the USS *Quincy* with his daughter Anna and set sail for Malta.[82]

The next day Churchill, as he was getting into bed, confided his fears to John Colville. "Make no mistake, all the Balkans, except Greece, are going to be Bolshevised; and there is nothing I can do to prevent it. There is nothing I can do for poor Poland either."[83] He was also less than enamored with Stalin's choice of location. Churchill, Harriman recorded in a cable to Roosevelt on January 24, "says if we had spent ten years on research we could not have found a worse place in the world than MAGNETO but that he feels that he can survive it by bringing an adequate supply of whiskey. He claims it is good for typhus and deadly on lice which thrive in those parts."[84]

In Berlin, Hitler was sinking. "This time the Führer gives the impression of being tired. The heavy workload has affected his health slightly," Goebbels wrote in his diary on January 25. More than ever, Hitler was seeing Stalin as the man he must not only beat but also emulate: "What the wide territory of Russia was to Stalin, the lesser territory of Germany is to us. We must fight as fanatically for Oberschlesien as Stalin fought for Moscow, and we will succeed."[85] The following day he was clutching at his final straw: "Stalin wants to bolshevise Europe at all costs. That is our big chance, for England and America cannot permit that. If they wish to offer resistance to it, they would have to call on German help," he told Goebbels. "The enemy coalition will and must break."[86]

Three and a half years on, Stalin's men were reaping their revenge for "Barbarossa." "There were terrible tales from the villages that had fallen into enemy hands," Traudl Junge recalled. "Hitler's features were set hard and full of hatred, and he kept saying, 'These uncivilized brutes cannot, must not be allowed to swamp Europe. I am the last bulwark against that danger.' He often quoted some remarks by Frederick the Great, whose picture hung over his desk: 'The commander who flings his last battalion into the fray will be the victor!'"[87] Christa Schroeder, his other secretary, watched Hitler's physical decline, which "continued daily, despite his despairing efforts to check it. In the last months he spoke only about the training of dogs, matters of nutrition, and the stupidity and vileness of the world."[88] The Red Army was now less than fifty miles from Berlin.

CHAPTER FIFTEEN

February 3–April 11, 1945

Saki airport, Crimea, February 3. Two planes touched down, the first bearing Churchill, the second Roosevelt. "The president looked old and thin and drawn; he had a cape or shawl over his shoulders and appeared shrunken; he sat looking straight ahead with his mouth open, as if he were not taking things in," observed Lord Moran, who was in the prime minister's party. "Everyone was shocked by his appearance."[1] They set out on the seven-hour drive to Yalta along what Churchill called the "Riviera of Hades."[2] The three Allied warlords, three aging men with their various illnesses and shared exhaustion, steeled themselves for their second face-to-face meeting; the futures of hundreds of millions of people lay in their hands.

At 6 p.m., after the long, bumpy journey through spectacular mountain scenery scarred by the devastation of war, Roosevelt's jeep drew up to the imposing facade of the Livadia Palace in Yalta, his home for the coming week. The president, and his daughter Anna who was accompanying him, noted with a mixture of surprise and awe that men and women from the Red Army lined the entire road from Saki to Yalta, saluting as the presidential car drove past. Churchill, who had brought his daughter Sara, was also struck by this "magnificent looking" display.[3]

Tsar Nicholas I's 50-room summer palace, with its marble and limestone walls and 20-foot ceilings, was a majestic setting for the conference. Roosevelt was more than satisfied with his accommodation. He even noticed with gratitude that the toilet in his bathroom had been built up in accordance with the needs of his disability. Churchill's warning of "typhus and deadly lice"[4] seemed no more than British prejudice. "I can't understand Winston's concern," Roosevelt told his head of security, Mike Reilly, "this place has all the comforts of home."[5] There was also, Reilly noted dryly, "an added comfort." The Russians "had hospitably assigned what seemed like a platoon of very competent butlers and waiters. They had evidently checked their guns at the door because, unlike at Tehran, they were not armed. Nevertheless they were all large-eared NKVD men, so I thanked them politely, told them our Filipino boys would make the Boss comfortable, and gave them the gate."[6]

As Roosevelt settled in, his daughter Anna went to speak to Harry Hopkins. Hopkins was now a sick man; the journey had left him tired and bad-tempered. He also believed that the president was ill-prepared for the conference. "He gave me a long song and dance that FDR must see Churchill in the morning for a long meeting to dope out how those two are going to map out the Conf," Anna noted in her diary of the trip, "made a few insulting remarks to the effect that after all FDR had asked for this job and that now, whether he liked it or not, he had to do the work, and that it was imperative that FDR and Churchill have some prearrangements before the big Conf started."[7] Anna, knowing her father's fears of offending Stalin, warned that "this course might stir up some distrust among our Russian brethren," but promised to discuss it with the president.[8]

As Churchill and his entourage unpacked in the Vorontsov Villa, a 25-minute drive from the Livadia Palace, Allied bombers were preparing to smash Hitler's capital. The old *Reich* Chancellery, as well as many official buildings in the center of Berlin, were shattered. Hitler was driven to spend more and more of his waking hours in the subterranean bunker system beneath the new Chancellery. This underground network had been built in 1943. Though Hitler had been sleeping there since his return to Berlin in January, he now rarely saw daylight, save for a few brief breaths of fresh air when he took his preferred form of company, his Alsatian "Blondie," for walks.

The next morning, February 4, Stalin arrived in Yalta, having traveled that morning by train from Moscow. "According to my father he [Stalin] was no longer interested in the details of conversations," noted Sergo Beria, who was again on spying duties for the NKVD. "From this time onwards he could force the Allies to accept whatever was important for him. Still, we had to remain vigilant." Sergo was struck most by a remark made by Churchill on Poland: "I recall hearing him say that the Russians wanted to swallow up such a big piece that they risked choking."[9] Sergo was confused; Churchill's concern was that Poland, in compensation for losing land to the east, was being offered in return too large a piece of Germany to digest.

At 3 p.m. Stalin paid a courtesy call on Churchill at the Voronstov Villa; they spent most of their 45 minutes discussing General Bernard Montgomery's plans for an offensive in the west. He then headed for the Livadia Palace and a private meeting with Roosevelt. The president was seated in the small study in the Palace. The two men shook hands, and in his attempt to set a comradely tone, Roosevelt told Stalin that, while sailing across the Atlantic, he had made a bet that the Red Army would be in Berlin before General Macarthur took Manila. Stalin chuckled, and modestly replied that Roosevelt would not win his bet.[10] Keen to demonstrate that Britain and America had no intention of ganging up on their Soviet ally, Roosevelt suggested that, as the armies on the western and eastern fronts were now so close, perhaps the time was ripe to initiate daily contact between the two commands. Stalin agreed. They set off to the main ballroom, the setting for the formal meetings of the Big Three.

The first session went off without argument, and the three men repaired for dinner, hosted by the president. With the vodka toasts under way, Roosevelt decided it was time for a little pleasantry. "There is one thing I want to tell you," he said to Stalin, "the prime minister and I have been cabling back and forth for years now. We have a term of endearment by which we refer to you and that is 'Uncle Joe.'"[11] This light attempt at camaraderie appeared to backfire. Stalin put on a show of stiffness and replied that he found this "unfriendly." Despite one of Roosevelt's aides' attempt to reassure him that it was rather like the nickname "Uncle Sam" that was applied by many to the United States, Stalin got up to leave.[12]

Roosevelt was shaken. "Please stay," he pleaded. Vyacheslav Molotov intervened to calm things down. "He is just pulling your leg," he told the president, "we have known for two years. All Russia knows you call him Uncle Joe."[13] The drinking continued and the frayed nerves settled until the subject of Poland came up. "We have seven million Poles in America—people who are vitally interested in the future of Poland," Roosevelt declared. "Of your seven million Poles," Stalin replied, "only seven thousand vote ... I looked it up and I know I am right."[14]

"A terrible party I thought," Anthony Eden noted afterwards, "the president vague and loose and ineffective. W understanding that business was flagging made desperate efforts and too long speeches to get things going again. Stalin's attitude to small countries struck me as grim, not to say sinister. I was greatly relieved when the whole business was over," he concluded.[15]

However, these opening appearances were deceptive, as was Roosevelt's apparent feebleness. The president had come to Yalta with two key objectives. The first and more immediate was to secure Russian entry into the war against Japan after Germany's defeat. He succeeded in this, partly by secretly bribing Stalin with offers of Japanese and Chinese territory that would be incorporated into the postwar Soviet Union. He did not consult his Chinese ally, Chiang Kai-shek, before making the offer.

The second and more important was to agree with Stalin the structure of a postwar United Nations organization, which was to be the practical outcome of Roosevelt's vision of the great powers acting as the world's "policemen." The heart of this new body was to be a Security Council on which the "policemen" would sit and prevent further wars breaking out. There were long negotiations over its structure and powers. Initially Stalin wanted all the republics of the Soviet Union to have a vote, which seemed hardly practical if the United States and Britain each only had one vote. In the end a compromise was reached which allowed a seat for three Soviet republics. There were also haggles over whether each policing nation should have a right of veto on Security Council proposals. Eventually Roosevelt managed to agree with Stalin an initial structure which was to be refined by further talks.

While Roosevelt succeeded in his two main objectives, the real question, whatever the written agreements, was whether Stalin would become the protector of peace and of the independence of nations or an oppressor building a new totalitarian empire. The crucible remained Poland, which was now occupied by Russian troops. The debate was not now over territory, although details remained to be ironed out; in the fifteen months since Churchill had first made his secret deal with Stalin that the new eastern border would be based broadly on the Curzon Line, that had become an accepted fact with which the London Poles had been forced to go along. What now mattered was whether Stalin would immediately broaden the sitting provisional government, which had been based on the Lublin Committee, to include the London Poles and whether he would guarantee that free elections would soon follow.

Two days later, during the third session in the Livadia Palace, Poland had risen to the top of the agenda. Roosevelt and Churchill were insisting not just on free elections but on objective, international monitoring of them. Stalin, while seeking to avoid such a sweeping commitment, nevertheless claimed that he and the Soviet nation really had undergone a change of heart. "For the Soviet government the question of Poland was one of honor," he said, "because the Russians had greatly sinned against Poland. The Soviet government," Stalin now proclaimed, "was trying to atone for those sins." He went on to say that his great interest in Poland stemmed from the fact that it had historically acted as the corridor for those forces attempting to invade Russia, and that he wanted to put an end to this pernicious state of affairs. "For that Poland must be strong," he asserted, explaining that as a result, "the Soviet Union is interested in the creation of a mighty, free and independent Poland."[16]

After the session had come to an end at 7:30 p.m., Eden was skeptical. "First talk on Poland. President and PM were both good," he noted, "but Stalin gave us a very dusty answer. I am sure that we must come back hard on this."[17] Alexander Cadogan was caustic about the president's efforts as chairman. "I think he is woollier than ever," he recorded, "Stalin looks well—rather greyer—and seemed to be in very good form."[18]

Roosevelt's stamina was clearly failing. Before dinner he had a massage, and insisted on a 30-minute rest. "The long meetings," he told one of his delegation, James Byrnes, "are really Winston's fault because he makes too many speeches." "Yes he does," replied Byrnes, who could see that the president was utterly exhausted. "But they are good speeches," Byrnes continued. "Winston doesn't make any other kind," Roosevelt answered with a smile.[19]

In Berlin Joseph Goebbels was trying to reach the *Reich* Chancellery for a meeting with Hitler. "My visit is rather dramatic," he recorded, "access to the Führer is completely obstructed by mountains of rubble. One has to find one's way to him through a kind of maze of trenches. The whole chancellery looks desolate. One thinks sadly of the evenings we spent among the very best circle of society in these rooms. Those rooms are now just ruins."[20] During the meeting, Hitler told Goebbels he was "convinced" that the front at the Oder could be held. He also explained his determination to "remain in Berlin and defend the city." "Stalin, Churchill and Roosevelt intend to destroy the German people," Hitler said of the air raids, "and against this we must deploy all the means at our disposal, no matter when or where." Hitler continued to measure himself against his Russian opponent: "He sees the situation for us as similar to that facing the Soviets in the winter of 1941," Goebbels noted. "There too, bolshevism was engaged in a life or death struggle, and through Stalin's determination succeeded in overcoming the deadly danger."[21]

Two days later, February 8, Hitler received Goebbels once again. The Führer was increasingly deluded about the military position. "He now looks utterly exhausted," Goebbels observed, "otherwise, he is convinced that we have half-way succeeded in restabilizing the situation in the east." Despite Hitler's conviction, Goebbels admitted privately in his diary that he was "a little skeptical. Just in the last few months the Führer has sometimes made mistakes in his judgment of our military possibilities."[22] It was the understatement of the war.

At 9 p.m. that day, Stalin hosted a dinner at the Yusupov Palace. That day's session had gone well. The Big Three had agreed that the provisional government in Poland would be widened to include all parties, including representatives of the Polish government in exile in London; once this had happened, Churchill and Roosevelt would withdraw their recognition of the London Poles. They had also agreed that a free election would swiftly follow, to be monitored by British and American observers. However, Roosevelt instantly let Stalin off the hook by telling him in a private letter, hand-delivered at the conference, that "the United States will never lend its support in any way to any provisional government in Poland that would be inimical to your interests."[23]

The dinner ran on until 1 a.m. and comprised 20 courses, 45 toasts, and endless congratulatory and emotional speeches. "It is no exaggeration or compliment of a florid kind," Churchill announced before the first toast, "when I say that we regard Marshal Stalin's life as most precious to the hopes and hearts of us all." A loud "hear, hear" erupted in the room. "I propose a toast," Stalin said soon after, "for the leader of the British Empire, the most courageous of all prime ministers in the world, embodying political experience with military leadership, who, when all Europe was ready to fall flat before Hitler, said that Britain would stand and fight."[24]

Goebbels was impatiently awaiting news of the conference. In the absence of anything concrete, he began drawing his own conclusions. "It is taking place behind closed doors and will probably last another week," he noted, just as the talks were drawing to a close. "They are agreed that Germany deserves only hatred and destruction. Roosevelt has proposed that the *Reich* be occupied until the year 2000; Stalin wants to flatten Berlin down to the last stone." Goebbels made a biting assessment of the Big Three: "One probably has to regard Churchill as the key to the puzzle. He is not a proper Englishman, but is half American, and his mentality and character make it completely impossible to talk sense with him. Stalin and Roosevelt have quietly purchased the world from him."[25]

Roosevelt was sure that Yalta had been a success. On the night of the multi-toast dinner he told his doctor, Admiral Ross McIntyre: "I've got everything I came for and not at too high a price. The one nettlesome problem is Poland. The settlement we have in mind leaves much to be desired."[26] He announced to Churchill and Stalin that he would be leaving the following afternoon. Churchill believed that there were too many loose ends to be tied up. At breakfast on February 11 he complained to Moran: "The president is behaving very badly. He won't take any interest in what we are trying to do."[27]

At noon, the Big Three sat side by side at the head of a grand table in the Livadia Palace. Flash bulbs popped and they exchanged triumphant smiles for the photographers. The final achievement was the signing of the Declaration on Liberated Europe. It promised that they would "solve by democratic means" the problems facing all countries liberated from Nazi tyranny. They agreed to uphold "the right of all peoples to choose the form of government under which they will live."[28] But what did words like "democracy" and "liberty" mean to a totalitarian dictator on one side and two constitutional democrats on the other? It was never spelt out.

Yet, as the three Allied warlords prepared to depart, Yalta seemed to herald a new era of cooperation. Cadogan, a seasoned and skeptical diplomat, noted: "I have never known the Russians so easy and accommodating. In particular Joe has been extremely good. He is a great man, and shows up very impressively against the background of the other two ageing statesmen. I think the conference has been quite successful. We have got an agreement on Poland which may heal differences, for some time at least, and assure some degree of independence to the Poles."[29]

"We will meet again soon," Roosevelt said to Stalin, "in Berlin."[30] The two men shook hands warmly and the president was helped into his wheelchair. His daughter Anna followed close behind as he left the room. Once Roosevelt had been driven off, Churchill could not remove himself fast enough. "I see no reason to stay a minute longer," he announced to his daughter Sara as they pulled up outside the Voronstov Villa. He sprang out of the car, shouting to his secretary: "I don't know about you—but I'm off."[31]

Two days later, February 13, Roosevelt, who was back on board the USS *Quincy*, now moored in Alexandria, sent a note of thanks to Stalin. "I wish again, upon leaving the hospitable shores of the Soviet Union, to tell you how deeply grateful I am for the many kindnesses which you showed me while I was your guest in the Crimea," he wrote. "I leave greatly heartened as a result of the meeting between you, the prime minister and myself."[32] As part of his ongoing mission to encourage nations to assert their independence of European imperialists, particularly British ones, he entertained rulers from Africa and the Middle East, writing home to Daisy Suckley: "Saw King Farouk, then Emperor Haile Selassie, and the next day, King Ibn Saud of Arabia with his whole court, slaves (black), taster, astrologer, and eight live sheep. Whole party was a scream!"[33] Despite the puckish humor, Daisy was anxious: "I am really worried about F.D.R. Even the papers say 'his aides are worried about his health.' In all the pictures that have come out, he looks really sick."[34]

That night Bomber Command mounted the most controversial and devastating raid of the war. Seven hundred and seventy-four bombers ignited Dresden into a giant fireball. Hitler was incensed, as was Goebbels, who mooted that tens of thousands of Allied prisoners of war should be executed in retribution. Hitler agreed. "We must scrap this idiotic convention," he said, referring to the Geneva Convention on the treatment of prisoners of war.[35] Only after pleas from Alfred Jodl, Joachim von Ribbentrop, Wilhelm Keitel and Karl Dönitz did the Führer abandon the idea.[36]

Churchill had flown from Athens to Alexandria. When they met for lunch aboard the USS *Quincy* he thought Roosevelt had a "placid, frail aspect."[37] After a brief discussion on the latest atom bomb research, in which they agreed that their collaboration would continue, they "parted affectionately."[38] It would be the last time the two men would see each other. Back on board his own ship, Churchill held a long salute in honor of the president as he and the *Quincy* slid serenely into the Mediterranean.

Despite his grumpiness, Churchill, like Roosevelt, thought that Yalta had worked and Stalin would keep his word. In Cairo two days later he remarked: "Poor Neville Chamberlain believed he could trust Hitler. He was wrong. But I don't think I'm wrong about Stalin." He believed that Stalin's admission of guilt over Russian crimes against the Poles, and his desire for atonement by the creation of a strong and free Poland, were sincere and important.

Back in Moscow, Stalin was also pleased. It seemed to him that his allies had, by nods and winks, and by the woolly nature of the agreements, tacitly accepted his effective sovereignty over eastern Europe. When Molotov expressed a worry that some of the wording could get in Russia's way, Stalin told him: "Never mind. We'll do it in our own way later."[39]

Roosevelt's voyage home was dispiriting. As the *Quincy* approached Algeria, Harry Hopkins told him: "Chip and I are getting off at Algiers." Chip was the State Department official and Russian interpreter, Charles Bohlen; he and Hopkins were indispensable members of Roosevelt's entourage whose help he needed in writing the speech on Yalta that he was due to deliver to Congress on his return. "Why?" Roosevelt demanded. "Well, I'm sick. I mean really sick. I want to stop off and go to Marrakech and rest," Hopkins explained, refusing to accept Roosevelt's protest that there could be nothing more relaxing than a sea voyage. When Anna joined her father, she thought he looked hurt; "I am going to need a lot of help with that speech," he said, "I kept no notes."[40] Hopkins, still only 54, was indeed ill and had only a year to live.

On February 20, as Churchill's plane neared the end of the thirteen-hour flight from Cairo to Lyneham airfield, Roosevelt suffered another blow. General Edwin "Pa" Watson, his closest crony, had died on board the *Quincy*. Anna watched with mounting anxiety as her father slipped into a deep malaise. When not talking about "Pa" he spent his time smoking cigarettes and staring at the ocean.[41] Three days later, he roused himself to give a short press conference to the three journalists who were on board. He expounded his plan to put Indo-China, part of the prewar French Empire, under an international trusteeship. "Stalin liked the idea," he said, "China liked the idea. The British don't like it." "Is that Churchill's idea on all territory out there; he wants them all back just as they were?" one of the journalists asked. "Yes," Roosevelt replied, "he is mid-Victorian on all things like that."[42]

At 2 p.m. the next day, February 24, Hitler summoned his *Gauleiter* to the *Reich* Chancellery. It would be the last address of this kind. Sitting at a small table, looking haggard and old, his left hand shook throughout. "You may see my hand tremble sometimes today," he announced, "and perhaps even my head now and then; but my heart—never!"[43] He gave a run down of National Socialist history, a promise of new weapons, and an announcement that, if Germany was to lose the war, it would be the fault of the German people themselves.[44]

Forty-eight hours later, Roosevelt finally found the energy to begin work on his report to Congress. He had summoned a White House speechwriter, Sam Rosenman, to fly from Washington to help him. "I understand Stalin," he told Rosenman as they worked together, "and he understands me."[45]

On February 27 the *Quincy* anchored at Newport News in Virginia. Roosevelt asked that he be allowed to board his train before "Pa" Watson's body was brought ashore. In London, Churchill was addressing the House of Commons. "The home of the Poles is settled," he told members. "Are they to be masters in their own house? Are they to be free as we in Britain and the United States or France are free? Are their sovereignty and their independence to be untrammelled or are they to become a mere projection of the Soviet state, forced against their will by an armed minority to adopt a Communist or totalitarian system?" It was the key question that had traveled with the Allied warlords from Yalta. Churchill told the House that "most solemn declarations have been made by Marshal Stalin and the Soviet state that the sovereign independence of Poland is to be maintained."[46]

Little more than two weeks after the conference's end, Churchill's anxiety was tangible. The reality of Stalin's promises on Poland was beginning to emerge. The next day, February 28, while Roosevelt attended "Pa" Watson's funeral, Churchill wrote him an anguished letter: "There are many stories put about of wholesale deportation by the Russians and of liquidations by the Lublin Poles of elements they do not like." At 2 a.m., before he went to bed, he told John Colville that, even though Stalin would have his way in Romania and Bulgaria as the *quid pro quo* for leaving Greece alone, "I have not the slightest intention of being cheated over Poland, not even if we go to the verge of war with Russia."[47]

In Washington Roosevelt retained his confidence that he had plumbed a latent goodness in the Soviet leader. He told his Cabinet: "Stalin has something else in his being besides this revolutionist, bolshevist thing. Perhaps it is do with his early training for the priesthood. I think that something entered into his nature of the way in which a Christian gentleman should behave."[48]

At 12:30 p.m. on March 1, 1945, Roosevelt wheeled into the House of Representatives. There was silence in the chamber as he was eased into a chair set up behind a desk covered with microphones. As he began his speech, he admitted for the first time in public the pain and extent of his disability. "Mr. Vice President, Mr. Speaker, Members of Congress, I hope you will pardon me for the unusual posture of sitting down during the presentation of what I wish to say, but I know you will realize it makes it a lot easier for me in not having to carry about ten pounds of steel around the bottom of my legs." Laughter rippled across the chamber. "And also," Roosevelt continued, "because of the fact I have just completed a 14,000-mile round trip." Sympathetic applause broke out.[49]

"I come from the Crimea conference with a firm belief that we have made a start on the road to a world of peace," he assured Congress. Yalta had

291

succeeded in continuing "to build the foundation for an international accord that would bring order and security after the chaos of war."[50] Many who watched him were shocked. The president drifted from the carefully written script at crucial points and his frailty was painfully obvious. "Sam and I were just sick," Grace Tully noted, after watching the speech with Rosenman, "he wasn't himself at all."[51]

That day Stalin was building his empire. His deputy foreign minister, Andrei Vyshinsky, was in Bucharest, installing a puppet government for Romania under the figurehead of the brow-beaten young King Michael, who had been muscled into allowing a communist takeover. There was no consultation with the British and Americans, as required by the Yalta agreements. However, as Churchill knew full well, Stalin had not interfered in Greece where he had used British forces to repress an attempted communist takeover. It was tit for tat.

Poland remained the key, and reports of growing Soviet oppression continued to filter out. The NKVD was rounding up potential opponents in their thousands. There was no sign of the promised free elections. "The mistrust of the Kremlin continues," Goebbels observed. "Meanwhile Stalin continues to achieve military *faits accomplis* which give him the upper hand with Roosevelt and Churchill." As for keeping Germany in the fight Goebbels recorded Hitler's agreement with his view that "we should create female battalions in Berlin. There are countless women now volunteering for duty at the front, and the Führer is also of the opinion that, so long as they come forward voluntarily, they will doubtless prove to be fanatical fighters."[52]

Not only was Hitler's mood constantly swinging; so too were his calculations on how to escape from his predicament. A few weeks before, he had judged that the British and Americans would soon have to unite with him to stop the march of Bolshevism. Now he told Goebbels that he was interested in "finding some means of coming to an agreement with the Soviet Union, and then continuing the struggle against England with the most brutal energy. For England has always been the mischief-maker in Europe. If England were finally swept out of Europe we'd all at least temporarily have some peace."[53]

On March 7, 1945, as American troops crossed the Rhine, General Georgy Zhukov visited Stalin's *dacha*. "He was not quite well," Zhukov observed.

After asking a few perfunctory questions about the situation in Pomerania and on the Oder, he said: "Let's stretch our legs a little. I feel sort of limp."[54] "From the way he looked, talked and moved you could tell that he was greatly fatigued," Zhukov recalled. "After four years of war he was badly overworked."[55]

The two men spent an hour walking around the grounds of the *dacha*. Zhukov was surprised when Stalin began reminiscing about his youth. "I've been meaning to ask you for a long time about your son Yakov," Zhukov said as they headed back to the *dacha* for tea. "Have you heard anything about his fate?" Yakov had been taken prisoner by the Germans and, at the time of Stalingrad, Stalin had refused to free him in exchange for releasing Field-Marshal Friedrich Paulus. "Yakov won't be able to get out of captivity," Stalin said quietly after a long pause. "They'll shoot him, the killers."[56] Yakov was already dead. He had committed suicide in April 1943 in a German prisoner of war camp. He had refused steadfastly during his imprisonment to cooperate with the Germans.

In London a large parcel arrived at Downing Street from Stalin bearing champagne, vodka and caviar. It did nothing to soften the mounting distrust of the Soviet leader's intentions. "The PM and Eden both fear that our willingness to trust our Russian ally may have been vain and they look with despondency to the future," John Colville wrote that night. "It looks as if Dr. Goebbels' disciples may still be able to say 'I told you so'; but, God knows, we have tried hard to march in step with Russia towards the broad and sunlit uplands. If a cloud obscures the sun when we reach them, the responsibility is with Moscow and the bitter, though for the Germans empty, triumph is with Berlin."[57] At the same time Averell Harriman was cabling Roosevelt: "The Lublin government every day is becoming more and more the Warsaw government and the ruler of Poland."[58] Churchill warned Roosevelt that, if the situation was not corrected, "it will soon be seen by the world that you and I by putting our signatures to the Crimea settlement have under-written a fraudulent prospectus."[59]

On March 10 Churchill wrote again: "It suits the Soviets very well to have a long period of delay so that the process of liquidation of elements unfavourable to them or their puppets may run its full course."[60] He was finding himself in an increasingly embarrassing political position as the volume of criticism rose within Parliament, and indeed his government, that he had effectively betrayed Poland at Yalta. He explained his problem to the president: "The feeling here is very strong ... four ministers have abstained from the divisions and two have already resigned."[61] Churchill asked that they send a joint message of protest to Stalin.

Roosevelt replied the next day: "I am fully determined, as I know you are, not to let the good decisions we reached at the Crimea slip through our hands."[62] However, he knew full well how much leeway Stalin had been given at Yalta; he told Churchill that they must wait and, for the moment, leave matters in the hands of their ambassadors in Moscow: "I feel that our personal intervention would best be withheld until every other possibility of bringing the Soviet government into line has been exhausted," he concluded. "I very much hope, therefore, that you will not send any message to Uncle Joe at this juncture."[63] As he wrote, his doctors and his secretary, Grace Tully, were keeping his diary as free from appointments as possible. He was now unable to shave or wash himself; those around him were desperately worried.[64]

In Germany, it was Heroes' Memorial Day. "It must be our ambition," Hitler told Goebbels, "to set an example for later generations to look to in similar crises and pressures, just as we today have to look to the past heroes of history."[65] In his proclamation that day to his generals he reminded them of what he considered the great betrayal, the "stab in the back," by Germany's leaders who had given in at the end of the First World War: "The year 1918 will not repeat itself."[66] He was also indulging in new fantasies about his allies. It was impossible for Britain or the United States to reverse their war policy "because both Roosevelt and Churchill have to give too much consideration to public opinion." However, the same did not go for Stalin, since he was a dictator. Therefore, Hitler deduced, "our goal must be to drive the Soviets back in the east and thereby cause them very high losses in lives and materiel. The Kremlin might then be more amenable to us." Goebbels recorded the upshot of the bargain with Russia that his Führer's logic was intended to bring about: "This special peace would not of course fulfil our 1941 aims, but the Führer hopes to achieve a partition of Poland, to be able to place Hungary and Croatia under German sovereignty, and to gain the freedom for operations against the west."[67]

Goebbels noted the one major flaw in the plan: "Where it falls down at present is that there is no possibility of effecting it."[68]

In London the next day, March 13, Churchill continued to fire cables at Roosevelt: "At Yalta we agreed to take the Russian view of the frontier line. Poland has lost her frontier. Is she now to lose her freedom?" he asked. Annoyed by Roosevelt's refusal to join him in writing to Stalin, he threatened to tell Parliament of this divergence in the British and American approach: "It would certainly be necessary for me to make it clear that we are in presence of a great failure and an utter breakdown of what was settled at Yalta, but that we British have not the necessary strength to carry the matter further and that the limits of our capacity to act have been reached."[69] This infuriated Roosevelt, who was fed up with Churchill's constant nagging about a deal on Poland which they had both signed and of whose flaws they had both been equally aware. He wanted to fire off an angry reply straightaway, but was persuaded to "sleep on it."[70]

Two days later, Roosevelt sent his reply, making clear his irritation at Churchill's threat to expose their alleged differences: "From our side there is certainly no evidence of any divergence of policy. We have been merely discussing the most effective tactics and I cannot agree that we are confronted with a breakdown of the Yalta agreement until we have made the effort to overcome the obstacles incurred in the negotiations in Moscow."[71] It was a warning to Churchill to stay in line.

The prime minister's behavior was making Roosevelt ever more determined to destroy European imperialism. In a conversation with the State Department official Charles Taussig, he explained that "one of the most important goals we must have in mind for the postwar world is to increase the purchasing power of great masses of people who now have negligible purchasing power."[72] Roosevelt said that "the brown people in the east" must be helped to achieve their independence.[73] If not, there would be the danger of hundreds of millions of "potential enemies." Pointedly, he remarked: "Churchill doesn't understand this."[74]

Churchill could sense that he was annoying the president. The next day, March 17, he wrote a personal and informal message apologizing for the burden he was creating: "I hope that the rather numerous telegrams I have to send you on so many of our difficult and intertwined affairs are not becoming a bore to you … our friendship is the rock on which I build for the future of the world so long as I am one of the builders." He then harked back to those happier times when their friendship was flowering against the backdrop of adversity: "I always think of those tremendous days when you devised Lend-Lease, when we met at Argentia, when you decided with my heartfelt agreement to launch the invasion of Africa, and when you comforted me for the loss of Tobruk by giving me the 300 Shermans of subsequent Alamein fame." The approach of victory, by contrast, seemed to bring only sourness.

In the White House Roosevelt was making a telling admission. "I got along absolutely splendidly with Stalin," he told two journalists, but conceded that the Russians were "going to do things in their own way in the areas they occupy." However, he explained that he had "got the impression that the Russians are now fully satisfied and that we can work out everything together. I am convinced we are going to get along," he concluded.[75] In other words, once Stalin had satisfied his appetite, he would need to devour no more. The problem remained that Poland appeared to be his choice of main course. Two days later in Berlin Goebbels used a different image to make the same analysis: "It's clear that in the present critical state of the war Stalin is staking everything on getting as much harvest as possible into his barns. Stalin long ago let down the iron curtain."[76] That phrase was being used by Goebbels long before Churchill made it famous.

In Moscow Averell Harriman was hardening his view of Stalin's ambitions. On March 21, he cabled Roosevelt: "We must come clearly to realize that the Soviet program is the establishment of totalitarianism, ending personal liberty and democracy as we know it." Two days later, as Churchill flew from Britain to Germany to meet General Montgomery at 21st Army headquarters at Straelem, Roosevelt was privately admitting that his assessment of Stalin could have been too rosy. He was lunching with his close friend, Anna Rosenberg. "Averell is right," he admitted, "we can't do business with Stalin. He has broken every one of the promises he made at Yalta."[77]

Twenty-four hours later, Churchill watched Montgomery's forces launch Operation "Plunder," an attempt to cross the lower Rhine in four separate places. To the alarm of the officers accompanying him, he spent two days pottering about Allied fortifications and wandering along the river. The smell of battle brought a reminder of contentment. "It was a relief to get Winston home safely," Alan Brooke noted in his diary, "I know that he longed to get into the most exposed position possible. I honestly believe that he would really have liked to be killed on the front at this moment of success. He had often told me that the way to die is to pass out fighting when your blood is up and you feel nothing."[78]

On March 27, an incident in Poland demonstrated more starkly than anything before the bad faith of the Soviet occupiers. Sixteen leaders of the Polish Underground were invited by Russian commanders to discuss local administrative arrangements. It was a trick. They were kidnapped by the NKVD and disappeared without trace for six weeks. They had been flown to Moscow, and would later be subject to a show trial and sent to the gulag.

Even though he realized that he was aggravating the president, Churchill refused to stop badgering him on the need to intervene personally with Stalin over Poland. The Russians were placing every possible obstacle and delay in the way of including former members of the London Poles in the provisional government in Warsaw. Free elections were still out of sight. Churchill told Roosevelt that it was "as plain as a pike staff" that Moscow's tactics were "to drag the business out while the Lublin Committee consolidate their power."

Finally Roosevelt agreed to send a protest. On March 29 he forwarded to Churchill, who was on his way to Chequers for the Easter weekend, a draft of his cable to Stalin. "I must make it quite plain to you that any such solution which would result in a thinly disguised continuance of the present Warsaw regime would be unacceptable," the telegram read. But Roosevelt still believed that he could persuade Stalin to fall in line: "Having understood each other so well at Yalta I am convinced that the three of us can and will clear away any obstacles which have developed since then."[79]

Evidence that a niggling doubt had now lodged in Roosevelt's mind surfaced the next day. He asked the lend-lease administrator, Leo Crowley: "How much do the Russians owe us?"[80] Crowley replied that it was somewhere in the region of eleven billion dollars. Roosevelt told him that Henry Morgenthau had suggested the Soviets be given ten billion more.

Crowley said he was opposed to this. Roosevelt agreed. "I have yet to get any concessions from Stalin," he remarked. "We are getting down to the tail end of the war. I do not want you to let out any more long-term contracts on Lend-Lease," he ordered Crowley, "further, I want you to shut off Lend-Lease the moment Germany is defeated."[81] He also conveyed his anxieties to an aide, Chester Bowles: "We've taken a great risk here, an enormous risk, and it involves the Russian intentions. I'm worried. I still think Stalin will be out of his mind if he doesn't cooperate, but maybe he's not going to; in which case, we're going to have to take a different view."[82]

Despite his worries, neither Roosevelt nor his commanders in Europe would do anything to thwart the Soviet land grab. On this day, Dwight Eisenhower sent a signal to Stalin, without consulting his British allies, saying that he was concentrating his forces on southern Germany rather than Berlin. Stalin could hardly believe his luck. He cabled back to Eisenhower: "Your plans completely coincide with the plans of the Red Army. Berlin has lost its former strategic importance. The Soviet High Command therefore plans to allow secondary forces in the direction of Berlin."[83] The Soviet leader instantly summoned his two marshals, Georgy Zhukov and Ivan Konev. "Well then," he said, "who is going to take Berlin: are we or the Allies?" "It is we who shall take Berlin," Konev replied.[84] The Red Army massed all its available strength for the race to Berlin.

Churchill and the British Chiefs of Staff had been infuriated by Eisenhower's unilateral decision. For Churchill, the political consequences were obvious and he tried to nudge both Roosevelt and Eisenhower to deploy forces so that the British and Americans could retrieve at least some of the territory that would otherwise fall into Russian hands. He cabled Eisenhower: "I deem it highly important that we should shake hands with the Russians as far east as possible."[85] Eisenhower, a future apostle of Cold War, was deaf to any such pleas.

After finishing his business in Washington on March 30, Roosevelt boarded the presidential train for Warm Springs, his retreat in Georgia where he had built the "Little White House" in 1932 and established a rehabilitation center for polio sufferers. On his arrival, some of those closest to him realized how ill he was. "When we disembarked at Warm Springs, I got my first inkling that things might not go too well," Roosevelt's chief of security, Mike Reilly, recalled.[86] Normally the president used his impressive upper body strength to help the transfer from car to wheelchair. Now, his muscles had gone: "It took every bit of strength I could muster to make the transfer that evening at Warm Springs. He was absolutely dead weight."[87]

Roosevelt's peace was now interrupted by the only unpleasant row in his entire relationship with Stalin. Three weeks before, the German commander in the south, General Albert Kesselring, had put out feelers for a negotiated surrender, using an SS general, Karl Wolff, to make contact with Allen Dulles, the head of the OSS in Berne, Switzerland. The Russians were informed of the approach but, as it seemed unlikely to lead to anything, they were not invited to take part in the initial, informal conversations. However, Stalin's paranoia was quickly aroused. He wrote to Roosevelt: "I cannot understand why the representatives of the Soviet Command have been excluded from the talks [in Berne].[88] In a situation of this kind allies should have nothing to conceal from each other."[89] The Allies had, in fact, not concealed anything. In Moscow Stalin told Zhukov: "This is some more proof of the backstage intrigues carried on between the Hitlerites and the British Government circles."[90]

In Berlin thoughts of surrender would never enter Hitler's mind. As always, he was complaining about his generals. "The Führer has to use a large part of his strength and time every day in supporting them and giving them some backbone," noted Goebbels. "It is, as he tells me, a real labor of Hercules. I also see how much he has suffered under the strain. I have never seen his hand shake as much as it did during this conversation."[91] That day Eva Braun arrived, uninvited, in Berlin. Hitler told her to return to Munich but she would not hear of it. "She was quite determined," Nicolaus von Below recalled, "that she wanted to be at Hitler's side and from then on she lived in the bunker in a room adjacent to Hitler's quarters."[92]

That day, Roosevelt tried to calm Stalin over the talks in Berne. "No negotiations for surrender have been entered into," he informed him, "and if there should be any negotiations, these will be conducted at Caserta with your representatives present throughout."[93] In a separate telegram Roosevelt repeated his concerns over events in Poland: "I wish I could convey to you how important it is for the successful development of our program of international collaboration that this Polish question be settled fairly and speedily."[94]

Churchill, too, wrote to Stalin on April 1 about Poland. "If our efforts to reach an agreement about Poland are to be doomed to failure," he warned, "I shall be bound to confess the fact to Parliament when they return from the Easter recess."[95] His concerns about Stalin's advance also surfaced in a letter he wrote that day to Roosevelt: "The Russian armies will no doubt overrun all Austria and enter Vienna. If they also take Berlin, will not their impression that they have been the overwhelming contributor to our common victory be unduly imprinted in their minds, and may this not lead them into a mood which will raise grave and formidable difficulties in the future?" he asked. "I therefore consider that from a political standpoint we should march as far east into Germany as possible and that should Berlin be in our grasp we should certainly take it."[96]

Whether because he genuinely smelt conspiracy, or whether he was using it as a tactic to deflect the pressure on Poland, Stalin now sent Roosevelt an extraordinary cable on the surrender negotiations in Berne. He claimed that he had information from his own military command that "negotiations did take place and that these ended in an agreement with the Germans, whereby the German Commander on the western front, Marshal Kesselring, is to open the front to the Anglo-American troops and let them move east while the British and Americans have promises, in exchange, to ease the armistice for the Germans."[97] Stalin was effectively making the lethal and false accusation that the British and Americans were doing a secret deal to free the Nazis to fight against Russia.

That day Roosevelt also received a cable from Averell Harriman with a catalogue of details showing a lack of Soviet cooperation. The ambassador in Moscow concluded: "The Soviets decide to do things not to obtain our good will but because they think their interests are being served. Conversely, the things we do to assist or please them do not obtain good will from them. Failure to stand our ground is interpreted as a sign of weakness."[98]

Roosevelt was so disgusted by Stalin's allegations that the next day, April 4, he allowed his staff for the very first time to send in his name angry words to the Soviet leader. "It would be one of the great tragedies of history if at the very moment of the victory, now within our grasp, such distrust, such lack of faith should prejudice the entire undertaking after the colossal losses of life, materiel and treasure involved," the telegram read. "Frankly I cannot avoid a feeling of bitter resentment toward your informers, whoever they are, for such vile misrepresentations of my actions or those of my trusted subordinates."[99]

In Berlin, Hitler was issuing commands to fight to the death. "For the defense of Vienna," Goebbels recorded, "the Führer has given his harshest order in the whole war. Our soldiers must stand here man for man, and anyone who leaves their post should be shot."[100] However, the resolve of Hitler's most loyal acolyte was beginning to waver: "I ask myself despairingly where it is all leading."[101]

In Moscow Stalin quickly saw his mistake in angering the man who had given him so much. He instantly apologized to Roosevelt: "In my message of April 3 the point was not about integrity or trustworthiness. I have never doubted your integrity or trustworthiness, just as I have never questioned the integrity or trustworthiness of Mr. Churchill." It was a well-timed climb-down. Once again Roosevelt could believe that Stalin would always respond to his appeals.

On April 11, "another perfect day,"[102] as Daisy Suckley recorded, at the Little White House, Roosevelt wrote, in words drafted by himself alone, to Churchill: "I would minimize the general Soviet problem as much as possible because these problems, in one form or another, seem to arise every day and most of them straighten out as in the case of the Berne meeting. We must be firm, however, and our course thus far is correct."[103] It was the authentic voice of the president, keeping his options open, but above all seeking to avoid confrontation with Stalin.

At 7:30 p.m. Henry Morgenthau called Roosevelt, who was in the middle of mixing cocktails. He was seated in a chair, his feet up, with a card table laid across his legs. "I was terribly shocked when I saw him, and I found that he had aged terrifically and looked very haggard," Morgenthau noted. "His hands shook so that he started to knock the glasses over."[104]

The next day, April 12, 1945, would shatter the world.

EPILOGUE

April 12, 1945

Thursday, April 12, 1945, dawned brightly at the Little White House. "Another beautiful day, with the promised heat. F woke up with a slight headache and a stiff neck, which probably comes from being over tired," Daisy Suckley noted in her diary. "The pouch from Washington won't arrive until after 11. At the moment everything is peaceful."[1]

As the sun hovered over Warm Springs, it was setting over Berlin. That evening, as the fighting grew ever nearer and Hitler faced his final days in the bunker, the Berlin Philarmonic Orchestra gave its last wartime concert. The program was Beethoven's Violin Concerto, Bruckner's Eighth Symphony and the finale to Wagner's *Götterdämmerung*.

In Moscow, Stalin was meeting a delegation of Yugoslav communists. He described to one of them, Milovan Djilas, his view of the realities of the new superpower world: "This war is not as in the past. Whoever occupies a territory also imposes on it his own social system. Everyone imposes his own system as far as his army has the power to do so. It cannot be otherwise."[2]

In London, Churchill was given sad news. Clementine's cousin, Tom Mitford, and a close family friend, Basil Dufferin, had both been killed in action. Events were not all bleak; that afternoon his daughter, Mary, was awarded the MBE.

At Warm Springs, Roosevelt was having his portrait painted. The artist said that he looked so much better, she was pleased she had not started work the day before. Late that night, Daisy Suckley recorded the day's events. "I was crocheting on the sofa. About 1 p.m. I glanced up from my work. F seemed to be looking for something: his head forward, his hands fumbling. I went forward and looked into his face. "Have you dropped your cigarette?" He looked at me with his forehead furrowed in pain and tried to smile."[3]

"I have a terrific pain in the back of my head," Roosevelt said quietly, raising his hand to touch the spot. He slumped forward, his eyes closed. By 3:15 p.m. Daisy noted: "F's breathing became very heavy and labored—I had a distinct feeling that this was the beginning of the end."[4] Twenty minutes later, his breathing gave out. "25 minutes of 4. It was the end. Franklin D Roosevelt, the hope of the world, is dead."[5]

In the concrete bunker deep below the *Reich* Chancellery, a telephone rang. It was midnight. Hitler picked up the receiver. Seconds later he slammed it down, unable to contain his excitement. "The war is not lost," he bellowed triumphantly at Albert Speer, "Roosevelt is dead!"[6] The boredom and gloom of the cold, dank rooms were displaced by elation. To Hitler it seemed that the hand of providence had once again intervened. "He was literally obsessed with the idea of some miraculous salvation," Albert Kesselring later told his Allied captors, "he clung to it like a drowning man to a straw."[7]

Ten days later, as the Allies' bombardment rocked the city above and the Red Army fought its way into Berlin, providence was finally failing the Führer. He barked at his secretaries: "Get changed at once. A plane is leaving in an hour and will take you south. All is lost, hopelessly lost."[8] The next day, he announced: "Gentlemen, it's over. I shall stay here in Berlin and shoot myself when the moment comes."[9] A week later, April 30, that moment arrived. When he was telephoned the news of Hitler's death, Stalin remarked: "So that's the end of the bastard." Churchill, on hearing the German statement that he had died "at his post," said: "I think he was perfectly right to die like that."

Hitler had spent his final hours in an orgy of self-justification. Everyone but himself was to blame for the catastrophe he had brought on his nation; his generals, his soldiers, the German people, and, of course, his enemies and the Jews. In his "Last Testament," written the day before he died, he declared: "It is untrue that I or anybody else in Germany wanted war in 1939. It was desired and instigated exclusively by those international statesmen who were either of Jewish origin or working for Jewish interests ... the responsibility for the outbreak of this war cannot rest on me. Furthermore, I never desired that after the first terrible World War a second war should arise against England or even against America."

By the end, the self-delusion was complete. Years later, in a discussion of "greatness," Churchill was asked whether Hitler was a "great" man. "No," he replied, "he made too many mistakes."[10]

In London, as Big Ben chimed the final seconds of April 12, Churchill was writing a cable to Clementine, who was visiting Moscow, to tell her of her cousin's death. There was a knock at the door; he was informed that his great ally had passed away. He placed the letter to Clementine on one side and began another, to Harry Hopkins. "I understand how deep your feelings of grief must be. I feel with you that we have lost one of our greatest friends and one of the most valiant champions of the causes for which we fight," he wrote. "I feel a very painful personal loss, quite apart from the ties of public action which bound us so closely together. I had true affection for Franklin."[11]

Something curious now happened. Even though transatlantic travel was still an eighteen-hour haul, Churchill's natural and overriding priority seemed obvious; to go on the journey he had made so often before and attend the funeral of the man with whom he had saved the world. Indeed, he had immediately written with this in mind to Halifax in Washington. Early the next morning, April 13, he received the ambassador's answer: he warmly approved of the idea, as did Harry Hopkins and the Secretary of State, Edward Stettinius. They all agreed on "the immense effect for good that would be produced." Halifax added: "Nor do I overlook the value if you came of your seeing Truman [the new president]." A flight was scheduled for 8:30 that evening.

At the last minute Churchill pulled out. He wrote to Hopkins that while it would have been "a solace to me to be present at Franklin's funeral ... everyone here thought my duty next week lay at home, at a time when so many ministers are out of the country." He gave King George VI a slightly different reason: that he had to "consider the tribute which should be paid to the late president, which clearly it is my business to deliver," in addition to the pressure of work.

John Colville recorded that it was only after "much deliberation" that Churchill decided not to go, but the reasons remain unsatisfactory. One simple fact, however, is clear: the emotional bond which Churchill always claimed tied him so closely to the president was not, even at that most poignant moment of his death, strong enough to impel him to drop everything else and make the funeral his priority. Perhaps there is an explanation which corresponds with that simple fact: that bond was not as strong as Churchill liked to claim.

The final year and a half of their relationship was not always pleasant. There had been the mocking at Tehran; the hostile cables after Roosevelt's re-election in November 1944; the view that Roosevelt was taking insufficient care at Yalta; and the disagreements that followed over Poland. Above all, there must have been constantly in Churchill's mind the feeling that, if only Roosevelt had adopted his alternative strategy, over which there had been the tempestuous arguments and bitter words of late 1943 and June 1944, Stalin's Bolshevik colossus might not at this moment be hanging over Europe.

Even after Roosevelt's death, Churchill kept pleading with Dwight Eisenhower to push Allied troops forward into Prague, Budapest and Vienna, not to mention Berlin. All these cities might have been occupied by the western allies but for the cardinal American rule, laid down by Roosevelt and, not surprisingly, followed by Truman, that such political considerations must never be allowed to influence military strategy. At the same time, of course, politics was dictating every move Stalin made. Therefore, Churchill might well have reflected on how much he really owed the dead president.

As for that alternative strategy, could it have succeeded? Majority opinion is skeptical that Churchill's eastern Mediterranean strategy of late 1943 could ever have led to the breakthrough he desired. However, the decision to go ahead with Operation "Dragoon," the invasion of southern France in the summer of 1944, rather than pursue the Italian campaign, was later condemned by one key man who was at the thick of the action: Mark Clark, the top American general in Italy. Clark wrote: "The weakening of the campaign in Italy in order to invade southern France, instead of pushing on into the Balkans, was one of the outstanding mistakes of the war. ... Stalin knew exactly what he wanted ... and the thing he most wanted was to keep us out of the Balkans. A campaign that might have changed the whole history of relations between the western world and the Soviet Union was permitted to fade away."[12]

The difference in hours meant that Moscow heard the news of Roosevelt's death the following day. "Jesus it was a shock," wrote Averell Harriman's daughter, Kathleen: "Red flags with black borders hung from all houses today throughout Moscow—something I'd have not guessed would happen." Stalin cabled Churchill: "Our people will always value highly and remember President F. Roosevelt's friendly attitude to the Soviet Union. As for myself, I am deeply afflicted by the loss of this great man, our common friend." The sentiments were genuine; and why should they not have been? Roosevelt had given Stalin almost everything he had ever asked for and exercised every facet of his manifold charm on him.

Now, Stalin gave one small thing in return. Among the various squabbles since Yalta, there had been bickering over the final structure of the United Nations. Stalin had decided not to send Vyacheslav Molotov to the inaugural gathering, which was about to take place in San Francisco. When Averell Harriman went to see him after Roosevelt's death, Stalin asked him if there was anything he could do. "Send Molotov to San Francisco," replied Harriman. Stalin agreed; Molotov went.

In the final days of his life, Roosevelt had realized that his great gamble of "giving" to the Soviet leader might be failing. But he had by no means given up on it and was not yet ready to confront him. Daisy Suckley judiciously summed it up in her diary a few days later:

"F. had his hopes and plans for world peace, and he couldn't give up until he had done everything in his power to get that peace started. He was working against time, and against his failing strength, and I think and know that all those who worked for him and with him for that goal will carry on as best they can. F. himself did not have too much faith in Stalin, but he thought that he and Stalin looked at things in the same practical way, and that for that reason, there was much hope that Stalin would follow along."

Daisy concluded with her own, sadly naïve hopes for the future: "Perhaps, now, Stalin will lead, along the line of F.'s ideas."[13]

On April 25 Russian and American soldiers linked up on the river Elbe. There were joyful scenes of celebration as officers and men from each side cracked bottles of champagne and danced together to the tunes of Russian accordions. It seemed to herald the new world of cooperation for which Roosevelt had been willing to give so much, but these images were deceptive. In the coming months and years Stalin would isolate the nations he had occupied in eastern Europe from the capitalist west and build a totalitarian empire.

Some believe that, had Roosevelt lived, he might have moderated Stalin's actions; but while Stalin made gestures and promises for Roosevelt, the Soviet leader always did what he wanted. Roosevelt's flaw, born of his own optimistic nature, was in believing that Stalin was at heart a politician like himself, albeit a harsh one. What he never understood, or perhaps chose not to understand as the consequences would have been too discomforting, was that deep inside Stalin lurked a combination, equaled only by Hitler, of cruelty, paranoia, ideology and greed for power.

In July 1945 the victors of war gathered at Potsdam, just outside Berlin. Roosevelt was dead. Hitler had shot himself. Churchill was about to be voted out of office by the British people. One man stood triumphant: Stalin, the new emperor of Russia and half of Europe.

In the same month of July in 1940, five years before, Hitler had paraded through Berlin in glory, the master of Europe, the "greatest warlord in history." Few could have suspected that those scenes signaled the close of one chapter in world history: the age of European empires. Stalin's triumph opened another: the age of two ideologically opposed superpowers, and a Cold War that would last nearly fifty years.

On one level the outcome had been decided by the march of events and mass armies. But the orchestrators were the four warlords. Their war of the mind had shaped a new world.

Notes

Prologue

1. Schroeder, Christa, *Er war mein Chef. Aus dem Nachlas der Sekretarin von Adolf Hitler*, Munich, 1989, p. 101
2. Ibid., p. 101
3. Colville, Sir John, *The Fringes of Power: 10 Downing Street Diaries 1939–1955*, London, 1985, p. 121
4. Gilbert, Martin, *Finest Hour: Winston S. Churchill 1939–1941*, London, 1983, p. 313
5. W. H. Thompson, *Sixty Minutes with Churchill*, London 1953, pp. 44–45
6. The unpublished diary of Ivan Maisky, taken from Gorodetsky, Gabriel, *Grand Delusion: Stalin and the German Invasion of Russia*, London, 1999, p. 270
7. Colville, *The Fringes of Power*, p. 122
8. Goebbels, Joseph, *Die Tagebücher von Joseph Goebbels, Teil 1: Aufzeichnungen 1923–1941*, ed. Elke Frohlich, Munich, 1998–2001, May 11, 1940
9. *Harold L. Ickes Diaries*, May 12, 1940
10. Ibid., May 12, 1940
11. Black, Conrad, *Franklin Delano Roosevelt: Champion of Freedom*, London, 2003, p. 91
12. Ward, Geoffrey C., *Closest Companion: The Unknown Story of the Intimate Friendship between Franklin Roosevelt and Margaret Suckley*, New York, 1995, p. 69
13. Lash, Joseph P., *Roosevelt and Churchill 1939–1941: The Partnership That Saved the West*, New York, 1976
14. Ward, *Closest Companion*, p. 125
15. Kimball, Warren, *Churchill and Roosevelt: The Complete Correspondence*, Princeton, New Jersey, 1984, vol. 1, p. 24
16. Ibid., vol. 1, p. 7
17. Document 226, *Documents on German Foreign Policy 1918–1945*, Series D (1937–1945), vol. IX, HMSO, London, 1956
18. Hitler, Adolf, *Mein Kampf*, translated by Ralph Manheim, London, 1992, p. 604
19. Goebbels, *Tagebücher, Teil 1*, 22 August 1939
20. Kershaw, Ian, *Hitler 1936–45: Nemesis*, London, 2000, pp. 211–212
21. Goebbels, *Tagebücher, Teil 1*, 22 August 1939
22. Sebag-Montefiore, Simon, *Stalin: The Court of the Red Tsar*, London, 2003, p. 276
23. Ibid., p. 276
24. Bullock, Alan, *Stalin and Hitler: Parallel Lives*, London, 1991, p. 676
25. Sebag-Montefiore, *Stalin*, p. 116
26. Ibid., p. 206
27. Davies, Norman, *Rising '44: The Battle for Warsaw*, London, 2003, pp. 83–84
28. Schroeder, *Er war mein Chef*, p. 152
29. Sebag-Montefiore, *Stalin*, p. 4
30. Dimitrov, Georgi, *The Diary of Georgi Dimitrov 1933–1949*, ed. Ivo Banac, London, 2003, p. 115
31. Goebbels, *Tagebücher, Teil 1*, 1 October 1939
32. Hitler, *Mein Kampf*, p. 598
33. Roberts, Geoffrey, *The Soviet Union and the Origins of the Second World War*, London, 1995, p. 103

34. Goebbels, *Tagebücher, Teil 1*, 15 March 1940
35. Keitel, Field Marshal, *Memoirs*, London, 1965, p. 110
36. Goebbels, *Tagebücher, Teil 1*, May 11, 1940
37. Gilbert, *Finest Hour*, p. 317

Chapter 1

1. Warlimont, Walter, *Inside Hitler's Headquarters 1939–1945*, Novato, California, 1964, p. 93
2. Hitler, Adolf, *Hitler's Table Talk 1941–1944: His Private Conversations*, London, 2000
3. Maisky, Ivan, *Memoirs of a Soviet Ambassador: The War 1939–1945*, London, 1967, p. 72
4. Gilbert, Martin, *The Churchill War Papers, Vol. II: Never Surrender May 1940–December 1940*, London, 1994, p. 22
5. Lukacs, John, *The Duel: Hitler vs. Stalin 10 May 1940–31 July 1940*, London, 1990
6. Ismay, General the Lord, *The Memoirs of General The Lord Ismay KG, PC, GCB, CH, DSO*, London, 1960, p. 116.
7. Colville, Sir John, *The Fringes of Power: 10 Downing Street Diaries 1939–1955*, London, 1985, p. 129
8. Gilbert, *Churchill War Papers, Vol. II*, pp. 70–71
9. Ibid., p. 35
10. Kimball, Warren, *Churchill and Roosevelt: The Complete Correspondence*, Princeton, New Jersey, 1984, Vol. 1, pp. 37–38
11. Lukacs, *Duel*
12. Ibid.
13. Ibid.
14. Burdick, Charles and Jacobsen, Hans-Adolf, *The Halder War Diary 1939–1942*, London, 1988, p. 149
15. Kimball, *Churchill and Roosevelt*, Vol. 1 p. 38
16. Colville, *The Fringes of Power*, pp. 134–135
17. *The Diaries of Lord Avon*, University of Birmingham, AP 20/1/1–32, May 18, 1940
18. Burdick and Jacobsen, *Halder War Diary 1939–1942*, p. 156
19. Lukacs, *Duel*

20. Colville, *Fringes of Power*, p. 138
21. Dilks, David, *The Diaries of Sir Alexander Cadogan 1938–1945*, London, 1971
22. Lukacs, *Duel*
23. Burdick and Jacobsen, *Halder War Diary 1939–1942*, p. 167
24. Engel, Major Gerhard, *Heeres-Adjutant bei Hitler 1938–1943*, Stuttgart, 1974
25. Gilbert, *Churchill War Papers, Vol. II*, p. 168
26. *The Diaries of Edward Lindley Wood, First Earl of Halifax*, Public Diary 1940–1945 A7.8.3–18, May 27, 1940
27. Gilbert, Martin, *Finest Hour: Winston S. Churchill 1939–1941*, London, 1983, p. 420
28. Lukacs, *Duel*
29. Goebbels, Joseph, *Die Tagebücher von Joseph Goebbels, Teil 1: Aufzeichnungen 1923–1941*, ed. Elke Frohlich, Munich, 1998–2001, May 29, 1940
30. Document 347, *Documents on German Foreign Policy 1918–1945*, Series D (1937–1945), Vol. X, HMSO, London, 1957
31. Merritt Miner, Steven, *Between Churchill and Stalin: The Soviet Union, Great Britain, and the Origins of the Grand Alliance*, London, 1988, p. 41
32. KV 2/483: Aleksei Aleksandrovich Doshchenko
33. Hinsley, F. H. and Simkins, C. A. G, *British Intelligence in the Second World War, Vol. 4: Security and Counter-Intelligence*, London, 1990, p. 20
34. Gorsky was the head of the NKVD "station" in London. He was recalled to Moscow in early 1940, but returned later that year after further training. He reactivated Blunt and was in close contact with many of the Cambridge spies. For more information on John Herbert King see KV 2/815–816 and TS 27/1217 (MI5 files on John Herbert King). Files released to National Archives, Kew from MI5 in 2002.
35. KV 4/185–196: *The Diaries of Guy Liddell*, November 1, 1942, Vol. 6, p. 902. Files released to the PRO in November 2002.

36. HO 45/25573: *Disturbances – Communist Party of Great Britain: Reports on Aims, Policy, Activities and Meetings*, KV 2/1038–1040: *Harry POLLITT: British* and KV 4/222: *Policy and Procedure for the Imposition of Home Office Warrants for the Interception of Mail and Telephone communications in the UK 1939–1945*.

37. KV 4/57: *Report on the Operations of F2B in Connection with Comintern Activities Generally and Communist Refugees in the UK*, p. 8. File released to National Archives, Kew in September 1999.

38. Hinsley and Simkins, *British Intelligence in the Second World War, Vol. 4*, pp. 305–307.

39. Churchill, Winston, *The Second World War*, London, 1953, Vol. 2, pp. 133–4.

40. Gilbert, *Churchill War Papers, Vol. II*, pp. 240–247

41. Goebbels, *Tagebüche, Teil 1*, June 5, 1940

42. Ibid., June 5, 1940

43. Engel, *Heeres-Adjutant bei Hitler 1938–1943*

44. Colville, *Fringes of Power*, p. 152

45. Public Papers of the President

46. Tully, Grace, *FDR My Boss*, New York, 1949, p. 99

47. Black, Conrad, *Franklin Delano Roosevelt: Champion of Freedom*, London, 2003, p. 555 and Sherwood, Robert E., *Roosevelt and Hopkins: An Intimate History*, New York, 2001, p. 140

48. Kimball, *Churchill and Roosevelt*, Vol. 1, p. 43

49. Colville, *Fringes of Power*, p. 153

50. Goebbels, *Tagebücher, Teil 1*, June 11, 1940

51. Kimball, *Churchill and Roosevelt*, Vol. 1, p. 45

52. Ibid., pp. 45–46

53. Ibid., p. 47

54. Ibid., p. 48

55. Colville, *Fringes of Power*, p. 157

56. Ibid., p. 158

57. Goebbels, *Tagebücher, Teil 1*, June 18, 1940

58. Ciano, Count Galeazzo, *Diary 1937–1943: The Complete, Unabridged Diaries of Count Galeazzo Ciano, Italian Minster for Foreign Affairs*, London, 2002, p. 363

59. Sebag-Montefiore, Simon, *Stalin: The Court of the Red Tsar*, London, 2003, p. 297

60. Khrushchev, Nikita, *Khrushchev Remembers: The Glasnost Tapes*, London, 1990, p. 54

61. Colville, *Fringes of Power*, p. 165

62. *The Presidential Diary of Henry Morgenthau*, June 18, 1940

63. PSF box 38

64. Colville, *Fringes of Power*, p. 166

65. Engel, *Heeres-Adjutant bei Hitler 1938–1943*

66. Speer, Albert, *Inside the Third Reich: Memoirs*, London, 1970, p. 172

67. Ibid., p.172

68. Churchill, Winston, *The Second World War*, London, 1953, Vol. 2, p. 135.

69. Lukacs, *Duel*

70. Merritt Miner, *Between Churchill and Stalin*, p. 65

71. Goebbels, *Tagebücher, Teil 1*, 2 July 1940

72. Maisky, *Memoirs of a Soviet Ambassado*, p. 98

73. Gilbert, *Churchill War Papers, Vol. II*, p. 475

74. Maisky, *Memoirs of a Soviet Ambassador*, p. 98

75. Davies, Kenneth S., *FDR the War President 1940–1943: A History*, New York, 2000 and Black, *Franklin Delano Roosevelt*, p. 566

76. Welles, Sumner, *The Time for Decision*, London, 1944, p. 123

77. Goebbels, *Tagebücher, Teil 1*, July 7, 1940

78. Burdick and Jacobsen, *Halder War Diary 1939–1942*, p. 227

79. Engel, *Heeres-Adjutant bei Hitler 1938–1943*

80. Colville, *Fringes of Power*, p. 195

81. Kershaw, Ian, *Hitler 1936–45: Nemesis*, London, 2000, p. 303

82. Goebbels, *Tagebücher, Teil 1*, July 7, 1940

83. Lukacs, *Duel* and Kershaw, *Hitler 1936–45*, p. 303

84. Ciano, *Diary 1937–1943*, p. 371

85. Colville, *Fringes of Power*, p. 200

86. Ciano, *Diary 1937–1943*, p. 371

87. Public Papers of the President

88. Burdick and Jacobsen, *Halder War Diary 1939–1942*, pp. 230–232

89. Goebbels, *Tagebücher, Teil 1*, July 29, 1940
90. Dilks, *The Diaries of Sir Alexander Cadogan OM 1938–1945*, p. 318
91. Kimball, *Churchill and Roosevelt*, p. 57
92. Burdick and Jacobsen, *Halder War Diary 1939–1942*, pp. 244–245

Chapter 2

1. Degras, Jane (ed.), *Soviet Documents on Foreign Policy 1917–1941, Vol. III 1933–1941*, London, 1953, p. 463
2. Below, Nicolaus von, *At Hitler's Side: The Memoirs of Hitler's Luftwaffe Adjutant 1937–1945*, London, 1980, p. 70
3. Colville, Sir John, *The Fringes of Power: 10 Downing Street Diaries 1939–1955*, London, 1985, p. 208
4. PSF Box 55
5. PSF Box 62
6. PSF Box 62
7. PSF Box 55
8. Colville, *Fringes of Power*, p. 215
9. Gilbert, Martin, *Finest Hour: Winston S. Churchill 1939–1941*, London, 1983, p. 716
10. Reynolds, David, *The Creation of the Anglo-American Alliance: A Study in Competitive Co-operation 1937–1941*, London, 1981
11. Merritt Miner, Steven, *Between Churchill and Stalin: The Soviet Union, Great Britain, and the Origins of the Grand Alliance*, London, 1988, pp. 78–79
12. Colville, *Fringes of Power*, pp. 221–223
13. *The Presidential Diary of Henry Morgenthau*, August 14, 1940
14. Roosevelt, Elliott (ed.), *The Roosevelt Letters: Being the Personal Correspondence of Franklin Delano Roosevelt, Vol. 3 1928–1945*, London, 1952, p. 329
15. Dilks, David, *The Diaries of Sir Alexander Cadogan OM 1938–1945*, London, 1971, p. 321
16. Gilbert, *Finest Hour*, p. 733
17. Roosevelt, *Roosevelt Letters*, Vol. 3, p. 329
18. Colville, *Fringes of Power*, p. 227
19. Voskresenskaya, Zoya, *Under Pseudonym Irina*, Moscow, 1997, p. 266
20. KV 4/185–196: *The Diaries of Guy Liddell*, August 26, 1940
21. Merritt Miner, *Between Churchill and Stalin*, p. 102
22. Gilbert, Martin, *Second World War*, London, 1989, p. 114
23. Below, *At Hitler's Side*, p. 71
24. Kershaw, Ian, *Hitler 1936–45: Nemesis*, London, 2000, p. 309 and Gilbert, *Second World War*, p. 122
25. Gilbert, *Second World War*, p. 122
26. Merritt Miner, *Between Churchill and Stalin*, p. 83
27. Ibid., p. 81
28. Maisky, Ivan, *Memoirs of a Soviet Ambassador: The War 1939–1945*, London, 1967, pp. 107–109
29. Alanbrooke, Field Marshal Lord, *War Diaries 1939–1945*, London, 2001, p. 108
30. Gilbert, *Second World War*, p. 125
31. Ciano, Count Galeazzo, *Diary 1937–1943: The Complete, Unabridged Diaries of Count Galeazzo Ciano, Italian Minster for Foreign Affairs*, London, 2002, p. 385
32. Gilbert, Martin, *The Churchill War Papers, Vol. II: Never Surrender May 1940–December 1940*, London, 1994, p. 876
33. *The Diaries of Henry L. Stimson*, September 27, 1940
34. Dimitrov, Georgi, *The Diary of Georgi Dimitrov 1933–1949*, ed. Ivo Banac, London, 2003, p. 129
35. Burdick, Charles and Jacobsen, Hans-Adolf, *The Halder War Diary 1939–1942*, London, 1988, p. 260
36. Kimball, Warren, *Churchill and Roosevelt: The Complete Correspondence*, Princeton, New Jersey, 1984, Vol. 1, p. 74
37. Colville, *Fringes of Power*, p. 259
38. Israel, Fred L., *The War Diary of Breckinridge Long: Selections from the Years 1939–1944*, Lincoln, Nebraska, 1966, p. 141
39. Public Papers of the President
40. Colville, *Fringes of Power*, pp. 262–264
41. Maisky, *Memoirs of a Soviet Ambassador*, p. 143

42. Document 211, *Documents on German Foreign Policy 1918–1945 Series D (1937–1945), Vol. XI: September 1, 1940–January 31, 1941*, London, 1961

43. Merritt Miner, *Between Churchill and Stalin*, p. 91

44. Kershaw, *Hitler 1936–45*, p. 330

45. Below, *At Hitler's Side*, p. 75

46. Ibid., p. 75

47. Kershaw, *Hitler 1936–45*, pp. 328–332

48. *The Diaries of Henry L. Stimson*, October 29, 1940

49. Gilbert, *Second World War*, p. 135 and Black, Conrad, *Frankiln Delano Roosevelt: Champion of Freedom*, London, 2003, p. 595

50. Colville, *Fringes of Power*, p. 283

51. Burdick and Jacobsen, *Halder War Diary 1939–1942*, pp. 273–274

52. Goebbels, Joseph, *Die Tagebücher von Joseph Goebbels, Teil 1: Aufzeichnungen, 1923–1941*, ed. Elke Frohlich, Munich, 1998–2001, November 1, 1940

53. Kershaw, *Hitler 1936–45*, p. 332

54. Kimball, *Churchill and Roosevelt*, Vol. 1, p. 81

55. Goebbels, *Tagebücher, Teil 1*, November 7, 1940

56. Dimitrov, *Diary 1933–1949*, pp. 132–33

57. Irving, David, *Hitler's War*, London, 2002, p. 343

58. Schmidt, P., *Hitler's Interpreter*, London, 1951, p. 211

59. Ibid., p. 211

60. Ibid., p. 211

61. *The Memoir of Y. Chadayev*, November 14, 1940

62. Ibid.

63. Schmidt, *Hitler's Interpreter*, p. 214 and Document 326, *Documents on German Foreign Policy 1918–1945 Series D, Vol. XI*

64. Ibid.

65. Schmidt, *Hitler's Interpreter*, p. 215 and Document 548, *Documents on German Foreign Policy 1918–1945 Series D, Vol. XI:*

66. Ibid.

67. Document 328, *Documents on German Foreign Policy 1918–1945 Series D (1937–1945), volume XI: September 1, 1940–January 31, 1941*, London, 1961

68. Document 328, *Documents on German Foreign Policy 1918–1945 Series D, Vol. XI*

69. Ibid.

70. Ibid.

71. Schmidt, *Hitler's Interpreter*, p. 215 and Document 326, *Documents on German Foreign Policy 1918–1945 Series D, Vol. XI*

72. Kershaw, *Hitler 1936–45*, p. 334

73. *Memoir of Y. Chadayev*, November 14, 1940

74. *Memoir of Y. Chadayev*, December 1940

75. Kershaw, *Hitler 1936–45*, p. 335

76. Kimball, *Churchill and Roosevelt*, Vol. 1, pp. 106–108

77. Ibid.

78. Kershaw, *Hitler 1936–45*, p. 335

79. Public Papers of the President

80. Kershaw, *Hitler 1936–45*, p. 335

81. Engel, Major Gerhard, *Heeres-Adjutant bei Hitler 1938–1943*, Stuttgart, 1974, December 18, 1940

82. *Memoir of Y. Chadayev*, February 1941

83. Hitler, Adolf, *Hitler's Table Talk 1941–1944: His Private Conversations*, London, 2000

84. Public Papers of the President

85. Goebbels, *Tagebücher, Teil 1*, December 29, 1940

86. Public Papers of the President

87. PSF Box 5

88. Public Papers of the President

89. Kershaw, *Hitler 1936–45*, p. 336

90. Burdick, and Jacobsen, *Halder War Diary 1939–1942*, p. 311

91. Sherwood, Robert E., *Roosevelt and Hopkins: An Intimate History*, New York, 2001, p. 232

92. Colville, *Fringes of Power*, p. 331

93. Ibid., p. 331

94. Dilks, *Diaries of Sir Alexander Cadogan OM 1938–1945*, p.348 and Black, *Frankiln Delano Roosevelt*, p. 615

95. Colville, *Fringes of Power*, pp. 331–332

96. Ibid., p. 334

97. See Moran, Lord, *Churchill at War 1940–1945,* London, 2002, p. 6 and Gilbert, *Finest Hour,* p. 991
98. Sherwood, *Roosevelt and Hopkins,* p. 237
99. Ross, Graham, *The Foreign Office and the Kremlin: British Documents on Anglo-Soviet Relations 1941–1945,* London, 1984
100. Gilbert, *Finest Hour,* p. 998
101. Kimball, *Churchill and Roosevelt,* Vol. 1, p. 131
102. Colville, *Fringes of Power,* p. 347
103. Kershaw, *Hitler 1936–45,* p. 349
104. Ibid., p. 348
105. Engel, *Heeres-Adjutant bei Hitler,* February 2, 1941
106. Burdick and Jacobsen, *Halder War Diary 1939–1942,* p. 320
107. Ibid., p. 320
108. *Diaries of Henry L. Stimson,* December 18, 1940
109. Kimball, Warren, *Forged in War,* London, 1997
110. Gorodetsky, Gabriel, *Grand Delusion: Stalin and the German Invasion of Russia,* London, 1999, p. 227
111. Gorodetsky, *Grand Delusion,* p. 228 and Sebag-Montefiore, Simon, *Stalin: The Court of the Red Tsar,* London, 2003, p. 304
112. Ibid.
113. Gorodetsky, *Grand Delusion,* p. 228
114. Sebag-Montefiore, *Stalin,* p. 304
115. Warlimont, Walter, *Inside Hitler's Headquarters 1939–1945,* Novato, California, 1964, pp. 150–151
116. Berle, B. B., and Jacobs, T. B. (eds), *Navigating the Rapids 1918–1971: From the Papers of Adolf A. Berle,* New York 1973, p. 362
117. Kimball, *Churchill and Roosevelt,* Vol. 1, p. 143
118. Goebbels, *Tagebücher, Teil 1,* March 10, 1941
119. Public Papers of the President
120. *The Diaries of Edward Lindley Wood, First Earl of Halifax, Public Diary 1940–1945* A7.8.3–18, March 16, 1941
121. Kimball, *Churchill and Roosevelt,* Vol. 1, p. 148
122. *Morgenthau Presidential Diary,* March 16, 1941
123. Gilbert, Martin, *The Churchill War Papers, Vol. 3: The Ever-Widening War 1941,* London, 2000, p. 363
124. Ibid.
125. Kershaw, Ian, *Hitler, 1936–45: Nemesis,* London, 2000, p. 334

Chapter 3

1. Kershaw, Ian, *Hitler 1936–45: Nemesis,* London, 2000, p. 362
2. Ibid., p. 362
3. Ibid., p. 363
4. Gilbert, Martin, *The Churchill War Papers, Vol. 3: The Ever-Widening War 1941,* London, 2000, pp. 403–415
5. Ibid., pp. 403–415
6. Ibid., pp. 403–415
7. Ibid., pp. 403–415
8. Kershaw, *Hitler 1936–45,* pp. 360–365
9. Burdick, Charles and Jacobsen, Hans-Adolf, *The Halder War Diary 1939–1942,* London, 1988, pp. 345–346
10. Ibid., pp. 345–346
11. Ibid., pp. 345–346
12. Ibid., pp. 345–346
13. *The Presidential Diary of Henry Morgenthau,* April 2, 1941
14. Colville, Sir John, *The Fringes of Power: 10 Downing Street Diaries 1939–1955,* London, 1985, pp. 369–370
15. PREM 3/403
16. Gilbert, *Churchill War Papers, Vol. 3,* pp. 447–448
17. Sebag-Montefiore, Simon, *Stalin: The Court of the Red Tsar,* London, 2003, p. 307
18. Merritt Miner, Steven, *Between Churchill and Stalin: The Soviet Union, Great Britain, and the Origins of the Grand Alliance,* London, 1988, p. 123 and see also Kershaw, *Hitler 1936–45*
19. Merritt Miner, *Between Churchill and Stalin,* p. 123

20. Eden, Anthony, *The Reckoning*, London, 1965, p. 255
21. Colville, *Fringes of Power*, p. 374
22. *The Diary of Harold L. Ickes*, April 21, 1941
23. *The Diaries of Henry L. Stimson*, April 21, 1941
24. *Diary of Harold L. Ickes*, April 22, 1941
25. Sebag-Montefiore, *Stalin*, pp. 309–310
26. Goebbels, Joseph, *Die Tagebücher von Joseph Goebbels, Teil 1: Aufzeichnungen, 1923–1941*, ed. Elke Frohlich, Munich, 1998–2001, April 22, 1941
27. Ibid., April 24, 1941
28. Kimball, *Churchill and Roosevelt*, pp. 176–177
29. *Halifax Papers: Correspondence, Ref: A4.410.4 – Papers as HM Ambassador at Washington*
30. Goebbels, *Tagebücher, Teil 1*, May 2, 1941
31. Kimball, *Churchill and Roosevelt*, pp. 179–180
32. Colville, *Fringes of Power*, pp. 381–382
33. Ibid., pp. 381–382
34. Kimball, *Churchill and Roosevelt*, pp. 181–182
35. Ibid., p. 8
36. Goebbels, *Tagebücher, Teil 1*, May 3, 1941
37. Colville, *Fringes of Power*, pp. 381–382
38. Chadayev quoted in Radzinsky, Edvard, *Stalin: The First In Depth Biography Based on Explosive New Documents from the Russian Archives*, London, 1996, p. 438
39. Burdick and Jacobsen, *Halder War Diary 1939–1942*, p. 383
40. Ibid., p. 384
41. Goebbels, *Tagebücher, Teil 1*, May 9, 1941
42. Kershaw, *Hitler 1936–45*, p. 371
43. Kershaw, *Hitler 1936–45*, p. 371 and Gilbert, *Churchill War Papers, Vol. 3*
44. Kershaw, *Hitler 1936–45*, p. 372
45. Beria, Sergo, *Beria My Father: Inside Stalin's Kremlin*, London, 2001, p. 67
46. *The Memoir of Y. Chadayev*, May 12, 1941
47. Ibid., May 12, 1941
48. Sebag-Montefiore, *Stalin*, p. 312

49. *Diary of Harold L. Ickes*, May 12, 1941
50. *Morgenthau Presidential Diary*, May 14, 1941
51. Sherwood, Robert E., *Roosevelt and Hopkins: An Intimate History*, New York, 2001
52. Kimball, *Churchill and Roosevelt*, p. 191
53. Casey, Steven, *Cautious Crusade: Franklin D. Roosevelt, American Public Opinion and the War against Nazi Germany*, Oxford, 2001, p. 11
54. Gilbert, Martin, *Finest Hour: Winston S. Churchill 1939–1941*, London, 1983, p. 1095
55. Public Papers of the President
56. Ibid.
57. *The Diaries of Edward Lindley Wood, First Earl of Halifax*, Public Diary 1940–1945 A7.8.3–18, May 27, 1941
58. *Diary of Harold L. Ickes*, May 27, 1941
59. *Diaries of Henry L. Stimson*, May 27, 1941
60. PSF Box 84
61. Goebbels, *Tagebücher, Teil 1*, May 29, 1941
62. Ibid., May 29, 1941
63. *Memoir of Y. Chadayev*, June 5, 1941
64. Dilks, David, *The Diaries of Sir Alexander Cadogan OM 1938–1941*, London, 1971, p. 382
65. Black, Conrad, *Franklin Delano Roosevelt: Champion of Freedom*, London, 2003
66. Degras, Jane (ed.), *Soviet Documents on Foreign Policy 1917–1941, Vol. III 1933–1941*, London, 1953, p. 489
67. Sebag-Montefiore, *Stalin*, pp. 313–314
68. Kershaw, *Hitler 1936–45*, p. 385
69. Sebag-Montefiore, *Stalin*, pp. 313–314
70. Kershaw, *Hitler 1936–45*, p. 386
71. Ibid., p. 387
72. Colville, *Fringes of Power*, p. 404
73. Goebbels, *Tagebücher, Teil 1*, June 21, 1941
74. Dimitrov, Georgi, *The Diary of Georgi Dimitrov 1933–1949*, ed. Ivo Banac, London, 2003, p. 165
75. Volkogonov, Dmitri, *Stalin: Triumph and Tragedy*, London, 1991, p. 402

Chapter 4

1. Volkogonov, Dmitri, *Stalin: Triumph and Tragedy*, London, 1991, p. 402 and Sebag-Montefiore, Simon, *Stalin: The Court of the Red Tsar*, London, 2003, pp. 314–320
2. Goebbels, Joseph, *Die Tagebücher von Joseph Goebbels, Teil 1: Aufzeichnungen 1923–1941*, ed. Elke Frohlich, Munich, 1998–2001, June 22, 1941
3. Chadayev quoted in Radzinsky, Edvard, *Stalin: The First In Depth Biography Based on Explosive New Documents from the Russian Archives*, London, 1996, pp. 445–448 and Sebag-Montefiore, *Stalin*, pp. 314–330
4. Chadayev quoted in Radzinsky, *Stalin*, pp. 445–448
5. Gorkov, Y., *Gosudarstvennyi Komitet Oborony postanovlyaet, 1941–1945*, Moscow, 2002
6. Dimitrov, Georgi, *The Diary of Georgi Dimitrov 1933–1949*, ed. Ivo Banac, London, 2003, p. 166
7. Chadayev quoted in Radzinsky, *Stalin*, pp. 445–448 and Sebag-Montefiore, *Stalin*, pp. 314–330
8. Ibid.
9. Kershaw, Ian, *Hitler 1936–45: Nemesis*, London, 2000, p. 387
10. Churchill, Winston S., *The Second World War, Vol. 3: The Grand Alliance*, London, 1950, p. 369
11. Gilbert, Martin, *The Churchill War Papers, Vol. 3: The Ever-Widening War 1941*, London, 2000, p. 838
12. *The Diaries of Harold L. Ickes*, June 22, 1941
13. *The Diaries of Guy Liddell*, KV 4/185–196, June 22, 1941
14. KV4/228, released May 2004
15. Gorkov, *Gosudarstvennyi Komitet Oborony postanovlyaet, 1941–1945* and Volkogonov, *Stalin*, p. 410
16. *The Memoir of Y. Chadayev*, June 23, 1941
17. Ibid., June 23, 1941
18. Gilbert, *Churchill War Papers, Vol. 3*, pp. 842–843
19. Colville, Sir John, *The Fringes of Power: 10 Downing Street Diaries 1939–1955*, London, 1985, p. 406
20. Hopkins Box 305
21. Hopkins Box 305
22. Hopkins Box 305
23. Junge, Traudl, *Until the Final Hour: Hitler's Last Secretary*, London, 2003, p. 65
24. Kershaw, *Hitler 1936–45*, p. 395
25. Document 7, *Documents on German Foreign Policy 1918–1945 Series D (1937–1945) Vol. XIII*, HMSO, 1963, p. 11
26. Casey, Steven, *Cautious Crusade: Franklin D. Roosevelt, American Public Opinion and the War Against Nazi Germany*, Oxford, 2001, p. 11. See also Kimball, Warren, *The Juggler*, London, 1991.
27. Chadayev quoted in Radzinsky, *Stalin*, p. 454
28. Gorkov, *Gosudarstvennyj Komitet Oborony postanovljaet 1941–1945*
29. Chadayev quoted in Radzinsky, *Stalin*, pp. 445–448
30. Alliluyeva, Svetlana, *Only One Year*, London, 1969, p. 369
31. Kershaw, *Hitler 1936–45*, pp. 397–398
32. Ibid, pp. 397–398
33. Ibid, pp. 397–398
34. Merritt Miner, Steven, *Between Churchill and Stalin: The Soviet Union, Great Britain, and the Origins of the Grand Alliance*, London, 1988, p. 143
35. Colville, *Fringes of Power*, p. 408
36. *Diaries of Guy Liddel*, KV 4/185–196, June 30, 1941
37. Merritt Miner, *Between Churchill and Stalin*, p. 144
38. *The Diaries of Henry L. Stimson*, June 30, 1941
39. Sebag-Montefiore, *Stalin*, p. 332
40. Beria, Sergo, *Beria My Father: Inside Stalin's Kremlin*, London, 2001, p. 71
41. Bullock, Alan, *Stalin and Hitler: Parallel Lives*, London, 1991, p. 794
42. Dimitrov, *Diary*, p. 172

43. Burdick, Charles and Jacobsen, Hans-Adolf, *The Halder War Diary 1939–1942*, London, 1988, pp. 446–447

44. *The Diaries of Edward Lindley Wood, First Earl of Halifax*, Public Diary 1940–1945 A7.8.3–18, July 7, 1941

45. Ministry of Foreign Affairs of the USSR, *Correspondence between Stalin, Roosevelt, Truman, Churchill and Attlee during World War Two: Correspondence with Winston S. Churchill and Clement Attlee (July 1941–November 1945)*, Moscow, 1957, p. 11

46. Merritt Miner, *Between Churchill and Stalin*, p. 145

47. Burdick and Jacobsen, *Halder War Diary 1939–1942*, pp. 448–459

48. Gilbert, Martin, *Second World War*, London, 1989, p. 209

49. Kershaw, *Hitler 1936–45*, p. 398 and see also Goebbels, *Tagebücher, Teil 2: Diktate 1941–1945*, ed. Elke Frohlich, Munich, 1993–1998, July 9, 1941

50. Gilbert, *Churchill War Papers, Vol. 3*, p. 920

51. Volkogonov, *Stalin*, p. 416

52. Ministry of Foreign Affairs of the USSR, *Correspondence between Stalin, Roosevelt, Truman, Churchill and Attlee during World War Two: Correspondence with Churchill*, p. 12

53. Gilbert, *Churchill War Papers, Vol. 3*, p. 921

54. Sherwood, Robert E., *Roosevelt and Hopkins: An Intimate History*, New York, 2001, p. 302

55. Kimball, Warren, *Churchill and Roosevelt: The Complete Correspondence*, Princeton, New Jersey, 1984, Vol. 1, p. 222

56. Burdick and Jacobsen, *Halder War Diary 1939–1942*, p. 474

57. Ministry of Foreign Affairs of the USSR, *Correspondence between Stalin, Roosevelt, Truman, Churchill and Attlee during World War Two: Correspondence with Churchill and Attlee*, pp. 12–13

58. Maisky, Ivan, *Memoirs of a Soviet Ambassador: The War 1939–1945*, London, 1967, p. 177

59. Ibid., p. 177

60. Ministry of Foreign Affairs of the USSR, *Correspondence between Stalin, Roosevelt, Truman, Churchill and Attlee during World War Two: Correspondence with Churchill and Attlee*, pp. 13–14

61. *Memoir of Y. Chadayev*, July 21, 1941

62. Eden, Anthony, *The Reckoning*, London, 1965, p. 273

63. Ibid., p.273

64. Volkogonov, *Stalin*, p. 422

65. Maisky, *Memoirs of a Soviet Ambassador*, p. 204

66. *Documents on German Foreign Policy 1918–1945 Series D (1937–1945) Vol. XIII*, HMSO, London, 1963, p. 203

67. Kershaw, *Hitler 1936–45*, p. 470

68. Ibid., p. 409

69. Burdick and Jacobsen, *Halder War Diary 1939–1942*, pp. 486–487

70. Engel, Major Gerhard, *Heeres-Adjutant bei Hitler 1938–1943*, Stuttgart, 1974, July 28, 1941

71. *The Presidential Diary of Henry Morgenthau*, August 4, 1941

72. Ibid., August 4, 1941

73. *Diaries of Henry L. Stimson*, August 1, 1941

74. PREM 3/485/6

75. Dilks, David, *The Diaries of Sir Alexander Cadogan OM 1938–1945*, London, 1971, p. 396

76. Ibid., p. 397

77. Engel, *Heeres-Adjutant bei Hitler 1938–1943*, August 8, 1941

78. Warlimont, Walter, *Inside Hitler's Headquarters 1939–1945*, Novato, California, 1964, p. 174

79. Volkogonov, *Stalin*, p. 415

80. Shtemenko, S. M., *The Soviet General Staff at War 1941–1945*, Moscow, 1975, p. 118

81. Roosevelt, Elliott, *As He Saw It*, New York, 1946, pp. 23–25

82. Ibid., pp. 23–25

Chapter 5

1. Lash, Joseph P., *Roosevelt and Churchill 1939–1941: The Partnership That Saved the West*, New York, 1976, p. 391

2. Roosevelt, Elliott, *As He Saw It*, New York, 1946, pp. 23–35

3. Ibid., p. 30

4. Ibid., pp. 35–36

5. Dilks, David, *The Diaries of Sir Alexander Cadogan OM 1938–1945*, London, 1971, p. 399

6. Burdick, Charles and Jacobsen, Hans-Adolf, *The Halder War Diary 1939–1942*, London, 1988, p. 506

7. Kershaw, Ian, *Hitler 1936–45: Nemesis*, London, 2000, p. 464

8. Dilks, *Diaries of Sir Alexander Cadogan OM 1938–1945*, p. 402

9. Kershaw, *Hitler 1936–45*, p. 411 and see also Goebbels, Joseph, *Die Tagebücher von Joseph Goebbels; Teil 2: Diktate 1941–1945*, ed. Elke Frohlich, Munich, 1993–1998

10. Goebbels, Joseph *Die Tagebücher von Joseph Goebbels; Teil 2 Diktate, 1941–1945*, ed. Elke Frohlich, Munich, 1993–1998, August 19, 1941

11. Goebbels, *Tagebücher, Teil 2*, August 19, 1941

12. Gilbert, Martin, *The Churchill War Papers, Vol. 3: The Ever-Widening War 1941*, London, 2000, p. 1081

13. Public Papers of the President

14. Gilbert, *Churchill War Papers, Vol. 3*, p. 1125

15. Roosevelt, Elliott (ed.), *The Roosevelt Letters: Being the Personal Correspondence of Franklin Delano Roosevelt, Vol. 3 1928–1945*, London, 1952, p. 385

16. Ministry of Foreign Affairs of the USSR, *Correspondence between Stalin, Roosevelt, Truman, Churchill and Attlee during World War Two: Correspondence with Winston S. Churchill and Clement Attlee (July 1941–November 1945)*, Moscow, 1957, pp. 18–19

17. Merritt Miner, Steven, *Between Churchill and Stalin: The Soviet Union, Great Britain, and the Origins of the Grand Alliance*, London, 1988, p. 155

18. Schroeder, Christa, *Er war mein Chef. Aus dem Nachlas der Sekretarin von Adolf Hitler*, Munich, 1989

19. Burdick and Jacobsen, *Halder War Diary 1939–1942*, p. 521

20. Maisky, Ivan, *Memoirs of a Soviet Ambassador: The War 1939–1945*, London, 1967, p. 188

21. Ministry of Foreign Affairs of the USSR, *Correspondence between Stalin, Roosevelt, Truman, Churchill and Attlee during World War Two: Correspondence with Churchill and Attlee*, pp. 20–22

22. Dilks, *Diaries of Sir Alexander Cadogan OM 1938–1945*, p. 404

23. Ministry of Foreign Affairs of the USSR, *Correspondence between Stalin, Roosevelt, Truman, Churchill and Attlee during World War Two: Correspondence with Churchill and Attlee*, pp. 22–23

24. *The Memoir of Y. Chadayev*, September 6, 1941

25. Public Papers of the President

26. Gilbert, *Churchill War Papers, Vol. 3*, p. 1205

27. Harriman, Averell and Abel, Elie, *Special Envoy to Churchill and Stalin 1941–1946*, New York, 1975, p. 89

28. Berezhkov, Valentin, *History in the Making: Memoirs of World War II Diplomacy*, Moscow, 1982, p. 144

29. Harriman and Abel *Special Envoy to Churchill and Stalin 1941–1946*, pp. 100–101

30. Hinsley F. H., *British Intelligence in the Second World War: Its Influence on Strategy and Operations, London, 1979–1990*, Vol. 2, p. 59

31. Gilbert, Martin, *Finest Hour: Winston S. Churchill 1939–1941*, London, 1983, p. 1210

32. Goebbels, *Tagebücher, Teil 2*, October 4, 1941

33. Ibid., October 4, 1941
34. Kershaw, *Hitler 1936–45*, p. 432
35. Burdick and Jacobsen, *Halder War Diary 1939–1942*, p. 545
36. Sebag-Montefiore, *Stalin—The Court of the Red Tsar*, London, 2003 p. 354
37. Ibid., p. 354
38. Ibid., p. 352
39. Hinsley, F. H. and Simkins, C. A. G, *British Intelligence in the Second World War, Vol. 4: Security and Counter-Intelligence*, London, 1990, p. 83
40. *Memoir of Y. Chadayev*, October 20, 1941
41. Ibid., October 20, 1941
42. Kimball, Warren, *Churchill and Roosevelt: The Complete Correspondence*, Princeton, New Jersey, 1984, Vol. 1, p. 253
43. Harriman and Abel, *Special Envoy to Churchill and Stalin 1941–1946*, pp. 108–110
44. Merritt Miner, *Between Churchill and Stalin*, p. 164
45. Ibid., p. 164
46. Public Papers of the President
47. Gilbert, *The Churchill War Papers, Vol. 3*, p. 1388
48. Merritt Miner, *Between Churchill and Stalin*, p. 164
49. Kimball, *Churchill and Roosevelt*, Vol. 1, p. 265
50. Hitler, Adolf, *Hitler's Table Talk, 1941–1944: His Private Conversations*, London, 2000, p. 110
51. Kershaw, *Hitler 1936–45*, p. 464
52. Public Papers of the President
53. Sebag-Montefiore, *Stalin*, p. 358
54. *The Diaries of Ivan Maisky*, November 9, 1941
55. Ministry of Foreign Affairs of the USSR, *Correspondence between Stalin, Roosevelt, Truman, Churchill and Attlee during World War Two: Correspondence with Churchill and Attlee*, pp. 33–34
56. Ibid., pp. 33–34
57. Kershaw, *Hitler 1936–45*, p. 436 and Gilbert, *Second World War*, p. 254
58. Goebbels, *Tagebücher, Teil 2*, November 9, 1941
59. *Diaries of Ivan Maisky*, November 11, 1941
60. Volkogonov, Dmitri, *Stalin: Triumph and Tragedy*, London, 1991, p. 456
61. Kershaw, *Hitler 1936–45*, p. 439
62. Burdick and Jacobsen, *Halder War Diary 1939–1942*, p. 563
63. *The Diary of Harold L. Ickes*, November 23, 1941
64. *The Presidential Diary of Henry Morgenthau*, November 25, 1941
65. *The Diaries of Henry L. Stimson*, November 23, 1941
66. Ministry of Foreign Affairs of the USSR, *Correspondence between Stalin, Roosevelt, Truman, Churchill and Attlee during World War Two: Correspondence with Churchill and Attlee*, p. 36
67. Kimball, *Churchill and Roosevelt*, Vol. 1 p. 279
68. Engel, Major Gerhard, *Heeres-Adjutant bei Hitler 1938–1943*, Stuttgart, 1974
69. Burdick and Jacobsen, *Halder War Diary 1939–1942*, p. 571
70. Ibid., p. 571
71. Kershaw, *Hitler 1936–45*, p. 440
72. *Morgenthau Presidential Diary*, December 3, 1941
73. Stinnett, Robert B., *Day of Deceit: The Truth About FDR and Pearl Harbour*, London, 2000, p. 181
74. Hull, Cordell, *Memoirs*, New York, 1948, Vol. 2, p. 1092
75. Sherwood, Robert E., *Roosevelt and Hopkins: An Intimate History*, New York, 2001, pp. 410–412
76. Ibid., pp. 410–412
77. Davis, Kenneth S., *FDR The War President 1940–1943: A History*, New York, 2000, p. 338
78. Sherwood, *Roosevelt and Hopkins*, p. 415

Chapter 6

1. Sherwood, Robert E., *Roosevelt and Hopkins: An Intimate History*, New York, 2001, p. 415

2. Winant, John G., *A Letter from Grosvenor Square: An Account of a Stewardship*, London, 1947, pp. 198–199

3. Gilbert, Martin, *Winston S. Churchill; Vol. VII: Road to Victory 1941–1945*, London, 1986, p. 1268

4. Ibid., p. 1268

5. Gilbert, Martin, *Second World War*, London, 1989, p. 274 and Kershaw, Ian, *Hitler 1936–45: Nemesis*, London, 2000, p. 422

6. Goebbels, Joseph, *Die Tagebücher von Joseph Goebbels, Teil 2: Diktate 1941–1945*, ed. Elke Frohlich, Munich, 1993–1998, December 8, 1941

7. Tully, Grace, *FDR My Boss*, New York, 1949, pp. 256–258

8. Ibid., pp. 256–258

9. OF 4675

10. Public Papers of the President

11. *The Diaries of Edward Lindley Wood, First Earl of Halifax*, Public Diary 1940–1945 A7.8.3–18, December 8, 1941

12. Berle Box 213

13. Files on the German declaration of war compiled by the Franklin D. Roosevelt Library and Museum

14. Alanbrooke, Field Marshal Lord, *War Diaries 1939–1945*, London, 2001, p. 209

15. Eden, Anthony, *The Reckoning*, London, 1965, p. 285

16. Ibid., p. 285

17. Engel, Major Gerhard, *Heeres-Adjutant bei Hitler 1938–1943*, Stuttgart, 1974, December 8,1941

18. Ibid., December 8, 1941

19. Ibid., December 8, 1941

20. Burdick, Charles and Jacobsen, Hans-Adolf, *The Halder War Diary 1939–1942*, London, 1988, p. 582

21. Goebbels, *Tagebücher, Teil 2*, December 10, 1941

22. Ibid., December 10, 1941

23. Halifax Papers: Correspondence, Ref: A4.410.4 – Papers as HM Ambassador at Washington

24. Goebbels, *Tagebücher, Teil 2*, December 10, 1941

25. Gilbert, Martin, *Winston S. Churchill, Vol. VII: Road to Victory 1941–1945*, London, 1986, p. 1273

26. Ibid., p. 1273

27. Kimball, Warren, *Churchill and Roosevelt: The Complete Correspondence*, Princeton, New Jersey, 1984, Vol. 1, p. 286

28. Document 572, *Documents on German Foreign Policy 1918–1945 Series D (1937–1945) Vol. XIII*, HMSO, London 1963, pp. 999–1000

29. Kershaw, *Hitler 1936–45*, p. 446 and Bullock, Alan, *Stalin and Hitler: Parallel Lives*, London, 1991, p. 838

30. Ibid.

31. Below, Nicolaus von, *At Hitler's Side: The Memoirs of Hitler's Luftwaffe Adjutant 1937–1945*, London, 1980, p. 118

32. Files on German declaration of war prepared by the Franklin D. Roosevelt Library and Museum

33. *Diaries of Edward Lindley Wood, First Earl of Halifax*, Public Diary 1940–1945 A7.8.3–18, December 11, 1941

34. Gilbert, *Winston S. Churchill, Vol. VII*, p. 1274

35. Goebbels, *Tagebücher, Teil 2*, December 13, 1941

36. Ibid., December 13, 1941

37. Ibid., December 13, 1941

38. Ministry of Foreign Affairs of the USSR, *Correspondence between Stalin, Roosevelt, Truman, Churchill and Attlee during World War Two: Correspondence with Churchill and Attlee*, p. 37

39. Eden, Anthony, *The Reckoning*, London, 1965, pp. 289–296

40. Rzheshevsky, Oleg (ed.), *War and Diplomacy: The Making of the Grand Documents from Stalin's Archives*, Amsterdam, 1996, Document 4

41. Burdick and Jacobsen, *Halder War Diary 1939–1942*, pp. 589–590

42. Ibid., p. 590

43. Below, *At Hitler's Side*, p. 121
44. Ibid., p. 121
45. Gilbert, *Winston S. Churchill, Vol. VII*, p. 16
46. Ibid., p. 16 and Churchill, Winston S., *The Second World War, Vol. 3: The Grand Alliance*, London, 1950, p. 630
47. Ibid.
48. Dilks, David, *The Diaries of Sir Alexander Cadogan OM 1938–1945*, London, 1971, p. 422
49. Gilbert, Winston S. *Churchill, Vol. VII*, p. 17
50. *Diaries of Edward Lindley Wood, First Earl of Halifax*, Public Diary 1940–1945 A7.8.3–18, December 22, 1941
51. Ibid., December 23, 1941
52. Ibid., December 25, 1941
53. Ibid., December 26, 1941
54. Gilbert, *Winston S. Churchill, Vol. VII*, pp. 29–30
55. *The Diaries of Harold L. Ickes*, December 26, 1941
56. Burdick and Jacobsen, *Halder War Diary 1939–1942*, p. 598
57. Ibid., pp. 596–598
58. *Diaries of Edward Lindley Wood, First Earl of Halifax*, Public Diary 1940–1945 A7.8.3–18, January 3, 1942
59. Ibid., January 4, 1942
60. Halifax Papers: Correspondence, Ref: A4.410.4 – Papers as HM Ambassador at Washington
61. Hitler, Adolf, *Hitler's Table Talk 1941–1944: His Private Conversations*, London, 2000, p. 179
62. Ibid., p. 180
63. Ibid., p. 181
64. Merritt Miner, Steven, *Between Churchill and Stalin: The Soviet Union, Great Britain, and the Origins of the Grand Alliance*, London, 1988, p. 194
65. See Moran, Lord, *Churchill at War 1940–1945*, London, 2002
66. *The Diaries of Henry L. Stimson*, January 5, 1942

67. Bialer, Seweryn (ed.), *Stalin and His Generals: Soviet Military Memoirs of World War II*, London, 1970, p. 331
68. Ibid., p. 332
69. Ibid., p. 332 and Bullock, Alan, *Stalin and Hitler: Parallel Lives*, London, 1991, p. 841 and Sebag-Montefiore, Simon, *Stalin: The Court of the Red Tsar*, London, 2003, p. 359
70. Gilbert, *Winston S. Churchill, Vol.VII*, p. 38
71. *Diaries of Edward Lindley Wood, First Earl of Halifax*, Secret Diary A7.8.19: Secret Diary 1941–1945, January 8, 1942
72. Casey, Steven, *Cautious Crusade: Franklin D. Roosevelt, American Public Opinion and the War against Nazi Germany*, Oxford, 2001, p. 49
73. *Diaries of Henry L. Stimson*, January 11, 1942
74. Halifax Papers: Correspondence, Ref: A4.410.4 – Papers as HM Ambassador at Washington
75. Hopkins Box 308 and Hopkins Box 380
76. Kimball, *Churchill and Roosevelt, Vol. 1*, p. 335
77. Ibid., p. 337
78. Perkins, Frances, *The Roosevelt I Knew*, New York, 1946, p. 368
79. Gilbert, Martin, *Winston S. Churchill, Vol. VII*, p. 239
80. Roosevelt, Elliott (ed.), *The Roosevelt Letters: Being the Personal Correspondence of Franklin Delano Roosevelt, Vol. 3: 1928–1945*, London, 1952
81. Burdick and Jacobsen, *Halder War Diary 1939–1942*, p. 604

Chapter 7

1. Ross, Graham, *The Foreign Office and the Kremlin: British Documents on Anglo-Soviet Relations 1941–1945*, London, 1984
2. *The Diaries of Guy Liddell*, KV 4/185–196, January 17, 1942
3. Goebbels, Joseph, *Die Tagebücher von Joseph Goebbels, Teil 2: Diktate, 1941–1945*, ed. Elke Frohlich, Munich, 1993–1998, January 20, 1942

4. Ibid., January 20, 1942
5. *The Presidential Diary of Henry Morgenthau,* January 27, 1942
6. Hitler, Adolf, *Hitler's Table Talk 1941–1944: His Private Conversations,* London, 2000, p. 260
7. Eden, Anthony, *The Reckoning,* London, 1965, p. 318 and Merritt Miner, Steven, *Between Churchill and Stalin: The Soviet Union, Great Britain, and the Origins of the Grand Alliance,* London, 1988, p. 198
8. Ibid.
9. Merritt Miner, *Between Churchill and Stalin,* p. 195
10. Alanbrooke, Field Marshal Lord, *War Diaries 1939–1945,* London, 2001, p. 225
11. Ibid., p. 225
12. Bullock, Alan, *Stalin and Hitler: Parallel Lives,* London, 1991, p. 850
13. Goebbels, *Tagebücher, Teil 2,* January 30, 1941
14. Ibid., January 30, 1941
15. Kimball, Warren, *Churchill and Roosevelt: The Complete Correspondence,* Princeton, New Jersey, 1984, Vol. 1, ,p. 345
16. Ibid., p. 346
17. Goebbels, *Tagebücher, Teil 2,* February 8, 1942
18. Ibid., February 14, 1942
19. Gilbert, Martin, *Churchill, Vol. VII: Road to Victory 1941–1945,* London, 1986, p. 59
20. Goebbels, *Tagebücher, Teil 2,* February 16, 1942
21. Gilbert, Martin, *Second World War,* London, 1989, p. 301
22. Kershaw, Ian, *Hitler 1936–45: Nemesis,* London, 2000, p. 504
23. Maisky, Ivan, *Memoirs of a Soviet Ambassador: The War 1939–1945,* London, 1967, p. 257
24. Kimball, *Churchill and Roosevelt,* Vol. 1, p. 362
25. Ibid., p. 364
26. FO 371/32876 and FO 371/32897
27. Merritt Miner, *Between Churchill and Stalin,* p. 208

28. Gilbert, *Winston S. Churchill, Vol. VII,* p. 66
29. *The Diaries of Lord Avon,* University of Birmingham, AP 20/1/1–32, February 27, 1942
30. Kimball, *Churchill and Roosevelt,* Vol. 1, p. 394
31. Merritt Miner, *Between Churchill and Stalin,* p. 216
32. *The Diaries of Edward Lindley Wood, First Earl of Halifax,* Secret Diary A7.8.19: Secret Diary 1941–1945, March 8, 1942
33. Ibid., March 8, 1942
34. Merritt Miner, *Between Churchill and Stalin,* p. 213
35. *Morgenthau Presidential Diary,* March 11, 1942
36. Ministry of Foreign Affairs of the USSR, *Correspondence between Stalin, Roosevelt, Truman, Churchill and Attlee during World War Two: Correspondence with Churchill and nt Attlee (July 1941–November 1945),* Moscow, 1957, p. 41
37. Maisky, *Memoirs of a Soviet Ambassador,* p. 253
38. *The Memoir of Y. Chadayev,* March 16, 1942
39. Kimball, *Churchill and Roosevelt,* Vol. 1, pp. 421–422
40. Kershaw, *Hitler 1936–45,* p. 495
41. Kimball, *Churchill and Roosevelt,* Vol. 1, p. 446
42. *The Diaries of Henry L. Stimson,* April 22, 1942
43. Kimball, *Churchill and Roosevelt,* Vol. 1, pp. 447–448
44. Ibid., pp. 447–448
45. Ibid., p. 449
46. Alanbrooke, *War Diaries 1939–1945,* p. 249
47. Goebbels, *Tagebücher, Teil 2,* April 17, 1942
48. Ibid., April 26, 1942
49. Dimitrov, Georgi, *The Diary of Georgi Dimitrov 1933–1949,* ed. Ivo Banac, London, 2003, p. 214
50. Goebbels, *Tagebücher, Teil 2,* April 27, 1942
51. Harriman, Averell and Abel, Elie, *Special Envoy to Churchill and Stalin 1941–1946,* New York, 1975, p. 135

52. Ministry of Foreign Affairs of the USSR, *Correspondence between Stalin, Roosevelt, Truman, Churchill and Attlee during World War Two: Correspondence with Churchill and Attlee (July 1941–November 1945)*, Moscow, 1957, p. 48
53. Ibid., p. 48
54. Dilks, David, *The Diaries of Sir Alexander Cadogan OM 1938–1945*, London, 1971, p. 453
55. *Memoir of Y. Chadayev*, May 22, 1942
56. Goebbels, *Tagebücher, Teil 2*, May 24, 1942
57. Ibid., May 24, 1942
58. Ibid., May 24, 1942
59. Rzheshevsky, Oleg (ed.), *War and Diplomacy: The Making of the Grand Documents from Stalin's Archives*, Amsterdam, 1996, Document 38
60. Alanbrooke, *War Diaries 1939–1945*, p. 260
61. Kimball, *Churchill and Roosevelt*, Vol. 1
62. Ibid., p. 503
63. *Diaries of Lord Avon*, University of Birmingham, AP 20/1/1–32, June 9, 1942
64. Ibid., June 9, 1942
65. Eden, *The Reckoning*, p. 330
66. Ibid., p. 330
67. Goebbels, *Tagebücher, Teil 2*, June 10, 1942
68. Alanbrooke, *War Diaries 1939–1945*, p. 266
69. *Diaries of Edward Lindley Wood, First Earl of Halifax*, Public Diary 1940–1945 A7.8.3–18, June 18, 1942
70. Ward, Geoffrey, C., *Closest Companion: The Unknown Story of the Intimate Friendship between Franklin Roosevelt and Margaret Suckley*, New York, 1995, p. 162
71. Gilbert, *Winston S. Churchill, Vol. VII*, pp. 128–129
72. Goebbels, *Tagebücher, Teil 2*, June 23, 1942

Chapter 8
1. *The Diaries of Edward Lindley Wood, First Earl of Halifax*, Public Diary 1940–1945 A7.8.3–18, June 21, 1942
2. Ward, Geoffrey, C., *Closest Companion: The Unknown Story of the Intimate Friendship*

between Franklin Roosevelt and Margaret Suckley, New York, 1995, p. 167
3. Ibid., p. 167
4. Ibid., p. 167
5. *The Diary of Henry L. Stimson*, June 22, 1942
6. Ibid., June 22, 1942
7. Burdick, Charles and Jacobsen, Hans-Adolf, *The Halder War Diary 1939–1942*, London, 1988, p. 627
8. Hitler, Adolf, *Hitler's Table Talk 1941–1944: His Private Conversations*, London, 2000, p. 527
9. Eden, Anthony, *The Reckoning*, London, 1965, p. 333
10. Goebbels, Joseph, *Die Tagebücher von Joseph Goebbels, Teil 2: Diktate 1941–1945*, ed. Elke Frohlich, Munich, 1993–1998, June 23, 1942
11. Hitler, *Hitler's Table Talk 1941–1944*, pp. 538–539
12. Warlimont, Walter, *Inside Hitler's Headquarters 1939–1945*, Novato, California, 1964, p. 243
13. Hitler, *Hitler's Table Talk 1941–1944*, p. 545
14. Gilbert, Martin, *Winston S. Churchill, Vol. VII: Road to Victory 1941–1945*, London, 1986, pp. 139–140
15. Kimball, Warren, *Churchill and Roosevelt: The Complete Correspondence*, Princeton, New Jersey, 1984, Vol. 1, p. 517
16. Goebbels, *Tagebücher, Teil 2*, July 2, 1942
17. Zhukov, Marshal Georgy, *The Memoirs of Marshal Zhukov*, London, 1971, p. 369
18. Burdick and Jacobsen, *Halder War Diary 1939–1942*, p. 632
19. Maisky, Ivan, *Memoirs of a Soviet Ambassador: The War 1939–1945*, London, 1967, p. 290
20. *Diaries of Edward Lindley Wood, First Earl of Halifax*, Secret Diary A7.8.19: Secret Diary 1941–1945, July 9, 1942
21. Kimball, *Churchill and Roosevelt*, Vol. 1, p. 528
22. *Diaries of Edward Lindley Wood, First Earl of Halifax*, Secret Diary A7.8.19: Secret Diary 1941–1945, July 15, 1942

23. *Diary of Henry L. Stimson*, July 15, 1942
24. Hopkins Box 308 and Hopkins Box 380
25. Below, Nicolaus von, *At Hitler's Side: The Memoirs of Hitler's Luftwaffe Adjutant 1937–1945*, London, 1980, pp. 149–150
26. Beevor, Anthony, *Stalingrad*, London, 1999, p. 138
27. Ibid., p. 138
28. Ministry of Foreign Affairs of the USSR, *Correspondence between Stalin, Roosevelt, Truman, Churchill and Attlee during World War Two: Correspondence with Winston S. Churchill and Clement Attlee (July 1941–November 1945)*, Moscow, 1957, pp. 52–55
29. Dilks, David, *The Diaries of Sir Alexander Cadogan OM 1938–1945*, London, 1971, p. 463
30. The unpublished diary of Ivan Maisky, July 19, 1942
31. Sherwood, Robert E., *Roosevelt and Hopkins: An Intimate History*, New York, 2001, p. 582
32. Ibid., p. 582
33. Alanbrooke, Field Marshal Lord, *War Diaries 1939–1945*, London, 2001, p. 282
34. Ministry of Foreign Affairs of the USSR, *Correspondence between Stalin, Roosevelt, Truman, Churchill and Attlee during World War Two: Correspondence with Churchill and Attlee*, p. 56
35. Ibid., p. 56
36. Unpublished diary of Ivan Maisky, July 23, 1942
37. HO 45/25574 – Docs on surveillance of CPGB
38. Kershaw, Ian, *Hitler 1936–45: Nemesis*, London, 2000, p. 528
39. Burdick and Jacobsen, *Halder War Diary 1939–1942*, p. 646
40. Volkogonov, Dmitri, *Stalin: Triumph and Tragedy*, London, 1991, p. 460
41. Dimitrov, Georgi, *The Diary of Georgi Dimitrov 1933–1949*, ed. Ivo Banac, London, 2003, p. 233

42. Warlimont, *Inside Hitler's Headquarters 1939–1945*, p. 249
43. Ibid., p. 249
44. Eden, *The Reckoning*, p. 338
45. Ibid., p. 338
46. *The Diaries of Lord Avon*, University of Birmingham, AP 20/1/1–32, July 10, 1942
47. Unpublished diary of Ivan Maisky, July 30, 1942
48. Ibid., July 30, 1942
49. Ibid., July 30, 1942
50. Ibid., July 30, 1942
51. Ministry of Foreign Affairs of the USSR, *Correspondence between Stalin, Roosevelt, Truman, Churchill and Attlee during World War Two: Correspondence with Churchill and Attlee*, p. 57
52. Ibid., p. 58
53. Churchill, Winston S., *The Second World War, Vol. IV: The Hinge of Fate*, London, 1950
54. Kimball, *Churchill and Roosevelt*, Vol. 1, p. 553
55. Gilbert, *Winston S. Churchill, Vol. VII*, pp. 161–162 and see also Moran, Lord, *Churchill at War 1940–1945*, London, 2002
56. Hitler, Adolf, *Hitler's Table Talk 1941–1944*, p. 609
57. Volkogonov, *Stalin*, p. 469
58. Warlimont, *Inside Hitler's Headquarters 1939–1945*, p.251
59. Ibid., p. 251
60. *The Diaries of Guy Liddell*, KV 4/185–196, August 11, 1942
61. Gilbert, *Winston S. Churchill, Vol. VII*, p. 173
62. Churchill, Winston S., *Second World War, Vol. IV*, pp. 428–9
63. Ibid., pp. 428–9
64. Berezhkov, Valentin, *History in the Making: Memoirs of World War II Diplomacy*, Moscow, 1982, pp. 194–200
65. Ibid., pp. 194–200
66. Ibid., pp. 194–200
67. Ibid., pp. 194–200
68. Ibid., pp. 194–200

69. Kimball, Warren, *Churchill and Roosevelt*, Vol. 1, p. 562
70. Gilbert, *Winston S. Churchill, Vol. VII*, p. 183
71. Ministry of Foreign Affairs of the USSR, *Correspondence between Stalin, Roosevelt, Truman, Churchill and Atlee during World War Two: Correspondence with Winston S. Churchill and Clement Atlee (July 1941–November 1945)*, Moscow, 1957, pp. 60–61.
72. Gilbert, *Winston S. Churchill, Vol VII*, p. 184
73. Ibid., p. 185
74. Dilks, *Diaries of Sir Alexander Cadogan OM 1938–1945*, pp. 471–474
75. Gilbert, *Winston S. Churchill, Vol VII*, p. 186
76. Alanbrooke, *War Diaries 1939–1945*, p. 301
77. Dilks, *Diaries of Sir Alexander Cadogan OM 1938–1945*, pp. 471–474
78. Alanbrooke, *War Diaries 1939–1945*, p. 301
79. Ibid., p. 301
80. Berezhkov, Valentin, *History in the Making: Memoirs of World War II Diplomacy*, pp. 194–200
81. Ibid., pp. 194–200
82. Dilks, *Diaries of Sir Alexander Cadogan OM 1938–1945*, pp. 471–474
83. Ibid., pp. 471–474
84. Alanbrooke, *War Diaries 1939–1945*, p. 306
85. Kimball, *Churchill and Roosevelt*, Vol. 1, p. 572
86. Goebbels, *Tagebücher, Teil 2*, August 19, 1942

Chapter 9

1. Goebbels, Joseph, *Die Tagebücher von Joseph Goebbels, Teil 2: Diktate 1941–1945*, ed. Elke Frohlich, Munich, 1993–1998, August 20, 1942
2. Ibid., August 20, 1942
3. Warlimont, Walter, *Inside Hitler's Headquarters 1939–1945*, Novato, California, 1964, p. 251
4. Ibid., p. 251
5. Ibid., p. 252
6. Ibid., p. 252
7. Engel, Major Gerhard, *Heeres-Adjutant bei Hitler 1938–1943*, Stuttgart, 1974, August 27, 1942
8. Kimball, Warren, *Churchill and Roosevelt: The Complete Correspondence*, Princeton, New Jersey, 1984, Vol. 1, p. 576
9. Zhukov, Marshal Georgy, *The Memoirs of Marshal Zhukov*, London, 1971, p. 377
10. Ibid., p. 377
11. Gilbert, Martin, *Winston S. Churchill, Vol. VII: Road to Victory 1941–1945*, London, 1986, p. 223
12. Hitler, Adolf, *Hitler's Table Talk, 1941–1944: His Private Conversations*, London, 2000, p. 680
13. Ibid., p. 680
14. Kimball, *Churchill and Roosevelt*, Vol. 1, p. 592
15. Ibid., p. 592
16. Ibid., p. 592
17. Kershaw, Ian, *Hitler 1936–45: Nemesis*, London, 2000, p. 533
18. Warlimont, *Inside Hitler's Headquarters 1939–1945*, p. 259
19. Ibid., p. 259
20. Engel, *Heeres-Adjutant bei Hitler 1938–1943*, September 8, 1942
21. *The Presidential Diary of Henry Morgenthau*, September 9, 1942
22. Zhukov, *Memoirs of Marshal Zhukov*, p. 384
23. Ibid., p. 384
24. *The Memoir of Y. Chadayev*, September 22, 1942
25. Ibid., September 22, 1942
26. Ibid., October 5, 1942
27. Kimball, *Churchill and Roosevelt*, Vol. 1, pp. 602–604
28. Ibid., pp. 602–604
29. Burdick, Charles and Jacobsen, Hans-Adolf, *The Halder War Diary 1939–1942*, London, 1988, p. 670
30. Warlimont, *Inside Hitler's Headquarters 1939–1945*, p. 258

31. Below, Nicolaus von, *At Hitler's Side: The Memoirs of Hitler's Luftwaffe Adjutant 1937–1945*, London, 1980, p. 154
32. Goebbels, *Tagebücher, Teil 2*, October 1, 1942
33. Eden, Anthony, *The Reckoning*, London, 1965, p. 343
34. 6Rzheshevsky, O. A., *Stalin i Cherchill: vstrechi, besedy, diskussii: dokumenty, kommentarii 1941–1945*, Moscow 2004, Document 156
35. Ibid., Document 156
36. Alanbrooke, Field Marshal Lord, *War Diaries 1939–1945*, London, 2001, p. 333
37. Warlimont, *Inside Hitler's Headquarters 1939–1945*, p. 267
38. Goebbels, *Tagebücher, Teil 2*, November 4, 1942
39. Ibid., November 4, 1942
40. Gilbert, *Winston S. Churchill, Vol. VII*, p. 248
41. Engel, *Heeres-Adjutant bei Hitler 1938–1943*, November 8, 1942
42. Gilbert, *Winston S. Churchill, Vol. VII*, p. 252
43. Kershaw, *Hitler 1936–45*, p. 539
44. Gilbert, *Winston S. Churchill, Vol. VII*, p. 254
45. Zhukov, *Memoirs*, p. 404
46. Below, *At Hitler's Side*, p. 158
47. Zhukov, *Memoirs*, pp. 405–406
48. Below, *At Hitler's Side*, p. 161
49. Ward, Geoffrey C., *Closest Companion: The Unknown Story of the Intimate Friendship between Franklin Roosevelt and Margaret Suckley*, New York, 1995, p. 187
50. Ibid., p. 187
51. Ibid., p. 187
52. Ibid., p. 187
53. Taussig Papers Box 5
54. Gilbert, *Winston S. Churchill, Vol. VII*, p. 267
55. Ministry of Foreign Affairs of the USSR, *Correspondence between Stalin, Roosevelt, Truman, Churchill and Attlee during World War Two: Correspondence with Churchill and Attlee*, p. 82, p. 43

56. Ibid., p. 44
57. *Memoir of Y. Chadayev*, December 31, 1942
58. Goebbels, *Tagebücher, Teil 2*, January 1, 1943
59. Ibid., January 1, 1943
60. Below, *At Hitler's Side*, p. 161
61. Goebbels, *Tagebücher, Teil 2*, January 7, 1943
62. Ward, *Closest Companion*, p. 194
63. *Memoir of Y. Chadayev*, January 9, 1943
64. Ibid., January 10, 1943
65. Ward, *Closest Companion*, p. 198
66. Gilbert, *Winston S. Churchill, Vol. VII*, p. 296
67. Goebbels, *Tagebücher, Teil 2*, January 23, 1943
68. Ibid., January 23, 1943
69. Ibid., January 23, 1943
70. Public Papers of the President, January 24, 1943
71. Goebbels, *Tagebücher, Teil 2*, January 24, 1943
72. Junge, Traudl, *Until the Final Hour: Hitler's Last Secretary*, London, 2003, p. 115
73. Gilbert, *Winston S. Churchill, Vol. VII*, p. 326
74. Ibid., p. 328
75. Ministry of Foreign Affairs of the USSR, *Correspondence between Stalin, Roosevelt, Truman, Churchill and Attlee during World War Two: Correspondence with Franklin D. Roosevelt and Harry S Truman (August 1941–December 1945)*, Moscow, 1957, p. 53
76. Engel, *Heeres-Adjutant bei Hitler 1938–1943*, February 1, 1943
77. Warlimont, *Inside Hitler's Headquarters 1939–1945*, pp. 300–307
78. Goebbels, *Tagebücher, Teil 2*, February 8, 1943
79. Ibid., May 9, 1943

Chapter 10
1. Kershaw, Ian, *Hitler 1936–45: Nemesis*, London, 2000, p. 579
2. Dilks, David, *The Diaries of Sir Alexander Cadogan 1938–1945*, London, 1971, pp. 520–521

3. Ministry of Foreign Affairs of the USSR, *Correspondence between Stalin, Roosevelt, Truman, Churchill and Attlee during World War Two: Correspondence with Winston S. Churchill and Clement R. Attlee (July 1941–November 1945)*, Moscow, 1957, 120–121

4. Ibid., pp. 121–122

5. Ibid., pp. 123–124

6. Ibid., p. 127

7. Nisbet, Robert, *Roosevelt and Stalin: The Failed Courtship*, New York, 1988, p. 6

8. Ministry of Foreign Affairs of the USSR, *Correspondence between Stalin, Roosevelt, Truman, Churchill and Attlee during World War Two: Correspondence with Franklin D. Roosevelt and Harry S. Truman (August 1941–December 1945)*, Moscow, 1957, pp. 63–64

9. Meacham, Jon, *Franklin and Winston: An Intimate Portrait of an Epic Friendship*, New York, 2004, pp. 226–227

10. Goebbels, Joseph, *Die Tagebücher von Joseph Goebbels, Teil 2: Diktate 1941–1945*, ed. Elke Frohlich, Munich, 1993–1998, May 10, 1943

11. *The Diary of Henry L. Stimson*, May 10, 1943

12. Ibid., May 12, 1943

13. KV 4/228

14. Gilbert, Martin, *Winston S. Churchill, Vol. VII: Road to Victory 1941–1945*, London, 1986, pp. 408–410

15. Goebbels, *Tagebücher, Teil 2*, May 20, 1943

16. Warlimont, Walter, *Inside Hitler's Headquarters 1939–1945*, Novato, California, 1964, pp. 331–339

17. Gilbert, Martin, *Winston S. Churchill, Vol. VII*, p. 418

18. Ministry of Foreign Affairs of the USSR, *Correspondence between Stalin, Roosevelt, Truman, Churchill and Attlee during World War Two: Correspondence with Roosevelt and Truman (August 1941–December 1945)*, Moscow, 1957, p. 66

19. *Diary of Henry L. Stimson*, May 27, 1943

20. Ibid., pp. 70–71

21. Kimball, Warren, *Churchill and Roosevelt: The Complete Correspondence*, Princeton, New Jersey, 1984, Vol. 1, p. 245

22. Below, Nicolaus von, *At Hitler's Side: The Memoirs of Hitler's Luftwaffe Adjutant 1937–1945*, London, 1980, p. 173

23. FO 800/301

24. *The Diaries of Guy Liddell*, KV 4/185–196, June 17, 1943

25. Harriman, Averell and Abel, Elie, *Special Envoy to Churchill and Stalin 1941–1946*, New York, 1975, p. 217

26. Ibid., p. 217

27. Ibid., p. 217

28. *The Diaries of Lord Avon*, University of Birmingham, AP 20/1/1–32, June 24, 1943

29. Kimball, *Churchill and Roosevelt*, Vol. 1, pp. 278–279

30. Ministry of Foreign Affairs of the USSR, *Correspondence between Stalin, Roosevelt, Truman, Churchill and Attlee during World War Two: Correspondence with Churchill and Attlee*, p. 138

31. Dilks, *Diaries of Sir Alexander Cadogan 1938–1945*, pp. 538–539

32. Ministry of Foreign Affairs of the USSR, *Correspondence between Stalin, Roosevelt, Truman, Churchill and Attlee during World War Two: Correspondence with Churchill and Attlee*, pp. 140–141

33. Goebbels, *Tagebücher, Teil 2*, June 25, 1943

34. Ibid., June 25, 1943

35. Kimball, *Churchill and Roosevelt*, Vol. 1, pp. 278–279

36. Colville, Sir John, *The Fringes of Power: 10 Downing Street Diaries 1939–1955*, London, 1985, p. 624

37. Kimball, *Churchill and Roosevelt*, Vol. 1, p. 290

38. PSF Box 36

39. Dilks, *Diaries of Sir Alexander Cadogan 1938–1945*, p. 540

40. Sebag-Montefiore, Simon, *Stalin: The Court of the Red Tsar*, London, 2003, p. 401

41. Ibid., p. 401

42. Junge, Traudl, *Until the Final Hour: Hitler's Last Secretary*, London, 2003, p. 114
43. Kershaw, *Hitler 1936–45*, p. 594
44. Warlimont, *Inside Hitler's Headquarters 1939–1945*, p. 344
45. Goebbels, *Tagebücher, Teil 2*, July 25, 1943
46. Gilbert, *Winston S. Churchill, Vol. VII*, p. 453
47. Ministry of Foreign Affairs of the USSR, *Correspondence between Stalin, Roosevelt, Truman, Churchill and Attlee during World War Two: Correspondence with Roosevelt and Truman*, p. 73
48. Ministry of Foreign Affairs of the USSR, *Correspondence between Stalin, Roosevelt, Truman, Churchill and Attlee during World War Two: Correspondence with Churchill and Attlee* , p. 142
49. *The Diaries of William Lyon Mackenzie King of Canada*, ref: MG26–J13, August 10, 1943
50. Goebbels, *Tagebücher, Teil 2*, August 10, 1943
51. Ward, *Closest Companion*, p. 229
52. Kimball, *Churchill and Roosevelt*, Vol. 1, pp. 391–398
53. Meacham, *Franklin and Winston*, p. 235
54. Ibid., p. 237
55. Ibid., p. 237

Chapter 11

1. *The Diaries of Guy Liddell*, KV 4/185–196, September 7, 1943
2. Ministry of Foreign Affairs of the USSR, *Correspondence between Stalin, Roosevelt, Truman, Churchill and Attlee during World War Two: Correspondence with Franklin D. Roosevelt and Harry S. Truman (August 1941–December 1945)*, Moscow, 1957, p. 90
3. Goebbels, Joseph, *Die Tagebücher von Joseph Goebbels, Teil 2: Diktate 1941–1945*, ed. Elke Frohlich, Munich, 1993–1998, September 10, 1943
4. Ibid., September 10, 1943
5. Kershaw, Ian, *Hitler 1936–45: Nemesis*, London, 2000, p. 601

6. Eden, Anthony, *The Reckoning*, London, 1965, p. 405
7. Ward, Geoffrey, C., *Closest Companion: The Unknown Story of the Intimate Friendship between Franklin Roosevelt and Margaret Suckley*, New York, 1995, pp. 238–239
8. Moran, Lord, *Churchill at War 1940–1945*, London, 2002, p. 144
9. Ibid., p. 144
10. Ibid., p. 145 and Gilbert, Martin, *Winston S. Churchill, Vol. VII: Road to Victory 1941–1945*, London, 1986, p. 503
11. Kimball, Warren, *Churchill and Roosevelt: The Complete Correspondence*, Princeton, New Jersey, 1984, Vol. 2, p. 447
12. Moran, *Churchill at War 1940–1945*, p. 146
13. Gilbert, *Winston S. Churchill,Vol. VII*, p. 509
14. Ibid., p. 510
15. *The Diary of Henry L. Stimson*, September 22, 1943
16. Goebbels, *Tagebücher, Teil 2*, September 23, 1943
17. *Diary of Henry L. Stimson*, September 28, 1943
18. PSF Box 38
19. Public Papers of the President
20. Gilbert, *Winston S. Churchill, Vol. VII*, p. 521
21. Harvey, John (ed.), *The War Diaries of Oliver Harvey 1941–1945*, London, 1978, p. 304
22. Kimball, *Churchill and Roosevelt*, Vol. 2, p. 503
23. Alanbrooke, Field Marshal Lord, *War Diaries 1939–1945*, London, 2001, p. 459
24. Gilbert, Winston S. Churchill, Vol. VII, p. 525 and Kimball, *Churchill and Roosevelt*, Vol. 1
25. Ministry of Foreign Affairs of the USSR, *Correspondence between Stalin, Roosevelt, Truman, Churchill and Attlee during World War Two: Correspondence with Winston S. Churchill and Clement R. Attlee (July 1941–November 1945)*, Moscow, 1957, p 171
26. Kimball, *Churchill and Roosevelt*, Vol. 1, p. 533

27. Dilks, David, *The Diaries of Sir Alexander Cadogan 1938–1945*, London, 1971, p. 568
28. Eden, *The Reckoning*, pp. 410–418
29. Alanbrooke, *War Diaries 1939–1945*, p. 461
30. Kimball, *Churchill and Roosevelt*, Vol. 1, p. 565
31. Goebbels, *Tagebücher, Teil 2*, October 27, 1943
32. Ibid., October 27, 1943
33. Ibid., October 27, 1943
34. *Diary of Henry L. Stimson*, October 28, 1943
35. Harvey, *War Diaries of Oliver Harvey 1941–1945*, p. 315
36. Hinsley, F. H. and Simkins, C. A. G., *British Intelligence in the Second World War, Vol. 4: Security and Counter Intelligence*, London, 1990, p. 285
37. HS 9/1645
38. We requested that file PREM 4/64/4 be opened. We were informed by the Cabinet Office that the files were now open, but had been lost. For more information see Hinsley and Simkins, *British Intelligence in the Second World War, Vol. 4*, pp. 283–291.
39. Ward, *Closest Companion*, pp. 250–251
40. Secret Service Records Box 21
41. *Diary of Henry L. Stimson*, November 4, 1943
42. MR Box 12
43. Beria, Sergo, *Beria, My Father: Inside Stalin's Kremlin*, London, 2001, p. 92
44. Zhukov, Marshal Georgy, *The Memoirs of Marshal Zhukov*, London, 1971, p. 486
45. Sebag-Montefiore, Simon, *Stalin: The Court of the Red Tsar*, London, 2003, p. 409
46. Below, Nicolaus von, *At Hitler's Side: The Memoirs of Hitler's Luftwaffe Adjutant 1937–1945*, London, 1980, p. 185 and Kershaw, *Hitler 1936–45*, p. 606
47. We requested that file PREM 4/64/4 be opened. We were informed by the Cabinet Office that the files were now open, but had been lost. For more information see Hinsley and Simkins, *British Intelligence in the Second World War, Vol. 4*, pp. 283–291.

48. Bower, Tom, *The Perfect English Spy: Sir Dick White and the Secret War 1935–1990*, London, 1995, p. 56
49. OF 200–3–N
50. Sherwood, Robert E., *Roosevelt and Hopkins: An Intimate History*, New York, 2001, p. 733
51. Alanbrooke, *War Diaries 1939–1945*, p. 473
52. *The Diaries of Edward Lindley Wood, First Earl of Halifax*, Secret Diary A7.8.19: Secret Diary 1941–1945, November 20, 1943
53. Soames, Mary, *Speaking for Themselves: The Personal Letters of Winston and Clementine Churchill*, London, 1999, p. 486
54. Meacham, Jon, *Franklin and Winston: An Intimate Portrait of an Epic Friendship*, New York, 2004, pp. 247–248
55. Dilks, *Diaries of Sir Alexander Cadogan 1938–1945*, pp. 577–578
56. Macmillan, Harold, *War Diaries: Politics and War in the Mediterranean: January 1943–May 1945*, London, 1984
57. Moran, *Churchill at War 1940–1945*, p. 160
58. Eden, *The Reckoning*, p. 423

Chapter 12

1. Reilly, Michael F. (as told by William J. Slocum), *Reilly of the White House*, New York, 1947, pp. 174–188
2. Beria, Sergo, *Beria, My Father: Inside Stalin's Kremlin*, London, 2001,
3. Harriman, Averell and Abel, Elie, *Special Envoy to Churchill and Stalin 1941–1946*, New York, 1975, p. 266 and Reilly, *Reilly of the White House*
4. Harriman and Abel, *Special Envoy to Churchill and Stalin 1941–1946*, p. 265
5. *The Tehran, Yalta and Potsdam Conferences*, Moscow, 1969, pp. 7–53
6. OF 200–3–N
7. Reilly, *Reilly of the White House*, pp. 174–188
8. Alanbrooke, Field Marshal Lord, *War Diaries 1939–1945*, London, 2001, pp. 484–485
9. Ibid., pp. 484–485

10. *Tehran, Yalta and Potsdam Conferences,* pp. 7–53
11. Alanbrooke, *War Diaries 1939–1945,* pp. 484–485
12. Moran, Lord, *Churchill at War 1940–1945,* London, 2002, pp. 171–173
13. Ibid., pp. 171–173
14. Kimball, Warren, *Churchill and Roosevelt: The Complete Correspondence,* Princeton, New Jersey, 1984, Vol. 1, p. 615
15. Goebbels, Joseph, *Die Tagebücher von Joseph Goebbels, Teil 2: Diktate 1941–1945,* ed. Elke Frohlich, Munich, 1993–1998, December 1, 1943
16. *The Diary of Henry L. Stimson,* December 5, 1943
17. Ibid., December 18, 1943
18. Warlimont, Walter, *Inside Hitler's Headquarters 1939–1945,* Novato, California, 1964, pp. 389–395
19. Perkins, Frances, *The Roosevelt I Knew,* New York, 1946, p. 382
20. Kershaw, Ian, *Hitler 1936–45: Nemesis,* London, 2000, p. 609
21. Ibid., p. 607
22. Dilks, David, *The Diaries of Sir Alexander Cadogan OM 1938–1945,* London, 1971, p. 592
23. Ministry of Foreign Affairs of the USSR, *Correspondence between Stalin, Roosevelt, Truman, Churchill and Attlee during World War Two: Correspondence with Winston S. Churchill and Clement Attlee (July 1941–November 1945),* Moscow, 1957, p. 181
24. Gilbert, Martin, *Winston S. Churchill, Vol. VII: Road to Victory 1941–1945,* London, 1986, p. 641
25. Warlimont, *Inside Hitler's Headquarters 1939–1945,* p. 407
26. Below, *At Hitler's Side,* p. 190
27. Gilbert, *Winston S. Churchill, Vol. VII,* pp. 651–652
28. Colville, Sir John, *The Fringes of Power: 10 Downing Street Diaries 1939–1955,* London, 1985, p. 467
29. *The Diaries of Lord Avon,* University of Birmingham, AP 20/1/1–32, January 20, 1944
30. Harriman and Abel, *Special Envoy to Churchill and Stalin 1941–1946,* p. 296
31. Ministry of Foreign Affairs of the USSR, *Correspondence between Stalin, Roosevelt, Truman, Churchill and Attlee during World War Two: Correspondence with Churchill and Attlee,* p. 189
32. Alanbrooke, *War Diaries 1939–1945,* p. 516
33. Goebbels, *Tagebücher, Teil 2,* January 25, 1944
34. Below, *At Hitler's Side,* pp. 190–191 and Kershaw, *Hitler 1936–45,* p, 618
35. Below, *At Hitler's Side,* pp. 193–194
36. Ministry of Foreign Affairs of the USSR, *Correspondence between Stalin, Roosevelt, Truman, Churchill and Attlee during World War Two: Correspondence with Churchill and Attlee,* pp. 191–192
37. Dilks, *Diaries of Sir Alexander Cadogan OM 1938–1945,* p. 604
38. Harriman and Abel, *Special Envoy to Churchill and Stalin 1941–1946,* pp. 323–324
39. Dilks, *Diaries of Sir Alexander Cadogan OM 1938–1945,* p. 606
40. *Diaries of Lord Avon,* February 18, 1944
41. Kimball, *Churchill and Roosevelt, Vol. 1,* p. 739
42. Harriman and Abel, *Special Envoy to Churchill and Stalin 1941–1946,* pp. 315–316
43. Goebbels, *Tagebücher, Teil 2,* March 4, 1944
44. Eden, Anthony, *The Reckoning,* London, 1965, p. 438
45. Ministry of Foreign Affairs of the USSR, *Correspondence between Stalin, Roosevelt, Truman, Churchill and Attlee during World War Two: Correspondence with Churchill and Attlee,* p. 208
46. Sebag-Montefiore, Simon, *Stalin: The Court of the Red Tsar,* London, 2003, p. 418
47. Ministry of Foreign Affairs of the USSR, *Correspondence between Stalin, Roosevelt, Truman, Churchill and Attlee during World War Two: Correspondence with Churchill and Attlee,* pp. 212–213

48. Below, *At Hitler's Side*, p. 195
49. Harriman and Abel, *Special Envoy to Churchill and Stalin 1941–1946*, p. 306
50. Churchill, Winston S., *The Second World War, Vol. V: Closing the Ring*, London, 1951, p. 705.
51. Kershaw, *Hitler 1936–45*, p. 632
52. Below, *At Hitler's Side*, p. 197
53. Ibid., p. 197
54. Harriman and Abel, *Special Envoy to Churchill and Stalin 1941–1946*, p. 328
55. Alanbrooke, *War Diaries 1939–1945*, p. 544
56. Kimball, *Churchill and Roosevelt*, Vol. 1, p. 149
57. Ibid., p. 152
58. Kimball, Warren, *Forged in War: Roosevelt, Churchill and the Second World War*, New York, 1997, p. 259
59. Gilbert, *Winston S. Churchill, Vol. VII*, p. 791
60. Stafford, David, *Ten Days to D–Day: Countdown to the Liberation of Europe*, London, 2003, p. 256
61. Kershaw, *Hitler 1936–45*, p. 639

Chapter 13

1. Below, Nicolaus von, *At Hitler's Side: The Memoirs of Hitler's Luftwaffe Adjutant 1937–1945*, London, 1980, p. 202
2. Public Papers of the President
3. Perkins, Frances, *The Roosevelt I Knew*, New York, 1946, p. 383
4. Goebbels, Joseph, *Die Tagebücher von Joseph Goebbels, Teil 2: Diktate 1941–1945*, ed. Elke Frohlich, Munich, 1993–1998, June 7, 1944
5. Kimball, Warren, *Churchill and Roosevelt: The Complete Correspondence*, Princeton, New Jersey, 1984, Vol. 1, p. 153
6. Ibid., p. 177
7. Ibid., p. 178
8. Ibid., p. 182
9. Ibid., pp. 198–199
10. *The Diary of Henry L. Stimson*, June 21, 1944
11. Kershaw, Ian, *Hitler 1936–45: Nemesis*, London, 2000, p. 645
12. Goebbels, *Tagebücher, Teil 2*, June 22, 1944

13. Ibid., June 22, 1944
14. Below, *At Hitler's Side*, p. 206
15. Ibid., pp. 204–205
16. Ibid., pp. 204–205
17. Kimball, *Churchill and Roosevelt*, Vol. 1, pp. 202–203
18. Ibid., pp. 212–213
19. Ibid., p. 213
20. Ibid., pp. 214–219
21. Ibid., pp. 214–219
22. Ibid., pp. 220–221
23. Ward, Geoffrey, C., *Closest Companion: The Unknown Story of the Intimate Friendship between Franklin Roosevelt and Margaret Suckley*, New York, 1995, p. 314
24. Kimball, *Churchill and Roosevelt*, Vol. 1, pp. 221–223
25. Ibid., pp. 221–223
26. Ibid., p. 225
27. Alanbrooke, Field Marshal Lord, *War Diaries 1939–1945*, London, 2001, pp. 564–565
28. Ibid., pp. 564–565
29. Kimball, *Churchill and Roosevelt*, Vol. 1, p. 227
30. MR Box 12
31. Junge, Traudl, *Until the Final Hour: Hitler's Last Secretary*, London, 2003, p. 125
32. Ward, *Closest Companion*, p. 316
33. *The Diaries of Edward Lindley Wood, First Earl of Halifax*, Public Diary 1940–1945 A7.8.3–18, July 3, 1944
34. Alanbrooke, *War Diaries 1939–1945*, p. 566
35. Zhukov, Marshal Georgy, *The Memoirs of Marshal Zhukov*, London, 1971, pp. 535–537
36. MR Box 13
37. Junge, *Until the Final Hour*, pp. 125–130 and Schroeder, Christa, *Er war mein Chef. Aus dem Nachlas der Sekretarin von Adolf Hitler*, Munich, 1989
38. Goebbels, *Tagebücher, Teil 2*, July 23, 1944
39. Kimball, *Churchill and Roosevelt*, Vol. 1, p. 253
40. Dilks, David, *The Diaries of Sir Alexander Cadogan OM 1938–1945*, London, 1971, p. 651

41. *The Diaries of Lord Avon*, University of Birmingham, AP 20/1/1–32, July 25, 1944
42. Goebbels, *Tagebücher, Teil 2*, July 25, 1944
43. Ibid., July 27, 1944
44. Ministry of Foreign Affairs of the USSR, *Correspondence between Stalin, Roosevelt, Truman, Churchill and Attlee during World War Two: Correspondence with Churchill and Attlee*, p. 245
45. Ibid., p. 246
46. Davies, Norman, *Rising '44: The Battle for Warsaw*, London, 2003, p. 66
47. PSF Box 48
48. Harriman, Averell and Abel, Elie, *Special Envoy to Churchill and Stalin 1941–1946*, New York, 1975, p. 333
49. PSF Box 48
50. Moran, Lord, *Churchill at War 1940–1945*, London, 2002, pp. 197–198
51. MR Box 31
52. Ministry of Foreign Affairs of the USSR, *Correspondence between Stalin, Roosevelt, Truman, Churchill and Attlee during World War Two: Correspondence with Churchill and Attlee*, p. 252
53. PSF Box 48
54. Ministry of Foreign Affairs of the USSR, *Correspondence between Stalin, Roosevelt, Truman, Churchill and Attlee during World War Two: Correspondence with Churchill and Attlee*, p. 254
55. Ibid., p. 254
56. *The Presidential Diary of Henry Morgenthau*, August 19, 1944
57. Kimball, *Churchill and Roosevelt*, Vol. 1, p. 288
58. Ministry of Foreign Affairs of the USSR, *Correspondence between Stalin, Roosevelt, Truman, Churchill and Attlee during World War Two: Correspondence with Churchill and Attlee*, p. 255
59. Kimball, *Churchill and Roosevelt*, Vol. 1, pp. 292–294
60. Ward, *Closest Companion*, p. 321
61. Kimball, *Churchill and Roosevelt*, Vol. 1, p. 294

Chapter 14
1. Goebbels, Joseph, *Die Tagebücher von Joseph Goebbels, Teil 2: Diktate 1941–1945*, ed. Elke Frohlich, Munich, 1993–1998, August 24, 1944
2. Ibid., August 24, 1944
3. Kimball, Warren, *Churchill and Roosevelt: The Complete Correspondence*, Princeton, New Jersey, 1984, Vol. 1, p. 295
4. *The Presidential Diary of Henry Morgenthau*, August 25, 1944
5. Kimball, *Churchill and Roosevelt*, Vol. 1, p. 296
6. Kershaw, Ian, *Hitler 1936–45: Nemesis*, London, 2000, p. 696
7. Junge, Traudl, *Until the Final Hour: Hitler's Last Secretary*, London, 2003, p. 145
8. Eden, Anthony, *The Reckoning*, London, 1965, p. 473
9. Kimball, *Churchill and Roosevelt*, Vol. 1, p. 309
10. Ibid., p. 310
11. Ibid., p. 313
12. Colville, Sir John, *The Fringes of Power: 10 Downing Street Diaries 1939–1955*, London, 1985, p. 508
13. Ibid., p. 510
14. *The Diaries of Lord Avon*, University of Birmingham, AP 20/1/1–32, September 10, 1944
15. MR Box 31
16. Ward, Geoffrey, C., *Closest Companion: The Unknown Story of the Intimate Friendship between Franklin Roosevelt and Margaret Suckley*, New York, 1995, p. 327
17. *The Diaries of William Lyon Mackenzie King of Canada*, ref: MG26–J13, September 11, 1944
18. Ibid., September 11, 1944
19. Kimball, *Churchill and Roosevelt*, Vol. 1, p 318
20. *Morgenthau Presidential Diary*, September 15, 1944
21. *Diaries of William Lyon Mackenzie King of Canada*, September 14, 1944
22. Alanbrooke, Field Marshal Lord, *War Diaries 1939–1945*, London, 2001, p. 593

23. Kershaw, Ian, *Hitler 1936–45*, p. 726
24. Meacham, Jon, *Franklin and Winston: An Intimate Portrait of an Epic Friendship*, New York, 2004, p. 302
25. Gilbert, Martin, *Winston S. Churchill, Vol. VII: Road to Victory 1941–1945*, London, 1986, p. 969
26. MR Box 31
27. MR Box 31
28. Below, Nicolaus von, *At Hitler's Side: The Memoirs of Hitler's Luftwaffe Adjutant 1937–1945*, London, 1980, p. 216
29. Moran, Lord, *Churchill at War 1940–1945*, London, 2002, pp. 232–233
30. Davies, Norman, *Rising '44: The Battle for Warsaw*, London, 2003
31. Kimball, *Churchill and Roosevelt*, Vol. 1, p. 339
32. Ministry of Foreign Affairs of the USSR, *Correspondence between Stalin, Roosevelt, Truman, Churchill and Attlee during World War Two: Correspondence with Franklin D. Roosevelt and Harry S Truman (August 1941–December 1945)*, Moscow, 1957, p. 162
33. Harriman, Averell and Abel, Elie, *Special Envoy to Churchill and Stalin 1941–1946*, New York, 1975, p. 354
34. Ministry of Foreign Affairs of the USSR, *Correspondence between Stalin, Roosevelt, Truman, Churchill and Attlee during World War Two: Correspondence with Roosevelt and Truman*, p. 163
35. MR Box 32
36. *The Diaries of Edward Lindley Wood, First Earl of Halifax*, Secret Diary A7.8.19: Secret Diary 1941–1945, October 9, 1944
37. Gilbert, *Winston S. Churchill, Vol. VII*, pp. 990–996
38. Ibid., pp. 990–996
39. Harriman and Abel, *Special Envoy to Churchill and Stalin 1941–1946*, p. 360
40. MR Box 32
41. Soames, Mary, *Speaking for Themselves: The Personal Letters of Winston and Clementine Churchill*, London, 1999, p. 506
42. Ministry of Foreign Affairs of the USSR, *Correspondence between Stalin, Roosevelt, Truman, Churchill and Attlee during World War Two: Correspondence with Winston S. Churchill and Clement R. Attlee (July 1941–November 1945)*, Moscow, 1957, p. 263
43. Gilbert, *Winston S. Churchill, Vol. VII*, p. 1032
44. Below, *At Hitler's Side*, p. 217
45. Ibid., p 217–219
46. Moran, Lord, *Churchill at War 1940–1945*, London, 2002, pp. 251–252
47. Harriman and Abel, *Special Envoy to Churchill and Stalin 1941–1946*, p. 366
48. Ibid., pp. 369–370
49. Kimball, *Churchill and Roosevelt*, Vol. 1, p. 377
50. Ibid., p. 378
51. Ibid., p. 385
52. Goebbels, *Tagebücher, Teil 2*, November 17, 1944
53. Eden, *Reckoning*, p. 496
54. Goebbels, *Tagebücher, Teil 2*, November 23, 1944
55. *The Diaries of Lord Avon*, University of Birmingham, AP 20/1/1–32, November 25, 1944
56. Kimball, *Churchill and Roosevelt*, Vol. 1, p. 419
57. MR Box 12
58. Kimball, *Churchill and Roosevelt*, Vol. 1, p. 425
59. Goebbels, *Tagebücher, Teil 2*, December 2, 1944
60. Gilbert, *Winston S. Churchill, Vol. VII*, pp. 1085–1086
61. Kimball, *Churchill and Roosevelt*, Vol. 1, p. 437
62. Ministry of Foreign Affairs of the USSR, *Correspondence between Stalin, Roosevelt, Truman, Churchill and Attlee during World War Two: Correspondence with Churchill and Attlee*, p. 283
63. Below, *At Hitler's Side*, p. 222

64. Kershaw, *Hitler 1936–45*,
p. 742
65. Ibid., p. 742
66. Ward, *Closest Companion*, p. 367
67. Goebbels, *Tagebücher, Teil 2*, December 20,
1944
68. PSF Box 39
69. Ministry of Foreign Affairs of the USSR,
*Correspondence between Stalin, Roosevelt,
Truman, Churchill and Attlee during World
War Two: Correspondence with Roosevelt and
Truman*, p. 181
70. Warlimont, Walter, *Inside Hitler's
Headquarters 1939–1945*, Novato,
California, 1964, p. 491
71. Ibid., pp. 491–492
72. Ibid., pp. 491–492
73. Kershaw, *Hitler 1936–45*, p. 685
74. Schroeder, Christa, *Er war mein Chef. Aus
dem Nachlas der Sekretarin von Adolf Hitler*,
Munich, 1989, p. 151
75. Eden, *Reckoning*, p. 504
76. Colville, *Fringes of Power*, p. 551
77. Dilks, *Diaries of Sir Alexander Cadogan
1938–1945*, p. 696
78. Below, *At Hitler's Side*, p. 226
79. Warlimont, *Inside Hitler's Headquarters
1939–1945*, pp. 500–501
80. Ibid., pp. 500–501
81. Ibid., pp. 500–501
82. Ward, *Closest Companion*, p. 390
83. Colville, *Fringes of Power*, p. 555
84. Harriman and Abel, *Special Envoy to
Churchill and Stalin 1941–1946*, p. 390
85. Goebbels, *Tagebücher, Teil 2*, January 25,
1945
86. Ibid., January 26, 1945
87. Junge, *Until the Final Hour*, p. 158
88. Schroeder, *Er War Mein Chef*, p. 200

Chapter 15
1. Moran, Lord, *Churchill at War 1940–1945*,
London, 2002, p. 267
2. Sebag-Montefiore, Simon, *Stalin: The Court
of the Red Tsar*, London, 2003, p. 425
3. Gilbert, Martin, *Winston S. Churchill, Vol.*

VII: *Road to Victory 1941–1945*, London,
1986, p. 1172
4. Reilly, Michael F. (as told by William J.
Slocum), *Reilly of the White House*, New
York, 1947, pp. 200–215
5. Ibid., pp. 200–215
6. Ibid., pp. 200–215
7. Anna Halsted Paper Box 64
8. Anna Halsted Paper Box 64
9. Beria, Sergo, *Beria, My Father: Inside
Stalin's Kremlin*, London, 2001, p. 105
10. Bishop, Jim, *FDR's Last Year: April
1944–April 1945*, London, 1974, p. 311
11. Ibid., p. 320
12. Ibid., p. 320
13. Ibid., p. 320
14. Ibid., p. 321
15. Eden, Anthony, *The Reckoning*, London,
1965, p. 512
16. *The Tehran, Yalta and Potsdam Conferences*,
Moscow, 1969, p. 93
17. Eden, *Reckoning*, p. 516
18. Dilks, David, *The Diaries of Sir Alexander
Cadogan 1938–1945*, London, 1971, p. 704
19. Bishop, *FDR's Last Year*, p. 348
20. Goebbels, Joseph, *Die Tagebücher von Joseph
Goebbels, Teil 2: Diktate 1941–1945*, ed. Elke
Frohlich, Munich, 1993–1998, February 6,
1945
21. Ibid., February 6, 1945
22. Ibid., February 8, 1945
23. Nisbet, Robert, *Roosevelt and Stalin: The
Failed Courtship*, Washington DC, 1988, p. 72
24. Bishop, *FDR's Last Year*, p. 384
25. Goebbels, *Tagebücher, Teil 2*, February 10,
1945
26. Bishop, *FDR's Last Year*, p. 403
27. Moran, *Churchill at War 1940–1945*, p. 281
28. *Tehran, Yalta and Potsdam Conferences*,
p. 54–146
29. Dilks, *Diaries of Sir Alexander Cadogan
1938–1945*, pp. 708–709
30. Black, Conrad, *Franklin Delano Roosevelt:
Champion of Freedom*, London, 2003, p. 1072
31. Gilbert, *Winston S. Churchill, Vol. VII*,
p. 1212

32. Ministry of Foreign Affairs of the USSR, *Correspondence between Stalin, Roosevelt, Truman, Churchill and Attlee during World War Two: Correspondence with Franklin D. Roosevelt and Harry S. Truman (August 1941–December 1945)*, Moscow, 1957, p. 192

33. Ward, Geoffrey, C., *Closest Companion: The Unknown Story of the Intimate Friendship between Franklin Roosevelt and Margaret Suckley*, New York, 1995, p. 396

34. Ibid., p. 395

35. Kershaw, Ian, *Hitler 1936–45: Nemesis*, London, 2000, p. 779

36. Ibid., p. 779

37. Gilbert, *Winston S. Churchill, Vol. VII*, p. 1222

38. Ibid., p. 1223

39. Resis, Albert (trans.), *Molotov Remembers: Inside Kremlin Politics – Conversations with Felix Chuev*, Chicago, 1993, p. 51

40. Bishop, *FDR's Last Year*, pp. 450–451

41. Ibid., p. 458

42. Ibid., pp. 459–461

43. Gilbert, Martin, *Second World War*, London, 1989, p. 644

44. Kershaw, *Hitler 1936–45*, p. 780

45. Bishop, *FDR's Last Year*, p. 462

46. Gilbert, *Winston S. Churchill, Vol. VII*, pp. 1233–1234

47. Colville, Sir John, *The Fringes of Power: 10 Downing Street Diaries 1939–1955*, London, 1985, p. 566

48. Black, *Franklin Delano Roosevelt*, p. 1080

49. Public Papers of the President

50. Public Papers of the President

51. Bishop, *FDR's Last Year*, p. 481

52. Goebbels, *Tagebücher, Teil 2*, March 5, 1945

53. Ibid., March 5, 1945

54. Zhukov, Marshal Georgy, *The Memoirs of Marshal Zhukov*, London, 1971, pp. 582–583

55. Ibid., pp. 582–583

56. Ibid., pp. 582–583

57. Colville, *Fringes of Power*, p. 570

58. Harriman, Averell and Abel, Elie, *Special Envoy to Churchill and Stalin 1941–1946*, New York, 1975, p. 427

59. Kimball, Warren, *Churchill and Roosevelt: The Complete Correspondence*, Princeton, New Jersey, 1984, Vol. 1, p. 547

60. Ibid., pp. 551–552

61. Ibid., pp. 551–552

62. Ibid., p. 562

63. Ibid., p. 562

64. Bishop, *FDR's Last Year*, p. 500

65. Kershaw, *Hitler 1936–45*, p. 783

66. Ibid., p. 783

67. Goebbels, *Tagebücher, Teil 2*, March 12, 1945

68. Ibid., March 12, 1945

69. Kimball, *Churchill and Roosevelt*, Vol. 1, p. 564

70. Bishop, *FDR's Last Year*, p. 501

71. Kimball, *Churchill and Roosevelt*, Vol. 1, p. 568

72. Taussig Papers Box 5

73. Taussig Papers Box 5

74. Taussig Papers Box 5

75. Bishop, *FDR's Last Year*, p. 507

76. Goebbels, *Tagebücher , Teil 2*, March 19, 1945

77. Harriman and Abel, *Special Envoy to Churchill and Stalin 1941–1946*, p. 444

78. Alanbrooke, Field Marshal Lord, *War Diaries 1939–1945*, London, 2001, p. 678

79. Ministry of Foreign Affairs of the USSR, *Correspondence between Stalin, Roosevelt, Truman, Churchill and Attlee during World War Two: Correspondence with Roosevelt and Truman*, pp. 201–202

80. Bishop, *FDR's Last Year*, p. 528

81. Ibid., p. 528

82. Meacham, Jon, *Franklin and Winston: An Intimate Portrait of an Epic Friendship*, New York, 2004, p. 338

83. Harriman and Abel, *Special Envoy to Churchill and Stalin 1941–1946*, p. 435; Beevor, Anthony, *Berlin: The Downfall 1945*, London, 2002, pp. 145–147 and Sebag-Montefiore, *Stalin*, p. 430

84. Beevor, *Berlin*, p. 146

85. Gilbert, *Winston S. Churchill, Vol. VII*, p. 1276

86. Reilly, *Reilly of the White House*, pp. 200–215
87. Ibid., pp. 200–215
88. Ministry of Foreign Affairs of the USSR, *Correspondence between Stalin, Roosevelt, Truman, Churchill and Attlee during World War Two: Correspondence with Roosevelt and Truman*, pp. 200–201
89. Ibid., pp. 200–201
90. Zhukov, *Memoirs*, pp. 588–589
91. Goebbels, *Tagebücher, Teil 2*, March 31, 1945
92. Below, *At Hitler's Side*, pp. 232–233
93. Ministry of Foreign Affairs of the USSR, *Correspondence between Stalin, Roosevelt, Truman, Churchill and Attlee during World War Two: Correspondence with Roosevelt and Truman*, pp. 204–205
94. Ibid., pp. 203–204
95. Ministry of Foreign Affairs of the USSR, *Correspondence between Stalin, Roosevelt, Truman, Churchill and Attlee during World War Two: Correspondence with Churchill and Attlee*, p. 310
96. Kimball, *Churchill and Roosevelt*, Vol. 1, p. 605
97. Ministry of Foreign Affairs of the USSR, *Correspondence between Stalin, Roosevelt, Truman, Churchill and Attlee during World War Two: Correspondence with Roosevelt and Truman*, p. 206
98. MR Box 12
99. Ministry of Foreign Affairs of the USSR, *Correspondence between Stalin, Roosevelt, Truman, Churchill and Attlee during World War Two: Correspondence with Roosevelt and Truman*, p. 207

100. Goebbels, *Tagebücher, Teil 2*, April 4, 1945
101. Ibid., April 8, 1945
102. Ward, *Closest Companion*, p. 414
103. Kimball, *Churchill and Roosevelt*, Vol. 1, p. 630
104. *The Presidential Diary of Henry Morgenthau*, April 11, 1945

Epilogue

1. Ward, Geoffrey, C., *Closest Companion: The Unknown Story of the Intimate Friendship between Franklin Roosevelt and Margaret Suckley*, New York, 1995, p. 416–420
2. Djilas, Milovan, *Conversations with Stalin*, London, 1962, p. 105
3. Ward, *Closest Companion*, pp. 416–420
4. Ibid., pp. 416–420
5. Ibid., pp. 416–420
6. Below, Nicolaus von, *At Hitler's Side: The Memoirs of Hitler's Luftwaffe Adjutant 1937–1945*, London, 1980, p. 234 and Kershaw, Ian, *Hitler 1936–45: Nemesis*, London, 2000, p. 791
7. Ibid., p. 792
8. Junge, Traudl, *Until the Final Hour: Hitler's Last Secretary*, London, 2003
9. Ibid.
10. Colville, Sir John, *The Fringes of Power: 10 Downing Street Diaries 1939–1955*, London, 1985
11. MR Box 13
12. Clark, Mark, *Calculated Risk*, London, 1951
13. Ward, *Closest Companion*

BIBLIOGRAPHY

UNPUBLISHED SOURCES

Canada
National Archives, Canada
The Diaries of William Lyon Mackenzie King of Canada

Russia
The diaries of Ivan Maisky
The memoir of Y. Chadayev

United Kingdom
Rothermere American Institute, University of Oxford
The Diaries of Henry L. Stimson

National Archives, Kew
PREM 3
PREM 4
CAB 163
CAB 66
CAB 93
CRIM1
FO 371
FO 954
HO 45
HO 144
HO 262
HO 45
HS 9
HW 17
KV 2
KV 4
MEPO 3

Borthwick Institute, University of York
The diaries of Edward Frederick Lindley Wood, 1st Earl of Halifax

Special Collections Department, University of York
The diaries of Lord Avon

<u>United States</u>
Library of Congress
Papers of Charles Eustis Bohlen
Papers of Joseph Edward Davies
Papers of Averell W. Harriman
Papers of William D. Leahy
Diaries of Robert P. Meiklejohn

Franklin D. Roosevelt Library and Museum
Map Room Files (MR)
President's Alphabetical File (PAF)
President's Official File (OF)
President's Personal File (PPF)
President's Secretary's File (PSF)
Adolf A. Berle Papers
Anna Roosevelt Halsted Papers
Harry L. Hopkins Papers (Sherwood Collection)
The Diaries of Harold L. Ickes
Henry Morgenthau Jr Papers
Morgenthau Presidential Diary
James Rowe Jr Papers
Secret Service Records
Charles W. Taussig Papers

PUBLISHED SOURCES

Alanbrooke, Field Marshal Lord, *War Diaries 1939–1945: Field Marshal Lord Alanbrooke*, London, 2001
Aldrich, Richard, J, *The Hidden Hand: Britain, America and Cold War Secret Intelligence*, London, 2001
Alliluyeva, Svetlana, *Only One Year*, London, 1969
Alliluyeva, Svetlana, *Twenty Letters to a Friend*, London, 1967
Beevor, Anthony, *Berlin: The Downfall 1945*, London, 2002
Beevor, Anthony, *Stalingrad*, London, 1998
Below, Nicolaus von, *At Hitler's Side: The Memoirs of Hitler's Luftwaffe Adjutant 1937–1945*, London, 1980
Bennett, John W. Wheeler, *Action This Day: Working with Churchill*, London, 1968
Berezhkov, Valentin, *History in the Making: Memoirs of World War II Diplomacy*, Moscow, 1982
Beria, Sergo, *Beria My Father: Inside Stalin's Kremlin*, London, 2001
Berle, Adolf, *Navigating the Rapids 1918–1971: From the Papers of Adolf A. Berle*, New York, 1973
Berthon, Simon, *Allies at War*, London, 2001

Bialer, Seweryn (ed.), *Stalin and His Generals: Soviet Military Memoirs of World War II*, London, 1970

Bishop, Jim, *FDR's Last Year: April 1944–April 1945*, London, 1974

Black, Conrad, *Franklin Delano Roosevelt: Champion of Freedom*, London, 2003

Blum, John Morton, *From the Morgenthau Diaries*, Boston, 1959-1965, 3 Volumes

Blum, John Morton, *The Price of Vision: The Diary of Henry A. Wallace 1942–1946*, Boston, 1973

Bullock, Alan, *Hitler: a Study in Tyranny*, London, 1964

Bullock, Alan, *Stalin and Hitler: Parallel Lives*, London, 1991

Burdick, Charles and Jacobsen, Hans-Adolf, *The Halder War Diary 1939-1942*, London, 1988

Cannadine, David, *In Churchill's Shadow: Confronting the Past in Modern Britain*, London, 2002

Carlton, David, *Churchill and the Soviet Union*, Manchester, 2000

Casey, Steven, *Cautious Crusade: Franklin D. Roosevelt, American Public Opinion and the War Against Nazi Germany*, Oxford, 2001

Charmley, John, *Churchill, The End of Glory: A Political Biography*, London, 1993

Chubarian, Alexander, O. and Harold Shukman, *Stalin and the Soviet-Finnish War, 1939–1940*, London, 2001

Churchill, Randolph, *The Rise and Fall of Sir Anthony Eden*, London, 1959

Churchill, Winston S., *The Second World War*, London, 1948–1954

Ciano, Count Galeazzo, *Diary 1937–1943: The Complete, Unabridged Diaries of Count Galeazzo Ciano, Italian Minster for Foreign Affairs*, London, 2002

Clark, Mark, *Calculated Risk*, London, 1951

Clayton, Tim and Craig, Phil, *End of the Beginning*, London, 2002

Colville, Sir John, *The Fringes of Power: 10 Downing Street Diaries 1939–1955*, London, 1985,

Davies, Norman, *Rising '44: The Battle for Warsaw*, London, 2003

Davis, Kenneth S., *FDR, the War President, 1940–1943: A History*, New York, 2000

Degras, Jane (ed.), *Soviet Documents on Foreign Policy 1917–1941: Volume III 1933–1941*, London, 1953

Dilks, David, *The Diaries of Sir Alexander Cadogan OM 1938–1945*, London, 1971

Dimitrov, Georgi, *The Diary of Georgi Dimitrov 1933–1949*, ed. by Ivo Banac, London, 2003

Djilas, Milovan, *Memoir of a Revolutionary*, New York, 1973

Djilas, Milovan, *Conversations with Stalin*, London, 1962

Dobbs, Michael, *Winston's War*, London, 2002

Documents On German Foreign Policy 1918-1945, Series D (1936–1941), Volumes IX–XIII, HMSO, London, 1956–1962

Dutton, David, *Anthony Eden: Life and Reputation*, London, 1997

Eden, Anthony, *The Reckoning*, London, 1965

Edmonds, Robin, *The Big Three: Churchill, Roosevelt and Stalin in Peace and War*, London, 1991

Engel, Major, *Heeres-Adjutant bei Hitler 1938–1943*, Stuttgart, 1974

Fest, Joachim, *Inside Hitler's bunker: The Last Days of the Third Reich*, London, 2004

Fest, Joachim, *Hitler*, London, 1974

Fleming, Gerald, *Hitler and the Final Solution*, London, 1985

Foot, M. R. D., *SOE: An Outline History of the Special Operations Executive 1940–46*, London, 1984

Freedman, Max, *Roosevelt and Frankfurter: Their Correspondence 1928–1945*, London, 1968

Freidel, Frank, *Roosevelt: A Rendezvous with Destiny*, Boston, 1990

Gilbert, Martin, *Finest Hour: Winston S. Churchill 1939–1941, Volume VI*, London, 1983

Gilbert, Martin, *Road to Victory 1941–1945, Volume VII*, London, 1986

Gilbert, Martin, *The Churchill War Papers, Volume II: Never Surrender May 1940–December 1940*, London, 1994

Gilbert, Martin, *The Churchill War Papers, Volume Three: The Ever-Widening War 1941*, London, 2000

Gilbert, Martin, *The Holocaust*, London, 1987

Gilbert, Martin, *Second World War*, London, 1989

Glantz, David and Heiber, Helmut, *Hitler and His Generals: Military Conferences 1942–1945*, London, 2002

Goebbels, Joseph *Die Tagebücher von Joseph Goebbels Teil 1 Aufzeichnungen, 1923–1941*, ed. Elke Frohlich, Munich, 1998–2001

Goebbels, Joseph *Die Tagebücher von Joseph Goebbels; Teil 2 Diktate, 1941–1945*, ed. Elke Frohlich, Munich, 1993–1998

Gorkov, Y., *Gosudarstvennyj Komitet Oborony Postanovljaet, 1941–1945. Zifry I Documenty*, Moscow, 2002

Gorodetsky, Gabriel, *Grand Delusion: Stalin and the German Invasion of Russia*, London, 1999

Grigorenko, Petro D., *Memoirs*, London, 1983

Gromyko, Andrei, *Memories*, London, 1989

Harriman, Averell and Abel, Elie, *Special Envoy to Churchill and Stalin 1941–1946*, New York, 1975

Hassett, William D, *Off the Record with FDR 1942–1945*, London, 1960

Hastings, Max, Armageddon, *The Battle for Germany 1944–45*, London, 2004

Heinrichs, Waldo, *Threshold of War: Franklin D. Roosevelt and American Entry into World War II*, New York, 1988

Herne, Gary, *A Death in Washington: Walter G. Krivitsky and the Stalin Terror*, New York, 2003

Hilger, Gustav and Meyer, Alfred G., *The Incompatible Allies: a Memoir-History of German-Soviet Relations, 1918–1941*, New York, 1953

Hinsley F. H., *British Intelligence in the Second World War: Its Influence on Strategy and Operations*, London, 1979–1990

Hinsley, F. H. and Simkins, C. A. G, *British Intelligence in the Second World War, Volume Four: Security and Counter-Intelligence*, London, 1990

Hitler, Adolf, *Mein Kampf*, translated by Ralph Manheim, London, 1992

Hitler, Adolf, *The Testament of Adolf Hitler: the Hitler-Bormann Documents February–April 1945*, London, 1961

Hull, Cordell, *The Memoirs of Cordell Hull*, London, 1948

Ickes, Harold L., *The Secret Diary of Harold L. Ickes*, New York, 1953–1955

Israel, Fred L., *The War Diary of Breckinridge Long: Selections from the Years 1939–1944*, Lincoln, 1966

Jenkins, Roy, *Churchill*, London, 2001

Joachimsthaler, Anton, *The last days of Hitler: The Legends, the Evidence, the Truth*, London, 1996

Junge, Traudl, *Until the Final Hour: Hitler's Last Secretary*, London, 2003

Keitel, Field Marshal, *Memoirs*, London, 1965

Kershaw, Ian, *Hitler 1936–45: Nemesis*, London, 2000

Kershaw, Ian, *Hitler 1889–1936: Hubris*, London, 1998

Khrushchev, Nikita, *Khrushchev Remembers*, London, 1971

Khrushchev, Nikita, *Khrushchev Remembers: The Glasnost Tapes*, London, 1990

Kimball, Warren, Chubarian, A. O. and Reynolds, David, *Allies at war: The Soviet, American, and British experience, 1939–1945*, Basingstoke, 1994

Kimball, Warren, *Churchill and Roosevelt: The Complete Correspondence*, Princeton, New Jersey, 1984

Kimball, Warren, *The Most Unsordid Act: Lend-Lease, 1939–1941*, Baltimore, 1969

Kimball, Warren, *The Juggler: Franklin Roosevelt as Wartime Statesman*, Princeton, N.J., 1991

Kimball, Warren, *Forged in War: Churchill, Roosevelt and the Second World War*, London, 1997

Lash, Joseph P., *Roosevelt and Churchill 1939–1941: The Partnership that Saved the West*, New York, 1976

Lash, Joseph, *Roosevelt and Churchill, 1939–1941: The Partnership That Saved the West*, London, 1977

Leahy, William D., *I Was There: The Personal Story of the Chief of Staff to Presidents Roosevelt and Truman*, London, 1950

Lih, Lars, T., Naumov, Oleg, V. and Khlevniuk, Oleg, V., *Stalin's Letters to Molotov, 1925–1936*, London, 1995

Loewnheim, Francis, L., Langley, Harold D. and Jonas, Manfred, *Roosevelt and Churchill: Their Secret Wartime Correspondence*, London, 1975

Lukacs, John, *The Duel: Hitler vs. Stalin 10 May 1940–31 July 1940*, London, 1990

Lukacs, John, *The Hitler of History*, New York, 1997

Maisky, Ivan, *Memoirs of a Soviet Ambassador: The War 1939–1945*, London, 1967

Manstein, Erich von, *Lost Victories*, Chicago, 1958

Meacham, Jon, *Franklin and Winston: An Intimate Portrait of an Epic Friendship*, New York, 2004

Merritt Miner, Steven, *Between Churchill and Stalin: The Soviet Union, Great Britain, and the Origins of the Grand Alliance*, London, 1988

Ministry of Foreign Affairs of the USSR, *Correspondence Between Stalin, Roosevelt, Truman, Churchill and Attlee During World War Two: Correspondence with Winston S. Churchill and Clement Attlee (July 1941–November 1945)*, Moscow, 1957

Ministry of Foreign Affairs of the USSR, *Correspondence Between Stalin, Roosevelt, Truman, Churchill and Attlee During World War Two: Correspondence with Franklin R. Roosevelt and Harry S Truman (August 1941–December 1945)* Moscow, 1957

Moran, Lord, *Churchill at War 1940–1945*, London, 2002

Nicolson, Harold, *Diaries and letters 1930-1964*, London, 1980

Nisbet, Robert, *Roosevelt and Stalin: The Failed Courtship*, Washington, DC, 1988

Overy, Richard, *Russia's War*, London, 1998

Overy, Richard, *The Dictators: Hitler's Germany and Stalin's Russia*, London, 2004

Perkins, Frances, *The Roosevelt I Knew*, New York, 1946

Perlmutter, Amos, *FDR and Stalin: A Not So Grand Alliance 1943–1945*, London, 1993

The Public Papers and Addresses of Franklin D. Roosevelt, New York, 1938–1950

Radzinsky, Edvard, *Stalin—The First In Depth Biography Based on Explosive New Documents from the Russian Archives*, London, 1996

Reilly, Michael F. (as told by William J. Slocum), *Reilly of the White House*, New York, 1947

Renwick, Sir Robin, *Fighting With Allies: America and Britain in Peace and War*, Basingstoke, 1996

Resis, Albert (trans.), *Molotov Remembers: Inside Kremlin Politics—Conversations with Felix Chuev*, Chicago, 1993

Reynolds, David, *The Creation of the Anglo-American Alliance, 1937–41: A Study in Competitive Co-operation*, London, 1981

Reynolds, David, *In Command of History: Churchill Fighting and Writing the Second World War*, London, 2004

Roberts, Andrew, *Hitler and Churchill: Secrets of Leadership*, London, 2003

Roberts, Geoffrey, *Victory at Stalingrad: The Battle that Changed History*, London, 2002

Roberts, Geoffrey, *The Soviet Union and the Origins of the Second World War: Russo-German Relations and the Road to War, 1933–1941*, Basingstoke: Macmillan, 1995

Roberts, Geoffrey, *The Unholy Alliance: Stalin's Pact with Hitler*, Bloomington, Ind., 1989

Roosevelt, Eleanor, *The Autobiography of Eleanor Roosevelt*, New York, 1992

Roosevelt, Elliott, *As He Saw It*, New York, 1946

Roosevelt, Elliott, *F.D.R., His Personal Letters*, New York, 1948

Ross, Graham, *The Foreign Office and the Kremlin: British Documents on Anglo-Soviet Relations 1941–1945*, London, 1984

Rusbridger, James and Nave, Eric, *Betrayal at Pearl Harbor: How Churchill Lured Roosevelt into War*, London, 1991

Rzheshevsky, O. A., *Stalin i Cherchill: Vstrechi, Besedy, Diskussii: Dokumenty, Kommentarii: 1941–1945*, Moscow 2004

Rzheshevsky, Oleg (ed.), *War and Diplomacy: The Making of the Grand Documents from Stalin's Archives*, Amsterdam, 1996

Schmidt, P., *Hitler's Interpreter*, London, 1951

Schroeder, Christa, *Er War Mein Chef. Aus dem Nachlas der Sekretarin von Adolf Hitler*, Munich, 1989

Sebag-Montefiore, Simon, *Stalin: The Court of the Red Tsar*, London, 2003

Service, Robert, *Stalin: a Biography*, London, 2004

Sherwood, Robert E., *Roosevelt and Hopkins: An Intimate History*, New York, 2001

Shtemenko, S. M., *The Soviet General Staff at War 1941–1945*, Moscow, 1985–86

Soames, Mary, *Clementine Churchill, by Her Daughter*, London, 1979

Soames, Mary, *Speaking for Themselves: The Personal Letters of Winston and Clementine Churchill*, London, 1998

Speer, Albert, *Inside the Third Reich: Memoirs*, London, 1970

Stafford, David, *Roosevelt and Churchill: Men of Secrets*, London, 1999

Stephan, Robert W., *Stalin's Secret War: Soviet Counterintelligence against the Nazis 1941–1945*, London, 2003

Stettinius, Edward, R., *The Diaries of Edward R. Stettinius, Jr.*, 1943–1946, New York, 1975

Stimson, Henry L., *On Active Service in Peace and War*, New York, 1947

Stinnett, Robert B., *Day of Deceit: The Truth About FDR and Pearl Harbor*, London, 2000

The Tehran, Yalta and Potsdam Conferences, Moscow, 1969

Taubman, William, *Khrushchev: The Man and His Era*, London, 2003

Thompson, W. H., *Sixty Minutes with Churchill*, London 1953

Thorpe, D. R., *Eden*, London, 2003

Trevor-Roper, Hugh, *Hitler's Table Talk, 1941–1944: His Private Conversations*, London, 2000

Trevor-Roper, Hugh, *The Last Days of Hitler*, London, 1987

Trevor-Roper, Hugh, *The Bormann Letters: The Private Correspondence between Martin Bormann and His Wife from January 1943 to April 1945*, London, 1954

Tully, Grace, *FDR My Boss*, New York, 1949

Volkogonov, Dmitri, *Stalin: Triumph and Tragedy*, London, 1991

Ward, Geoffrey, C., *Closest Companion: The Unknown Story of the Intimate Friendship between Franklin Roosevelt and Margaret Suckley*, New York, 1995

Warlimont, Walter, *Inside Hitler's Headquarters 1939–1945*, Novato, Calif., 1964

Weizsacker, Ernst von, *Memoirs*, London 1951

Welles, Sumner, *The Time for Decision*, London, 1944

Winant, John G., *A Letter From Grosvenor Square: An Account of a Stewardship*, London, 1947

Zhukov, Marshal Georgy, *The Memoirs of Marshal Zhukov*, London, 1971

INDEX